The History of British Women's Writing, 1610–1690

The History of British Women's Writing
General Editors: **Jennie Batchelor** and **Cora Kaplan**

Advisory Board: Isobel Armstrong, Rachel Bowlby, Carolyn Dinshaw, Margaret Ezell, Margaret Ferguson, Isobel Grundy, and Felicity Nussbaum

The History of British Women's Writing is an innovative and ambitious monograph series that seeks both to synthesize the work of several generations of feminist scholars, and to advance new directions for the study of women's writing. Volume editors and contributors are leading scholars whose work collectively reflects the global excellence in this expanding field of study. It is envisaged that this series will be a key resource for specialist and non-specialist scholars and students alike.

Titles include:
Caroline Bicks and Jennifer Summit (*editors*)
THE HISTORY OF BRITISH WOMEN'S WRITING, 1500–1610
Volume Two

Mihoko Suzuki (*editor*)
THE HISTORY OF BRITISH WOMEN'S WRITING, 1610–1690
Volume Three

Ros Ballaster (*editor*)
THE HISTORY OF BRITISH WOMEN'S WRITING, 1690–1750
Volume Four

Jacqueline M. Labbe (*editor*)
THE HISTORY OF BRITISH WOMEN'S WRITING, 1750–1830
Volume Five

Forthcoming titles:
Elizabeth Herbert McAvoy and Diane Watt (*editors*)
THE HISTORY OF BRITISH WOMEN'S WRITING, 700–1500
Volume One

Mary Joannou (*editor*)
THE HISTORY OF BRITISH WOMEN'S WRITING, 1920–1945
Volume Eight

History of British Women's Writing
Series Standing Order ISBN 978–0–230–20079–1 hardback
(*outside North America only*)

You can receive future titles in this series as they are published by placing a standing order. Please contact your bookseller or, in case of difficulty, write to us at the address below with your name and address, the title of the series and the ISBN quoted above.

Customer Services Department, Macmillan Distribution Ltd, Houndmills, Basingstoke, Hampshire RG21 6XS, England

---

The History of British Women's Writing, 1610–1690

Volume Three

Edited by

Mihoko Suzuki
Professor of English and Director of the Center for the Humanities
at the University of Miami

First published 2011 by
PALGRAVE MACMILLAN

Palgrave Macmillan in the UK is an imprint of Macmillan Publishers Limited,
registered in England, company number 785998, of Houndmills, Basingstoke,
Hampshire RG21 6XS.

Palgrave Macmillan in the US is a division of St Martin's Press LLC,
175 Fifth Avenue, New York, NY 10010.

Palgrave Macmillan is the global academic imprint of the above companies
and has companies and representatives throughout the world.

Palgrave® and Macmillan® are registered trademarks in the United States,
the United Kingdom, Europe and other countries.

ISBN 978–0–230–22460–5   hardback

This book is printed on paper suitable for recycling and made from fully
managed and sustained forest sources. Logging, pulping and manufacturing
processes are expected to conform to the environmental regulations of the
country of origin.

A catalogue record for this book is available from the British Library.

A catalog record for this book is available from the Library of Congress.

10   9   8   7   6   5   4   3   2   1
20 19 18 17 16 15 14 13 12 11

Transferred to Digital Printing in 2011

Contents

Part III   New Perspectives on Literary Genres

Part IV   Revisioning Contexts

List of Figures

Series Preface

One of the most significant developments in literary studies in the last quarter of a century has been the remarkable growth of scholarship on women's writing. This was inspired by, and in turn provided inspiration for, a post-war women's movement, which saw women's cultural expression as key to their emancipation. The retrieval, republication, and reappraisal of women's writing, beginning in the mid-1960s, have radically affected the literary curriculum in schools and universities. A revised canon now includes many more women writers. Literature courses that focus on what women thought and wrote from antiquity onwards have become popular undergraduate and postgraduate options. These new initiatives have meant that gender – in language, authors, texts, audience, and in the history of print culture more generally – are central questions for literary criticism and literary history. A mass of fascinating research and analysis extending over several decades now stands as testimony to a lively and diverse set of debates, in an area of work that is still expanding.

Indeed so rapid has this expansion been, that it has become increasingly difficult for students and academics to have a comprehensive view of the wider field of women's writing outside their own period or specialism. As the research on women has moved from the margins to the confident centre of literary studies it has become rich in essays and monographs dealing with smaller groups of authors, with particular genres and with defined periods of literary production, reflecting the divisions of intellectual labour and development of expertise that are typical of the discipline of literary studies. Collections of essays that provide overviews within particular periods and genres do exist, but no published series has taken on the mapping of the field even within one language group or national culture.

A History of British Women's Writing is intended as just such a cartographic standard work. Its ambition is to provide, in ten volumes edited by leading experts in the field, and comprised of newly commissioned essays by specialist scholars, a clear and integrated picture of women's contribution to the world of letters within Great Britain from medieval times to the present. In taking on such a wide-ranging project we were inspired by the founding, in 2003, of Chawton House Library, a UK registered charity with a unique collection of books focusing on women's writing in English from 1600 to 1830, set in the home and working estate of Jane Austen's brother.

JENNIE BATCHELOR
UNIVERSITY OF KENT

CORA KAPLAN
QUEEN MARY, UNIVERSITY OF LONDON

Acknowledgments

First and foremost, thanks are due to the contributors who have been wonderful collaborators in bringing this volume to completion. In addition, I would like to acknowledge the many scholars who have enriched the scholarship of seventeenth-century English women writers, in particular, Hilda Smith and Sara Mendelson, who have not only been pioneers in establishing the field, but also have been supportive mentors to younger scholars. Thanks are also due to Jennie Batchelor and Cora Kaplan, general editors of *The History of British Women's Writing*, for their expert guidance throughout the process, and to Paula Kennedy at Palgrave Macmillan for her assistance.

Notes on Contributors

Bernadette Andrea is Professor of English at the University of Texas at San Antonio, where she chaired the Department of English, Classics, and Philosophy. Her research focuses on women's writing from the sixteenth through the eighteenth century, with emphasis on Western European interactions with the Ottoman Empire. She has also published articles and book chapters on contemporary Algerian, Egyptian, and Turkish women writers. She is the author of *Women and Islam in Early Modern English Literature* (2007); *English Women Staging Islam, 1696–1707* is forthcoming from the Centre for Reformation and Renaissance Studies/University of Toronto.

Victoria E. Burke is an Associate Professor of English at the University of Ottawa. She has published widely on early modern women's manuscript writing. Recent articles include those published in the journal *Literature Compass* and the books *Ars Reminiscendi: Mind and Memory in Renaissance Culture*, *The Cambridge Companion to Early Modern Women's Writing*, and *Material Readings of Early Modern Culture: Texts and Social Practices 1580–1730*. She is also the co-editor of the essay collection *Early Modern Women's Manuscript Writing* (2004), and a contributing editor to the anthology *Early Modern Women's Manuscript Poetry* (2005).

Katharine Gillespie is an Associate Professor of seventeenth-century English and Colonial American Literature at Miami University of Ohio, who specializes in writings by women associated with religious and political dissent. She is the author of *Domesticity and Dissent in the Seventeenth-Century: English Women Writers and the Public Sphere* (2004), as well as articles on Anne Bradstreet, Mary Rowlandson, Elizabeth Cromwell, and Lucy Hutchinson. She is the editor of *Writings by Katherine Chidley* (2009) and is completing work on a monograph entitled *Lucretia and Beyond: Women Write the English Republic, 1638–1681*.

Pamela Hammons is Associate Professor of English at the University of Miami and author of *Gender, Sexuality, and Material Objects in English Renaissance Verse* (2010); *Poetic Resistance: English Women Writers and the Early Modern Lyric* (2002); and essays in *SEL, ELH, Criticism, Clio, Women's Writing, Literature Compass,* and *Write or Be Written*. She is currently working on a modernized edition of Katherine Austen's 'Book M' (1664) for the series The Other Voice in Early Modern Europe, and a book on traveling early modern women writers.

Theodora A. Jankowski, Professor of English and Director of Academic Affairs at Penn State Wilkes-Barre, is the author of *Pure Resistance: Queer Virginity in Early Modern English Drama* (2000) and *Women in Power in the Early Modern Drama* (1992). She has written numerous articles on Shakespeare, Lyly, Webster, Cavendish, and Marvell which have appeared in various collections and such journals as *Renaissance Drama, Shakespeare Studies, Studies in Philology, Early Drama*, and *Medieval and Renaissance Drama in England*. She is completing work on a collection of essays on Lyly's plays and doing more work on the uses of queer theory in the early modern period.

Clare R. Kinney is Associate Professor of English at the University of Virginia. She is the author of *Strategies of Poetic Narrative: Chaucer, Spenser, Milton, Eliot* (1992) and has edited *Ashgate Critical Essays on Women Writers in England, 1550–1700*, Volume 4, *Mary Wroth* (2009). She has published many articles on the Sidney circle (including Wroth and Mary Sidney Herbert), Spenser, Shakespeare, narrative and dramatic romance, and the interplay of gender and genre in early modern texts.

Cristina Malcolmson is Professor of English at Bates College. She has written two books on George Herbert, and has edited, with Mihoko Suzuki, *Debating Gender in Early Modern England, 1500–1700* (2002). Her essays on studies of skin color in the early Royal Society have appeared in *Fault Lines and Controversies in the Study of Seventeenth-Century Literature*, edited by Claude J. Summers and Ted-Larry Pebworth (2002), and *Humans and Other Animals in Eighteenth-Century Britain*, edited by Frank Palmeri (2006). A collaborative article written with Ruth Paley (first author) and Michael Hunter on 'Parliament and Slavery 1660–c.1710' appeared in the journal *Slavery and Abolition*. She is writing a book on race and gender in the early Royal Society.

Megan Matchinske is Professor of English and Comparative Literature at the University of North Carolina at Chapel Hill where she teaches courses in early modern literature and the philosophy of history. She is the author of *Writing, Gender and State in Early Modern England: Identity Formation and the Female Subject* (1998) and *Women Writing History in Early Modern England* (2009). She is currently at work on an edition of the Mary Carleton bigamy trials for the Other Voice series and a monograph that examines moments of rupture in historical memory – early modern interruptions to and failures in political, religious, economic, and cultural transfer.

Shannon Miller is Department Chair and Professor of English at Temple University. She is the author, most recently, of *Engendering the Fall: John Milton and Seventeenth Century Women Writers* (2008), as well as articles on writers such as Margaret Cavendish, Aphra Behn, and Aemilia Lanyer. She is working on a book project that examines seventeenth-century pamphlets and marginalia entitled 'On the Margins of History'.

Patricia Phillippy is Professor of English Literature at Kingston University, London. Her most recent publications are *Painting Women: Cosmetics, Canvases, and Early Modern Culture* (2006) and *Women, Death and Literature in Early Modern England* (2002). She has completed an edition of Elizabeth Cooke Hoby Russell's letters and works, forthcoming as *The Writings of an English Sappho* in The Other Voice in Early Modern Europe series. She is at work on a monograph which studies the intersection between early modern women's writing in funeral monuments and manuscripts.

Margaret Reeves is an Assistant Professor in the Department of Critical Studies at the University of British Columbia. She has published articles on the literary history of fiction and on several women writers, including Aphra Behn and Elizabeth Cary, and co-edited with Mark Crane and Richard Raiswell a collection of essays entitled *Shell Games: Studies in Scams, Frauds, and Deceits (1300–1650)*. Her current research focuses on political satiric discourse in seventeenth-century women's writing and Elizabeth Cary's manuscript histories of King Edward II.

Paul Salzman is Professor of English Literature at La Trobe University, Melbourne, Australia. His most recent book is *Reading Early Modern Women's Writing* (2006). He has worked extensively on early modern women and has just completed an online edition of Mary Wroth's poetry. His current project is a book on literature and politics in the 1620s.

Mihoko Suzuki is Professor of English and Director of the Center for the Humanities at the University of Miami. She is the author, most recently, of *Subordinate Subjects: Gender, the Political Nation, and Literary Form in England, 1588–1688* (2003) and the co-editor (with Hilda L. Smith and Susan Wiseman) of *Women's Political Writings, 1610–1725* (2007). She has also edited the volumes on Mary Carleton and Elizabeth Cellier for Ashgate's Early Modern Englishwoman facsimile series, and the volume on Anne Clifford and Lucy Hutchinson for Ashgate Critical Essays on Women Writers in England, 1550–1700. Her current project, *Antigone's Example*, is a comparative study of women and civil war in seventeenth-century England and France.

Susan Wiseman is Professor of Seventeenth-Century Literature, Birkbeck College, University of London. Her most recent book is *Conspiracy and Virtue: Women, Writing and Politics in Seventeenth-Century England* (2006). She has co-edited *Women, Writing History: 1640–1740* (1992) and is the author of numerous articles on seventeenth-century women's literary and political writing.

Joanne Wright is Associate Professor of Political Science at the University of New Brunswick. She is the author of *Origin Stories in Political Thought: Discourses on Gender, Power, and Citizenship* (2004). Her current work explores the political thought of Margaret Cavendish. She is also co-editing (with Nancy Hirschmann) a volume of feminist interpretations of Thomas Hobbes.

Marion Wynne-Davies holds the Chair of English Literature in the Department of English at the University of Surrey. Her main areas of interest are early modern literature and women's writing. She has published two editions of primary material, *Renaissance Drama by Women: Texts and Documents* (with S. P. Cerasano) (1995) and *Women Poets of the Renaissance* (1998), as well as several collections of essays in the same field. She has written four monographs, *Women and Arthurian Literature* (1996), *Sidney to Milton* (1996), *Women Writers of the English Renaissance: Familial Discourse* (2007), and *Margaret Atwood* (2010).

Chronology

1677	Aphra Behn, *The Rover, or the Banished Cavaliers*
	Anne Wentworth, *A Vindication of Anne Wentworth*
1678–80	Popish Plot and Exclusion Crisis
1678	Aphra Behn, *The Feigned Courtesans*
	Anne Bradstreet, *Several Poems*
1679	Lucy Hutchinson, anonymous publication of *Order and Disorder*
	Ephelia, *Female Poems on Several Occasions*
1680	Elizabeth Cellier, *Malice Defeated*
	[Elizabeth Cary], *The History of the Life, Reign, and Death of Edward II* (composed 1627)
[1681]	Ephelia, 'Advice to his Grace'
1681–1716	Elinor James, petitions to monarchs, Parliament, lord mayor, citizens, and aldermen of London
1682	Aphra Behn, *The City Heiress*
	Anne Docwra, *A Looking-Glass for the Recorder and Justices of the Peace*
1683	Anne Docwra, *An Epistle of Love and Good Advice*
	Hannah Allen, *Satan his Methods and Malice Baffled*
1684	Aphra Behn, *Love-Letters Between a Nobleman and His Sister*, Part I
	Aphra Behn, *Poems upon Several Occasions, with a Voyage to the Isle of Love*
1685	Death of Charles II and accession of James II; Monmouth Rebellion
	Aphra Behn, *Love Letters*, Part II
1687	Isaac Newton, *Principia Mathematica*
	Aphra Behn, *Love Letters,* Part III
	Elinor James, *Mrs James's Defence of the Church of England*; *Mrs James's Vindication of the Church of England*
	Elizabeth Cellier, *To Dr. — An Answer to his Queries, concerning the Colledg of Midwives*; 'A Scheme for the Foundation of a Royal Hospital' [pub. 1745, *Harleian Miscellany*]
1688–89	Glorious Revolution: accession of William III and Mary II; Bill of Rights passed
1688	Aphra Behn, *Oroonoko, or The Royal Slave*

1689   John Locke, *Two Treatises of Government*
Joan Whitrowe, *The Humble Address of the Widow Whitrowe to the King William*

1690   Battle of the Boyne: William defeats Irish and French forces
Aphra Behn, *The Widow Ranter*
Joan Whitrowe, *To Queen Mary: The Humble Salutation and Faithful Greeting*
Anne Conway, *Principia philosophiae antiquissimae et recentissimae de Deo, Christo et Creatura id est de materia et spiritu in genere* [composed 1671–75; English translation, *The Principles of the Most Ancient and Modern Philosophy*, pub. 1692]

Introduction

Mihoko Suzuki

Varieties of women's writing, 1610–1690

Women's writing during the period covered by this volume, 1610–1690, is marked by the great variety in kinds and genres, in manuscript and in print: from literary works such as poetry, drama, and fiction, to memoirs, letters, pamphlets, and broadsides. Their authors span the social spectrum from aristocratic women writing memoirs and letters to lower-rank women petitioning Parliament on behalf of their imprisoned husbands. The religious and political allegiances of these authors range from strict Anglicans and monarchists to dissenters and supporters of Parliament and even Catholics who were persecuted for their faith. Although the greatest number of publications appeared during the central years of the Civil War and Interregnum (1642–60), the decades before 1640 as well as the years following the Restoration of Charles II in 1660 also constitute significant periods for women's writing.

The 1610s saw the publication of two important texts for women's literary history: Aemilia Lanyer's book of poetry, *Salve Deus Rex Judaeorum* (1611), and Elizabeth Cary's closet play, *The Tragedy of Mariam* (1612).[1] Lanyer dedicates her volume to a large number of aristocratic women and defends Eve against accusations that she was responsible for the Fall. Lanyer is only the second woman writer (after Isabella Whitney) to publish a volume of poetry, and her account of the Fall has been compared to that of Milton's later in the century; her country house poem, 'To Cookeham', can be compared to Ben Jonson's contemporaneous 'To Penshurst'. Cary, who later became a Catholic, dramatizes the tragic fate of Mariam, who rebels against her husband Herod and is falsely accused by him of adultery and executed. Cary's is the first play published by a woman after Mary Sidney's *Tragedie of Antonie* (1595), a translation from the French. *Mariam* includes lines that closely resemble those in Shakespeare's *Othello*; since the two plays were published the same year, it is not clear whether Shakespeare borrowed from Cary or Cary from Shakespeare.

The proto-feminist thrust of these works anticipates the Swetnam debate, sparked by the 1615 publication of Joseph Swetnam's *Arraignment of Lewd, idle, froward, and unconstant Women*. Swetnam's *Arraignment*, which went through ten editions, was answered by the publication of three defenses of women – one written by Rachel Speght, a minister's daughter, and two written by the pseudonymous Ester Sowernam and Constantia Munda. These were followed by the anonymous *Hic Mulier* and *Haec Vir* (1620), which take up the controversy concerning cross-dressing, as exemplified by the titles' inversion of the gender of the adjectives.[2] Although the rejoinders to Swetnam were each published in only one edition – indicating that the market for misogyny was larger than that for pro-women writings – the pamphlet debate on gender marks an important watershed for women's writing in seventeenth-century England. Even though Sowernam and Munda might have been males masquerading as women, they nevertheless wrote from the subject position of women and had the effect of galvanizing women's identity as a subordinate group with common interests. The negative interpellation by Swetnam's pamphlet and the responses to it – whether serious or tongue-in-cheek – therefore had effects that were real, if unintended.

At the same time that these texts were being published and circulated among a middle-class audience, Lady Anne Clifford was writing her Knole Diary, covering the years 1616–19, which remained in manuscript – copied and transmitted by her female descendants – until the twentieth century when it was edited and published by a descendant of her husband, Vita Sackville-West. Clifford recorded her experience of being deprived by her father of her rightful inheritance of her titles and estates; she resisted pressure from not only her husband, but also King James and the Archbishop of Canterbury to sign over her rights. In addition to the Knole Diary, Clifford produced the 'Great Book', a massive genealogical history of her ancestors culminating in herself that also includes journal entries of her life as a landed aristocrat intended for her own family and descendants.[3]

The 1620s saw the publication of Mary Wroth's *Urania* (1621), an ambitious romance that includes her sonnet cycle, 'Pamphilia and Amphilantus'. As niece of Philip and Mary Sidney, Wroth bases her work on her uncle's *Arcadia* but also on Spenser's *Faerie Queene*.

The vexed position of a woman writer, even an aristocratic one with an impeccable literary pedigree, is evidenced in her being reviled by Lord Denney and publishing only the first volume, which she subsequently withdrew; the second volume remained in manuscript until its publication in 1999.[4] Diana Primrose's *The Chaine of Pearle* (1630) challenged Jacobean patriarchy in yet another way by celebrating the virtues of Elizabeth. Indeed, the legacy of Elizabeth had a profound effect on the ability of women to counter misogynist attacks such as Swetnam's and even to imagine political possibilities for themselves throughout the seventeenth century.[5]

In apparent contrast to these works by Lanyer, Cary, Speght, Clifford, Wroth, and Primrose that pushed against the restrictions of Jacobean patriarchy, mother's advice books by Dorothy Leigh (*The Mother's Blessing* [1616]), Elizabeth Clinton (*The Countess of Lincolnes Nurserie* [1622]), and Elizabeth Jocelin (*The Mother's Legacie for her Unborne Childe* [1624]), affirmed the maternal role as one fully within the prescriptions of accepted femininity.[6] Nevertheless, it is important to acknowledge the connections between the pamphlet debate and these texts, in their affirmation of women as mothers who not only give birth to children but educate them into culture. These texts challenged the conventionally hierarchized gendered binary between textual production (by male writers) and biological reproduction (by mothers), thereby enabling their authors to resist the injunction against female authorship.[7]

The period during the English Civil Wars and Interregnum (1642–60) has often been neglected by traditional histories of English literature, which have focused more closely on the periods designated by monarchical reigns, such as the Jacobean and Caroline. Yet these years saw a remarkable increase in women's publications.[8] The breakdown of censorship in 1640–41 allowed petitions to Parliament, including those composed and signed by women, to be published in their own right and as part of newsbooks.[9] The petitions by Leveller women (1648–49) were published both as broadsides and as part of collections of writings by Leveller men. While strategically emphasizing their wifely and domestic role, the female petitioners indict the extralegal actions of the state against their husbands. The impact of these petitions can be gauged by the appearance of satiric petitions purported to be by women.[10]

The largest number of publications by women in this period consisted of those authored by sectarians. The connection between women's petitions and sectarian women's writing can be seen in the example of Katherine Chidley, a dissenting seamstress, who published three works promoting the separation of church and state; she later participated in the Leveller women's protests and may have helped compose their petitions.[11] The Baptist Elizabeth Poole published texts counseling Cromwell against executing Charles I.[12] Also critical of Cromwell, Anna Trapnel, a Fifth Monarchist, became a celebrity for speaking as in a trance; her words were transcribed, resulting in four publications.[13] Not all were critical of Cromwell or the regicide. The millenarian Mary Cary defended the execution of Charles in *The Little Horns Doom and Downfall* (1651), dedicated to Elizabeth Cromwell, Bridget Ireton, and other wives of parliamentarian leaders.[14]

In addition to these published works, writings in manuscript such as Brilliana Harley's letters to her husband and son claim our attention. In the 'Siege Letters' addressed to her husband, the Puritan MP Robert Harley, she indicates her keen interest in the conflict between King and Parliament, and Parliament's assertion of its prerogatives against Charles. She also addresses Charles and his agents who command her to cede her estate Brampton Bryan to the Crown, protesting the abrogation of her rights as a property owner.[15]

Not only dissenters and parliamentarians, but also royalist women such as Mary Pope published tracts expressing pro-monarchist critiques of Parliament.[16] Anna Weamys (Mrs A.W.), author of *A Continuation of Sir Philip Sydney's Arcadia* (1651), wrote in the genre of romance to affirm her royalist allegiances.[17] The most prominent (and prolific) royalist writer during this period was Margaret Cavendish, Duchess of Newcastle, the wife of Charles I's general and Charles II's governor. During the Interregnum, even during her exile in Antwerp, Cavendish published five folio volumes in various genres and subjects: *Poems and Fancies* (1653), *Philosophical Fancies* (1653), *Philosophical and Physical Opinions* (1655), *The Worlds Olio* (1655), and *Natures Pictures* (1656); many of the works she composed during these years (e.g., her plays) were published after the Restoration.[18] Jane Cavendish, Margaret's stepdaughter, wrote poetry and a play, 'The Concealed Fansyes' – the latter with her sister, Elizabeth Brackley – included in manuscript presentation volumes for their father.[19]

The manuscript volume 'Poems Breathed forth by the Nobel Haddassas' by Hester Pulter, another notable royalist writer, includes a strikingly wide variety of genres: satires, love-poetry, elegies, emblems, allegories, and a substantial romance, 'The Unfortunate Florinda'. The dates of this manuscript, 1655–78, indicate that Pulter's authorship began during the Interregnum and continued well after the Restoration of Charles II.[20]

As evident in the example of Pulter, the impetus for women to produce impressive and substantial works during the Interregnum did not abate after the Restoration of the monarchy in 1660. Most notably, Cavendish's writing and publishing career spans the Interregnum and Restoration, for she published in the 1660s and the 1670s revised editions of many of her volumes that originally appeared in the 1650s. During the same period, she also published eight folio volumes of new writing, including additional works on natural science, one of which included her speculative utopia *The Blazing World* (1666), as well as collections of fictional orations (*Orations of Divers Sorts* [1662]) and letters (*CCXI Sociable Letters* [1664]), and the biography of her husband (1667).[21]

From the opposite pole of the political spectrum, Lucy Hutchinson also wrote during the 1660s a biography of her husband, the parliamentarian Colonel John Hutchinson, for her family.[22] She composed an epic poem based on Genesis – comparable to Milton's *Paradise Lost* – and published a portion of it anonymously, as *Order and Disorder* (1679).[23] Her translation of Lucretius's *De Rerum Natura* and her elegies written after her husband's death remained in manuscript until recently.[24]

Although writings by sectarian women abated after the Restoration, Margaret Fell published *A Declaration and an Information* (1660) which gives a detailed and graphic description of the violence and torture suffered by Quaker prisoners as well as letters reminding Charles II of his promise to protect the Quakers and attacking the judge for ruling against them. In her most well-known work, *Women's Speaking Justified* (1666), she defended the right of women to speak in church and to become preachers and ministers. Although Fell was the most prominent, many other Quaker writers, such as Elizabeth Hooton, Dorothy White, and Anne Docwra, wrote works that were circulated in manuscript among the missions or were published.[25]

Upon his return from exile in France, where a thriving theater included actresses, Charles not only reopened the London theaters – closed by the Puritans in 1642 – but permitted actresses for the first time to perform on the English stage. These conditions in Restoration London facilitated the rise of the first female professional playwright, Aphra Behn, who led the way for Catherine Trotter and Mary Pix later in the century. In addition to a large number of plays, the prolific Behn wrote poetry, short fiction, as well the epistolary novel, *Love Letters between a Nobleman and his Sister* (1687).[26]

Behn set her novella *Oroonoko* (1688) in Surinam and her play *The Widow Ranter* (1689) in Virginia; Anne Bradstreet's poems composed in New England were published in London in 1650 with an expanded edition published in Boston in 1678.[27] Other women wrote during this period from the margins of Britain – Katherine Philips from Wales and Lady Anne Halkett from Scotland. During the Civil Wars and Interregnum, the Stuart court was in exile in France, but it was only after the Restoration that the effects of this transculturalism manifested themselves in women's writing: Philips translated plays by Corneille for the London stage;[28] Halkett described in her memoirs her experiences supporting the Jacobite cause in Scotland; Mary Carleton convincingly represented herself as a 'German Princess' as recounted in her *Case of Madam Mary Carleton* (1663) dedicated to Prince Rupert of the Rhine;[29] and Elizabeth Cellier, a midwife married to a Frenchman, authored a number of political and midwifery tracts, and after the Glorious Revolution accompanied James II into exile in France.[30]

The political upheavals during the early 1680s generated by the Popish Plot (which revolved around the accusation that Catholics were conspiring to assassinate Charles II in order to place his Catholic brother James on the throne) and the Exclusion Crisis (caused by Parliament's attempt to exclude James from the succession) brought concern about the outbreak of another civil war. The conditions that reproduced the disorder of the Civil Wars again encouraged a spate of publications by women. The previously mentioned Elizabeth Cellier's *Malice Defeated* (1680) and her subsequent publications were written in response to the Popish Plot. Elizabeth Cary's *Historie of Edward II* (composed 1626–27) was published in 1680, during the Exclusion Crisis – though attributed to her husband, Lord Falkland.[31] Through her extensive correspondence, Lady Rachel Russell helped transform her husband William – executed for treason in 1683 as a participant in the Rye House Plot (to assassinate Charles and James after the failure of the Exclusion Bill) – into a national Whig martyr. After the Glorious Revolution (1688–89), her husband was officially rehabilitated and she became an important political figure.[32]

Elinor James, a printer's widow who published numerous petitions during 1682–1715 to the King, the Parliament, and her fellow citizens of London, produced a number of pamphlets surrounding the Glorious Revolution, the endpoint of this volume. In these, she strongly advised against setting aside James II in favor of William, and admonished William not to accept the crown.[33] In the wake of the Glorious Revolution, Joan Whitrowe published tracts addressing William (1689) and Mary (1690), claiming the 'Liberty' to counsel the monarchs, for she intends 'what is good for the King and his People'.[34] In Whitrowe's statement, we may see an exemplary reaffirmation of women's right and prerogative, first claimed during the seventeenth century, to participate in public political discourse.

Virginia Woolf and 'Judith Shakespeare'

Virginia Woolf in her 1929 *A Room of One's Own* wrote concerning what she considered the hypothetical woman writer in early modern England: 'Aubrey hardly mentions her. She never writes her own life and scarcely keeps a diary; there are only a handful of her letters in existence. She left no plays or poems by which we can judge her'.[35] Woolf's belief – mistaken, in retrospect, as I have indicated in the foregoing section – in the absence of women writers led her to ask 'who shall measure the heat and violence of the poet's heart when caught and tangled in a woman's body?' and to imagine Judith, Shakespeare's 'extraordinarily gifted sister' who, pregnant, 'killed herself one winter's night and lies buried at some cross-roads' (49–50). Though she writes favorably of Aphra Behn and disparagingly of Margaret Cavendish, Woolf apparently was not aware of the many writers who would be 'rediscovered' toward the end of the twentieth century. While Woolf's praise of Behn – 'All women together ought to let flowers fall upon the tomb of Aphra Behn ... for it was she who earned them the right to speak their minds' (69) – continues to be quoted approvingly by contemporary scholars, her assessment of Cavendish as 'hare-brained' (64) and the statement that her work 'stand[s] congealed in quartos and folios that nobody ever reads' (65) has been emphatically challenged by the outpouring of scholarship on Cavendish in the last decade as well as by the establishment of the International Margaret Cavendish Society which will hold its eighth biennial meeting in 2011. And even Woolf's characterization of Behn as a foremother for women writers needs to be revised by our awareness of the many who were writing even earlier than Behn in the seventeenth century, such as Aemilia Lanyer and Elizabeth Cary. Woolf's bald statement, 'Letters did not count', elaborating on her assertion that Dorothy Osborne 'wrote nothing' (65) – though she later refers to Sir Walter Raleigh's letters as examples of 'pure, self-assertive virility' (106) – is belied by the increasing amount of scholarship on early modern women's letters. And her assumption that a statement in a recently published imaginary novel, 'Chloe liked Olivia', bespoke a great change – 'Chloe liked Olivia perhaps for the first time in literature' (86) – has also proven to be in need of revision by scholars who have called attention to same-sex desire in early modern women's writing.

In *Writing Women's Literary History* (1998), Margaret J. M. Ezell challenged the 'evolutionary model' of narrative historiography that was the basis for Woolf and later scholars of women's literary history, in which earlier writers are judged on the basis of nineteenth-century conceptions of authorship and of literature.[36] These conceptions, centered on publication in the competitive marketplace, Ezell argues, have led to the overlooking or exclusion of 'a literary world before 1700, one in which men and women participated together' (38). Moreover, Ezell importantly showed that an earlier, eighteenth- and nineteenth-century 'tradition of anthologizing women's verse and recording women writers' works and lives' and the 'large body of writing by women and studies of women authors' available to readers then became lost to Woolf and to later scholars.[37] Thus the accomplishments of writers such as Cavendish and Katherine Philips were more evident and their works more readily available in the eighteenth and nineteenth centuries than they were during much of the twentieth century.

Ezell characterizes George Ballard's *Memoirs of Several ladies of Great Britain Who have been Celebrated for their Writings or Skill in the Learned Languages, Arts and Sciences* (1752) as 'the most developed and subsequently influential presentation of early women writers' (78). Working in the British Library, I came across an extensive manuscript 'Catalogue of Ladies famous for their writings, or skill in the learned languages' apparently compiled in 1749 for Ballard, which includes many of the seventeenth-century writers we study today, such as 'Eliz. Carew [Carey]', Anne Clifford, Mary Wroth, Margaret Cavendish, Katherine Philips, and 'Astrea Behn'. Significantly, while the list also includes 'Anne Broadstreet [Bradstreet]' it does not mention Aemilia Lanyer or any of the Civil War writers, except Katherine Chidley. But it also includes many writers unfamiliar to us, such as 'Lady Packington', 'Lady Gethin', 'Lady Hay', etc.[38] Ballard's volume does not include discussion of some writers on the manuscript list, such as Cary, Clifford, Wroth, Bradstreet, or even Behn, but it does include an additional writer active during the Civil War, Eleanor Davies.[39]

The memoir and biography of her husband by Lucy Hutchinson, another writer who has come to prominence recently, was published in 1806 and 1906, but not included by Woolf in her discussion of women authors, perhaps because Hutchinson's published work was not properly 'literary'. Neither does Woolf discuss Anne Clifford, whose autobiography she used as she was writing *Orlando*.[40] Woolf's omission of these writers indicates the shift that has occurred in what scholars now consider 'women's writing', which not only includes 'literature' in the traditional sense, but also memoirs and letters, and works that remained in manuscript as well as those that were printed.

The history of the history of seventeenth-century British women's writing, 1982–2010

Just as Woolf's assertion, 'Women cannot write the plays of Shakespeare' (48) was prompted by her feminism, evident in her account of being chased away by a beadle from the library at 'Oxbridge' and of the many negative representations of women by male authors in the books she read in the British Museum, so the scholars who later in the century would take up the study of women writers were influenced by second-wave feminism and the rise of women's history that sought to recover women's achievements that had been lost. For example, intellectual historian Hilda L. Smith, the author of the pioneering *Reason's Disciples* (1982) also has written concerning her experiences as a feminist activist when a graduate student at the University of Chicago.[41] Patricia Crawford, in 'Women's Published Writings, 1600–1700' (1985) – included in an influential volume on early modern women's history edited by Mary Prior – found a dramatic rise in the number of published writings after 1640, which with some falling off persisted into the Restoration; during the 1680s and 1690s their number matched and exceeded the level of the 1640s.[42] Sara Mendelson, who later co-authored with Crawford *Women in Early Modern England* (1998), featured Cavendish as one of her three 'case studies' in *The Mental World of Stuart Women* (1987); correcting Woolf's assessment, she argued for Cavendish's importance as a writer and her influence on Hutchinson and others.[43] Elaine Hobby, the first scholar of English literature to produce a monograph in this emerging field of scholarship, discussed in her *Virtue of Necessity* (1988) an extensive range of genres – including prophecies, autobiographies, and 'skill books' on housewifery, medicine, and midwifery – in which women wrote between the execution of Charles I and the Glorious Revolution.[44]

In the subsequent two decades, scholarship on seventeenth-century English women writers has truly come into its own. Smith and Susan Cardinale's extensive annotated bibliography of 637 works by women, and nearly 1,000 works for and about women, proved to be an invaluable resource for scholars in identifying texts for further study;[45] it also would prove influential in widening the study of women's writing beyond what was traditionally considered 'literature'.

Even so, as Germaine Greer stated in the Introduction to *Kissing the Rod* (1988), her pioneering anthology of women's poetry in the seventeenth century – the century of 'Donne, Milton, and Dryden': poetry represents 'the highest bastion of the cultural establishment'.[46] Aware of the historical importance of this project, Greer states: 'We are at the beginning of the long process of literary archeology rather than the end'.[47] Indeed, the works of Julia Palmer and Anne Southwell, which Greer and the other editors searched for but could not find, have now been discovered and published; and Hester Pulter, unknown to the editors, has recently been recognized as an important poet deserving scholarly attention, though an edition of her works still awaits publication.[48]

Two monographs and two collections of essays appeared in 1992 on early modern English women writers. Both Elaine Beilin's *Redeeming Eve* and Tina Krontiris's *Oppositional Voices* include discussion of earlier, sixteenth-century writers, concluding with chapters on Elizabeth Cary, Aemilia Lanyer, and Mary Wroth.[49] *Women, Texts & Histories 1575–1760*, edited by Clare Brant and Diane Purkiss, and *Women, Writing, History, 1640–1740*, edited by Isobel Grundy and Susan Wiseman, span longer periods, extending into the eighteenth century. These collections already presage the expansion of the field beyond the triumvirate of Cary, Lanyer, and Wroth and beyond 'literary' works strictly speaking: the writings studied include those by English nuns, female prophets, and writers such as Mary Carleton, who will receive scholarly attention in the subsequent decade. Already, both collections include work on Cavendish, predictive of her importance to the field in more recent years.

Along with these monographs and collections appeared Susanne Woods's 1993 edition of Lanyer's poetry which proved to be instrumental in making Lanyer available for twentieth-century scholars as well as for use in the classroom. Woods's volume marked the inauguration of Oxford University Press's series, Women Writers in English 1350–1850, which in subsequent years published volumes on a number of writers spanning the seventeenth century, such as Arbella Stuart, Rachel Speght, Eleanor Davies, Anna Weamys, and Jane Sharp. Barbara Lewalski's influential *Writing Women in Jacobean England* (1995) includes chapters on Queen Anne and other aristocratic writers such as Arbella Stuart and Anne Clifford, as well as the three treated by Beilin and Krontiris.[50]

Even while this scholarship took as its subject women writers per se, Wendy Wall's *Imprint of Gender* (1993), though focused primarily on the period before 1610, foregrounded the concept of 'gender', discussing Lanyer and Wroth as examples of how 'the strict limitations placed on women's social and mental activities' and 'the overwhelming weight of prohibition against authorship' mark their works by contrast to those by 'A Man In Print' (e.g., Michael Drayton) in the literary marketplace.[51]

This concern with gender was already present in Greer's recognition that many works published under women's names were in fact written by men and Diane Purkiss's contention that the pamphlets signed by women in the 'woman debate' cannot be assumed to be the work of women: 'the gendering of their authors remains open to question'.[52]

Paul Salzman in his recent *Reading Early Modern Women's Writing* (2007) disaggregates the category of 'woman writer' by calling attention to differences among the writers, especially in class position. His book also discusses writing in many genres, as well as works in both print and manuscript. His contribution to this volume concerns the possibilities of networks and affiliations among women writers.

Class, race, and sexuality

Taking up the challenge of third-wave feminism that raised questions concerning an essentialist female identity and experience, the next generation of scholars began to address issues of class and race as they intersected with gender, as well as issues of sexuality. Susan Wiseman made an early argument that Cavendish in her plays 'wishes to support the idealized class order, but to disrupt gender ideologies'.[53] In articles on Aemilia Lanyer, Lisa Schnell challenged Lewalski who maintained that Lanyer sought to construct a proto-feminist 'community of women' through her poetry; Schnell argued, rather, that Lanyer's attitude toward the aristocratic women from whom she sought patronage was resentful and at times hostile.[54] These have been followed by Hero Chalmers's *Royalist Women Writers* (2004) – on Cavendish, Philips, and Behn – and my *Subordinate Subjects* (2003) on women's writing in relation to those by non-aristocratic males.[55]

The various ways in which female authors – Cary, Wroth, and Behn – negotiated race were first explored by some of the essays collected by Margo Hendricks and Patricia Parker in *Women, 'Race', and Writing in the Early Modern Period* (1994).[56] Bernadette Andrea deployed an expanded notion of authorship as she argued that Queen Anne subverted the patriarchal prerogative of her husband James by appropriating Africanness in her performance of Jonson's *Masque of Blackness*.[57] Andrea, who contributes a chapter on women and Islam to this volume, emphasized this ambivalent position of English women writers who advanced a 'feminist orientalism' at the expense of Muslim women.[58] Joyce Green MacDonald, in *Women and Race in Early Modern Texts* (2002), uses critical race theory to discuss a similar 'complication of female authorship by race' in the works of Behn and Philips.[59]

In a departure from the virtually exclusive focus on the heterosexual woman that characterized the first generation of scholarship, Theodora Jankowski in *Pure Resistance* (2000) coined the now oft-used term 'queer virgins' to designate those who resist compulsory heterosexuality in patriarchy.[60] She contributes a chapter to this volume on sexuality and economics – and the conjunction of prostitution and marriage. Harriette Andreadis and Valerie Traub called attention to the presence of homosexual relations and homoerotic desire between women.[61] Andreadis examined the work of Cavendish, Manley, Behn, and Killigrew to argue that these writers expressed female same-sex erotics through evasive erotic language; and Traub, while discussing Philips, also uncovered a rich (pre)history of lesbianism in early modern England.

Literacy

Women's literacy in early modern England has been an active field of scholarly investigation, following Margaret Ferguson's demonstration that rates of women's literacy were higher than previously assumed.[62] In addition to Speght, the defenses of women by 'Constantia Munda' and 'Ester Sowernam' indicate that there was a female readership for these works, even though it might not have been as large as the market for Swetnam's misogynist attack, for his work went through ten editions while the defenses were each published only once. Other popular books targeting a female readership include Richard Brathwaite's *The English Gentlewoman* (1631) and John Taylor's *The Needles Excellency* (?1629), which celebrates needlework as a skill practiced by queens and aristocrats, and which went through twelve editions by 1640. Recent scholarship on the Civil War, Interregnum, and Restoration has contributed a great deal to our knowledge of works published during these years that were targeted to a female readership. Ezell suggests that popular advice books that were heretofore considered to have been intended for male audiences, such as the 1650s editions of the *Academy of Complements*, were in fact marketed to young female readers, exemplifying the important connection between literacy and social mobility during a period that saw 'astonishing upheavals in social decorum and customs occasioned by the war'.[63] In the final years of the Commonwealth, Sarah Jinner published *An Almanack or Prognostication* (1658, 1659, 1660), which defended women's publication in 'the Celestial Sciences' citing the example of Maria Cuniz, the Silesian astronomer and the author of *Urania propitia* (1650); in her almanac Jinner prominently featured medical advice specifically for women, concerning menstruation and reproduction. Jinner's medical entries in her almanacs anticipate the post-Restoration publication of medical texts directed to a female readership such as Jane Sharp's manual, *The Midwives Book: Or the Art of Midwifry Discovered* (1671) and Mary Trye's *Medicatrix, or the Woman-Physician* (1675),[64] as well as Elizabeth Cellier's defense of the expertise of midwives over male physicians, *To Dr. — (1688)*. Anne Maxwell, who printed the works of Cavendish, published grammars such as *Reading and spelling English made easie* (1673) as well as Hannah Wolley's *The Gentlewomans companion: or, A guide to the female sex: containing directions of behaviour... with letters and discourses upon all occasions. Whereunto is added, a guide for cook-maids, dairy-maides, etc.* (1673), targeted to women of different ranks.[65]

Print culture and manuscript coteries

As Crawford indicated, women participated in the explosion of print culture during the English Civil Wars, but even earlier in the century, Lanyer published *Salve Deus Rex Judaeorum* (1611), Elizabeth Cary published *The Tragedie of Mariam* (1613), and Rachel Speght participated in the Jacobean pamphlet debate on gender initiated by Joseph Swetnam's *Arraignment of Lewde, idle, froward, and unconstant Women* (1615).[66] Lanyer sought patrons by including numerous dedications to aristocratic women in her volume of poetry (the combination of dedications not identical in all surviving copies) and Speght may have been recruited to join the profitable publishing venture of the Swetnam controversy.[67] In any case, the publication of these two works are landmark events in the history of British women's writing. Megan Matchinske traces in her chapter for this volume the continuities in the discourses between the Jacobean pamphlet debate on gender and the poetry of Lanyer and Diana Primrose. Much work has already been accomplished on the outpouring of print publications by women during the Civil Wars and Interregnum, for example in Marcus Nevitt's *Women and the Pamphlet Culture of Revolutionary England, 1640–1660* (2006). Many of these women – e.g., Anna Trapnel and Eleanor Davies – were sectarian writers publishing on the cusp of religion and politics. Others, such as Elizabeth Poole and the women petitioners, sought to intervene directly in political developments through the medium of print. Even after the Restoration, women such as Mary Carleton continued to publish their works. The Exclusion Crisis served as a catalyst for the publishing activities of middle-class women such as the midwife Elizabeth Cellier and the printer's widow Elinor James. In a series of important articles,

Maureen Bell has shown the important role women played in the book trade during this period.[68]

In *The Patriarch's Wife: Literary Evidence and the History of the Family* (1987), Ezell examined an essay by Mary More, 'A Woman's Right', contained in a manuscript miscellany designed for circulation.[69] Ezell has been instrumental in our understanding of manuscript circulation as a form of publication,[70] and the Perdita Project at Nottingham Trent University, directed by Elizabeth Clarke, has contributed a great deal in identifying and making accessible over 230 digitized manuscripts by writers such as Julia Palmer and Hester Pulter. These developments have led to the publication of two anthologies of manuscripts edited by Jill Seal Millman and Gillian Wright and by Helen Ostovich and Elizabeth Sauer.[71] Victoria Burke, who edited with Jonathan Gibson a collection of essays on women's manuscript culture, contributes a chapter on this subject to this volume.[72] And Clare Kinney discusses in her chapter both the published Part I and unpublished Part II of Mary Wroth's *Urania*, indicating that writers cannot be easily divided into those who participated in either print culture or manuscript coteries.

Genres

As already mentioned, poetry was one of the first literary genres to receive attention from scholars and teachers of early modern women's writing: Greer's anthology was followed by others, most notably one edited by Marion Wynne-Davies. Scholarship on poetry included a collection of essays, *Write or Be Written*, and *Poetic Resistance*, by Pamela Hammons, who contributes a chapter on poetry to this volume.[73] The other major genre of women's writing to be studied was drama, as indicated in the anthology and collection of contextual texts edited by Wynne-Davies and S. P. Cerasano and the books on drama by Nancy Cotton and Jacqueline Pearson.[74] Recent work on women's closet drama by Marta Straznicky and Karen Raber has advanced our understanding concerning this sub-genre that enabled women to engage in playwriting when the public stage was not available to them.[75] Wynne-Davies contributes a chapter to this volume reassessing the field of early modern women's dramatic writing. The seventeenth century also saw the beginning of women's contribution to the writing of fiction, most notably by Mary Wroth and Aphra Behn. Clare Kinney argues that Wroth engages in a 'defense of poesy' – referring to the well-known example by her uncle Philip Sidney – in her romance fiction *Urania* and sonnet sequence *Pamphilia to Amphilanthus*. Margaret Reeves takes up the fiction of Behn to discuss its intersection with satire and history. As the field has expanded, other genres, both literary and non-literary – e.g., memoirs, mother's advice books – have become objects of scholarship.[76] Following the recent attention that women's letters have received from scholars, Susan Wiseman raises the question in her chapter of the status of letters as women's writing.[77]

Interdisciplinary approaches: religion, politics, law, history, science and medicine, art and architecture

Scholarship on early modern women's writing has always been inter-disciplinary: historians have used literary works and literature scholars have been attentive to the historical context of the authors and their writings. Closely corresponding to the expansion of the field in terms of the different genres that scholars are considering is the interdiscipli-nary nature of these investigations. For example, religion was an early focus of scholarship on these writers, even before the current renewal of interest by early modern scholars on the subject. Initially the argument was made that religious subjects, along with translations from other languages, enabled women to pursue appropriately self-effacing author-ship. However, studies of sectarian women writers during the Civil Wars, Catholic recusant women, and Quaker women quickly dispelled this notion.[78] As Patricia Crawford argues, 'religion was their most pow-erful justification for activity outside their conventional roles'.[79] Indeed, the most recent studies of women and religion by Erica Longfellow and Shannon Miller emphasize the political dimension of women's religious writings.[80] Miller's chapter in this volume examines women's contributions to the intersection of religion and political thought. And Katharine Gillespie, whose *Domesticity and Dissent* (2004) argued for the political engagement of sectarian women writers, who spoke out 'against Presbyterian ministers, judges, members of Parliament, kings, and even their own ministers', identifies a discourse of Fifth Monarchism among women writing during the Civil Wars in her chapter for this volume.[81]

If women's religious writings had implications for politics, so did their writings in other genres.[82] Recent scholars of seventeenth-century women's writing no longer take at face value Richard Brathwaite's injunction in *The English Gentlewoman* (1631) against women engaging in 'discourse on State-matters' and 'state-political action', nor Margaret Cavendish's disclaimer that 'I have not been bred, being a Woman, to public Affairs, Associations, or Negotiations'.[83] Indeed, since the mid-1990s and especially in the last several years, scholars have been calling attention to the political implications and ambitions of their writing.[84] These scholars share a common concern with redefining the public and private divide: Carol Barash in her study of seventeenth- and eighteenth-century women's poetry argued that the apparently different spheres of male vs. female, public vs. private, and books vs. manuscripts were interwoven – rather than mutually exclusive.[85] In *Subordinate Subjects* I discussed women's pre-Civil War poetry and pamphlet literature as well as pamphlets produced after the Restoration and during the Exclusion Crisis as interventions in the political conversations of their time. My chapter for this volume examines Katherine Philips's translations of Corneille as 'Civil War writings' that also reflect upon the relation between the metropole and the colony. Susan Wiseman's *Conspiracy and Virtue* (2007) argues that women's theoretical exclusion from the political sphere elicited and shaped 'figurative, oblique, complex' political responses from women on issues concerning 'law, liberty, subjecthood, property, nature, reason, land'.[86] Wiseman's chapter in this volume on women's letters foregrounds precisely these issues.

These works, as well as the four-volume collection of manuscript and printed political writings by seventeenth-century women edited by Smith, Suzuki, and Wiseman (2007), place women into what many have considered the most important framing of seventeenth-century structure and values: politics and political theory. Scholars are examining as political writing works by women in different genres – letters, petitions and other pamphlets, poetry, essays, plays, and other literary works – that do not necessarily follow the familiar form of the systematic treatise in which Hobbes and Locke wrote. These texts examine topics such as 'the power and legitimacy of the state, the most effective forms of government, and the relative power of rulers and their subjects or citizens'.[87] This reevaluation has already begun to take place for Margaret Cavendish, whose *Blazing World* and *Orations* have been collected in a volume of *Cambridge Texts in the History of Political Thought* edited by Susan James.[88] Joanne Wright's contribution to this volume takes up the question of Cavendish's intervention in the question of war and its justifications.

Early modern women's legal standing cannot be easily separated from their political status. Amy Louise Erickson's *Women and Property in Early Modern England* (1993) has been an important guide for scholars of women's writing, as has Barbara J. Todd's challenge to the stereotype of the 'remarrying widow', in which she emphasizes the greater freedom and independence that widows enjoyed.[89] Indeed, Anne Clifford's account of her female ancestors indicates that they accomplished much as widows; she herself enjoyed a lengthy widowhood, ruling her estates as a baron in her own right and using her will to endow almshouses for lay widows and her female servants.[90] In *Bell in Campo*, Cavendish similarly portrays a widow who wills the enormous sum of £1,000 to her maid so that she will not be compelled to marry.[91]

During the Civil Wars, female petitioners cited legal precedents and the writings of Edward Coke in advancing their points. It is noteworthy that even after the Restoration, non-aristocratic women such as Mary Carleton and Elizabeth Cellier displayed their expertise in the law during their trials. A Canterbury fiddler's daughter, Mary Carleton in her *Case of Madam Mary Carleton* (1663) claims that her father was a 'Licentiat and Doctor of the Civil Law' and repeatedly calls attention to her familiarity with the legal system and its terminology. In *Malice Defeated* (1680) the midwife Elizabeth Cellier invokes the rights of the accused as well as statutes by 'Mr. Cook' (Edward Coke), and claims during her trial that her knowledge of English law was indispensable to her husband, a Frenchman. Anne Docwra also recounts how her father, a justice under Charles I, encouraged her to read statute books when she was young; she later authored *A Looking-glass for the Recorder and Justices of the Peace, and Grand Juries for the Town and County of Cambridge* (1682). Thus although the legal profession was closed to women, some women attained legal knowledge and in some cases defended themselves successfully in court. Legal texts such as *Lawes Resolution of Womens Rights Or the Lawes Provisions for Women* (1632) targeted, at least in part, a female readership.

While Catherine Macaulay's *History of England* has often been designated as the first history written by an Englishwoman, Natalie Zemon Davis first treated Hutchinson and Cavendish as historians; Sheila Ottway and Helen Wilcox discussed in addition works by Anne Halkett, Anne Fanshawe, Brilliana Harley, Dorothy Osborne, and Anne Clifford as women's histories.[92] Megan Matchinske's *Women Writing History in Early Modern England* (2009) also takes an expansive view of women's historical writing to include 'poetic verse, mothers' legacy, diary, and apology', a view congruent with that of scholars who have argued for considering genres other than the political treatise – plays, essays, petitions, letters – as political writing.[93] Margaret Reeves's contribution to this volume examines the conjunction of history with the genres of satire and fiction in the prose narratives by Cary and Behn.

Just as scholars are turning to fields such as politics, law, and historiography that were assumed to be inhospitable to early modern women, so scholars are investigating early modern women's involvement in medicine and science. Elaine Hobby has edited Jane Sharp's midwifery texts; more recently, Rebecca Laroche examines women's engagement in their writings with the medical authority of herbal texts.[94] Historian of science Londa Schiebinger began her discussion of women in early modern science, *The Mind has No Sex?* (1991) with Margaret Cavendish;[95] Cristina Malcolmson's chapter in this volume investigates Cavendish's understanding of race in the context of her scientific interests.

Art history and architecture represents another interdisciplinary field of study that promises fruitful inquiry. Anne Clifford's commission of the 'Great Picture' and her architectural projects have already been studied by a number of scholars as instances of her authorship.[96] Patricia Phillippy, whose *Painting Women* (2006) examined the connections between women's writing and painting, takes up the question of women's design of funereal monuments and the inscriptions they authored as the subject of her chapter for this volume.[97]

Transcultural and global approaches

While these interdisciplinary approaches have necessitated scholars to gain expertise in disciplines not their own, the crossing of geographical boundaries has required knowledge of languages and cultures other than English, or at times, even European. In suggesting directions for future scholarship on early modern women, Jane Stevenson and Merry Wiesner-Hanks have called for placing women and their writings in a larger, transnational context.[98] As Stevenson states, such work will entail 'cross-cultural comparative work', to investigate the 'variety of interfaces between early modern Englishwomen and the wider world', for 'early modern people themselves were aware of comparative perspectives'.[99] Indeed, David Norbrook has already explored the notion of a European women's 'republic of letters' in the mid-seventeenth century; and Julie Campbell and Anne Larsen's new collection of essays centers on women's 'transnational community of letters'.[100] My chapter on Katherine Philips takes as its point of departure the question of transculturalism between France and England, especially in terms of the near-contemporary civil wars that the two countries experienced during the seventeenth century. Beyond Europe, Bernadette Andrea's *Women and Islam* (2007) and Kate Chedzoy's *Women Writing in the British Atlantic World* (2007) promise that the turn to 'internationalism' and 'global approaches' that Wiesner-Hanks has called for as the next step in the scholarship of early modern women will prove to be a fruitful avenue of inquiry.[101] Andrea's chapter for this volume makes a further contribution to this endeavor.

With the globalization and internationalization of scholarship, scholars have been able to exchange ideas at conferences drawing participants from all over the world. For example, Paul Salzman hosted a conference in New Zealand that produced an oft-cited volume of essays, and the conference 'Still Kissing the Rod' at Oxford University resulted in a special issue of *Women's Writing*. The International Cavendish Society conference alternates between Europe and North America; some essays based on papers given at the Paris conference were included in a special double issue on Cavendish of *In-Between* (volume 9, 2000) published by the University of New Delhi.

Institutional frameworks for scholarship and teaching: conferences, academic journals, book series, editions, anthologies

Scholarly associations which regularly sponsor conferences for readers of this volume include the already mentioned International Cavendish Society, the Aphra Behn Society for Women and the Arts 1660–1830, and the interdisciplinary Society for the Study of Early Modern Women which holds a biennial conference, 'Attending to Women'.

Just as conferences encourage the timely dissemination of new discoveries and new approaches, so, the establishment of academic journals such as *Women's Writing* and *Early Modern Women: An Interdisciplinary Journal* enable the consolidation of these findings. Blackwell's online journal, *Literature Compass*, whose seventeenth-century section was first edited by Ezell and is now edited by Elizabeth Clarke, has published a number of important articles on seventeenth-century women writers, both established, such as Philips, and newly discovered, such as Pulter. Ashgate has published a large number of books on seventeenth-century women writers in its book series, Women and Gender in the Early Modern World and its facsimiles series, The Early Modern Englishwoman in Print; recently it brought out a six-volume collection of critical essays that include volumes on Lanyer, Wroth, Clifford and Hutchinson, Cary, and Cavendish.[102]

The ability to access printed texts through Early English Books Online and women's manuscript writings through the Perdita Project has been a boon to scholars and students who do not have direct access to these materials. Yet these online resources, which are available only by subscription, do not obviate the need for editions with full scholarly apparatus. The early, though limited, edition of Aphra Behn, by Montague Summers, published in 1915 and reissued in 1967 undoubtedly encouraged the scholarship on Behn; and since the early 1990s Behn scholars have had access to Janet Todd's edition of her works.[103] The recent explosion of scholarship on Lanyer, Cary, and Cavendish – as well as their frequent appearance on course syllabi – was made possible by the readily available editions of their works. Some editions now under preparation include the collected works of Hutchinson edited by David Norbrook and the collected works of Philips edited by Elizabeth Hageman. Other writers in need of new scholarly editions of their complete works include Anne Bradstreet and Margaret Cavendish.

The publication of MLA's *Teaching Tudor and Stuart Writers* (2000), edited by Margaret Hannay and Susanne Woods, confirms that at least the earlier part of the century is being taught regularly in courses on women writers or in literature courses more generally. The importance of anthologies in establishing a field of scholarship as well as a claim to be included in course syllabi has been well established by *Kissing the Rod*. Also of immense significance was Paul Salzman's inclusion in his Oxford World Classics *Anthology of Seventeenth-Century Fiction* (1991) of Book I of Wroth's *Urania* and Cavendish's *Blazing World*, before there were any modern editions of either text. The anthology of texts from the Swetnam controversy, *Half Humankind* (although it mysteriously omits Speght, the only writer whose identity as a woman writer is certain), made these texts available for the classroom. A number of anthologies have appeared in the last decade, though at times the excerpts are too short or the same texts by certain writers, such as Cavendish, tend to be repeatedly anthologized.[104] Broadview Press has published a number of texts suitable for use in the classroom by Cary, Clifford, and Cavendish.[105] Elizabeth Hageman has joined Margaret King and Albert Rabil, Jr. as general editor for a series of English texts to be published in the series The Other Voice in Early Modern Europe, suitable for use by both scholars and teachers.[106]

Rethinking periodization: moving forward

This volume does not follow the traditional divisions of literary scholarship that have discussed together Elizabethan and Jacobean writings, and grouped together those of the Restoration and the eighteenth century. Rather, it cuts across boundaries of periodization to treat the period 1610–1690, beginning with the Jacobean pamphlet debate on gender, which enabled female and female-voiced tracts to advance women's subject position as a group, to include at its center the tumultuous mid-century Civil Wars and Interregnum as an important watershed for women's writing – whose effects continued to be felt during the Restoration, Exclusion Crisis (1680), and the Glorious Revolution (1688–89) – that encouraged women writers to enter public political debates.[107] This volume is divided into four parts. Part I focuses on various links and connections between and among women writers during this period: Paul Salzman examines the continuities and discontinuities in the category 'woman writer'; Megan Matchinske traces the shared rhetoric used by authors of pamphlets (not necessarily women) involved in the Jacobean gender debate and women poets who wrote in the wake of the debate. Shannon Miller and Katharine Gillespie each focus on the important links among women writers created by a shared discourse of religion: Miller traces women writers' use of the biblical narrative of the Fall and Gillespie identifies a common discourse of Fifth Monarchism used by writers during the English Civil Wars.

Part II takes up related modes and sites of writing, which had been considered 'private' or excluded from the privileged category of 'literature', to which recent scholars of seventeenth-century women's writing have been paying increased attention with productive results. Victoria Burke's chapter discusses a great variety of manuscripts, which we now know were circulated, if not published in printed form. Susan Wiseman examines women's letters, which dealt with matters that were not confined to the 'domestic', and raises the question of their 'literary' value, as well as their value more widely. Patricia Phillippy studies funereal monuments as a unique site for women's writing, providing women a means to represent themselves and to forge female alliances.

The chapters in Part III reassess established literary genres from new perspectives. Clare Kinney suggests that Wroth's sonnet sequence and romance constitute defenses of poetry; Pamela Hammons, after surveying the existing scholarship on women's poetry, both in print and in manuscript, goes on to demonstrate a materialist approach, and shows how lyric poems can represent property and property rights. Marion Wynne-Davies takes stock of the great range of scholarship on women playwrights, in particular the recent interest in performance studies, and suggests directions for further work. Finally, Margaret Reeves argues for going beyond a focus on the development from romance to novel to a recognition of a relationship among the genres of fiction with history and satire, which have not been traditionally associated with women.

Part IV places seventeenth-century women's writing in new and still developing contexts: Theodora Jankowski discusses the intersection between sexuality and economics; Cristina Malcolmson investigates seventeenth-century women's contributions to early modern science and their interest in the question of race; Joanne Wright demonstrates the heretofore unrecognized military expertise evidenced in the writings of Cavendish; my own chapter reads Katherine Philips's Restoration translations as writings on civil war from a postcolonial and archipelagic perspective; and Bernadette Andrea shows English women writers' abiding engagement with Islam throughout the seventeenth century.

The chapters of this volume by many of the scholars working at the forefront of this field offer a guide to the direction scholarship on seventeenth-century women's writing is taking at the beginning of the twenty-first century. While Greer in editing *Kissing the Rod* implicitly sought to correct what she considered the overemphasis on history at the expense of literature in the scholarship on women's writing, the chapters in this volume demonstrate that an attention to history and historical contexts is in fact not incompatible with attention to literary questions such as genre. Indeed, scholars of the next generation will no doubt continue to expand these contexts as well as turn their attention to new authors and texts that still await discovery in archives and among manuscript collections labeled 'domestic papers'.[108]

Notes

1. Susanne Woods, ed., *The Poems of Aemilia Lanyer: Salve Deus Rex Judaeorum* (New York: Oxford University Press, 1993). Barry Weller and Margaret W. Ferguson, eds, *The Tragedy of Mariam with The Lady Falkland Her Life* (Berkeley: University of California Press, 1994).
2. Excerpts from Swetnam's text as well as from Sowernam, Munda, *Hic Mulier*, and *Haec Vir* are included in Katherine Usher Henderson and Barbara F. McManus, eds, *Half Humankind: Contexts and Texts of the Controversy About Women in England, 1540–1640* (Urbana: University of Illinois Press, 1985). For Speght, see Barbara Kiefer Lewalski, ed., *The Polemics and Poems of Rachel Speght* (New York: Oxford University Press, 1996).
3. D. J. H. Clifford, ed., *The Diaries of Lady Anne Clifford* (Stroud: Sutton, 1990). For the portion of the 'Great Book' not included in D. J. H. Clifford's edition, see Hilda L. Smith, Mihoko Suzuki, and Susan Wiseman, eds, *Women's Political Writings, 1610–1725* (London: Pickering and Chatto, 2007), I: 5–107.
4. Josephine Roberts, ed., *The First Part of the Countess of Montgomery's Urania* (Binghamton, NY: Center for Medieval and Early Renaissance Studies, 1995); Roberts, ed., completed by Suzanne Gossett and Janel Mueller, *The Second Part of the Countess of Montgomery's Urania* (Tempe, AZ: Renaissance English Text Society, 1999).
5. See Mihoko Suzuki, 'Elizabeth, Gender and the Political Imaginary in Seventeenth-Century England', in *Debating Gender in Early Modern England, 1500–1700*, ed. Cristina Malcolmson and Mihoko Suzuki (New York: Palgrave Macmillan, 2002), 231–53.
6. The texts by Leigh, Clinton, and Jocelin are included in Betty S. Travitsky, ed., *Mother's Advice Books* (Aldershot: Ashgate, 2001).

7. Naomi J. Miller, 'Hens should be served first: Prioritizing Maternal Production in the Early Modern Pamphlet Debate', in *Debating Gender*, ed. Malcolmson and Suzuki, 161–84.
8. Patricia Crawford, 'Women's Published Writings, 1600–1700', in *Women in English Society, 1500–1800*, ed. Mary Prior (London: Methuen, 1985), 211–82.
9. For texts of women's petitions published from 1641 to 1653, see *Women's Political Writings*, ed. Smith et al., II: 1–44.
10. See Mihoko Suzuki, *Subordinate Subjects: Gender, the Political Nation, and Literary Form in England, 1588–1688* (Aldershot: Ashgate, 2003), 145–51.
11. Katharine Gillespie, ed., *Katherine Chidley* (Aldershot: Ashgate, 2009), xi.
12. *Women's Political Writings*, ed. Smith et al., II: 47–65.
13. Ibid., II: 217–85.
14. Ibid., II: 181–200.
15. Ibid., I: 109–202.
16. Ibid., III: 67–163.
17. Anna Weamys, *The Continuation of Sir Philip Sidney's Arcadia*, ed. Patrick Cullen (New York: Oxford University Press, 1994).
18. For excerpts from Cavendish's works, see Sylvia Bowerbank and Sara Mendelson, eds, *Paper Bodies: A Margaret Cavendish Reader* (Peterborough, ON: Broadview, 2000). See also Anne Shaver, ed., *The Convent of Pleasure and Other Plays* (Baltimore: Johns Hopkins University Press, 1999).
19. S. P. Cerasano and Marion Wynne-Davies, eds, *Renaissance Drama by Women: Texts and Documents* (New York and London: Routledge, 1996), 127–56.
20. Excerpts from Pulter's poetry can be found in Jill Seal Millman and Gillian Wright, eds, *Early Modern Women's Manuscript Poetry* (Manchester: Manchester University Press, 2005), 111–27; and Jane Stevenson and Peter Davidson, eds, *Early Modern Women Poets: An Anthology* (New York: Oxford University Press, 2001), 187–95.
21. *The Blazing World* and selections from the *Orations* can be found in Susan James, ed., *Margaret Cavendish Political Writings* (New York: Cambridge University Press, 2003). See also Kate Lilly, ed., *The Blazing World and Other Writings* (London: Penguin, 1992) and James Fitzmaurice, ed., *Sociable Letters* (Peterborough, ON: Broadview, 2004).
22. N. H. Keeble, ed., *Memoirs of the Life of Colonel Hutchinson with a Fragment of Autobiography* (London: J. M. Dent; Rutland, VT: Everyman, 1995).
23. David Norbrook, ed., *Order and Disorder* (Oxford: Blackwell, 2000), includes both the published cantos and those that remained in manuscript.
24. Hugh de Quehen, ed., *Lucy Hutchinson's Translation of Lucretius: De rerum natura* (London: Duckworth; Ann Arbor: University of Michigan Press, 1996); David Norbrook, 'Lucy Hutchinson's Elegies and the Situation of the Republican Woman Writer (with text)', *English Literary Renaissance* 27 (1997): 468–521.
25. The writings by Fell, Hooton, White, Docwra, are available in *Women's Political Writings*, ed. Smith et al., vol. III.
26. The complete works of Aphra Behn have been published in seven volumes under the editorship of Janet Todd (London: Pickering, 1992–96).
27. Joseph R. McElrath, Jr. and Allan P. Robb, eds, *The Complete Works of Anne Bradstreet* (Boston: Twayne, 1981).

28. Patrick Thomas, ed., *The Collected Works of Katherine Philips* (Stump Cross: Stump Cross Books, 1993), vol. III.
29. Mihoko Suzuki, ed., *Mary Carleton* (Aldershot: Ashgate, 2006).
30. Mihoko Suzuki, ed., *Elizabeth Cellier* (Aldershot: Ashgate, 2006).
31. Margaret W. Ferguson, ed., *Works by and attributed to Elizabeth Cary* (Aldershot: Ashgate, 1996).
32. For selections of Russell's letters, 1671–91, see *Women's Political Writings*, ed. Smith et al., III: 83–108. See also Lois G. Schwoerer, *Lady Rachel Russell, 'One of the Best of Women'* (Baltimore: Johns Hopkins University Press, 1988).
33. Paula McDowell, ed., *Elinor James* (Aldershot: Ashgate, 2005), 62–79.
34. Joan Whitrowe, *The Humble Address of the Widow Whitrowe to King William*, in *Women's Political Writings*, ed. Smith et al., III: 207.
35. Virginia Woolf, *A Room of One's Own* (New York: Harcourt Brace, 1927), 47. Subsequent references are cited parenthetically in the text. A question similar to Woolf's was asked by art historian Linda Nochlin in 'Why Have There Been No Great Women Artists?' *Art News* 69 (January 1971): 22–39, 67–71, reprinted in *Women, Art, and Power and Other Essays* (Boulder: Westview Press, 1988), 147–58. Challenging the notion of 'genius' and 'greatness' ascribed to male artists, Nochlin, like Woolf, called attention to the institutional obstacles women faced in entering the artistic profession.
36. Margaret J. M. Ezell, *Writing Women's Literary History* (Baltimore: Johns Hopkins University Press, 1998), 18–23. Subsequent references are cited parenthetically in the text.
37. Ibid., 68: 'Between 1675 and 1875, there were at least twenty-five biographical encyclopedias and anthologies specifically devoted to chronicling the lives and labors of literary Englishwomen.'
38. British Library Add. MSS 4244 fol. 23.
39. George Ballard, *Memoirs of Several ladies of Great Britain Who have been Celebrated for their Writings or Skill in the Learned Languages, Arts and Sciences*, ed. Ruth Perry (Detroit: Wayne State University Press, 1985).
40. Nicky Hallett, 'Anne Clifford as Orlando: Virginia Woolf's Feminist Historiology and Women's Biography', *Women's History Review* 4 (1995): 505–24.
41. Hilda L. Smith, 'Regionalism, Feminism, Class: The Development of a Feminist Historian', in *Voices of Women Historians: The Personal, the Political, and the Professional*, ed. Eileen Boris and Nupur Chaudhuri (Bloomington: Indiana University Press, 1999), 30–42.
42. Crawford, 'Women's Published Writings', 212, see esp. fig. 7.1.
43. Sara Mendelson, *The Mental World of Stuart Women: Three Studies* (Amherst: University of Massachusetts Press, 1987), 61.
44. Elaine Hobby, *Virtue of Necessity: English Women's Writing, 1648–88* (Ann Arbor: University of Michigan Press, 1989).
45. Hilda L. Smith and Susan Cardinale, eds, *Women and the Literature of the Seventeenth Century: An Annotated Bibliography based on Wing's Short-title Catalogue* (New York: Greenwood, 1990).
46. Germaine Greer, Susan Hastings, Jeslyn Medoff, and Melissa Sansone, eds, *Kissing the Rod: An Anthology of Seventeenth-Century Women's Verse* (New York: Farrar, Straus, and Giroux, 1988), 1. The landmark nature of this publication event can be gleaned from its commemoration by an international

conference held at St. Hilda's College, Oxford: *Still Kissing the Rod?*: Early Modern Women's Writing, in 2005, and in the special issue of *Women's Writing* (14.2 [2007]), *Still Kissing the Rod?: Early Modern Women's Writing*, ed. Elizabeth Clarke and Lynn Robson.

47. Greer, in *Kissing the Rod*, ed. Greer et al., 31.
48. *The 'Centuries' of Julia Palmer*, ed. Victoria Burke and Elizabeth Clarke (Nottingham: Trent Editions, 2001); *The Southwell-Sibthorpe Commonplace Book: Folger Ms. V.B. 198*, ed. Jean Klene (Tempe, AZ: Medieval and Renaissance Texts and Studies, 1997). On the importance of Pulter, see Nigel Smith, 'The Rod and the Canon', *Women's Writing* 14.2 (2007): 232–45.
49. Elaine Beilin, *Redeeming Eve: Women Writers of the English Renaissance* (Princeton: Princeton University Press, 1987). Beilin's final chapter discusses defenses of women and mother's advice books.
50. Barbara Lewalski, *Writing Women in Jacobean England* (Cambridge, MA: Harvard University Press, 1995).
51. Wendy Wall, *Imprint of Gender: Authorship and Publication in the English Renaissance* (Ithaca: Cornell University Press, 1993), 289.
52. Greer, in *Kissing the Rod*, ed. Greer et al., 20; Diane Purkiss, 'Material Girls: The Seventeenth-Century Woman Debate', in *Women, Texts and Histories, 1575–1760*, ed. Clare Brant and Diane Purkiss (London: Routledge, 1992), 71.
53. Susan Wiseman, 'Gender and Status in Dramatic Discourse: Margaret Cavendish, Duchess of Newcastle', in *Women, History, Writing, 1640–1740*, ed. Isobel Grundy and Susan Wiseman (Athens, GA: University of Georgia Press, 1992), 177.
54. Lisa Schnell, '"So Great a Diffrence is There in Degree": Aemilia Lanyer and the Aims of Feminist Criticism', *Modern Language Quarterly* 57.1 (1996): 23–35; Lisa Schnell, 'Breaking "the rule of *Cortezia*": Aemilia Lanyer's Dedications to *Salve Deus Rex Judaeorum*', *Journal of Medieval and Renaissance Studies* 27.1 (1997): 77–101.
55. Hero Chalmers, *Royalist Women Writers, 1650–1689* (Oxford: Clarendon Press, 2004). For discussion of Cavendish's 'ambiguous royalism', see Suzuki, *Subordinate Subjects*, 182–202.
56. See also Margo Hendricks, 'Alliance and Exile: Aphra Behn's Racial Identity', in *Maids and Mistresses, Cousins and Queens: Women's Alliances in Early Modern England*, ed. Susan Frye and Karen Robertson (New York: Oxford University Press, 1998), 259–73. On Wroth, see Kim Hall, *Things of Darkness: Economies of Race and Gender in Early Modern England* (Ithaca: Cornell University Press, 1995), chapter 4, 'Race and the English Woman Writer'.
57. Bernadette Andrea, 'Black Skin, the Queen's Masques: Africanist Ambivalence and Feminine Author(ity) in the Masques of *Blackness* and *Beauty*', *English Literary Renaissance* 29 (1999): 246–81.
58. Bernadette Andrea, *Women and Islam in Early Modern English Literature* (Cambridge: Cambridge University Press, 2007).
59. Joyce Green MacDonald, *Women and Race in Early Modern Texts* (Cambridge: Cambridge University Press, 2002), 7n.
60. Theodora Jankowski, *Pure Resistance: Queer Virginity in Early Modern English Drama* (Philadelphia: University of Pennsylvania Press, 2000).
61. Harriette Andreadis, *Sappho in Early Modern England: Female Same-Sex Literary Erotics 1550–1714* (Chicago: University of Chicago Press, 2001); Valerie

Traub, *The Renaissance of Lesbianism in Early Modern England* (Cambridge: Cambridge University Press, 2002).

62. Margaret W. Ferguson, *Dido's Daughters: Literacy, Gender, and Empire in Early Modern England and France* (Chicago: University of Chicago Press, 2003). See also Eve Rachele Sanders, *Gender and Literacy on Stage in Early Modern England* (Cambridge: Cambridge University Press, 1998); Heidi Brayman Hackel, *Reading Material in Early Modern England: Print, Gender, Literacy* (Cambridge: Cambridge University Press, 2005).

63. Margaret J. M. Ezell, 'Never Boring: Or Imagine my Surprise: Interregnum Women and the Culture of Reading Practices', in *Imagining Selves: Essays in Honor of Patricia Meyer Spacks*, ed. Rivka Swenson and Elise Lauterbach (Newark: University of Delaware Press, 2009), 155–69.

64. See Lisa Forman Cody, ed., *Writings on Medicine* (Aldershot: Ashgate, 2002).

65. For more on this subject, see Margaret Ferguson and Mihoko Suzuki, 'Literacy, Literature and Social Status', in *Palgrave Advances in Early Modern Women's Writing*, ed. Suzanne Trill (Basingstoke: Palgrave Macmillan, forthcoming, 2011).

66. Although the title page of *Mariam* identifies the author as 'that learned, virtuous, and truly noble lady, E.C.', the dedication addressed to her 'sister-in-law', 'My Worthy Sister, Mistress Elizabeth Cary', all but identifies the author of the work.

67. On the Swetnam controversy, see Linda Woodbridge, *Women and the English Renaissance: Literature and the Nature of Womenkind, 1540–1620* (Urbana: University of Illinois Press, 1984), 81–103; Cristina Malcolmson and Mihoko Suzuki, *Debating Gender in Early Modern England, 1500-1700* (New York: Palgrave Macmillan, 2002).

68. Maureen Bell, 'Women in the English Book Trade, 1557–1700', *Leipziger Jahrbuch zur Buchgeschichte* 6 (1996): 13–45; 'Women and the Opposition Press after the Restoration', in *Writing and Radicalism*, ed. John Lucas (London: Longman, 1996), 39–60; 'Mary Westwood, Quaker Publisher', *Publishing History* 23 (1988): 5–66; 'Hannah Allen and the Development of a Puritan Publishing Business, 1646–51', *Publishing History* 26 (1989): 5–66; 'Elizabeth Calvert and the Confederates', *Publishing History* 32 (1992): 5–49; '"Her usual practices": The Later Career of Elizabeth Calvert', *Publishing History* 35 (1994): 5–64.

69. Margaret J. M. Ezell, *The Patriarch's Wife: Literary Evidence and the History of the Family* (Chapel Hill: University of North Carolina Press, 1987), 144–60.

70. Margaret J. M. Ezell, *Social Authorship and the Advent of Print* (Baltimore: Johns Hopkins University Press 1999).

71. Jill Seal Millman and Gillian Wright, eds, *Early Modern Women's Manuscript Poetry* (Manchester: Manchester University Press, 2005); Helen Ostovich and Elizabeth Sauer, eds, *Reading Early Modern Women: An Anthology of Texts in Manuscript and Print, 1550–1700* (New York and London: Routledge, 2004).

72. Victoria E. Burke and Jonathan Gibson, eds, *Early Modern Women's Manuscript Writing: Selected Papers from the Trinity/Trent Colloquium* (Aldershot: Ashgate, 2004).

73. Barbara Smith and Ursula Appelt, eds, *Write or be Written: Early Modern Women Poets and Cultural Constraints* (Aldershot: Ashgate, 2001); Pamela Hammons, *Poetic Resistance: English Women Writers and the Early Modern Lyric* (Aldershot: Ashgate: 2002). For poetry from later in the century, see

Carol Barash, *English Women's Poetry, 1649–1714: Politics, Community, and Linguistic Authority* (Oxford: Clarendon Press, 1996); Sarah Prescott and David Shuttleton, eds, *Women and Poetry, 1660–1750* (New York: Palgrave Macmillan, 2003).

74. Nancy Cotton, *Women Playwrights in England, c.1363–1750* (Lewisburg, PA: Bucknell University Press, 1980); Jacqueline Pearson, *The Prostituted Muse: Images of Women and Women Dramatists, 1642–1737* (New York: St. Martin's Press, 1988).

75. Marta Straznicky, *Privacy, Playreading, and Women's Closet Drama, 1550–1700* (Cambridge: Cambridge University Press, 2004); Karen Raber, *Dramatic Difference: Gender, Class, Genre in the Early Modern Closet Drama* (Newark: University of Delaware Press, 2001). On the performability of closet drama, see Alison Findlay and Stephanie Hodgson-Wright, with Gweno Williams, *Women and Dramatic Production, 1550–1700* (Harlow: Longman, 2000).

76. On memoirs, or 'life-writing', see Elspeth Graham, Hilary Hinds, Elaine Hobby, and Helen Wilcox, eds, *Her Own Life: Autobiographical Writings by Seventeenth-Century Englishwomen* (New York: Routledge, 1989); Sharon Seelig, *Autobiography and Gender in Early Modern Literature: Reading Women's Lives, 1600–1680* (Cambridge: Cambridge University Press, 2006); Michelle M. Dowd and Julie A. Eckerle, eds, *Genre and Women's Life Writing in Early Modern England* (Aldershot: Ashgate, 2007).

77. James Daybell, ed., *Early Modern Women's Letter Writing, 1450–1700* (New York: Palgrave Macmillan, 2001).

78. On sectarian women, see Phyllis Mack, *Visionary Women: Ecstatic Prophecy in Seventeenth-Century England* (Berkeley and Los Angeles: University of California Press, 1992); Hilary Hinds, *God's Englishwomen: Seventeenth-Century Radical Sectarian Writing and Feminist Criticism* (Manchester: Manchester University Press, 1996); Teresa Feroli, *Political Speaking Justified: Women Prophets in the English Revolution* (Newark: University of Delaware Press, 2006). On Catholic women, see Frances Dolan, *Whores of Babylon: Catholicism, Gender, and Seventeenth-Century Print Culture* (Ithaca: Cornell University Press, 1999). On Quaker women, see Mary Garman, Judith Applegate, Margaret Benefiel, and Dortha Meredith, eds, *Hidden in Plain Sight: Quaker Women's Writings* (Wallingford, PA: Pendle Hill, 1996); Bonnelyn Young Kunze, *Margaret Fell and the Rise of Quakerism* (Stanford: Stanford University Press, 1994); Catie Gill, *Women in the Seventeenth-Century Quaker Community: A Literary Study of Political Identities 1650–1700* (Aldershot: Ashgate, 2006).

79. Patricia Crawford, *Women and Religion in England, 1500–1720* (London and New York: Routledge, 1993), 210.

80. Erica Longfellow, *Women and Religious Writing in Early Modern England* (Cambridge: Cambridge University Press, 2004); Shannon Miller, *Engendering the Fall: John Milton and Seventeenth-Century Women Writers* (Philadelphia: University of Pennsylvania Press, 2008).

81. Katharine Gillespie, *Domesticity and Dissent in the Seventeenth Century: English Women's Writing and the Public Sphere* (Cambridge: Cambridge University Press, 2004), 10.

82. For a more extended discussion on this topic, see Mihoko Suzuki, 'What's Political in Seventeenth-Century Women's Political Writing?' *Literature Compass* 6 (2009): 1–15.

83. Richard Brathwait, *The English Gentlewoman* (1631), 89–91; Margaret Cavendish, *Playes* (1662), B1.
84. See, for example, Hilda L. Smith, ed., *Women Writers and the Early Modern British Political Tradition* (Cambridge: Cambridge University Press, 1998).
85. Carol Barash, *English Women's Poetry, 1649–1714: Politics, Community, and Linguistic Authority* (Oxford: Clarendon Press, 1996). Danielle Clarke, *The Politics of Early Modern Women's Writing* (Harlow: Longman, 2001) focuses on the period 1558–1640, to examine the 'writers' engagement, through literary means, with matters of state, culture, religion, and subjecthood ... [and] the process of political signification in which women's texts participate, whether consciously or not', as well as whether 'politics might be encoded in generic choices, forms of circulation and exchange, and modes of articulation' (1). Catharine Gray, *Women Writers and Public Debate in Seventeenth-Century Britain* (New York: Palgrave Macmillan, 2007) suggests that women were 'reliant on private affiliation to ground their public identity', emphasizing the multiplicity of 'politically marked communities' (3).
86. Susan Wiseman, *Conspiracy and Virtue: Women, Writing, and Politics in Seventeenth-Century England* (Oxford: Oxford University Press, 2007), 3, 2.
87. Hilda L. Smith and Mihoko Suzuki, 'Introduction', in *Women's Political Writings*, ed. Smith et al., I: xiii.
88. Yet even this volume does not quite indicate the wide-ranging political import of Cavendish's plays, essays in *The Worlds Olio*, and her other writings. See Mihoko Suzuki, 'The Essay Form as Critique: Reading Cavendish's *The Worlds Olio* through Montaigne and Bacon (and Adorno)', *Prose Studies* 22.3 (December 1999): 1–16; Joanne H. Wright, 'Reading the Private in Margaret Cavendish: Conversations in Political Thought', in *British Political Thought in History, Literature and Theory*, ed. David Armitage (Cambridge: Cambridge University Press, 2006), 212–34.
89. Amy Louise Erickson, *Women and Property in Early Modern England* (London and New York: Routledge, 1993); Barbara J. Todd, 'The Remarrying Widow: A Stereotype Reconsidered', in *Women in English Society*, ed. Prior, 54–92.
90. Mihoko Suzuki, 'Anne Clifford and the Gendering of History', *CLIO: A Journal of Literature, History, and the Philosophy of History* 30.2 (Winter 2001): 215–16. See also Mary Chan and Nancy E. Wright, 'Marriage, Identity, and the Pursuit of Property in Seventeenth-Century England: The Cases of Anne Clifford and Elizabeth Wiseman' and Paul Salzman, 'Early Modern (Aristocratic) Women and Textual Property', in *Women, Property, and the Letters of the Law in Early Modern England*, ed. Nancy E. Wright, Margaret W. Ferguson, and A. R. Buck (Toronto: University of Toronto Press, 2004), 162–82; 281–95.
91. Suzuki, *Subordinate Subjects*, 193–94. See Lloyd Davis, 'Women's Wills in Early Modern England', in *Women, Property*, ed. Wright et al., 219–36.
92. Natalie Zemon Davis, 'Gender and Genre: Women as Historical Writers, 1400–1820', in *Beyond their Sex: Learned Women of the European Past*, ed. Patricia H. Labalme (New York: New York University Press, 1980), 153–82; Helen Wilcox and Sheila Otway, 'Women's Histories', in *Cambridge Companion to Writing of the English Revolution*, ed. N. H. Keeble (Cambridge: Cambridge University Press, 2001), 148–61. On Hutchinson, see also Devoney Looser, *British Women Writers and the Writing of History, 1620–1820*

(Baltimore: Johns Hopkins University Press, 2000), 28–60. On Clifford's reading and writing of history, see Suzuki, 'Anne Clifford'.

93. Megan Matchinske, *Women Writing History in Early Modern England* (Cambridge: Cambridge University Press, 2009), 162n.

94. Elaine Hobby, ed., *The Midwives Book: Or the Whole Art of Midwifry Discovered* (New York: Oxford University Press, 1999); Rebecca Laroche, *Medical Authority and Englishwomen's Herbal Texts, 1550–1650* (Aldershot: Ashgate, 2009).

95. Londa Schiebinger, *The Mind has No Sex? Women in the Origins of Modern Science* (Cambridge, MA: Harvard University Press, 1991).

96. Alice T. Friedman, 'Constructing an Identity in Prose, Plaster, and Paint: Lady Anne Clifford as Writer and Patron of the Arts', in *Albion's Classicism: The Visual Arts in Britain, 1550–1660*, ed. Lucy Gent (New Haven: Yale University Press, 1995), 359–76; Anne Myers, 'Construction Sites: The Architecture of Anne Clifford's Diaries', *ELH* 73 (2006): 581–600. Both are reprinted in *Ashgate Critical Essays on Women Writers in English 1550–1700*, vol. 5: *Anne Clifford and Lucy Hutchinson*, ed. Mihoko Suzuki (Aldershot: Ashgate, 2009).

97. Patricia Phillippy, *Painting Women: Cosmetics, Canvases, and Early Modern Culture* (Baltimore: Johns Hopkins University Press, 2005).

98. Jane Stevenson, 'Still Kissing the Rod? Whither Next?' *Women's Writing* 14.2 (2007): 290–305; Merry E. Wiesner-Hanks, 'A Renaissance Woman (Still) Adrift in the World', *Early Modern Women: An Interdisciplinary Journal* 1 (2006): 137–57.

99. Stevenson, 'Still Kissing the Rod?', 291. Stevenson has contributed to this investigation through her *Women Latin Poets: Language, Gender, and Authority from Antiquity to the Eighteenth Century* (Oxford: Oxford University Press, 2005) and her anthology co-edited with Peter Davidson, *Early Modern Women Poets*, which includes works in Latin. Wiesner-Hanks discusses the various pressures, including pedagogical ones (the need to teach 'world history' and the mandate 'to prepare students for the "global" economy') behind the 'transcultural' direction scholarship is taking ('A Renaissance Woman', 138–39]).

100. David Norbrook, 'Women, the Republic of Letters, and the Public Sphere in the Mid-Seventeenth Century', *Criticism* 46.2 (2004): 223–40; Julie Campbell and Anne Larsen, eds, *Early Modern Women and Transnational Communities of Letters* (Aldershot: Ashgate, 2009).

101. Bernadette Andrea, *Women and Islam in Early Modern English Literature* (Cambridge: Cambridge University Press, 2007); Kate Chedgzoy, *Women's Writing in the British Atlantic World: Memory, Place and History, 1550–1700* (Cambridge: Cambridge University Press, 2007).

102. *Ashgate Critical Essays on Women Writers in England, 1550–1700*: *Anne Lock, Isabella Whitney and Aemilia Lanyer* (vol. 3, 2009, ed. Micheline White), *Mary Wroth* (vol. 4, 2009, ed. Clare R. Kinney); *Anne Clifford and Lucy Hutchinson* (vol. 5, 2009, ed. Suzuki); *Elizabeth Cary* (vol. 6, 2009, ed. Karen Raber); *Margaret Cavendish* (vol. 7, 2009, ed. Sara Mendelson).

103. Janet Todd, ed., *The Works of Aphra Behn*, 7 vols. (Columbus: Ohio State University Press, 1992).

104. James Fitzmaurice, Carol L. Barash, Eugene R. Cunnar, Nancy A. Gutierrez, and Josephine A. Roberts, eds, *Major Women Writers of Seventeenth-Century*

England (Ann Arbor: University of Michigan Press, 1997); Paul Salzman, ed., *Early Modern Women's Writing: An Anthology, 1560–1700* (Oxford: Oxford University Press, 2000); Stephanie Hodgson-Wright, ed., *Women's Writing of the Early Modern Period, 1588–1688: An Anthology* (New York: Columbia University Press, 2002). On poetry, see: Marion Wynne-Davies, ed., *Women Poets of the Renaissance* (London and New York: Routledge, 1999); Danielle Clarke, ed., *Isabella Whitney, Mary Sidney and Aemilia Lanyer: Renaissance Women Poets* (Harmondsworth: Penguin, 2000). On drama, see: S. P. Cerasano and Marion Wynne-Davies, eds, *Renaissance Drama by Women: Texts and Documents* (London and New York: Routledge, 1996); Cerasano and Wynne-Davies, eds, *Readings in Renaissance Women's Drama: Criticism, History, and Performance* (London and New York: Routledge, 1998).

105. Elizabeth Cary, *The Tragedie of Mariam*, ed. Stephanie Hodgson-Wright (2000); Anne Clifford, *The Memoir of 1603 and the Diary of 1616–1619*, ed. Katherine O. Acheson (2006); Margaret Cavendish, *Paper Bodies: A Margaret Cavendish Reader*, ed. Sylvia Bowerbank and Sara Mendelson (2000); Margaret Cavendish, *Bell in Campo and the Sociable Companions*, ed. Alexandra G. Bennett (2002); Margaret Cavendish, *Sociable Letters*, ed. James Fitzmaurice (2004).

106. These include, for example, Katherine Austen, edited by Pamela Hammons; Mary Carleton, edited by Megan Matchinske; Margaret Fell, edited by Jane Donawerth and Rebecca Lush; Elizabeth Poole, edited by Katharine Gillespie; Hester Pulter, edited by Alice Eardley; Elizabeth Cooke Hoby Russell, edited by Patricia Phillippy. A full list of these texts can be found at the Center for Reformation and Renaissance Studies website: http://www.crrs.ca/publications/bookseries/ov.htm.

107. On this last period, see Susan Staves, *A Literary History of Women's Writing in Britain, 1660–1789* (Cambridge: Cambridge University Press, 2006), chapter 1: 'The Restoration to the death of Behn, 1660–1689'.

108. Margaret J. M. Ezell, 'Domestic Papers: Manuscript Culture and Early Modern Women's Life Writing', in *Genre and Women's Life Writing in Early Modern England*, ed. Julie A. Eckerle and Michelle M. Dowd (Aldershot: Ashgate, 2007), 33.

Part I

Networks, Debates, Traditions, Discourses

1
Identifying as (Women) Writers

Paul Salzman

Did early modern women writers see themselves as having a particular identity? In this chapter I trace some of the possible identities available to early modern women who wrote. It might make more sense, in this context, to talk of 'identifications' rather than identities. In general it is true to say that the category 'early modern women writers' is a modern concept that would have had no meaning for the writers under consideration here.[1] Many women who wrote in the seventeenth century would not have seen themselves as 'writers', especially those who produced diaries, letters, advice to children, receipt/recipe books, or even religious works of many kinds. On the other hand, a number of early modern women did see themselves as authors who might have a literary career. In a suggestive article on the question of authorship and early modern women, Susanne Woods et al. show how Anne Dowriche, Mary Sidney, Aemilia Lanyer, and Margaret Cavendish 'presented themselves as authors'.[2] However, it is difficult to determine whether they saw themselves specifically as *women* authors, and if that category may have been empowering. In the case of Cavendish, one could argue that there was a *dis*-identification with other women writers, while for Mary Sidney, the identification was with her brother Philip, rather than with a notion of female authorship. But, as I will discuss later in the case of Mary Wroth, there were some women who appear to have seen themselves as part of a tradition of female authorship, amongst other identifications.

In this chapter I want to look at four broad categories of early modern women's writing in relation to the writers' identifications. The first encompasses the idea of authorship as noted above, and includes writers who did seem to aspire to a model career that had certain affiliations with those being constructed by some male authors in the period.

My examples of this are Mary Sidney, Mary Wroth, Anne Bradstreet, Margaret Cavendish, Lucy Hutchinson, Katherine Philips, and Aphra Behn. This selection will also allow me to consider how the concept of 'female authorship' may have changed in the course of the seventeenth century.

The second category, which is particularly evident in the early seventeenth century, involves less powerful women who attempted to authorize their writing by associating it with the works of other, more powerful women. The most notable example of this is Aemilia Lanyer, but one could also see writers involved in the debates over the nature of women, such as Rachel Speght, as using a version of this authorizing strategy.

The third category includes writers who worked in genres which could be seen to have a particular relationship with women and their activities, such as recipe books, mother's advice books, diaries, and letters. These writings might have manuscript or print circulation, or both.

The fourth category concerns writers who are gathered together through political or religious issues. These writers may not necessarily categorize themselves as writers at all; for example, some religious groups may see themselves as witnesses. But as scholars have revealed in considerable detail over the last twenty years, the outbreak of women's prophecy and political activities, as well as their engagement with radical religious sects, marked an empowering moment in the development of women's writing, especially during and after the Civil War period. In some cases, I will argue that here we may also be looking at forms of self-conscious authorship, a notable case being the career of Anna Trapnel.

As even now more and more writing by women in the seventeenth century is being unearthed, it is clear that many women wrote, and wrote in every possible mode and genre. But that does not mean that they all saw themselves as writers. I want to begin with the group most associated with the notion of authorship, and I will examine how far that category might include female authorship. Two members of the Sidney family, Mary Sidney and her niece Mary Wroth, were able to assume a certain right to authorship that went along with their family status. As Mary Ellen Lamb has pointed out in her study of the relationship between gender and authorship within the Sidney family, both inspiration and authority passed from Philip Sidney to the rest of the family; in the case of the female members of the family who wrote, Lamb notes that 'Sir Philip Sidney's name provided a competing discourse enabling authorship.'[3] This is literally the case with Philip's sister Mary, as she notes in her poem in memory of him, 'To the Angel Spirit of the Most Excellent Sir Philip Sidney': 'what is mine / inspired by thee, thy secrett power imprest'.[4] Mary Sidney took over her brother's translation of the Psalms (which then circulated in manuscript); she edited his unfinished revision of his prose romance *Arcadia* and published it, rebutting the version published by Philip's friend Fulke Greville; and she published her own translations. The construction of Philip Sidney as author, martyr for the Protestant cause in Europe, and exemplar of the Elizabethan aristocratic ideal, was a careful act with political implications, both when it began late in Elizabeth's reign, and as it continued into the reign of James. Under James in particular, the Sidney/Herbert families used literary patronage and their own writing as part of their interest in the fortunes of European Protestantism, and also as an aid to advance their position within the court.[5]

The process by which Mary Sidney instituted herself as an author was very different from that described by Richard Helgerson in his influential account of how Spenser, Jonson, and Milton constructed their careers as 'self-crowned laureates'.[6] Mary Sidney begins, as I have already mentioned, with the adoption and promotion of her brother's oeuvre. Her 1593 edition of his romance *Arcadia* contains a preface decrying the version published without her permission: a 'disfigured face', which moved her 'to take in hand the wiping away those spottes' (¶4).[7] Accordingly, this newly edited *Arcadia* is indeed hers: 'The Countesse of Pembrokes Arcadia: done, as it was, for her: as it is, by her' (¶v). While 'by her' means by her authority, as the authorizer, Mary Sidney is close to being a stand-in for the author. By the 1598 edition, the *Arcadia* was joined by Philip's other works: 'Certain Sonnets', 'The Defence of Poetry', 'Astrophil and Stella', and 'The Lady of May'. It is this volume that can be seen as Philip's monument: the collection of his literary remains. But by this time Mary had also published her own work, joining, in a sense, her own authorship with his authority.

In 1592 Mary Sidney published her translation of Philippe de Mornay's 1576 treatise *Excellent discourse de la vie et de la Mort* as *A Discourse of Life and Death*. This was reprinted in 1600, 1606, 1607, and 1608. Then in 1595 she published her translation of Robert Garnier's *Marc Antoine* as *Antonie*. While these translations were published, Mary's continuation of her brother's translation of the Psalms (he translated the first 43, Mary completed the remaining 107) circulated widely in manuscript, but was not published in the seventeenth century. This combined translation inextricably joined Mary with Philip, and at the same time bestowed upon her a mantle of piety which, along with her brother's fame, 'justified' her writing.

This legacy had a powerful influence on Mary Wroth, who can, I think, be seen as modeling her writing career on that of her uncle, but with the example of her aunt acting as a sanction for her endeavors. Wroth's work will be discussed in detail in Clare Kinney's chapter, but here I want to consider her as a compelling example of how a woman in the seventeenth century might profess authorship – and the negative reaction that this provoked from some quarters. Wroth has received considerable attention over the past thirty years, in part as a reflection of the sheer quality and scope of her writing, but also because she fits so well into accepted notions of literary production. I believe that this is actually a response to Wroth's own sense of herself as a literary writer in what might be called the Sidney tradition. Unlike her aunt, Wroth did not produce translations or works of piety; rather, she seems to have set out to mirror her uncle's achievements. But this does not mean that she separated herself from her aunt, because she clearly derived literary status from her aunt's own ongoing literary activities, and also from her position as Philip's literary trustee.

I don't have the space here to look at Wroth's life and writing in any detail, but it is important to note that, although she was married (unhappily, it seems) to Robert Wroth, she regarded herself as a Sidney. This is apparent both through her writing and within her writing through her many autobiographical representations, and also in her attachment to her first cousin, Mary Sidney's son William Herbert, with whom she had an affair that, after her husband's death, resulted in two illegitimate children. Writing as a woman forms a vital aspect of Wroth's literary work, especially through her depiction of herself as the character Pamphilia, who is both 'author' of Wroth's sonnet sequence and a major actor in her prose romance *Urania*.

Wroth began by writing poetry. The fact that Wroth begins her career with what was finally gathered together as a sonnet sequence points to her literary ambitions. While the sonnet sequence was associated with male writers, there were examples of sonnets by women to serve as models for Wroth, perhaps most notably the sonnet ascribed to Queen Elizabeth, 'I grieve and dare not show my discontent'. But Wroth's ambition, even at this early stage of her writing, is indicated by her production of a complete sequence, structured similarly to that of Philip, and also to a sequence written by her father, Philip's brother Robert. Wroth was probably writing her poetry from about 1610, when she was twenty-three years old and had been married for six years, although she may well have begun writing much earlier than that. Her poetry was reasonably well known from 1611 onwards, when various literary figures such as Ben Jonson and John Davies alluded to it.[8] Again this is a reflection of her activities as a patron (continuing the tradition of her aunt's patronage), but it also can be seen as acknowledgment of her literary ambition. Jonson in particular praised her in a sonnet of his own, stating that her poetry made him a 'better poet'.[9]

But Wroth's ambitions stretched beyond poetry to her immense, complex prose romance *Urania*. While *Urania* pays homage to Philip's *Arcadia* in various ways, from its title to its form, it moves the genre on from Sidney's version of romance, especially through Wroth's interest in the depiction of real characters and events shadowed within the romance in thinly disguised form.[10] This enabled her to engage with court scandals, political debates, and the entire geopolitical situation in the early seventeenth century. Wroth's publication of the first part of *Urania* in 1621 is a more dramatic and public claim to authorship than the manuscript circulation of her poetry, and must have been inspired by Mary Sidney's example as author and editor. (It is perhaps a coincidence, but the seventh edition of *Arcadia* was published in 1621, and this was also the year of Mary Sidney's death.) The impressive folio of *The Countess of Montgomery's Urania* (the full title, which echoes the printed title of Philip's romance: *The Countess of Pembroke's Arcadia*), has an elaborate engraved title page which depicts a key event in the narrative. Such a volume calls up the authority invested in volumes by writers like Jonson (who published his folio in 1616), or indeed in the volume of Philip Sidney's works, which had become so successful in the early seventeenth century.[11]

Like the volumes of *Arcadia* published under Mary Sidney's auspices, the *Urania* volume contained Wroth's poetry as well as her prose narrative. However, Wroth's experiment with the depiction of actual people and scandalous events from the Jacobean court brought on a fiery response from Sir Edward Denny, who objected to his depiction in the romance. Denny specifically condemned Wroth for writing a 'lascivious' work rather than the 'holy' works of her aunt. This may indicate that Wroth's affiliation with her aunt's literary activities did not protect her from the anxiety and potential opposition that surrounded female *authorship* (as opposed to female writing). She was not exactly silenced, because she wrote a lengthy manuscript continuation of *Urania*, but she was forced into a kind of public silence and the continuation was never published.

Wroth offered women who aspired to authorship a dual legacy. On the one hand, she exemplified the literary aspirations of her family, acquired praise for her poetry, and published an impressive folio evoking the status of her uncle's collected works; on the other hand, she attracted opprobrium for venturing into print, and was forced to apologize for what she had done. Her exchange with the irate Edward Denny clearly circulated amongst interested people, because Denny's catch-phrase 'Work o th' Workes leave idle bookes alone / For wise and worthyer women have writte none' was repeated twice by Margaret Cavendish as an expression of her anxiety over female authorship.[12] From 1621 until the 1650s, women writers became increasingly visible, especially in response to radical political and religious upheaval, and I will describe their activities below, but the kinds of self-conscious authorship that I have been discussing do not seem to have been taken up until mid-century.

The 1650s saw a number of women assuming self-conscious authorship in a variety of modes. Perhaps the most spectacular, in terms of her ambition, is Margaret Cavendish, who began by publishing two volumes in 1653: *Philosophical Fancies* and *Poems and Fancies*. Cavendish went on to publish eleven more volumes of philosophy, poetry, drama, essays, letters, biography, autobiography, and stories, and revised versions of a number of these volumes. While her prefaces often express anxiety about publication, in fact her volumes proclaim her rights to authorship over and over again, including her use of an elaborate engraving of herself in a classical pose (discussed in Theodora Jankowski's chapter). The volumes became more and more impressive physical objects, but even *Poems and Fancies* is substantial, and one can see the multiple dedications and prefaces as proclamations of a claim to self-representation, rather than just protestations of unworthiness. As time went on, Cavendish's desire for 'fame' increased, and this is reflected in the grand appearance of her folios, as well as her writing in every current literary genre.

David Norbrook has examined the fascinating parallels between the royalist Cavendish's literary career and that of the republican Lucy Hutchinson.[13] Like the other women I have been considering as authors, Hutchinson's ambitions are reflected in the range of genres in which she wrote, even though they are all tied together by her religious and political affiliations. In the 1650s she translated Lucretius's *De Rerum Natura*, a daunting task both linguistically and intellectually. After the Restoration, when her husband was imprisoned for his role in the Civil War, Hutchinson wrote his biography (in a fascinating parallel, Cavendish wrote her husband's biography), and then wrote a long religious poem, *Order and Disorder*, which is gradually emerging as a significant example of religious epic to stand alongside Milton's *Paradise*

Lost.[14] While on the whole Hutchinson's work circulated in manuscript, rather than print, her authorial ambitions seem to have been as substantial as Cavendish's, albeit directed by quite different intellectual, poetic, and ideological motivations.

Katherine Philips was a precocious poet, writing verse from an early age and gathering around her a circle of admirers, on whom she bestowed romance names and carried out a series of intense relationships, especially with Anne Owen ('Lucasia') and Mary Aubrey ('Rosania') – Philips herself was 'Orinda'. While Philips first published a poem in 1651 as one of the numerous dedicatory verses for the posthumous collection of William Cartwright's works – Philips's was the first poem and the collection itself was a roll-call of royalist sympathizers – she concentrated on positioning herself as a manuscript poet. During the 1650s, Philips wrote poems to the various members of her coterie, especially to Lucasia and Rosania, and the poems circulated extensively in manuscript. Philips herself compiled poems for presentation. Philips has been seen as a poet of personal intimacy, and in some respects as a poet of lesbian desire, but in recent years she has also been seen as a political poet who was highly self-conscious about her engagement with royalist politics.[15] Both these sides of Philips involved her considerable poetic skills, and an extremely controlled positioning of her poetry in relation to both literary achievement and personal influence. Not only did Philips aspire to some status as a poet, but her ambitions were reinforced by the admiration of her coterie.

However, when Philips accompanied Anne Owen to Dublin upon Owen's second marriage, her writing shifted to a far more public arena. She translated Corneille's *La mort de Pompée*, which was performed to considerable acclaim and was published in 1663. In 1664 a collection of Philips's poetry was published in London. Philips protested that this was unauthorized, although scholars have been unable to decide whether or not this was a disingenuous protestation.[16] After Philips's sudden death in 1664 from smallpox, a posthumous volume was published in 1667 which gathered together the poems and her translations, including *Pompey* and the incomplete *Horace*. This was a true monument to Philips's status; it included an engraved frontispiece depicting Philips as a classical bust and the title page notes her as 'most deservedly Admired'.

Cavendish, Hutchinson, and Philips overshadowed Anne Bradstreet in their own time, but Bradstreet assumed a place within the American literary canon that made her unique among early modern women writers until their comparatively recent championing by scholars. Bradstreet emigrated to America with her husband in 1630. Her poems circulated amongst her family in manuscript in the 1640s, but were then compiled and brought to England to be published as *The Tenth Muse* in 1650. While this volume purports to be published by Bradstreet's brother-in-law, its structure seems entirely authorial, and it contains a defiant Prefatory poem by Bradstreet, now often quoted, which defends her right, as a woman, to be a poet:

> I am obnoxious to each carping tongue,
> Who sayes, my hand a needle better fits,
> A Poets Pen, all scorne, I should thus wrong:
> For such despight they cast on female wits:
> If what I doe prove well, it won't advance,
> They'l say its stolne, or else, it was by chance. (4)

The bulk of *The Tenth Muse* is made up of an ambitious series of poems now termed *Quaternions*, exploring the four elements, humors, ages of man, seasons, and monarchies. These are intellectually challenging and are joined by a series of elegies which in 1650 have some political import, notably Bradstreet's elegy on Queen Elizabeth and on Philip Sidney, although Susan Wiseman has offered a compelling interpretation of their political stance as safer and more acceptable than the millenarian work of Bradstreet's relative by marriage, Elizabeth Avery.[17] Bradstreet's conception of herself as a poet was enhanced with a follow-up volume in 1678, adding the more personal poems about her husband and children which so appealed to her admirers in the twentieth century, such as Adrienne Rich.[18]

All the writers I have discussed so far had some powerful affiliations which allowed them to construct themselves as authors: Mary Sidney and Mary Wroth could both claim familial status and a certain imprimatur derived from the relationship of their own writings to those of Philip Sidney. The shift from aunt to niece did, however, involve a specific authorization of women as writers, even if Wroth found that authorization to have flaws. Margaret Cavendish benefited from the status provided by her husband, and also his direct encouragement. She clearly saw herself as working within a tradition that included Wroth, and Edward Denny's condemnation of Wroth seems to have spurred Cavendish on in her defense of her right to publish. Philips was supported by an admiring coterie of royalists who were pulled into a Platonic circle with her as its center; in Philips's case it is perhaps true to say that women as objects of desire were more empowering than women as writers. Hutchinson had a kind of intellectual strength that was grounded in an acute political consciousness. Bradstreet was able to draw on a spiritual authority, but also evoked a powerful woman from the past in her elegy for Queen Elizabeth. In their different ways, these women were, if not always consciously, at least through print and man-uscript circulation of their work, establishing something like a tradition of women's writing, even if that tradition was discontinuous.

The difficulty of constructing an authorial position is much more evi-dent in the career of Aphra Behn, whose background and poverty placed her in a much more vulnerable position than even the more modestly situated women discussed so far. Behn, as a woman who established a career as a professional dramatist and occasional poet, translator, and writer of prose fiction, had to keep fighting for the legitimacy of her output. Behn began as a playwright after an adventurous if financially precarious life which included service as a spy. Her first play, *The Forc'd Marriage*, was performed in 1670, at a stage when the Restoration theater scene was particularly vibrant. It was a great success, and Behn had at least fourteen plays performed over the following decade. During this period, Behn also wrote poetry, much of which was collected in her volume *Poems Upon Several Occasions* (1684), and she achieved some sta-tus in the Restoration literary world, testified to by being commissioned by Dryden to take part in the collective translation of Ovid. Despite this, Behn had to keep fighting for her right to be a female author in the misogynistic Restoration literary scene. In the prologue to *The Dutch Lover* (1673) Behn defends herself against accusations personified by the Fop who says 'they were to expect a woful Play, God damn him, for it was a womans'. Behn responds by asking why 'women having equal education with men, were not as capable of knowledge' (Preface). In *The Lucky Chance* (1686) Behn offers perhaps her most moving state-ment of her right to be accepted into the male world of letters: 'All I ask is the Priviledge for my Masculine Part the Poet in me.' Here she also states 'I value Fame as much as if I had been born a Hero.' While these statements seem to grow out of a desire to be accepted into a masculine tradition, Behn was also conscious of a female tradition of writers, mak-ing her most eloquent reference in an aside during her translation of part of Cowley's Latin poem *Of Plants*, which is underlined by the note 'The translatress in her own Person Speaks':

> Let me with *Sappho* and *Orinda* be
> Oh ever sacred Nymph, adorn'd by thee
> And give my Verses Immortality.[19]

In evoking the fame of Katherine Philips (Orinda) together with the legendary Sappho, Behn indicates that a tradition of women writers was within reach for her by this stage of the seventeenth century. The tradition that Behn could look back on continued to grow at the end of the seventeenth century, although Behn's own reputation as a disreputable writer of scandalous works was to color response to her as a role model in the eighteenth century.[20]

But even at the beginning of the seventeenth century there were writers who sought to create a space for themselves by association with these more significant women authors. The most interesting example of this process is the volume published by Aemilia Lanyer in 1611: *Salve Deus Rex Judaeorum*. Lanyer's religious poem about the Passion, and the accompanying country house poem, 'The Description of Cookham', were preceded by no fewer than eleven dedicatory poems addressed to Queen Ann; Princess Elizabeth; virtuous ladies 'in general'; Arbella Stuart; Susan Bertie, Countess of Kent; Mary Sidney; Lucy, Countess of Bedford; Margaret Clifford, Countess of Cumberland; Katherine, Countess of Suffolk; Anne Clifford, Countess of Dorset (Margaret's daughter), who is also the subject of the Cookham poem; and to the 'virtuous' reader. The nine powerful women addressed by Lanyer form a kind of intellectual, literary, and royal/aristocratic affiliation for her poetry, so that she actually evokes a female community for her writing within the conventions of dedications to powerful patrons. In particular, Lanyer produces an elaborate, highly symbolic tribute to Mary Sidney, noting her Psalm translations and really attaching her poetic wagon to Mary Sidney's star.

Lanyer's attempt to join a circle of powerful women seems to have been unsuccessful, as she did not publish anything else, and no other writing by her has survived, although there are some details of her impecunious life, which included some time running a school.[21] During the remainder of the seventeenth century, a series of connections were made by women writers with both other women writers and women readers. In the area of print, this was an intermittent process, including, for example, the possibly trumped-up debate over the nature of women joined by Rachel Speght, or admirers of later women writers such as the pseudonymous Philo-Philippa, who wrote an admiring poem about Katherine Philips.[22] But in manuscript, many women wrote in a variety of genres and often saw themselves as part of a circle that might extend quite widely, or might simply be confined to members of the family. Amongst family circles, one could cite Elizabeth Brackley/Egerton and her sister Jane Cavendish, who together early in the 1640s produced a miscellany that included an impressive play, 'Concealed Fancies'.[23] This is a good example of relatively private familial literary practices, although even here one must note that 'private' is a word to be used with caution, as much of this manuscript writing (including 'Concealed Fancies') circulated beyond the family.

This process is also evident in generic writing that addressed issues specifically seen as part of a woman's domain. We can in these cases detect an implied female writing community, even if there was no actual contact between the women who wrote in these modes. The most visible of these was what has become known as the 'mother's advice book'. These are pious works addressed by mothers to their children, but while a number of them were manuscripts intended for use within the family, some of them proved enormously popular when printed. The two most notable of these in terms of their editions and readership are Dorothy Leigh's *The Mother's Blessing*, first published in 1616, which had twenty-three editions between then and 1647, and Elizabeth Jocelin's *Mother's Legacy to her Unborn Child*, published in 1624, which had seven editions. Leigh in particular is self-conscious about her use of the genre to argue for female spiritual authority, in part through her account of the Virgin Mary, and also about her decision to publish, which was made, she states, in order to ensure that her advice would circulate when her sons most needed it (and by implication, in order to ensure that other children would also receive it).[24] Clearly Leigh was extremely successful in gauging the market for this specifically female genre, and she creates a safe and authorized space for women as mothers and women as writers. Jocelin's volume is quite different, in so far as it registers the dangers of childbirth during the period by anticipating that Jocelin might die in childbirth, and so the book will be her testament addressed to her unborn child. And in a horrible irony, Jocelin did indeed die soon after the birth of her baby, and her book was published posthumously, with an introduction by the theologian Thomas Goad. Mother's advice books are the clearest example of the construction and dissemination of a specifically female writing community, but this is also evident in genres such as receipt books, which tended to circulate within families in manuscript, although they too were published, most notably late in the century, as evidenced by the voluminous work of Hannah Woolley in the 1660s and early 1670s.[25]

Finally I can only mention very briefly the extraordinary participation by women in the religious and political upheavals of the Civil War and its aftermath.[26] The political events of this period saw a dramatic increase in women's visibility in areas of radical debate, especially through their participation in new sects (notably Baptist and Quaker communities), through their preaching, prophesying, and writing. Political participation was also important, especially the actions of women petitioners on behalf of John Lilburne in 1649. Such political participation bonded women together in a common purpose, and the purpose and also the anxious responses created a consciousness amongst these women and in society of the potential for women's involvement in the public sphere, through pamphlet polemic as well as other religious and political writing.[27] Recently, both Mihoko Suzuki and Susan Wiseman have detailed the way in which early modern women participated in the public sphere, especially in the mid-seventeenth century, through a variety of activities with political import, most especially via pamphlet controversies.[28] In a discussion of female community within these groups, Elaine Hobby cites Margaret Cavendish's vivid evocation of this participation from the preface to *Poems and Fancies* (by 'effeminate' Cavendish means feminine/ female):

> this Age hath produced many effeminate Writers, as well as Preachers, and many effeminate Rulers, as well as Actors. And if it be an Age when the effeminate spirits rule, as most visibly they doe in every Kingdome, let us take the advantage, and make the best of our time, for feare their reigne should not last long.[29]

Women who participated in sectarian activity during this period drew strength from the communities within which they preached, wrote, and prophesied. In some of those communities, such as the Quakers, there was a specific ideological/theological framework allowing women to assert their right to be heard, with the result that there was a clear sense of connection between women, and an authorization of their activities. In other communities, most notably the Fifth Monarchist group surrounding Anna Trapnel, one charismatic woman was empowered, but remained a single presence, rather than part of a female community. Trapnel's fierce political denunciations and her visions of radical change were manifested in a series of publications, some of them transcriptions of her words taken down during her visions, but all amounting to perhaps the most powerful authorial presence achieved by any woman during this period.[30]

Women certainly identified themselves as 'women writers' at this time, but their affiliations were varied, and the possibility for networks of women writers was patchy during the seventeenth century. But it seems clear that an identification as a woman writer became increasingly possible during the course of the century. In all cases the identifications and affiliations that allowed women to write, let alone have their writing transmitted through print or manuscript, were multiple.

Notes

1. I discuss this issue in more detail in *Reading Early Modern Women's Writing* (Oxford: Oxford University Press, 2006), ch. 1.
2. Susanne Woods, Margaret Hannay, Elaine Beilin, and Anne Shaver, 'Renaissance Englishwomen and the Literary Career', in *European Literary Careers*, ed. Patrick Cheney and Frederick de Armas (Toronto: University of Toronto Press, 2002), 302.
3. Mary Ellen Lamb, *Gender and Authorship in the Sidney Circle* (Madison: University of Wisconsin Press, 1990), 21; see also the discussion of Sidney's influence in Gavin Alexander, *Writing After Sidney: The Literary Response to Sir Philip Sidney* (New York: Oxford University Press, 2006).
4. *Collected Works of Mary Sidney Herbert*, ed. Margaret P. Hannay et al. (Oxford: Oxford University Press, 1998), I.110.
5. See, for example, Michael G. Brennan, *Literary Patronage in the English Renaissance: The Pembroke Family* (London: Routledge, 1988).
6. Richard Helgerson, *Self-Crowned Laureates: Spenser, Jonson, Milton, and the Literary System* (Berkeley: University of California Press, 1983).
7. References to *Arcadia* (1593).
8. See the account in *The Poems of Mary Wroth*, ed. Josephine Roberts (Baton Rouge: Louisiana State University Press, 1983), 16–22.
9. Ben Jonson, 'A Sonnet, to the Noble Lady, the Lady Mary Wroth', *Underwoods* xxviii, *Poems*, ed. George Parfit (Harmondsworth: Penguin, 1975), 165.
10. For an account of the romance genre's engagement with women and women's engagement with it, including a detailed discussion of *Urania*, see Helen Hacket, *Women and Romance Fiction in the English Renaissance* (Cambridge: Cambridge University Press, 2000).
11. While a great deal of work has been done on Jonson's folio, for my purposes, Joseph Loewenstein's account of the relationship between copyright, intellectual property, early modern printing, and authorship has been especially useful: see his *Ben Jonson and Possessive Authorship* (Cambridge: Cambridge University Press, 2002); see also Kevin Pask, *The Emergence of the English Author* (Cambridge: Cambridge University Press, 1996), which describes the construction of the poet as author through contemporaneous and later biographical accounts of the writer.
12. *Poems*, ed. Roberts, 32; by 'Workes' Denny means needlework, etc.; Cavendish quoted a version of this couplet in both her *Poems and Fancies* (1653) and *Sociable Letters* (1664).
13. David Norbrook, 'Margaret Cavendish and Lucy Hutchinson: Identity, Ideology, and Politics', *In-Between* 9 (2000): 179–203.
14. See Shannon Miller's chapter for a discussion of *Order and Disorder*.
15. See Catharine Gray, *Women Writers and Public Debate in 17th-Century Britain* (New York: Palgrave Macmillan, 2008), ch. 3.
16. On this debate see especially Elizabeth H. Hageman, 'Treacherous Accidents and the Abominable Printing of Katherine Philips's 1664 Poems', in W. Speed Hill, ed., *New Ways of Looking at Old Texts III* (Tempe: RETS, 2004), 85–95.

17. The poem to Elizabeth circulated in manuscript form well before its publication. On the overall political implications of Bradstreet's collection, especially in relation to 'Protestant poetic history' (198), see Susan Wiseman, *Conspiracy and Virtue: Women, Writing, and Politics in Seventeenth Century England* (Oxford: Oxford University Press, 2006), 182–209.

18. See Rich's Preface to the 1967 edition of Bradstreet's poetry, ed. Jeannine Hensley (Cambridge, MA: Harvard University Press).

19. Abraham Cowley, *Works Parts 2 and 3* (1689), 149.

20. For responses to Behn in the eighteenth century see Jane Spencer, *Aphra Behn's Afterlife* (Oxford: Oxford University Press, 2000).

21. For a thorough biography, see Susanne Woods, *Lanyer: A Renaissance Woman Poet* (Oxford: Oxford University Press, 1999).

22. See Megan Matchinske's and Shannon Miller's chapters on the gender debate in this volume; Philo-Philippa's poem was printed with other commendatory verses at the beginning of the 1667 edition of Philips's works.

23. See the discussions in Margaret Ezell, '"To be your daughter in your pen": The Social Function of Literature in the Writings of Elizabeth Brackley and Lady Jane Cavendish', *HLQ* 51 (1988): 281–96; and Alexandra Bennett, '"Now Let My Language Speak": The Authorship, Rewriting and Audience[s] of Jane Cavendish and Elizabeth Brackley', *EMLS* 11.2 (2005): 3.1–13. Bennett produces convincing evidence that the poems are Jane's and only the plays are collaborations by the two sisters.

24. For a particularly fine account of the political and spiritual purport of Leigh's book, see Gray, *Women Writers and Public Debate*, ch. 1.

25. 'Receipt' is the contemporary term for recipe, but is worth using because it underlines the fact that these books were not just to do with cookery, but also contained important instructions for medicines of various kinds, underlining how important women's knowledge of such potions was during this period (see Cristina Malcolmson's chapter in this volume). Printed receipt books have only recently received much scholarly attention; see in particular Catherine Field's useful account, '"Many Hands Hands": Writing the Self in Early Modern Women's Recipe Books', in Michelle Dowd and Julie Eckerle, eds, *Genre and Women's Life Writing in Early Modern England* (Aldershot: Ashgate, 2002), 49–63; and a particularly interesting analysis of the political implications of two recipe books, one purporting to originate from Queen Henrietta Maria (and defending her during her exile in France), and one purporting to originate from Cromwell's wife Elizabeth (and satirizing the Cromwell household), by Laura Knoppers, 'Opening the Queen's Closet: Henrietta Maria, Elizabeth Cromwell, and the Politics of Cookery', *RQ* 60 (2007): 464–99.

26. See the chapters by Susan Wiseman and Rachel Trubowitz in this volume.

27. See in particular Sharon Achinstein's pioneering essay, 'Women on Top in the Pamphlet Literature of the English Revolution', *Women's Studies* 24 (1994): 130–61; and Marcus Nevitt, *Women and the Pamphlet Culture of Revolutionary England, 1640–1660* (Aldershot: Ashgate, 2006).

28. Mihoko Suzuki, *Subordinate Subjects: Gender, the Political Nation, and Literary Form in England, 1588–1688* (Aldershot: Ashgate, 2003); Wiseman, *Conspiracy and Virtue*.

29. Margaret Cavendish, *Poems and Fancies* (1653), Aa; noted in Elaine Hobby, '"Come to Live a Preaching Life": Female Community in Seventeenth Century

Radical Sects', in Rebecca D'Monté and Nicole Pohl, eds, *Female Communities, 1600–1800* (London: Macmillan, 2000), 78.

30. Amongst a number of recent accounts of Trapnel, see in particular Hilary Hinds, *God's Englishwomen: Seventeenth-Century Radical Sectarian Writing and Feminist Criticism* (Manchester: Manchester University Press, 1996); and Erica Longfellow, *Women and Religious Writing in Early Modern England* (Cambridge: Cambridge University Press, 2004), ch 5. See also Rachel Trubowitz's chapter in this volume.

2
Channeling the Gender Debate: Legitimation and Agency in Seventeenth-Century Tracts and Women's Poetry

Megan Matchinske

In 1615, twelve years after James I ascended to the throne of England, Joseph Swetnam published *The Arraignment of Lewd, idle, froward, and unconstant Women*, a venomous, but not highly original polemic against women, accusing them, among other things, of bringing men to spiritual and secular ruin.[1] Two years and several editions later, three authors, Rachel Speght, Ester Sowernam, and Constantia Munda, returned the favor with tracts of their own.[2] Their ostensibly female-authored responses took Swetnam and his unconscionable *Arraignment* to task, shifting the focus of their attacks to accommodate separate and not always harmonious agendas.[3] The upshot of that engagement was a refiguring of the *querelle des femmes* ('woman' debate) along three discrete yet coexistent trajectories.[4] The comparative nature of the Speght, Sowernam, and Munda tracts (they are generically, historically, and geographically parallel) renders them ideal for discussions of appropriate subjectivity for English women at the beginning of the seventeenth century. Despite the same object of discussion, Swetnam's *Arraignment*, these authors create unique and competing lines of defense. Because each author relies on different frames, the definitions between defenses vary in substance as well as kind. Looking at the debate texts in dialogue and noting the ways that they strategically imagine possibilities, can offer us an opportunity to resuscitate notions of volition and effect, conceptual categories that have suffered serious neglect in the wake of recent theoretical concerns over an essentialized subject.

Foregrounding three distinct sites of authority that the tracts employ in making their case – religion, law, and status – I will consider, first, what is at stake in the decision for early modern women to align themselves with a given legitimating authority, and, second, how causative strategies in both public and private realms, derive from, depend on, and mitigate that shaping. Finally, using the debate's proscriptive categories as a springboard to address the gendering of female authority across seventeenth-century English print culture, I will in closing turn to two contemporaneous 'literary' works by women – Aemilia Lanyer's *Salve Deus Rex Judaeorum* and Diana Primrose's *Chaine of Pearle* – for signs of lawful, godly, and well-bred conduct and, on occasion, for its flagrant disregard.

Authority

In the first of the three tracts to be published, *A Mouzell for Melastomus*, Speght legitimates her right to speak through God. It is not by choice that this young, untested David volunteers to speak out against the *Arraignment*'s 'vaunting *Goliath*. ... Armed with the truth ... and the Word of Gods Spirit', she is obliged as a Christian to defend the elect from Swetnam's blasphemies.[5] Using a predestinarian logic not only to justify her own willingness to enter into the *querelle* as a defender of women but also to qualify the degree of blame that falls on women through original sin, Speght displays an assurance of grace – a certainty that she has been chosen and that God has made this choice evident to her.[6] Speght's focus here is particularly timely in light of contemporaneous soteriological debates over issues of salvation.

Anticipating the moderate Puritan line ratified at Dort in the following year, Speght's Calvinism poses as central the relative culpability of original sin. In order to emphasize ideas of volition, her own as well as that of her fellows, she foregrounds a logical rather than a temporal order for Godly decree.[7] She discursively delays the moment of election until after the Fall, a point that will carry special gender weight in her discussion of Genesis. Insisting first that Eve's sin, committed in ignorance, was 'imperfect, and unable to bring a deprivation of a blessing received, or death on all mankind, till ... [Adam] had transgressed' (5), and second that Adam's trespass was self-determined ('for by the free will, which before his fall hee enjoyed, he might have avoided, and beene free from beeing burnt' [5]), Speght creates a template for election that mimics the circumstances of the Fall and provides readers with an infralapsarian and gender-specific logic for its fulfillment. Eve's ignorant sin has not only secured a lesser sentence for women (as 'by her seede ... the serpents head [will] be broken' [6]) but also eased the way to female redemption. Adam's fall, in contrast, is damning: '[w]hosoever blasphemeth God,' Speght reminds readers, 'ought by his Law, to die; The *Bayter of Women* [like Adam] hath blasphemed God, *Ergo*, he ought to die the death' (38). By breaking Swetnam's head, Speght simultaneously vindicates Eve and illustrates her own saintliness as one of God's chosen.

Six weeks after the publication of Speght's initial defense, a second writer entered the fray.[8] In the pseudonymous *Ester hath hang'd Haman*, Ester Sowernam invokes not God but a lesson in civics. Privileging issues of social agency and effect, she focuses her sights on those institutions that enable or inhibit action on behalf of women.[9] Promising appropriate female conduct in a domestic setting, Sowernam outlines complementary duties for husbands and fathers as providers and protectors. Sowernam's insistence on mutual obligation paves the way for a practical revision of gender roles, evinced in changed laws and reformed behavior.

Where Speght bases her defense on religious authority, specifically creedal Calvinism, Sowernam justifies her right to rebuttal 'at the barre of fame and report' (27), defending women from the social ramifications of Swetnam's libelous (no longer blasphemous) remarks.[10] She is asked to speak out on behalf of women: 'that the world might be satisfied in respect of the wrongs done unto us, and to maintaine our honourable reputation, it was concluded that my selfe should deliver before the Judges, to all the assembly, speeches to these effects following' (31).

As a pseudo-legal document arraigning Swetnam before various aspects of his own conscience, Sowernam's account follows court procedure but keeps its subject comfortably within the domestic; it addresses issues of slander and marital abuse, generally the domain of Chancery (the only court where married women might seek legislative redress) and it restricts that defense to interrogating the internal workings of Swetnam's mind, legitimate purview for such investigation in its feminized interiority.[11] By continually emphasizing the primacy of the husband as legally responsible (liable, like Swetnam, to the weight of the law), Sowernam effectively shifts the burden of gender reform onto men – men already married or soon to be married who are most able to do something about it.[12]

Sowernam's institutional focus allows her to play one authority (domestic) off against another (legal), redefining both in the process. At one point, discussing the aftermath of the Fall not its theological antecedents, she emphasizes men's material failure to negotiate the social roles of husband *and* judge effectively. For Sowernam, it is not Eve's naïveté in eating the apple that deserves interrogation but rather Adam's faulty judgment in turning against his wife to accuse her before God: 'It was no good example in Adam,' she writes, 'who having received his wife from the gift of God ... would presently accuse ... & put her in all danger; but the woman was more bound to an upright judge, then to a loving husband' (34). Sowernam seems here to be demanding from men some sort of intermediary stance that will embrace both judgment and compassion – both paternal law and uxorial commitment – a synthesis that the equity courts with their focus on domestic matters were ideally suited to navigate.[13]

The third and last ostensibly female-authored response to Swetnam's diatribe, Munda's *The Worming of a mad Dogge*, channels both the spiritual and the familial into a validation of privilege. Munda's tract, the most overtly secular of the three treatises, foregrounds its own satiric erudition.[14] Where Speght and Sowernam apologize for intruding in an all-male domain, Munda, a proclaimed gentlewoman's daughter, drops any pretense of female disclaimer to launch instead into a bold statement of attack. She offers an ultimatum that leaves Swetnam directly responsible for the behavior that he seeks to condemn:

> Know therefore that wee will cancell your accusations, travers your bils, and come upon you for a false inditement, and thinke not tis our waspishnesse that shall sting you; no sir, untill we see your malepert sausinesse reformed, which will not be till you doe *make a long letter to us*, we will continue *Juno'es*.[15]

Munda's status-based success comes in her decision to frame her account via writing and rank. Recognizing herself as a 'wit' and making distinctions between an innate literary talent conferred by gentle blood and the base birth of 'every foule-mouthed male-content [who] may disgorge his *Licambean* poyson in the face of all the world' (1), Munda associates good writing with good breeding, outlining a textual hierarchy that will eventually separate Grub Street hacks (of whom Swetnam is an example *par excellence*) from their literary and social superiors.[16] In this construction, Juno-like behavior comes with the territory; gentility demands its champion, especially when someone of Swetnam's questionable background threatens its borders.

Agency: public and private

The authorizing principles of religion, law, and status create in their wake field-specific consequences and responsibilities. Where Munda foregrounds appearance, often at the expense of any notion of interiority at all and where Sowernam valorizes each site separately, Speght, in turn, sees one as mirroring the other and both outside human understanding in God's hands. This framing necessarily affects her ability to imagine action. Insisting that Swetnam is no better authorized to understand the mysteries of the soul than the thoughts of the women that he denigrates, she accuses him of arrogating God's will: 'As for your audacitie in judging of womens thoughts, you thereby shew your selfe an usurper against the King of heaven, the true knowledge of cogitations being appropriate unto him alone' (34). 'Thoughts' and 'cogitations' are material representations of the soul; they embody the spiritual on earth. Swetnam is 'an usurper' in attempting to judge them much less to display them publicly before others: 'It was the saying of a judicious Writer,' Speght informs him, 'that whoso makes the fruit of his cogitations extant to the view of all men, should have his worke to be as a well tuned instrument, in all places according and agreeing, the which I am sure yours doth not' (39). Because Swetnam is not elect, because he speaks off-key, his words deserve censorship.

In Speght's account, notions of interiority are either the dangerous rambling of a diseased mind or the material illustration of a higher power – a power manifest through biblical exegesis. As one of the elect, Speght interprets scripture correctly, deciphering its meanings from a host of often-disharmonious possibilities. As she sees it, faithful interpretation is both private and absolute. Accordingly, though she may accuse Swetnam of transgressing human bounds in judging what he cannot know, she herself speaks with impunity. The difference resides in the distinction she makes between the private as self-determined (hubristic and unconscionable) and the private as the domain of God's spirit (something only the elect possess). Within this godly space, gender difference momentarily becomes less significant, more open to revision.

In contrast to Speght's Calvinist determinism, Sowernam's reliance on institutional reform necessitates a proto-contractual framing of social spheres and of the gender obligations particular to them. Within the wider commonwealth, men are to pass laws, honor contracts, and take responsibility for the women in their care.[17] Women, in contrast, must attend to the household. In *Ester hath hang'd Haman*, Sowernam posits the domestic as a site for female expression and mobility. In this realm, she says, women are 'designed, to be helpers, comforters, joyes, and delights, and in true use and government they ever have beene and ever will be' (10).[18] At the same time she situates moral comprehension within that female space, gendering ideas of invigilation. Women alone have access to the essence of things.[19]

Because women are better able to discern, they necessarily provide a service to the men in their lives: indeed, young men 'are never free-men, nor ever called honest men, till they be married: for that is the chief portion which they get by their wives. When they are once married, they are forthwith placed in the ranke of honest men ... And the reason presently added, for hee hath a wife; shee is the sure signe and seale of honestie' (23). Sowernam's promise of women's moral integrity plays directly into her presentation of Swetnam's trial before a female tribunal. Assigning Swetnam two 'Judgesses, *Reason* and *Experience*' (28), Sowernam genders and internalizes the jurisdictional authority of the legal system, re-invoking it as the voice of conscience, as a legitimate form of civic discipline that justifies female prerogative in the area of moral reform: '[a]s for *Experience*,' she writes, 'one property she hath above all the rest, no man commeth before her but she maketh him ashamed' (28).

Where Sowernam spatially divides female and male responsibility, interior from exterior, Munda ignores gender completely when it comes to issues of agency – or so it would seem. What initially worries her, in fact, is Swetnam's failure to keep private things private; it is the inappropriate nature of his writing that so distresses. Accusing Swetnam of a 'private spirit that ... interpret[s] by enthusiasmes', Munda reiterates the necessity of keeping both spheres separate and the personal very much to oneself (28). Munda is here using a familiar High Church attack on public expressions of private faith to demarcate between good print and bad. She is particularly alarmed at the potential exposure of private revelations, Swetnam's in particular, within the arena of bookselling. 'These wide open-dores,' she writes, 'these unwalled townes, these rudderlesse shippes, these uncoverd vessels, these unbrideled horses doe not consider that the tongue being a very little member should never goe out of that same ivory gate, in which ... divine wisedome and nature together hath enclosed' (4–5).

By drawing distinctions between an elite and able coterie of writers and the multitude of dissolute pamphleteers who must instead 'labor diligently' both to support themselves and to create a coherent sentence, Munda foregrounds decorum above everything else. Those with sufficient education and public expertise to keep private matters under wraps and out of sight, those who can display their rhetorical skills with nary a loss of textual control, merit a free and uncensored press and the public approbation that comes with literary skill. Unfortunately, discursively, beyond this exceptional speaker, that public voice remains a masculine domain, the possession of classically trained, socially polished, and adept male writers. For all three authors concepts of the private remain distinct and isolable, intellectually and geographically separate from either shared speech or public tavern. In each instance that which is within (hidden from view) is invariably and familiarly feminized. For Speght difference is made manifest in the material circumstances surrounding both men and women of this world and the spiritually transcendent realm above and beyond them. For Sowernam the difference is one of kind; male and female prerogative and locale are, or at least ought to be, distinct, each deserving of equal and complementary attention. Finally, for Munda the difference between realms is hierarchical; the public precedes the private in both importance and authority. In a culture ever more willing to categorize and define, it is no wonder that all three authors are so adamant in drawing boundaries between realms, dividing them hierarchically, appositionally, or transcendentally. That said, the cumulative effect of all three strategies ensures heightened division; the private necessarily becomes more private, the public, more public.

The Swetnam debate, with its different allegiances, exaggerates the kind of gender maneuvering that it is at work in navigating social constraint. The writers who respond to Swetnam's *Arraignment* pick and choose among different strategies in staking their claims – strategies that are available beyond the debate. Indeed, if we turn to other early seventeenth-century women authors, we can find similar borrowings – borrowings that speak to the social currency of religious, legal, and privilege-specific tropes in navigating gender restraint. The categories then are neither unique to the debate nor solely the domain of polemic. They are, instead, the conventional building blocks of early modern identity, available for 'conscious' and 'considered' appropriation across literary domains.[20]

Poetic borrowings

As poets, Aemilia Lanyer and Diana Primrose have access to a more fluid stylistic palette than do the polemicists. Backed into epistemological corners, they can simply write themselves out by switching metaphors, shifting voice or similarly navigating across ideological terrain. Indeed, generic flexibility, a willingness to engage in mixed forms, illustrates the early modern poet's writerly skills, her ability to maneuver and adapt advantageously. As a result of this greater generic freedom, poets may adopt Speght's religious iconographies to legitimate their work *and* borrow from Munda's aesthetic elitism in order to justify their transgressions. Using the Swetnam respondents as our template, we can investigate how and when boundaries become reified, noting as well the adaptive potential that each choice enables.

Lanyer published her *Salve Deus Rex Judaeorum* in 1611, five years before the Swetnam debate erupted in full. This imaginative retelling of the Passion includes both a detailed exordium in praise of women and a sustained defense of Eve. Incorporating elements common to all three debate writers, Lanyer's poetry offers a composite portrait of gender strategy at work. It alludes to good breeding, social obligation, *and* religious right to demand a more equitable, charitable, and institutionally secure position for women.

Like Speght, Lanyer invokes God's word, ceding at least some of its responsibility for her success to that higher power.[21] Over the course of her narrative Lanyer repeatedly falls back on godly authority, reminding her readers that their support of her text reflects their own spiritual worth. The most explicit rendering of this comes in Lanyer's prose dedication to Margaret Clifford, her principal dedicatee. She offers her patron Christ incarnate, 'whose infinit value is not to be comprehended within the weake imagination or wit of man' (34). Noting that her subject matter 'giveth grace to the meanest & most unworthy hand that will undertake to write thereof', and that God's 'Sunne [will] retaine his own brightnesses and most glorious luster, though never so many blind eyes looke upon him', she also ensures for her text a positive reception: 'Therefore good Madame, to the most perfect eyes of your understanding, I deliver the inestimable treasure of all elected soules' (35). Because the countess's eyes are not 'blind' and her imagination not 'weake', because, in fact, her understanding is 'perfect' in Christ, Lanyer's account should be welcomed.

Lanyer strengthens women's worth more broadly by foregrounding their role as defenders of Christ.[22] Relying on Sowernam's separate realms and the increasing importance of women as moral guardians, Lanyer underscores the particular qualities that women bring to the table. Describing in full the torments that Jesus faced as he made his way to the place of execution, Lanyer notes that it was 'women, by their piteous cries / Did moove their Lord, their Lover and their King, / To take compassion, turne about, and speake / To them whose hearts were ready now to breake' (93.981–84). Women, by virtue of their compassion elicit a response from their Lord when no man can do likewise. Lanyer explains, 'Your cries inforced mercie, grace, and love / From him, whom greatest Princes could not moove: / To speake one word, nor once to life his eyes / Unto proud Pilate, no nor Herod, king; / Could make him answere to no manner of thing' (93.975–80). Compassion is, according to this author, female domain, a gender-weighted attribute outside and beyond men's ken.

Lanyer uses the 'separate spheres' argument to make a case not simply for women's more perfect access to compassion but also, and more pertinently, for men's responsibility for protecting and defending women from abuse. Reminding readers in a general apology that most of the ill attributed to women could be better traced to men (recall Sowernam's blame-placing), Lanyer also underscores the myriad connections, biblical and historical, that men have erased in order to vilify the female sex. They must '[f]orget ... they were borne of women, nourished of women, and that if it were not by the means of women, they would be quite extinguished out of the world' (48). Indeed, it is precisely this obligation to women that Christ so vehemently embraces in the Passion; Christ, we are told, was

> begotten of a woman, borne of a woman, nourished of a woman, obedient to a woman ... [H]e healed woman, pardoned women, comforted women: yea, eve when he was in his greatest agonie and bloodie sweat, going to be crucified, and also in the last houre of his death, [he] tooke care to dispose of a woman: after his resurrection, [he] appeared first to a woman, sent a woman to declare his most glorious resurrection to the rest of his Disciples. ... All which is sufficient to inforce all good Christians and honourable minded men to speake reverently of our sexe, and especially of all virtuous and good women. (49–50)

For Lanyer, then, Christ's actions on the cross remind men of women's virtuous qualifications – qualifications that are further reinforced via status.

Birth and breeding accordingly loom large in this discussion, as does literary skill, all three cordoning off an elite domain where the privileged are accorded special access. As the non-noble daughter of a court musician, however, Lanyer complicates membership in this group by evoking a classically based and humanist inspired volunteerism that mirrors Christ's willing and salvific abasement.[23] Like Munda, Lanyer repeatedly associates virtue with high status, arguing that it must be passed on from one generation to the next.[24] Lacking appropriate conduct, social rank loses its definition.[25] 'How doe we know,' asks Lanyer's poet-narrator, that the biological offspring of noble parentage 'spring out of the same / True stocke of honour, being not of that kind? ... / If he that much enjoyes, doth little good, / We may suppose he comes not of that blood' (43.43–44, 47–48). Lanyer's figuring makes explicit use of Munda's status privilege to separate the noble from the base, but the dividing principle in this instance is merit-driven. Virtuous behavior, not simply the fact of one's birth, confers title and signals nobility.

Lanyer draws a careful distinction here as it seems as important that she maintain ties to privilege (through the language of breeding and inheritance) as that she extend that privilege to include her own endeavors. Lanyer may not be born to the manor, but her framing insists on just such a metaphorical link. In her dedication to the Lady Anne Clifford, she locates the countess's status not simply in virtue but also in a genetically ennobled predisposition that has been passed on by a worthy mother. Good breeding here supplants good birth but parallels it as a mark of nobility. 'To you, as to God's steward I doe write', Lanyer explains, commending Clifford's pastoral care, 'In whom the seeds of virtue have bin sowne, / By your most worthy mother, in whose right, / All her faire parts you challenge as your owne' (43.57–60).

For Lanyer, the most visible evidence of noble blood comes in charity, particularly, we might suspect, charitable actions directed toward impoverished female poets. She offers up a kind of literary blackmail that confers title only when fulfilled in full: 'And as your Ancestors at first possest / Their honours, for their honourable deeds, / Let their faire virtues, never be transgrest, / Bind up the broken, stop the wounds that bleeds, / Succour the poore, [and] comfort the comfortlesse, / ... So shal you shew from whence you are descended, / And leave to all posterities your fame, / So will your virtues alwais be commended, / And every one will reverence your name' (44.73–84); 'if you patronize my work,' she promises, 'you will prove yourself worthy of the Clifford title'.

While Lanyer embraces a standard topos of apology in this text, denigrating her little book and scant abilities, the demurrals only go so far. Throughout, Lanyer evinces a secure sense of her own literary skill, a skill that she equates with both divine inspiration and technical expertise. Like Munda's self-conscious rhetorical flourishes, Lanyer's claims to poetic mastery add ballast to her arguments about women's worth and promise her dedicatees immortality. Certain of both her subject matter and the means by which she will convey it, she too can assert an inherited literary excellence: 'And knowe, when first into this world I came, / This charge was giv'n me by th'Eternall powrs, / Th'everlasting trophie of thy fame, / To build and decke it with the sweetest flowers / That virtue yeelds' (113.1458–61). Comparing her patron, Margaret, Countess of Cumberland (Anne Clifford's mother) to the biblical Susanna, and, by extension, her own prophetic voice to that of Daniel, Lanyer validates her own stature: 'Although … [Susanna's] virtue doe deserve to be / Writ by that hand that never purchas'd blame, / In holy Writ, where all the world may see / Her perfit life, and ever honoured name: / Yet she was not to be compar'd to thee [Lady Margaret], / Whose many virtues doe increase thy fame' (117.1537–42). In promising that Clifford is more worthy than her biblical predecessor, Lanyer elevates her own dedication to the status of 'holy writ'. Virtue, here, a heritable artifact, becomes the domain of an elite coterie, carefully qualified by good breeding and consummate writing skills.

Lanyer's *Salve Deus Rex Judaeorum* calls on religion, law, and status to make its arguments, moving more or less seamlessly from one to another.[26] Using a pastiche approach to highlight female virtue and legitimate its own authority, her poem offers readers in that selective mix both fluidity and flexibility. It reminds us that rhetorical strategy is in fact a malleable resource – something that individual writers can both selectively employ and manipulate to suit particular ends. It also suggests by extension that subjectivity, the identities that we inhabit over time and across history, is negotiable, shaped to at least some extent by the particular choices that we make as to what to believe, value, and promote.

Published well over a decade after the Swetnam debate in 1630, Primrose's *Chaine of Pearl*, an encomium to Queen Elizabeth, takes advantage of many of the same categories, evoking once again elements from all three writers' repertoires.[27] Primrose begins her poem by underscoring Elizabeth's godliness: 'The goodliest Pearle in faire Eliza's Chaine; / is true Religion' (1). Like Speght, she initially locates the Queen's willingness to act in religious faith. Noting from the beginning of Elizabeth's reign the ill effects of superstition, Primrose tells us that the Queen, 'undaunted bravely did advance / Christs Glorious Ensigne, maugre all the feares / Or Dangers which appear'd' (3). While Elizabeth's religious response is at first gender-coded (she initially 'swaid the Scepter with a Ladies hand'), the sharpening disagreement between Catholic and Protestant perspectives finally incites the Queen to action: 'Against Recusants; and with Lyons heart,' we are told, 'Shee bang'd the *Pope*, and tooke the Gospells part' (4).

In its focus on regulatory procedures, Primrose's account simultaneously reveals both a deep regard for established institutional safeguards and recognition of women's responsibilities in that mix, just the sort of public/private complementarity that Sowernam advocates. In an effort to condemn the absolutist policies of the reigning monarch, Charles I, Primrose emphasizes not simply Elizabeth's actions but her self-discipline. The qualities (pearls) that she identifies – among them, prudence, temperance, and patience – reiterate Elizabeth's 'womanly' ability to curb her instincts, to draw inward and defer. Like Sowernam, Primrose places a high regard on established hierarchies (parliamentary, legal, and, in her case, episcopal) for support or qualification, but she especially reiterates the Queen's cooperative and sphere-specific restraint in navigating them. It is Elizabeth's willingness to offer her subjects the benefit of the doubt in matters of law, to eschew explicit religious decree and to heed advice from her counselors that best define her.[28]

While Primrose relies in part on both a privileging of religious and legal obligations, she also values Munda's elite literary aesthetic. Observing in the seventh and eighth pearls the success of the Queen's oratory – in particular Elizabeth's battle-readiness in the speech at Tilbury and her last recorded words before the House of Commons – Primrose stresses the power of noble language to move listeners: 'When ... Shee / Gave Audience in State and Majestie: / Then did the Goddesse *Eloquence* inspire / Her Royall Brest ... On her Sacred Lips / Angels enthron'd, most Heavenly *Manna* sips / Then might you see her *Nectar-flowing* Veine / Surround the Hearers; in which sugred Streame, / Shee able was to drowne a World of men, / And drown'd, with Sweetnes to revive agen' (10). Privileging the '*Atticke Eloquence*' of an erudite Elizabeth over the 'rude rambling *Rhetoricke*' of the 'mere *Slavonian*' (10), Primrose creates a female monarch who relegates outsiders to incoherence and displays in her own eloquence the military might of the nation.

Nearly fifteen years after the Swetnam debate runs it course, Primrose provides readers with a pointed albeit veiled critique of Charles I's policies and practices in the figure of the long departed Queen. She demands religious right (illustrated in an active and dedicated opposition to all things Catholic), Speght's purview, institutional safeguards (evoked in wise counsel, just law, and fair trial) and moral guardianship (in the form of an explicitly gendered regulatory system that relies on personal invigilation), both derivative of Sowernam, and she privileges Munda's aesthetic judgment (the skillful craftsmanship of a worthy and gentle-born poet-orator). In an environment openly hostile to general counsel (Charles had prorogued Parliament the year before the poem's publication, and it would not meet again until 1640), to legal recourse for private citizens (the little supervised power of the Caroline prerogative courts offered minimal protections against arbitrary incarceration or arrest), to religious freedom (Charles had outlawed parliamentary discussion of any point of controversial doctrine, including predestination, and had also, via Laud, begun campaigning against lay rents supporting parish ministries), and to women's rights (broken marriage contract and increasingly effective strictures that limited movement beyond the domestic space), Speght's, Sowernam's, and Munda's reformist agendas join forces to both critique and empower.[29]

The frames addressed here – religion, law, and status – are both conventional and long lived – honored, perhaps, only in the breach, in their formulaic display within the *querelle*. Certainly we understand these schematic renderings as such and can as critics of early modern gender easily identify the restrictions they impose. What we don't do as often, though, is to reanimate those familiar power centers with their sometimes stereotypical mindsets as trajectories of choice, available for gender appropriation and possessing in their complacency a surprising social force. In a disciplinary environment as theoretically savvy as our own, as sensitive, in fact, to essentializing gestures of cause and effect, it is useful to resuscitate the very real material repercussions of such authorial choosing, to recognize once again the singular choices that individual writers can and do make. For individual writers did choose, opting in their arguments for this line of reasoning over that. By looking carefully at the closed circumstances of the gender debate, narrowed as it is by place, time, and format, we can recognize the boundedness of singular patterns of thought, the internal logic of choice as it operates within and across any given conceptual category or author.

Notes

1. Joseph Swetnam, *The Arraignment of Lewd, idle, froward, and unconstant Women* (London, 1615).
2. While the earliest popular defense written by an Englishwoman, *Jane Anger her Protection for Women* (1589), no doubt paved the way for the female-authored tracts considered here, it was hardly the only impetus. Given almost half a century of successful female reign in England, a current (male) monarch whose attitudes toward women's status were at best indifferent, and even, perhaps, a few well-publicized London love scandals (most notably Overbury's murder), it is no wonder that the second decade of the seventeenth century saw no fewer than twenty separate publications on the controversy, three by women, several with extensive printings and multiple editions (Louis B. Wright, *Middle-Class Culture in Elizabethan England* [Ithaca: Cornell University Press, 1935], 490).
3. As two of the authors, Munda and Sowernam, wrote under pseudonyms, specific gender attribution is impossible. I will, nevertheless, assume female authorship throughout as both narrators 'regardless of gender, construct … [themselves] as female and as such establish … [themselves] in those terms'

(Megan Matchinske, *Writing, Gender and State in Early Modern England: Identity Formation and the Female Subject* [Cambridge: Cambridge University Press, 1998], 195 n.3). Several critics have questioned the gender identity of Sowernam and Munda. See, for instance, Linda Woodbridge, *Women and the English Renaissance: Literature and the Nature of Womankind, 1540–1620* (Urbana: University of Chicago Press, 1985), 93; and Diane Purkiss, 'Material Girls: The Seventeenth-Century Gender Debate', in *Women, Texts and Histories, 1575–1760*, ed. Clare Brant and Diane Purkiss (London: Routledge, 1992), 69–101.

4. For a formal definition of the genre, see Woodbridge, *Women and the English Renaissance*, 13–14. Wright, in contrast, locates these texts in terms of their popular appeal (*Middle-Class Culture*, 465–507). Other writers who discuss the controversy in England include Barbara J. Baines, *Three Pamphlets on the Jacobean Antifeminist Controversy* (Delmar, NY: Scholars' Facsimiles & Reprints, 1978); Katherine Usher Henderson and Barbara F. McManus, eds, *Half Humankind: Contexts and Texts of the Controversy About Women in England, 1540–1640* (Urbana: University of Illinois Press, 1985); Constance Jordan, *Renaissance Feminism: Literary Texts and Political Models* (Ithaca: Cornell University Press, 1990); Cristina Malcolmson and Mihoko Suzuki, eds, *Debating Gender in Early Modern England, 1500–1700* (New York: Palgrave Macmillan, 2002); Simon Shepherd, ed., *The Women's Sharp Revenge: Five Women's Pamphlets from the Renaissance* (London: Fourth Estate, 1985); and Lee Utley, *The Crooked Rib: An Analytical Index to the Argument About Women in English and Scots Literature to the End of the Year 1568* (Columbus: Ohio State University Press, 1944).

5. Rachel Speght, *A Mouzell for Melastomus* (1617), in *The Polemics and Poems of Rachel Speght*, ed. Barbara Kiefer Lewalski (New York: Oxford University Press, 1996), 4. Subsequent references are cited parenthetically in the text.

6. For 'wythoute some tast of thys divine providence in predestination, there can be no faithe, but ... a doubtful waveringe, leading to despare' (Anthony Gilbey, *A Briefe Treatyse of Election and Reprobation wythe certane answers to the objections of the adversaries of this doctrine* [1556], cited in Dewey D. Wallace, Jr., *Puritans and Predestination: Grace in English Protestant Theology, 1525–1695* [Chapel Hill: University of North Carolina Press, 1982], 26).

7. The Synod of Dort (1618) endorsed this de facto infralapsarian position averring, if only textually, that God's choosing occurs *after* humans have 'fallen through their own fault from their primitive state of rectitude into sin and destruction' (*Canons of Dort*, http://www.reformed.org/documents/index. html?mainframe=http://www.reformed.org/documents/synod_of_dort. html, 1.7).

8. Speght's tract was registered on 14 November 1616, Sowernam's on 4 January 1616 (i.e., 1617], and Munda's on 29 April 1617 (Edward Arber, *A Transcript of the Registers of the Company of Stationers of London; 1554–1640*, vol. 3 [London, 1876], 276, 277b, 281b).

9. 'In my first Part I have ... strictly observed a religious regard ... Now I am come to this second Part, I am determined to solace my selfe with a little libertie', Sowernam insists. Sowernam, *Ester hath hang'd Haman* (London, 1617), 16. Subsequent references are cited parenthetically in the text.

10. Sowernam's connection with the legal community is a matter of some conjecture as she is clearly familiar with the court calendar and its procedures.

11. See my *Writing, Gender and State*, for a discussion of interiority as a gendered space (14).
12. Marriage settlements comprised one of the most active sites of change in early modern case law (Anne Laurence, *Women in England, 1500–1760: A Social History* [New York: St. Martin's Press, 1994], 229). Amy Louise Erickson speculates that there were 'probably more than 7000 surviving bills of complaint from the plaintiff and/or answers from the defendant which ... [were] specifically about a marriage settlement in the seventeenth century' (*Women & Property in Early Modern England* [London: Routledge, 1993], 116). In addition to settlements, trusts enabled women to be left freehold land from which they could collect income and bequeath property to others. Chancery, in particular, became a key site for determining the legality of such transactions. See also Carroll Camden, 'The Marriage Contract, Marriage, Marriage Customs', in *The Elizabethan Woman: A Panorama of English Womanhood, 1540–1640* (Houston: Elsevier Press, 1952); Ralph A. Houlbrooke, *The English Family, 1450–1700* (London: Longman, 1984); and R. H. Smith, 'Marriage Processes in the English Past: Some Continuities', in *The World We Have Gained: Histories of Population and Social Structure*, ed. Lloyd Bonfield, Richard M. Smith, and Keith Wrightson (New York: B. Blackwell, 1986).
13. Sowernam's 'equitable' defense, like the courts it so obviously mimics, relies on a willingness to follow the spirit not the letter of the law.
14. Munda flaunts her obvious grounding in the classics, in Greek and Latin as well as contemporary Italian and French.
15. Constantia Munda, *The Worming of a mad Dogge* (London, 1617), 5. Subsequent references are cited parenthetically in the text. In her response, Munda references two law terms: the first, the 'traversing note', which presumes the defendant's failure to plead, postulating an answer regardless, and the second, the false indictment, which acknowledges the untruthfulness of a defendant's oath-bound declarations as perjury and thus subject to prosecution. In both cases, Munda envisions the efficacy of written testimony to intervene and remediate.
16. Munda explains, 'printing that was invented to be the store-house of famous wits, the treasure of Divine literature ... is become the receptacle of every dissolute Pamphlet' (1).
17. For Sowernam, 'it is not the loosening of affective ties that is paramount ... but rather the promise that vows once made will not be unmade' (Matchinske, *Writing, Gender and State*, 97).
18. Shannon Miller reads these lines differently in her chapter in this volume, noting instead their connection to the language of government and politics.
19. Women not men are best able to 'make difference betwixt colours and conditions', Sowernam insists, 'betwixt a faire shew, and a foule substance' (38).
20. Miller usefully underscores the extent to which conventional attacks against women might be redeployed to surprisingly different ends.
21. Were she to err in her religious constructions, she would be liable: 'Yet some of you methinks I heare to call / Me by my name, and bid me better looke / Lest unawares I in an error fall'. Aemilia Lanyer, *The Poems of Aemilia Lanyer: Salve Deus Rex Judaeorum*, ed. Susanne Woods (New York: Oxford University Press, 1993), 15.73–75. Subsequent references are cited parenthetically in the text.

22. Mary gives birth to God's son; Pilate's wife warns the governor to have nothing to do with the sentencing; and the daughters of Jerusalem weep for their martyred lord and receive his blessing (84.772–87.833, 93.981–84, and 94.995–1000).

23. *The Poems of Aemilia Lanyer*, ed. Woods, xv.

24. She offers a long list of particulars beginning with 'Zeale' and ending, pointedly perhaps, with 'bountie' and 'charitie' (940.91–95).

25. This connection between good birth and good breeding recalls Aristotle's virtuous citizen (*Aristotles Politiques, or Discourses of Government*, trans. Loys Le Roy [London, 1596], especially 55–58). Audrey Tinkham discusses this connection in her article, '"Owning" in Lanyer's *Salve Deus Rex Judaeorum* ('Hail God King of the Jews')', *Studies in Philology* 106.1 (2009): 52–75. See also Mike Pincombe, *Elizabethan Humanism* (London: Longman, 2001), and Janet M. Atwill, 'Rhetoric and Civic Virtue', in *The Viability of the Rhetorical Tradition*, ed. Richard Graff et al. (Albany: State University of New York Press, 2005), 75–92.

26. Like all of the works considered here, Lanyer's poem survives in a single edition. It was not reprinted, and there is no evidence that it won her the accolades to which she had aspired. I wonder whether her original dedicatees appreciated her praises or found them instead offensive? Perhaps the very multiplicity of authorizing principles that Lanyer evoked created obstacles, obstacles that made for mixed messages and unintended consequences. How could women be so perfect, so beyond nature (Munda), if they were God's fallen creatures (Speght) or if they suffered the indignities of an unequal gender system where men possessed all the power and continued to exert it improperly (Sowernam)? How could men be blamed for everything (Sowernam), if God's master plan was at work (Speght) or if nobility and literary genius continued to be at women's disposal (Munda)? Creating an insoluble puzzle, the contradictory points of authority that Lanyer employed in her narrative both enable and undermine in asserting their claims. Leeds Barroll concurs, locating Lanyer's failure specifically in the way that she prioritizes dedicatees ('Looking for Patrons', in *Aemilia Lanyer: Gender, Genre, and the Canon*, ed. Marshall Grossman [Lexington: University of Kentucky Press, 1998], 39ff.).

27. Diana Primrose, *A Chaine of Pearle, Or a Memoriall of the peerles Graces, and Heroick Vertues of Queene Elizabeth of Glorious Memory* (London, 1630). Subsequent references are cited parenthetically in the text. William Camden's *Annals of Queen Elizabeth*, published in the same year as Swetnam's *Arraignment*, is a likely source for this encomium.

28. In 'The third Pearle, Prudence', Primrose notes that Elizabeth believed that good governance is 'best, where more combine' and where 'Experience and deepe Policy / Are well approved' (5).

29. Mark Kishlansky, *A Monarchy Transformed: Britain, 1603–1714* (London: Penguin Books, 1996), 114, 128.

3
All about Eve: Seventeenth-Century Women Writers and the Narrative of the Fall

Shannon Miller

Adam and Eve's fall and expulsion from the Garden of Eden, one of the most common motifs and subjects for art and literature in the early modern period,[1] was simultaneously the basis of much seventeenth-century political thought: Robert Filmer and John Locke both positioned this narrative at the center of debates about political organization and legitimacy. Yet a parallel use of the Fall story exists in a range of female-authored texts throughout the seventeenth century. Early in the century, writers like Rachel Speght, Ester Sowernam, and Aemilia Lanyer use the Fall narrative to discuss women's engagement in political involvement and issues of authority. Following the English Civil War, the Fall will serve radically different purposes for writers with opposed political views and affiliations: republican Lucy Hutchinson and royalist Margaret Cavendish deploy portraits of Eve to intervene in the very debates that mark Robert Filmer's monarchical and John Locke's republican writings. The portrait of Eve in the Garden of Eden thus becomes a remarkably flexible tool for women writers to address women's role within the political or, what will later be termed, public sphere.[2] This chapter thus extends the work begun by Hilda L. Smith's collection on *Women Writers and the Early Modern British Political Tradition;*[3] by suggesting that the political narrative of the Garden and Fall enables women writers to interrogate and contribute to seventeenth-century political debates, I will argue for the centrality of gender in the formation of modern political thought.[4]

Reappropriating the Garden narrative becomes a significant opportunity for Rachel Speght and Ester Sowernam, who publish responses to Joseph Swetnam's 1615 *The Arraignment of Lewd, idle, froward, and unconstant Women.*[5] Despite the fact that the story of Adam and Eve's sin in the Garden had invariably led to the assertion of women's culpability for the Fall and consequent subordination to men, the portion of their tracts that turn to this story is significantly higher than in Joseph Swetnam's attack on women or in other male-authored defenses of women. In Swetnam's thirty-page attack on women, for example, only four brief references to the story appear.[6] By contrast, Rachel Speght and Ester Sowernam consider the story of Adam and Eve to be, literally, the central argument for women, the first line of defense in protecting women from attacks by Swetnam and others.[7] The bulk of Speght's 1617 *A Mouzel for Melastomus*, whose argument for women is almost entirely based on the events of the Creation and the Fall, counters Swetnam's examples. Meanwhile, his paragraph-long attack based on the Bible prompts Sowerman's biblical defense running five pages and two chapters in her *Ester hath hang'd Haman*.

As women take on the mantle as women's defenders, Speght and Sowernam expand their use of the Fall story into alternate narratives of Eve returning to an Edenic place. In Speght's 'A Dreame', a 1621 sequel to her earlier 1617 response to Swetnam, the poem describes a woman in a prelapsarian Garden space 'Where *Knowledge* growes, and where [the female narrator] mayst it gaine.'[8] Here, '*Desire* ... told me 'twas a **lawfull** avarice, / To covet *Knowledge* daily more and more' (229–32; my emphasis). Evoking a setting that recalls Eden through its beauty – 'the pleasure of the place' with its 'fragrant flowers of sage and fruitfull plants' (169, 189) – 'A Dreame' entirely remaps the constellation of forbidden knowledge, temptation, and sin presented in Genesis. The poem thus treats positively the acquisition of knowledge by this Eve-like figure.

Like Speght, Sowernam will also re-enter the Garden. Her access to this site will provide her the terms with which she can defend all women: '*I haue entred into the Garden of* Paradice, *and there haue gathered the choysest flowers which that Garden may affoord, and those I offer to you.*'[9] Calling attention to Eve's birth in the Garden as an argument for placing her above the dust-formed Adam, Sowernam calls Eve a '*Paraditian Creature*' (A4r). Eve is frequently treated as exemplary of all women in this tradition of attacks and defenses, but Sowernam turns this convention to her strongest advantage. Women can be defended *because* of their association with Eve and the site of the Garden itself: 'So that woman neither can or may degenerate in her disposition from that naturall inclination of the place, in which she was first framed, she is a Paradician, that is, a delightfull creature, borne in so delightfull a country' (B3v). All women are 'Paradician', holding aspects of prelapsarian perfection as they enter into marriage in this world. The association effectively counters arguments against women, positioned as they are in Sowernam's text as prelapsarian figures and thus equivalent to the unfallen Eve.

Both Speght and Sowernam, then, cleverly rework the convention of attacks against women, where women are blamed as seducers of men. As they argue for themselves, these female defenders take on the identity of Eve herself. Speght thereby rewrites and reinterprets Eve's acquisition of knowledge in the Garden and Sowernam redefines all women through a redeemed Eve figure with whom they share an '*esse*' or essense (B3v). Speght and Sowernam thus utilize, even embrace, this reconfigured identity of Eve within their texts.

The greater emphasis these women place on the story of the Fall than do male writers in the tradition has powerful consequences for the antifeminist tradition. But their use of the Fall invokes the political overtones of this narrative, which more radically heightens the importance of this genre. The Tudor period aligned the 'political and the social realms of human experience', consequently positioning the family as the basis for government.[10] This political model rested on women's domestic subservience to men to justify the very basis of political rule. As a result, the story of the Fall itself was every bit as important for the organization of familial relations as it was for political authority. In the Stuart period, the basis of this theory becomes explicitly theorized, a process in which these women writers seem to participate. For this line of political theory draws women into the very structure of political organization as it acknowledges women's position in the family as justifying monarchical authority. As I will suggest first in the defense by Ester Sowernam and then in the poetry of Aemilia Lanyer, these texts invoke the language of women's marital, social, and analogous political subordination in the context of the story of the Fall, differing here again from Joseph Swetnam who had banished women from the political sphere by evading the very language of biblical subordination. By invoking the Garden narrative more extensively than do men in this tradition, these women writers remind their readership that the very basis of political organization depends on their position within the social fabric of the family and, by extension, the state.[11]

In the female-authored defense tracts, the exoneration of Eve, or even the elevation of Eve over Adam, usually works in concert with the acceptance of man's sovereignty over women: though women defenders in the *querelle des femmes* will rewrite the narrative of the Fall, they do not usually challenge the terms of male sovereignty. Speght discusses Adam's sovereignty, while Sowernam asserts it and the consequent position of women: 'She is commanded to obey her husband' (9[C1r]).[12] Yet in Sowernam's tract, she simultaneously establishes links between women and 'government'; though women will be bound to obey, they are not completely distanced from the language of government. Women are praised for the 'true use and gouernment they ever haue beene and euer will be' (10[C1v]), a reference to women's relation to a political sphere that follows dirrectly upon Sowernam's use of the story of Adam and Eve. When she describes a Swetnam-style attack, in which women have been accused of being 'so weak in their government', she invokes the narrative of the Fall through her description of men who 'tempt' and 'allure' women (38[F3v]). The language of women's connection to government is thus consistently interwoven with references to the Fall.

I want to suggest, via patriarchalist theory's grounding analogy of the family and the state, that Sowernam's connecting of women to the public sphere invokes the political implications of the Fall narrative on which the analogy relied. We hear, alongside women's subservience to men, language of women's political involvement within her tract. She is 'determined to solace my selfe with a little libertie' (16[C4v]), a word that will retroactively take on a political valence as Sowernam lists women who remain actively involved within this public sphere. Sowernam's list of political women begins with two Margarets, queen to Henry VI and mother to Henry VII, moving on to Mary, Queen of Scots and Elizabeth I. These women are frequently more talented politicians, as 'Margaret the wise, wife to *Henrie* the sixt, who if her Husbands fortune, valour, and foresight, had beene answerable to hers, had left the Crowne of *England* to their owne Sonne, and not to a stranger' (20[D2v]). Sowernam resists the marginalization of women from a political or public sphere, creating space for women in the discussions of governmental organization.

Attacks, which were offered by men, follow the opposite strategy. They rarely mention Adam's sovereignty over women, while keeping women outside of any political activity. In Swetnam's *Arraignment*, women are consistently located in a household realm, as the bulk of Swetnam's attacks are directed at women's behavior within (a postlapsarian) marriage. In the very few instances in which he describes women who engage a world outside of the domesticity of marriage, he relocates them outside of any public identity: the beautiful and rich Flora is transformed into a prostitute, becoming a signifier of only private sexual deviance. Swetnam's attack thus has the opposite effect to Sowernam's positioning of women within the political world.

By distancing women's behavior from any form of, or the language of, submission to men, Swetnam effectively breaks the connection between the formation of the state and women's analogous position within the family that forms the basis of patriarchal theory. Alternately, the analogy between gender relations and political authority explicitly serves Sowernam's purposes. By invoking women's direct involvement in political events or the analogy of the state and family that places them under male authority, the defenses position women as central to the formation of state organization. For women's relevance to the structure of the state is fundamentally grounded in the state/family analogy. In the attacks, where the consequences of the organization of the family, analogous to the state because of the Fall, are avoided, women are distanced from the social or political organization of the state.[13] The discrepancy between the defenses and the attacks suggests that defenders of women rely on the analogy in order to illustrate women's central importance to cultural order – even if that order entails their subordination. When the attacks evade the issue of gendered authority, women's position as a cornerstone of cultural organization is negated. Thus even though patriarchal theory can hardly be considered liberating, it does in fact make women a vital basis for governmental organization, a political consequence not lost on authors like Speght and Sowernam who engage the incipient patriarchal theory of the early seventeenth century.

These two aspects of the defenses, rewriting the Genesis story of Adam and Eve and highlighting women's position within governmental organization through the analogy of family and state, are explicitly interwoven in Aemilia Lanyer's *Salve Deus Rex Judaeorum*. Her 1611 Passion poem overtly integrates the narrative of the Fall, the language of political identity, and the issue of women's culpability.[14] While Lanyer will challenge the status of women's subordination in a way Speght and Sowernam do not, her text makes the same link as they do: the narrative of the Fall is profoundly political because it defines women's relationship to the state. Lanyer's quite radical triangulation of these issues occurs within the digression entitled 'Eves Apology', positioned half-way through *Salve Deus*. In this frequently discussed passage, Lanyer narrates the terms of her defense of Eve; she is now to be forgiven for her earlier transgression as a result of men's actions during the crucifixion: 'Till now your indiscretion sets us free, / And makes our former fault much lesse appeare.'[15] Eve, described as 'simply good', is presented in a rewritten narrative of the Fall, just as Speght and Sowernam rewrote the Genesis story (765). We hear that 'If *Eve* did erre, it was for knowledge sake, / The fruit beeing faire perswaded him to fall' (797–98). Her culpability is diminished because of her pure motives, especially when compared with Adam's greater fault: 'surely *Adam* can not be excusde' since he 'was most too blame' (777–78) for the choice to eat the forbidden fruit.

Culpability is, of course, the central issue at the heart of the Fall, resulting in women's subordination to men. In exonerating Eve and all women, Lanyer first removes the consequences of the Fall from Eve and then proceeds to explicitly politicize the stakes of this suspension.[16] In language that resonates suggestively with Sowernam's desire for 'a little liberty' (16[C4v]), Lanyer declares that the crucifixion means men must

> ... let us have our Libertie againe,
> And challendge to your selves no Sov'raigntie; ...
> Your fault beeing greater, why should you disdaine
> Our beeing your equals, free from tyranny? (825–26, 829–30)

Lanyer rejects the male 'Sov'raigntie' granted over women because of the Fall; like Eve's simple goodness and the Passion, these show men's 'fault' to be much 'greater' than women's (826, 829). Lanyer thereby positions the Fall in an explicitly politicized context as she demands 'Libertie' for women, equality with men and, almost prophetically given James's emergent absolutism, 'free[dom] from tyranny' (825, 830). According to Gordon Schochet, the 'appearance of a truly absolutist political theory and practice' in England occurs with James's ascension to the throne (86) and quickly comes to be refracted into these early seventeenth-century texts. Freeing women from aspects of this developing theory, Lanyer offers a political identity to women as a function of the Genesis narrative: like Speght's and Sowernam's embracing of patriarchal thought, Lanyer's poem also highlights women's relationship to the state, now according them their 'Sov'raigntie'.

Restaged Edenic spaces elsewhere in Lanyer's volume also restore women to forms of political 'Libertie'. In the country house poem 'Description of Cooke-ham' that completes her volume, three women – the Countess of Cumberland, her daughter Anne, and the narrator/ author Aemilia Lanyer – enter an Edenic space. The characters and actions of these three will rewrite the narrative of the Fall. The poet asks of the countess, 'How often did you visite this faire tree?', a transformed tree of knowledge that exists within 'that delightfull Place' where 'Pleasure' 'abound[s]'.[17] Paradisical in imagery, the poem is also elegiac in tone as the women are forced to leave the Garden. The poem invokes the legal realities facing the countess, whose husband refused to allow her to retain possession of this estate. But this eviction is in no way the consequence of their sinning, as the traditional Fall story would imply. Free from any fault or transgression, these women are redeemed just as Eve is forgiven in Lanyer's 'Apology'. Of the countess we hear that 'In these sweet woods how often did you walke, / With Christ and his Apostles there to talke' (81–82), while 'In [Anne's] faire breast', we are told, 'true virtue then was hous'd' (96). Redeemed and spiritually elevated, these women carry no associations with a fallen Eve, only a prelapsarian one.

Political references and imagery are shown to be the very consequence of re-envisioning the Fall. For in the poem, the countess's 'Libertie' and 'Sov'raigntie' will be restored; further, her vindication as an Eve-like figure amplifies the vindication of all women already accomplished in the earlier 'Eve's Apology'. 'Cooke-ham's' focus on visual 'prospects' offered to the countess fuses the first garden and (its) politics. From a 'stately Tree', the countess has 'such goodly Prospects' over her land which give her 'A Prospect fit to please the eyes of Kings' (53, 54, 72). With this 'Prospect', the countess acquires specific social and political authority accorded to property ownership; like a (male) landowner, she is able to visually survey, and thus possess, her land from this 'Prospect'. In acquiring this usually male gaze over the land, the countess receives the kind of authority granted to Eve in *Salve Deus*; both are redeemed through the rewriting of the story of the Fall, which bestows upon them a form of political power. The 'Sov'raigntie' granted to the countess is also enhanced by the invocation of regnal power in this passage: the 'Prospect fit to please the eyes of Kings' available to her recalls, even usurps, the very site of sovereign power located in the monarch. An unfallen woman, the countess can evade the consequences of the Fall that would position her in subjection – marital or political. As in 'Eves Apologie', then, Margaret's political and spiritual authority are shown to buttress one another.

I am arguing, then, that significant aspects of political theory are interwoven into Lanyer's poetry and the writings of female defenders in the *querelle des femmes*. Discerning a central principle within patriarchal theory – that women are embedded in, rather than excluded from, political organization – these women engage its core analogy for their own purposes. These writers understand the stakes of deploying a rewritten narrative of the Fall in order to articulate women's position within seventeenth-century English culture. These early seventeenth-century experiments with the Fall narrative by Speght, Sowernam, and

Lanyer become diversely deployed by writers such as Lucy Hutchinson, Margaret Cavendish, and Aphra Behn.[18] If the texts by Speght, Sowernam, and Lanyer were composed during the earliest deployments of patriarchalist theory, the second half of the seventeenth century experienced theoretical and actual clashes of patriarchialist versus republican or contractual thought. The Fall story continues to serve these women's literary, but I would also argue political, interventions into one of the most important questions of the seventeenth century: on what basis can one justify the organization of government? An equally important, and related, question also dominates their writing: what position do women have within this governmental structure?

While I have suggested that early women writing in the *querelle des femmes* accept aspects of the logic of patriarchal theory in order to assert themselves into a political or public sphere, Lucy Hutchinson's republicanism clearly barred any concession to the primary theory supporting monarchy. Her *Order and Disorder*, whose subtitle includes a description of the poem as 'Meditations upon the Creation and the Fall', explicitly turns to the narrative of Genesis while engaging issues of political organization and women's involvement in that process. In an explicit counter to patriarchal theory, this poem, portions of which were published in 1679, denies the solely paternal authority over children that lay at the heart of this body of political thought. As Gordon Schochet has explained, patriarchal theory is grounded in the analogy between a father's rule over his family and the political application of this analogy to justify a monarch's right to rule over his subjects. The primary premise directing all this body of thought, represented most fully by the writings of Robert Filmer, was the equivalent, identical relationship of the family and state. The metaphoric logic at the base of patriarchal theory utilizes the biblical story to provide the ideological ground for monarchical authority. In fact, the basis for monarchical power was established not simply by the Bible, but in the Garden itself. According to Filmer, since God had granted the right of dominion to Adam, all subsequent patriarchs had the right to rule as monarchs, their power derived from the initial patriarch: 'This lordship which Adam by creation had over the whole world, and by right descending from him the patriarchs did enjoy, was as large and ample *as the absolutist dominion of any monarch* which hath been since the creation.'[19] Hutchinson's turn to the story of the Creation and the Fall allows her to dispute this monarchical argument by asserting a particular role for women through the first marriage and then the birth of Eve's sons, which is repeated in the broader representation of mothers in the poem. Unlike Filmer or any other patriarchal theorist of the period, Hutchinson denies that dominion is only vested in Adam. Hutchinson has Adam and Eve receive God's commands together in the poem: God 'give[s] you right to all her fruits and plants, / Dominion over her inhabitants ... Are all made subject under your command'.[20] Either the 'you' here refers to Adam and Eve, in which case Filmer's narrative of the single male monarch is undercut, or the 'you' represents men and women (i.e., humankind) receiving the grant of dominion. In either case, her account of the first marriage and the dispensing of authority counters the singular award of authority upon which all of Filmer's theory rests. Hutchinson's anti-monarchical sentiment, then, shapes her representation of this award of dominion to both Adam and Eve as the Garden narrative allows her to intervene in questions of female authority and woman's relationship to the state.

Hutchinson's second move to insert women into what will be the formation of human communities in *Order and Disorder* occurs at the birth of children. The poem paints Eve as embodying a kind of agency that will undermine a second major principle of patriarchalist thought: the elision of the mother. Filmer bases his theory on 'the law which enjoys obedience to kings' delivered in the terms of '"honour *thy father*" [Exodus, xx, 12] as if all power *were originally in the father*'; this gives 'power of the father over his child' (11–12; my emphases). The shift from parental to paternal authority, accomplished by truncating the commandment 'honor thy father and mother' to only 'honour thy father', becomes the basis of Filmer's theory of family and political obligation and power. Only by locating authority solely in the male parent can the power given to Adam become analogous to the singular power residing with the king.[21]

Hutchinson's narrative of the Fall allows her to intervene directly in the heart of these patriarchalist assumptions, positioning the mother as central in both the account of the relationship between Adam and Eve and that of later mothers. A very detailed account of childbearing in canto 5 is followed by a statement about woman's role as genetrix, one that underscores the relationship between (female) procreative power and authority:

> The next command is, mothers should maintain
> Posterity, not frighted with the pain,
> Which, though it make us mourn under the sense
> Of the first mother's disobedience,
> Yet hath a promise that thereby she shall

Recover all the hurt of her first fall
When, in mysterious manner, from her womb
Her father, brother, husband, son shall come. (5.221–28)

As in Lanyer, a rewriting of 'the first mother's disobedience' is imperative, but it is not to the redemptive nature of Mary that Hutchinson turns. Instead, the recuperative power of women's wombs, rather than Christ's grace produced through Mary's sinless conception, becomes her form of rewriting Genesis's punishment. All males, we are told, 'come' from Eve's 'womb'. Thus the future of the human race, its future history and thus existence, derives from her body.

The canto 6 account of Cain and Abel's own genesis underscores the importance of Eve's body while highlighting the form of familial power she, and all mothers, derive through this process. Canto 6 becomes the central moment in the poem commenting on the biological and political implications of generation. Hutchinson rejects the elision of mothers within Filmer's discussion of authority in her account of Cain and Abel's birth. First, Adam's singular identity and power as a parent is fundamentally renarrated by Hutchinson. Her Genesis account now insists on inserting the biological 'mother' explicitly into the narrative. While Hutchinson will offer Cain as 'man's first fruit', an epithet that does not highlight Eve's generative power, the sequence introduces the language of parental, not paternal, possession and authority. Eve asserts possession over her and Adam's 'fruit': 'Then brought she forth; and Cain she called his son, "For God", said she, "gives *us* possession"' (6.25–26; my emphasis). The marriage ceremony in canto 3 had stressed the importance of reproduction: 'Children in one flesh shall two parents join', declares God, as man and woman are fused into one and offered 'Dominion over [the Earth's] inhabitants' (3.416; 422). Subjugation to their husbands, to which women are condemned after the Fall, does not entail the erasure of either the mother nor allegiance owed to the mother; the mutuality implied by the marriage contract continues to mark the processes of and in the family. Thus, at the very moment that Adam is made a 'father', and consequently becomes able to claim monarchical authority in patriarchal theory, Hutchinson's Eve insists that children owe obligation to father and mother. Both have 'possession' of the child as Eve shows she remembers the marriage ceremony.

Eve's maternal claim to a form of dominion over the child is reinforced by her naming of both Cain and Abel: 'and Cain she called his son'; 'Abel she called the next' (6.25; 29). Naming is traditionally acknowledged as a form of power within the Genesis story: Adam's naming of the animals is often viewed as enacting his 'dominion' over them. Thus, Eve's act of naming indicates a form of her authority over children. While Hutchinson does not erase the biblical punishment that 'your husband … shall rule over you', the production of children throughout *Order and Disorder* provides an assertion of individualized power for the mother, one that joins the two parents in the more mutual union connoted by 'one flesh'.

This emphasis on a form of maternal power for Eve is then extended in the narrative to all mothers. Hutchinson's Genesis poem consistently alters biblical language in describing the production of children. Language in the Bible asserts that women produce children for men, as in the account of Sarah's production of a child where 'Sarah your wife shall *bear you a son*', 'For Sarah conceived and *bore Abraham a son*.'[22] This language of the child produced for the father is modified in a number of ways within Hutchinson's poem. Sarah does not bear a son for Abraham; rather they share in the joyful birth, as in canto 14 where '*they* call their son' Isaac since his 'name implies / *Their* gladness' (14.257–58; my emphases). Hutchinson further deploys language offering Sarah continued, even individualized, possession over her son: God states that 'I will thy Sarah bless / And *her son* shall the promised land possess, / And mighty nations out of her shall grow. / Upon *her nephews* I will thrones bestow, / My covenant establish with *her seed*' (12.179–83; my emphases). These modifications to biblical language indicate that mothers maintain a possession of and over their children, one which they share with, but do not have to concede to, their husband or master.

Each of these modifications to Genesis sustains Hutchinson's explicit challenge to Filmerian political theory, in accordance with her account of Adam and Eve's acquisition of dominion and the birth of their children. In her introduction of women's authority over their children, Hutchinson anticipates by at least a decade Locke's refutation of Filmer's use of the Genesis story in the first *Treatise of Government*.[23] There, Locke insists that 'the *Father*' would have 'a joynt Dominion with the Mother' over their children;[24] while Locke will dilute this maternal authority once he divides the public from the private sphere in the *Second Treatise*, Hutchinson's innovation in portraying the family shows the political possibilities in engaging Genesis. Here, she anticipates a major theoretical innovation by the father of modern liberal political thought.

This emphasis on the role of the mother in Hutchinson's poem is reworked by her contemporary, Margaret Cavendish, who focuses on the relationship between a husband and wife. The political as well as personal identities of the Emperor and Empress in Cavendish's 1666 *Blazing World* sustain Hutchinson's interrogation of aspects of political thought through a Genesis-inflected narrative. In this proto-science fiction prose narrative, a kidnapped woman finds herself in a prelapsarian 'Paradise' where the issues of Eve's culpability are restaged as the very status of women's 'subjugation' is reconsidered. Like Speght, Lanyer, and Hutchinson, Cavendish's revision of the narrative is redemptive for Eve as for all women, as she engages the political debates dominating the later seventeenth century.

The main figure in the *Blazing World*, the Empress who finds herself in *'Paradise'* after being kidnapped from her home world, follows in the very tradition of Speght and Sowernam's Eves who can reenter the Garden.[25] The kingdom in which she finds herself, and where she becomes its Empress through marriage, has never experienced the Fall, the peace of the community on her arrival a marker of its prelapsarian identity. The opening part of the narrative flirts with the temptation of dangerous knowledge that can lead to a (or the) Fall. The new practices of experimental science, briefly allowed by the Empress, threaten the community's stability, as it is cast as forbidden knowledge. This moment offers a reenactment of an averted fall from the original Garden that is complemented by the Empress's second encounter with knowledge and its appropriate boundaries. At the literal center of the *Blazing World*, in another rewriting of the Genesis story, the Empress again takes on Eve-like characteristics as she queries 'Immaterial Spirits' about the Fall. Yet for a second time, the Eve-like Empress will find appropriate boundaries to knowledge, refusing to ask more than she should 'for fear I should commit some error' (86). The narrative of the Fall is replayed, only to be effectively avoided by the querying Eve figure. Paradise thus remains prelapsarian, as Eve – in the figure of the Empress – is evacuated of her postlapsarian significance.

Cavendish's restaging of the story of the Fall has profound implications for hierarchy within marriage and, as a result, significant implications for the political sphere represented in Cavendish's *'Paradise'* (9). Since the Fall has not come to *'Paradise'*, neither has the necessary postlapsarian subjugation of women to their husbands. In this prelapsarian space, a wife can receive 'absolute power to rule and govern all that World as she pleased' (13) as the Empress does from the Emperor. In the prelapsarian Blazing World, the Empress's 'absolute power' will not destroy this 'peaceful Society', characterized by 'united Tranquillity, and Religious Conformity' (102). Thus Cavendish provides an alternative marital and political structure that can exist because of the restaged sojourn in the Garden. By acceding to the boundaries of knowledge, and eschewing the 'disobedience' that caused the first Fall, the Empress can replay Eve's role by redeeming women from the subsequent hierarchy imposed upon marital and political structures.

Thus while Hutchinson uses the role of the wife and mother to insert women into the formation of civil society, Cavendish offers a frequently singularly ruling Empress unfettered by the consequences of the Fall's asserted gender hierarchy.[26] The utter disappearance of the Emperor throughout most of the first book of the *Blazing World* underscores the suspension of postlapsarian strictures on a gendered hierarchy within marriage. And this suspension makes it possible for a woman to assume political authority. When the Emperor does reappear, his interactions with his wife resemble those between consulting heads of state as they discuss a plan to invade the Empress's native homeland of ESFI.[27] The narrative thus exposes how intimately an alternative view of female political power depends upon the structure of the first marriage. The form of autonomy that the Empress receives from her husband is simultaneously marital and political: the Empress operates independently throughout the narrative, traveling to other worlds and invading hostile countries. No femme covert she, these actions are possible precisely because the Blazing World is Paradise. The limitations of a gendered hierarchy of power established by the Fall are transgressable precisely because the Empress did not violate (appropriate) boundaries of knowledge. Rewriting the narrative of the Fall thus simultaneously makes possible the rewriting of women's relation to political authority.

Women's interventions in the very terms of political debates between Filmerian and contractual thinkers, such as John Locke, become even more pointed at century's end, as evidenced in Aphra Behn's challenge to the story of the Garden and the Fall as the basis for governmental organization. In terms even more extreme than in the writings of Hutchinson and Cavendish, Behn deploys the Garden motif as a weapon against a staunchly patriarchalist account of women's cultural position in her popular roman-à-clef *Love Letters Between a Nobleman and his Sister*, published between 1684 and 1687.[28] Centered around a well-known adulterous liaison and elopement, Behn's novel parodies the relationship between patriarchial authority and its justifying narrative of Adam, Eve, and the Garden. In a narrative of successive 'Edenic' marriages, we see them doubled, first between a sister-in-law and brother-in-law (Philander), and then tripled through Philander's second mistress. Through this narrative, Behn fractures the stabilizing institution of marriage upon which Filmer based his patriarchalist political theory. By undermining Filmer's ability to depend on the story of the Garden, her novel disputes Eve as permanently subject to a husband's power, denying the possibility of making marital and governmental spheres analogous. Turning, as do Filmer and Locke, to the originary story of the Garden and the Fall, Behn engages the political implications of marriage through her use of a perversely rewritten Edenic narrative. Behn thus completely revises the attraction of patriarchial thought for early seventeenth-century women. Behn appears to deploy her extensive literary output to position herself within the public sphere; Speght and Sowernam had maintained that connection by supporting aspects of early patriarchalist thought.

The seventeenth century in England is frequently viewed as one of the richest periods for the development of political theory; a century crowned by the publication of Locke's *Two Treatises of Government* saw political uprisings, executions, and civil wars waged over questions of governmental authority and organization. While the treatment of male authors in the early modern period has traditionally included these writers' representation of political conflict and ideals, this emphasis on the political sphere in imaginative literature is less evident in criticism on women writers. Beyond simply representing the conflicts over state formation, however, we need to adjust our sights to realize how many of these writers were active interlocutors in a sustained debate that formed the basis of major political concepts born out of the seventeenth century.

Notes

1. See Philip Almond, *The Idea of the Fall: Adam and Eve in Seventeenth-Century Thought* (Cambridge: Cambridge University Press, 1999) for a range of discourses that deployed the Genesis narrative.
2. Much excellent work has been done on the development of distinct private and public spheres in the seventeenth and eighteenth centuries. Jürgen Habermas has positioned this division between the two spheres in the early eighteenth century, while Katharine Gillespie in *Domesticity and Dissent in the Seventeenth Century: English Women Writers and the Public Sphere* (Cambridge: Cambridge University Press, 2004) moves this division of spheres into the mid-seventeenth century.
3. Hilda L. Smith, ed., *Women Writers and the Early Modern British Political Tradition* (Cambridge: Cambridge University Press, 1998).
4. Much work has been done in the last two decades on women writers' reconfiguration of patriarchy for the purposes of defending womankind or disputing aspects of the cultural assumptions about women. See Mihoko Suzuki on Aemilia Lanyer and Rachel Speght, who 'base this challenge to the ideology of patriarchy on a common strategy of textual interpretation, by reinterpreting the authoritative texts of their culture – in particular the Bible'

(*Subordinate Subjects: Gender, the Political Nation, and Literary Form in England, 1588–1688* [Aldershot: Ashgate, 2003]), 130.

5. For an in-depth discussion of Rachel Speght and Ester Sowernam's strategies within their responses to Swetnam's text, see Megan Matchinske's chapter in this volume.

6. John Swetnam, *The Arraignment of Lewd, idle, froward, and unconstant Women* (London, 1615), B1r. Subsequent references are cited parenthetically in the text.

7. While the biography of Rachel Speght confirms that she is a woman, critics debate the sex of Ester Sowernam and Constantia Munda. Yet the connections established between gender and governmental organization are present in Sowernam's tracts whether the name is a pseudonym or not.

8. Rachel Speght, 'A Dreame', in *The Polemics and Poems of Rachel Speght*, ed. Barbara Kiefer Lewalski (New York: Oxford University Press, 1996), 170. Subsequent references are cited parenthetically in the text.

9. Ester Sowernam, *Ester hath hang'd Haman: or An Answer to a lewd Pamphlet* (London, 1617), A4r. Subsequent references are cited parenthetically in the text.

10. Gorden Schochet, *Patriarchalism in Political Thought: The Authoritarian Family and Political Speculation and Attitudes Especially in Seventeenth-Century England* (New York: Basic Books, 1974), 54. Schochet suggests that the general alignment of the family with the state became explicitly theorized at the beginning of the Stuart period once contract theorists articulated a position that needed to be resisted by an emergent group of patriarchalist theorists.

11. For a cogent explanation of the 'originary' narrative of Genesis as the foundation for patriarchalist theory, see Schochet, *Patriarchalism in Political Thought*.

12. For a different emphasis on women's engagement of the household in these early seventeenth-century *querelle des femmes* texts, see Matchinske's chapter in this volume.

13. Constance Jordan, *Renaissance Feminism: Literary Texts and Political Models* (Ithaca, NY: Cornell University Press, 1990), 287, traces the 'depoliticization of marriage' in seventeenth-century marriage and domestic tracts.

14. Like Matchinske, I see Lanyer combining many of the strategies that writers such as Speght, Sowernam, and Munda deployed in their texts published a few years later.

15. Aemilia Lanyer, *Salve Deus Rex Judaeorum*, in *The Poems of Aemilia Lanyer*, ed. Susanne Woods (Oxford: Oxford University Press, 1993), ll. 761–62. Subsequent references are cited parenthetically in the text.

16. A few critics have noted the specifically political echoes within Lanyer's writings. See Suzuki, *Subordinate Subjects*, 120 and Achsah Guibbory, 'The Gospel According to Aemilia: Women and the Sacred', in *Aemilia Lanyer: Gender, Genre, and the Canon*, ed. Marshall Grossman (Lexington: University Press of Kentucky, 1998), 191–211.

17. Lanyer, 'Description of Cooke-ham', in *Poems of Aemilia Lanyer*, ed. Woods, 32, 42. Subsequent references are cited parenthetically in the text.

18. Though there are many women publishing in the 1640s and 1650s, their writings deal somewhat less centrally with the story of Adam, Eve, and the Fall, and thus I am not considering them in this essay.

19. Sir Robert Filmer, *Patriarcha and Other Writings*, ed. Johann Sommerville (Cambridge: Cambridge University Press, 1991), 7; my emphasis. Subsequent references are cited parenthetically in the text.
20. Lucy Hutchinson, *Order and Disorder*, ed. David Norbrook (Malden, MA: Blackwell, 2001), 3.421–22, 426. Subsequent references are cited parenthetically in the text.
21. See Catherine Belsey, *The Subject of Tragedy* (London: Methuen, 1985), 155, on the effect of employing only the male portion of the fifth commandment.
22. New King James Bible, 17:18, 21:2, 21:3; my emphasis. Subsequent references are cited parenthetically in the text.
23. Locke's *Two Treatises* was published in 1690 but was composed much earlier.
24. John Locke, *Two Treatise of Government*, ed. Peter Laslett (Cambridge: Cambridge University Press, 1988), I:55.
25. Margaret Cavendish, *The Description of A New World, Called The Blazing World* (London, 1666), 9. Subsequent references are cited parenthetically in the text.
26. For an alternate view of Cavendish as insisting on her unique status as a monarch within the text, see Catherine Gallagher, 'Embracing the Absolute: The Politics of the Female Subject in Seventeenth Century England', *Genders* 1 (March 1988): 24–29.
27. As numerous critics have noted, this appears to be an acronym for England, Scotland, France, and Ireland.
28. Filmer's *Patriarcha* was published in 1679. See Johann Sommerville's introduction to Robert Filmer's *Patriarcha and Other Writings* for a discussion of the date of Filmer's tracts, probably composed in the 1630s and 1640s.

4
English Civil War Women Writers and the Discourses of Fifth Monarchism

Katharine Gillespie

Recent revisions of the early modern literary canon have unearthed new information about the ways in which women – England's 'daughters' as it were – participated alongside its sons in the debates over kingship that roiled the years leading up to and constituting the English Civil War and Commonwealth periods.[1] Defying the association of female authors with loose-lipped shrews and whores, a surprising number of women helped construct the public sphere of print, letter-writing, manuscript circulation, petitioning, face-to-face debate, and other venues of expression which both fomented and formed a corollary to the military struggle against the Crown in the 1640s and the political struggle to implement a republic in the 1650s. Assessing women's contributions has involved retrieving their stories from the archive as well as contesting disciplinary divisions among discourses. Just as literary scholars now understand Milton's most ambitious poems to be as 'republican' as his explicitly polemical prose disquisitions, so too have feminist literary critics called for a broader definition of what constitutes political writing in order to take into account the variety of strategies that Civil War women writers used to critique monarchy. While some oppositional women writers used instrumental argumentation, others drew upon genres not readily associated with political philosophy in order to register perspectives upon the workings of government and its relationship to the individual as well as to other social, cultural, economic, and religious spheres. By assimilating their voices, scholars have deepened our understanding of the investment made by 'God's Englishwomen' and men alike in limiting or eliminating patriarchalist rule as well as the types of practices through which that investment was articulated.

In particular, women writers played a pivotal role in shaping and popularizing the influential discourse of 'Fifth Monarchism'. While eschatological ideas were foundational to Christianity, the idea that Christ would return to rule over a new order alongside his elect gained momentum after the Reformation and 'turned into fervor' during the English revolutionary period of the 1640s, 'with dates being set for the fulfillment of biblical prophecies, with the return of Christ itself taking place within the next sixty years'.[2] These ideas were not only religious but also political in their implications. As Jonathan Scott has recently argued, 'In England, almost all republican writing was overtly religiously engaged. The most powerful reason for laying earthly monarchy in the dust was to realize the monarchy of God.'[3] Women writers were in the vanguard of this 'Revolution of the Saints', the phrase Michael Walzer uses to describe how Fifth Monarchism and other radical scripture-based discourses rationalized dissent by positing God as a higher power whose royal law superseded that of flesh and blood monarchs.[4] Whereas the four major monarchies on earth – Assyria, Persia, Greece, and Rome – were ruled over largely by corrupt tyrants, the fifth and final monarchy would be governed by King Jesus and his saints; together they would usher in a thousand-year-long era of peace and justice in 'Sion' or the 'New Jerusalem' before the anti-Christ came to claim his own and the world would come to an end. Millenarian women and/or their publishers often directed their writings at both the general public and the ruling powers, believing that their vital messages were transmitted to these female 'instruments' from God and were thus designed to liberate both leaders and the people they governed from earthly tyranny and deliver them into the new promised age of religious and political reformation.[5]

Lady Eleanor Davies was one of the first women to employ Fifth Monarchist discourse to critique royal power, publishing over 70 tracts of religious and political commentary from 1625–1651, much of which took the complex form of prophesy.[6] Davies's first tract, *A Warning to the Dragon and all his Angels*, maps out the basic tenets of Fifth Monarchism that would guide much of her work. Derived from a synthesis of Nebuchadnezzar's dream in the Book of Daniel and the Book of Revelation, Davies's Fifth Monarchist vision believed that England's central role in bringing about the final monarchy was to complete the Protestant reformation of the Established Church. Published in 1625, just after Charles I's installation, *A Warning* celebrates the new King as the 'Angel of God' who, like his father James before him, would be 'God's lieutenant' on earth and defender of 'the saints' against the 'beast' of the Catholic Church.[7] Writing herself into the typological narratives that structured Fifth Monarchist discourse, Davies offered herself to Charles as a latter-day Daniel. Just as the Old Testament seer had guided Nebuchadnezzar away from idol worship, she would inspire her 'Lord the King' to continue his father's work of purifying the church of its 'popish' taint as a prelude to Christ's return. In 1633, she traveled to Amsterdam to publish *Given to the Elector Prince Charles of the Rhyne* (1633), a tract criticizing Charles for refusing to follow his father's example and behaving instead like Belshazzar, the debauched king who failed to heed the ghostly 'handwriting on the wall' and end his idolatry and lavish living.[8] Upon her return to England, she presented Archbishop William Laud with a note warning him (accurately) that he would be punished for his expensive enhancement of the baroque display of church ritual and his heavy-handed crackdown on dissenters (Parliament executed him in 1645). For these two acts, she was arrested, heavily fined, tried by 'his Highness Commissioners for Causes Ecclesiastical'[9] and imprisoned in Gatehouse.

Upon her release, Davies continued her campaign of iconoclasm. In 1635, after Lichfield Cathedral blocked the view of the Ten Commandments with the installation of a large crucifix and rich altar hangings, she protested by occupying the bishop's throne and pouring tar and wheat paste over the woolen cloths. As she wrote afterwards in her *Spirituall Antheme*, 'Devils administer. adjure. yee see / Epicure swine feeding ... Soe howese of god polluted smell & view'.[10] In tracts such as *Samsons Legacie* (1643), she offered her services as a seer to Parliament, believing that its members would finally be the ones who would prepare the ground for Christ's return by implementing the 'Sovereign Remedy' of purging residual Catholicism out of the church and ceasing to 'fill Prisons, with those call'd by them, *Puritans:* and now, *Round-Heads'*.[11] She had given up on Charles because, just as Samson had come under the 'thralldom' (88) of the Philistine Jezebel and hence failed as a 'Saviour or Deliverer', so too had Charles shown '*great Imbecilitie in subjecting himselfe*' to the '*waywardnesse*' (89) of Henrietta Maria. In 1647, as the 'Faith' continued to 'lay at stake', she shifted her hope for reformation to Oliver Cromwell, dedicating her *Excommunication out of Paradice* to him as a man of 'high merit' who would finally usher in Christ's reign and revealing to him the glorious moment of 'the Spirit and the Bride saying, Come, and if any man thirst &c. out of his belly (he that believeth) shall flow rivers of living water'.[12] In 1646 and again in 1650, Davies was imprisoned for debt and soon after wrote about these experiences bitterly.[13] But, after Parliament's New Model Army defeated the royalist troops and executed Charles I in 1649, she wrote numerous tracts celebrating the regicide and heralding the new era as a sign that the implementation of the fifth and final monarchy was nigh: 'Of which days come about again, this great Revolution ushering the day of Judgement, his coming in the Clouds.'[14]

Davies's texts anticipate the way in which references to the New Jerusalem or 'Sion' formed one of the most common 'chambers of imagery' for biblically constituted 'programs' that defined popular republicanism throughout the 1640s and 1650s.[15] Many Sionists imagined that the time that would lie between the demise of Stuart rule and the return of Christ would be defined by new forms of religious freedom. In 1641, Katherine Chidley (fl. 1616–53) became the first woman to use print to endorse religious 'independency'.[16] Chidley was a religious and political activist who dissented from the Established Church throughout the 1620s, 1630s, and 1640s; supported the parliamentarian cause against the royalists during the English Civil Wars of the 1640s; and sided with the liberal Levellers against the more authoritarian regime of Oliver Cromwell during the 1650s.[17] She took up the pen against Thomas Edwards, an influential Presbyterian who wanted to replace the episcopacy with a presbytery rather than with a complete separation of church from state as was demanded by radical separatists. After Edwards launched his campaign against 'Independency' in his *Reasons against the Independent Government of Particular Congregations* in 1641, Chidley replied by writing her *Justification for the Independent Churches of Christ* (1641), a lengthy tract in which she accused Edwards and his allies of setting their 'wits a work to withstand the bright comming of *Christ's Kingdome* (into the hearts of men)' and promulgated the alternative idea that, in the true dispensation of the Fifth Monarchy, it was not only 'lawfull' but the 'duty' of dissenters to separate from a church which did not allow them to 'preach or teach in the name (or by the power) of the Lord Jesus' and to build instead a 'land where they have Toleration'.[18] Although 'the King hath power (according to the Law) over the bodies, goods, and lives of all his subjects; yet it is Christ the King of Kings that reigneth over their consciences' (26). Granting people freedom of conscience would not, as detractors claimed, 'take away that power & authority which God hath given to Husbands, Father, and Masters over wives, children, and servants', rather as I Corinthians 7 'plainly declares', the 'wife may be a believer, & the husband an unbeliever' (26). As she concludes, 'I pray you tell me what authority this unbelieving husband hath over the conscience of his believing wife; It is true he hath authority over her in bodily and civill respects but not to be a Lord over her conscience' (26).

Just after Chidley's *Justification* appeared, Thomas Edwards issued *Antapologia* (1644), another attack on Independency. Chidley responded by publishing *A new-yeares-gift, or A brief exhortation to Mr. Thomas Edwards* (1644) in which she accused Edwards of having failed the first time around to convince readers that the Church of England was the only 'true church' and that separatists sinned by refusing to fund it through the '*Jewish yoakes of tithes paying*'.[19] 'As the hill of Syon appeareth more eminently', she wrote, ordained ministers were clearly growing fearful that they would have to seek alternative sources for their 'demanding dues'.[20] In her final publication, a broadside entitled *Good Counsell, to the Petitioners for Presbyterian Government* (London, 1645), Chidley mocked Edwards's claim that allowing religious freedom would compromise children, claiming that he and other anti-tolerationists were concerned only about two 'Children': 'MAINTENANCE and POWER'.[21]

As Chidley's writings attest, a highly controversial subject of the 1640s 'pamphlet wars' was the fact that some dissenting churches believed unlicensed lay preaching was one of the liberties that heralded the arrival of Christ's kingdom. Numerous attempts to denigrate and outlaw 'mechanic' ministers, both male and female, vied with celebrations of women preachers in the robust marketplace of ideas.[22] Women dissenters were among those who fought back against characterizations of self-styled female ministers as seductive 'Jezebels'.[23] In *To Sions Lovers* (1644), the Baptist, Sarah Jones, endorsed 'shee preachers' and criticized those churches that 'know not how to elect, choose, ordain, invest Pastors, Teachers, Elders, Deacons, Male and Female, qualified according to Holy Writt'.[24] In 1647, another young Baptist, the fifteen-year-old Sarah Wight, underwent a weeks-long, trance-inducing fast in which she delivered a series of visions to a bedside audience, including a number of those currently prosecuting the war against the Crown.[25] Her words were recorded by the dissenting minister, Henry Jessy, and published as *The Exceeding Riches of Grace Advanced by the Spirit of Grace, In an Empty Nothing Creature* (1647).[26] In her visions, Wight imagined herself as a sovereign in her own right who possessed the authority to speak due to the true royal authority of God that resided within her as a child of grace. She celebrated her rise from a 'nothing creature' to a bride of Christ by typing herself as an analogue to Judah, the harlot, and to Jerusalem itself whose 'skirts were full of bloud, her streets were full of bloud. Yet the Fountain is open for Judah and Jerusalem.'[27]

In 1649, just after Parliament won the Civil War, the power of the 'she preacher' entered the public political sphere when the New Model Army's General Council, headed by the soon-to-be head of state, Oliver Cromwell, met to debate the King's fate. For unknown reasons, Elizabeth Poole, a seamstress turned prophetess for a Particular Baptist congregation in Abingdon, appeared in Whitehall on 29 December 1648, and again on 5 January 1649, to try and dissuade the Council from regicide.[28] Soon after, Poole published an account of these sessions in *A Vision: Wherein is Manifested the Disease and Cure of the Kingdome* (1648).[29] In the arguments she made to the officers, Poole drew upon claims made by religious dissenters that God's higher law allowed them to separate from an 'unregenerate' spouse in order to argue that the Army should divorce rather than execute their 'husband', Charles I.[30] Poole was not alone in manipulating marriage codes to imagine a form of government by consent. On the one hand, royalists such as Henry Ferne contended that there was 'no warrant for the Armes now take up by Subjects' because the King was a *'sponsus Regni'* and 'wedded to the kingdom by a ring at his Coronation', thus, 'what our Saviour said of their light and unlawfull occasions of Divorse, *non suit ob initio*, it was not so from the beginning, may be said of such a reserved power of resistance, it was not so from the beginning'.[31] On the other hand, parliamentarians such as Herbert Palmer argued that 'a Wife is tyed to her Husband by a "Covenant of God"' that is 'more ancient, and no lesse strong then that of Politick Government', thus, 'she may by the Law of God and Conscience ... secure her Person from his violence by absence ... or any other meanes of necessary defence'.[32] Likewise, Poole argued that, while England was the King's wife and hence should not kill her husband, 'she' had a right to separate from him if he became tyrannical.

Poole retained the patriarchalist metaphor of the King as *'sponsus Regni'* – as she said to the officers, 'The king is your Father and Husband, which you were and are to obey' (4) – but she added that this obedience was to take place 'in the Lord, and no other way' (4). Thus, when the King proved a tyrant by forgetting 'his subordination to divine Fatherhood and headship' and using the people as 'wife for his own lust', then 'thereby is the yoak' 'taken' from the people's 'necks' (4–5). While it was true that a wife could not kill her husband because he was 'the head of her body', she could nonetheless 'commit an unsound member to Sathan (though the head) as it is flesh; that the spirit might be saved in the day of the Lord' (5). By taking the conventional formulation of the king's head as the seat of reason and using it to declare the head a rotten 'member' that could removed, Poole made a case that the wife's right to exit an abusive marriage formed the basis of the sovereign–subject relationship. Self-defense was legitimate as the wife was entitled to 'hold the hands' of her husband so that he 'pierce not' her 'bowels with a knife or sword to take [her] life' (6). Nor, however, could she kill him.

Poole failed to deter the Generals from execution and, in an apparent attempt to discredit her, was accused of sexual licentiousness by the head of her former congregation, a Cromwell loyalist. In *An Alarum of War* and *An(other) Alarum of War*, both published just after Charles was beheaded in 1649, she went back into print to defend her reputation and exonerate her godliness by typing herself as Isaiah, the prophet who warned Judean kings against overreaching.[33] While Poole was not heard from again, many religious dissenters had just begun to share Eleanor Davies's hope that Cromwell would now prove the champion of toleration and harbinger of the New Jerusalem. One such was Mary Cary, a seamstress and member of the actual Fifth Monarchist movement that emerged in the late 1640s and early 1650s as one of many new groups who wished to mold the young republic in accordance with its principle.[34] The Fifth Monarchists saw themselves as the elect who would reign at Christ's side in Sion and lobbied for a series of reforms designed to convert England into a worthier nation, including the implementation of a government modeled after the *Sanhedrin* of 70 nominated saints, the institution of poor relief and civil marriage, and the abolition of tithes.[35]

While historians often refer to the group as the 'Fifth Monarchy men', Cary was one of the leading spokespersons for the group's ideals.[36] In 1651, she published *The little horns doom & dovvnfall* which, as the title page advertised, argued that, 'the late Kings doom and death, was so long ago, as by Daniel pred-eclared' [sic].[37] This as well as a second text included in the same volume, *A New and More Exact Mappe, Or, Description of New Jerusalems Glory* was dedicated to Cromwell's wife and daughter who, Cary presumed, shared her millennial vision that the new era represented 'the present footsteps of God in this world, in order to the setting up of the kingdom of our Lord Jesus, and the making of all dominions to serve and obey him'.[38] Like Chidley, Cary believed that the arrival of Christ's Fifth Monarchy would coincide with the dissolution of the state church. In her first publication, *A Word in Season to the King of England* (1647), she attacked mandatory tithes and insisted that the men who 'sit at the Sterne' of government 'make no Laws' controlling 'the consciences' of the people 'for that were to take the Crown off the head of Jesus Christ' and place it on their 'own head'.[39] In *The Resurrection of the Witness* (1648), she exhorted Parliament to resist the temptations of power and remember their role as liberators: 'Consider you what your condition was about seven or eight year ago; at what time you were trampled upon by the Bishops (which was a treading underfoot of the Beast). Call to mind how some of you were pilloried, and had your eares cropt and many of you imprisoned, and fined, and by severall other waies were persecuted.'[40] In *Twelve humble proposals* (1653), she petitioned the Nominated Parliament to act as 'forerunners' of Christ's reign by refusing to enrich themselves through political spoils, passing an act for poor relief, protecting lay preachers and private churches, repealing tithes, simplifying the body of laws so as to reduce the need for lawyers, and other such 'humble' propositions.[41]

Across the Atlantic, Puritans who had gone into exile to avoid punishment continued to consort with their English counterparts to build the New Jerusalem. Anne Bradstreet's poetry collection, *The Tenth Muse Lately Sprung up in America* (1650), was an important vehicle for expressing this transatlantic Fifth Monarchist vision.[42] Her poem 'The Four Monarchies' drew on the Book of Daniel to craft a Fifth Monarchist vision of history in which one empire inevitably gives way to another as their respective kings fail to perform as regents of divine rule.[43] She describes the 'Golden Age' as a 'young' time when 'Man did not strive for Soveraignty' and blames its demise upon Cush, that 'mighty hunter' who through 'his toyls' subjected both 'Beasts and Men' to 'his spoyls', thereby laying the foundation for 'Babel' (65) and its long line of corrupt kings. In her account of the Persian monarchy, Bradstreet continues to recount her almost unrelenting genealogy of royal terror. While Artaxerxes is described as ruling over a relatively peaceful era and Darius, an elected king, receives praise for rebuilding Solomon's temple (96), the rest of the Persian kings, like those of the 'third Monarchy, the Grecian', are indicted for engendering the sort of chaos that Hobbes attributed to life in a state of nature rather than the ostensibly stabilizing rule of monarchs. Even Alexander the Great's power was fleeting, '[a]s Daniel, before had Prophesied' (150). Given the collection's publication date of 1650, the inaugural year of the new republic, it is perhaps significant that in the final section of the poem, 'The Roman Monarchy, being the Fourth, and last', Bradstreet tracks the rise of the senate alongside the history of Roman kings and ends with the rape of Lucretia by Sextus the son of '*Tarquinius Superbus*, the last *Roman* King' (179).[44] As she writes, Lucretia's husband was so 'incens'd' to 'quit this wrong' that he, along with *Junius Brutus*, 'rose, and being strong, / The *Tarquins* they from *Rome* with speed expel, / In banishment perpetuall, to dwell; / The Government they change, a new one bring, / And people sweare, ne're to accept of a King' (179).

Bradstreet's 'A Dialogue Between Old England and New: Concerning Their Present Troubles, Anno 1642', is an overtly pro-parliamentarian endorsement of transatlantic Sionism. England is figured as a sick and distressed mother who turns to her daughter, New England, for a cure. New England proffers a number of possible explanations for her mother's illness, including England's enduring struggles among royals for power. Her mother finally confesses that the cause is her own 'sin' of failing to purify the Church of England and persecuting 'the Saints of the most high' (183–84). After England asks her daughter, 'for sacred Zions sake' (187), to bring her devastated mother 'relief', her daughter calls for the two to join forces – 'O cry: the sword of God, and *Gideon*' – and root out the 'Prelates, head tail, branch, and rush' (188). By doing so, those who made a living out of oppressing dissenters will 'want their pay' and 'Peace' and 'Parliament' will 'prevail' (190).

Many of those who believed that Cromwell and Parliament would break what they perceived to be the endless cycle of royal and prelatical corruption were quickly disappointed. In 1653, Cromwell proclaimed himself 'Lord General' and, rather than hold elections as promised, hand-picked 140 'persons fearing God' to assemble at Westminster. Many dissenters, including the Fifth Monarchists, approved of the idea of a 'Nominated Parliament', as well as the fact that these nominees proposed to abolish tithes, the Court of Chancery, the universities, and the public ministry and to institute civil marriage. But the Nominated Parliament never framed a new constitution, thus, at the end of its term, power was returned to Cromwell who dissolved Parliament and ruled thereafter as 'Lord Protector'. Tellingly, the regalia for his 1657 reinstallation as Protector included a sword, scepter, and purple robe. In a series of quite lengthy pamphlets published in the early 1650s, the Fifth Monarchist prophetess, Anna Trapnel (fl. 1642–58) developed an extensive critique of Cromwell's growing pretensions.[45] Trapnel had been an early advocate of the new leader; in 1650, she envisioned Cromwell as an incarnation of Gideon who would successfully defeat the Scots but then divest the army of political power and hand it over to Parliament. Her prognostication appeared to be coming true when Cromwell emerged triumphant at Dunbar. But her opinion shifted – and her career as a nationally recognized prophetess began – when a number of Fifth Monarchist men were arrested on the suspicion that their often violent rhetoric would lead to armed insurrection. When Vavasour Powell was remanded to Whitehall for questioning in 1653, Trapnel was waiting with other members of the group in an anteroom when she was 'seized upon by the Lord' and began praying and singing. Her friends took her from Whitehall to a nearby inn where she stayed for twelve days, fasting and delivering 'songs', prayers, warnings, and indictments in hours' long trance-like sessions while a recorder wrote down as much as could be heard amid the large numbers of people who crowded her bedside to hear her admonitions.

Publicized in tracts such as *Strange and wonderful nevves from VVhite-Hall* (1654) and *The Cry of a Stone* (1654), Trapnel's prophecies utilized Fifth Monarchist discourse as a vehicle for criticizing Cromwell and calling for the true Fifth Monarchy of Christ's reign to begin.[46] As she apostrophizes in *The Cry of a Stone*, 'OH *sing for* Sion *Songs my soul / and magnifie that Grace / Which will bring* Sion *back again / into the glorious place*' (25). In that same text, she writes that if Cromwell were not 'back-sliden', he 'would be ashamed of his great pomp and revenue, while the poore are ready to starve' (51). She exhorts the Lord Protector's soldiers to not '*aspire for to / so high a title have / as King, or Protector: but oh / unto Christ that do leave*' (29) and adds scathing indictments of clergymen, merchants, and officers of the law. As she reiterates, 'Let us have one only King' (29).

Under increasing surveillance by Cromwell's spies, Trapnel journeyed to Cornwall to continue her public preaching. As she wrote in *Anna Trapnel's Report and Plea* (1654), her account of this venture, many came to hear her message about the new social order that would prevail when the 'Kingdom' was 'restored to the Old Israel' and 'Judges and Rulers might be as at the beginning, as Moses, and Joshua, and Samuel, and Gideon, and other faithful ones, as made mention of in the Scripture'.[47] Local ministers, she claimed, 'called to the Rulers' to 'take' her 'up' for fear that her competition meant they would 'lose their fleece'.[48] During another of her bed-based sessions, she was questioned by the local justices and examined by the witch-trying woman but claimed to have remained insensate to any external influences other than the messages she received from God. She was forcibly removed to the session house and tried but was reportedly released as a result of public outrage. However, she was soon arrested again by Cromwell and transported to Bridewell, London's infamous prison for the insane, where she produced a collection of prose prayers, letters, and self-defenses that were eventually published as *A Legacy for Saints* (1654).[49] After her release, she staged a series of sessions in which she delivered prophecies while surrounded by an audience, portions of which were published in *A Voice for the King of Saints* that same year and the entire transcriptions of which survive in an untitled manuscript numbering over 900 pages.[50] While she disappeared from the historical record in 1658, she left behind a substantial body of work that centered around the vision of a day when she and others like her could preach without fear of reprisal: 'Then there shall be no deriders, nor mockers, to scoffe at the fifth monarchy'.[51]

The end of Trapnel's career as a visionary in 1658 coincided with Cromwell's death. Because he died without naming a successor, the Council of State nominated his eldest son, Richard, who proved a disaster and quickly resigned. While many republicans attempted a series of last-ditch efforts to save 'the good old cause', some millenarians insisted that the death of the self-proclaimed Protector was a sign that the 'overthrow of the Antichrist' was finally at hand.[52] Thomas Weld seized upon 'these cold declining times' as an opportunity to try and 'comfort' those who 'mourn in Sion' by publishing *A Wise Virgin's Lamp Burning*, a 331-page document fashioned out of a set of loose papers reportedly discovered 'in the closet' of a young woman named Anne Venn sometime 'after her death' at or around the age of 32.[53] Born around 1624, Venn was the daughter of the New Model Army's Colonel John Venn and his second wife, Margaret. Her papers document the search she undertook from 1638 to 1653 for a religious experience that would help her make sense of the 'trouble' that 'lay' upon her 'spirit' due to the war that Satan had declared upon her soul at around the age of nine (7). Venn's work falls neatly into the category of spiritual autobiography. At the same time, the text's introductory materials as well as her own writings construct striking parallels between her personal search for religious truth and the nascent republic's struggle for independence from the Crown and the building of the New Jerusalem, an enterprise in which her publishers apparently continued to invest. The title was taken from the gospel of Matthew where Christ recounts the parable of the wise virgins who prepared themselves for the second coming of the bridegroom by keeping their lamps filled with oil. Although the last entry in Venn's diary is dated 'the 22nd of this tenth month of 1654', the publication of the text four years later coincided not only with Cromwell's death but also with the crafting of the so-called 'Savoy Declaration', a document that tried to revive the sagging hopes of the Independents who had penned the pro-toleration *Apologeticall Narration* in 1643.[54] Savoy's drafting committee consisted of Thomas Goodwin, William Bridge, Philip Nye, Joseph Caryl, William Greenhill, and John Owen, many of whom are listed by Venn as ministers who taught her that, in order for the New Jerusalem to arrive, even the most humble of individuals needed to be free to seek religious truth for him/herself.

Venn's 'pilgrimage' began at the age of nine when she encountered Robert Dod's commentary on the Decalogue first published in 1604. In his advice to wives on how to respond to the fifth commandment, Dod invoked Eve by proclaiming that, for a wife, 'her husbands charge, is Gods charge; and when he speaks, God speaks to him', thus 'if she rebel against his commandment, she rebels against God' (2). After reading this, Venn 'curse[d] the day of [her] birth' and expressed resentment for the assurance her brothers enjoyed that they 'should without all doubt go to Heaven' while she, due to the 'original corruption' that she 'brought into the world with her' was condemned to hell. However, when she was 'some 12 or 13 years old', she encountered other books which taught her that seeking pilgrims – both male and female – could submit themselves to the 'trials of self' that would enhance their chances of surviving the quest for the New Jerusalem.

Her years-long war with Satan was fully declared in '1638, or 1639', years, she writes, which were also 'times of great fears and sadness' for religious dissenters who 'met often and spake to one another in secret and kept days of humiliation and seeking the Lord in the behalf of the nation and his poor people in it' (5). Venn persuaded her parents to allow her to attend their underground church and claimed to have found there much 'refreshment' (5) and fortification against Satan's sieges against her soul. She was helped through this difficult period by the Presbyterian minister, Christopher Love, who lived in her family's house for two years while also serving as the chaplain to her father's regiment. In 1642, Love traveled with both the regiment and the family to Windsor where, as several news books reported, Colonel Venn helped the 'saints' defeat Prince Rupert and his 'anti-Christian party', just as Love helped her to defeat the 'anti-Christian party' that waged war within Venn's soul.[55]

Her subsequent relocation to London in 1645 dovetailed with her father's move to London to join the Army Committee as well as with the erection of the Presbyterian Church as the struggling republic's official religion. Venn, however, embarked upon a rejection of Presbyterianism that paralleled the rejection of the Presbyterian settlement staged both by her father, whose break with Love Venn claims to have brought about, and by radical millenarian ministers such as Thomas Goodwin who believed in freedom of conscience or 'the glorious liberties of the saints' on the grounds that any one individual was too blind to dictate religious truth to another in the shadowy time before Christ's return when Sion could only be 'glimpsed' by fallen humans.[56] While Venn's narrative broke off in 1653, the 'progress' she subsequently undertook by traveling from minister to minister, listening to their messages and weighing their merits, enacted the paradoxical idea upon which radical ministers hoped to found the republic, as an order whose 'foundation' would be 'settled' through the mobility and rigors of individual seeking, including a woman's. As Venn wrote, 'What though it be said work to work in the darkest Mines of Corruption and Temptation, to be continually fighting and wrestling with those Enemies of my Lords, and of my soul, and shall I not be willing to do his work as the Jews did theirs in building the Wall of Jerusalem, that he will have me to work with one hand, and with the other to hold a weapon, with my shield always by my side in a continual fighting posture?' (222).

The New Jerusalem failed to materialize in England and a number of republicans expressed unease with what they took to be Zionists' implicit claim that their subjection to God as the one true king entitled them to an 'exemption from all secular power'.[57] At the same time, liberty of conscience as it was 'often expressed in the language of natural law' was promulgated not only by dissenters but also by such prominent republicans as John Milton, Henry Vane, and Algernon Sidney, and it was eventually folded into the pivotal thought of John Locke.[58] Early on, a number of dissenting women were jeered, fined, castigated as seducers and witches, and jailed for propagating this influential idea through print and putting it into action through unorthodox interventions into the political sphere. Their voices have yet to enter into mainstream histories of the 'commonwealth principles' that fueled the breakdown of monarchy, even as that breakdown came to be so heavily associated with the death of paternalism and the rise of the specter of a woman holding a book in one hand and a light in the other.

Notes

1. *Women's Political Writings, 1610–1725*, ed. Hilda L. Smith, Mihoko Suzuki, and Susan Wiseman (London: Pickering & Chatto, 2007). Major studies of seventeenth-century radical women writers include Hilda L. Smith, *Reason's Disciples: Seventeenth-Century Feminists* (Urbana: University of Illinois Press, 1982); Hilary Hinds, *God's Englishwomen: Seventeenth-Century Radical Sectarian Writing and Feminist Criticism* (Manchester: Manchester University Press, 1996); Stevie Davies, *Unbridled Spirits: Women of the English Revolution, 1640–1660* (London: The Women's Press, 1998); Danielle Clark, *The Politics of Early Modern Women's Writing* (Harlow: Longman, 2001); Mihoko Suzuki, *Subordinate Subjects: Gender, the Political Nation and Literary Form in England, 1558–1688* (Aldershot: Ashgate, 2003); Katharine Gillespie, *Domesticity and Dissent in the Seventeenth Century: English Women's Writing and the Public Sphere* (Cambridge: Cambridge University Press, 2004); Teresa Feroli, *Political Speaking Justified: Women Prophets and the English Revolution* (Newark: University of Delaware Press, 2006); Susan Wiseman, *Conspiracy & Virtue: Women, Writing, and Politics in Seventeenth-Century England* (Oxford: Oxford University Press, 2006); Catharine Gray, *Women Writers and Public Debate in Seventeenth-Century Britain* (New York: Palgrave Macmillan, 2007); Shannon Miller, *Engendering the Fall: John Milton and Seventeenth-Century Women Writers* (Philadelphia: University of Pennsylvania Press, 2007).

2. Barry H. Howson, *Erroneous and schismatical opinions: The Question of Orthodoxy Regarding the Theology of Hanserd Knollys* (Leiden: Brill, 2001), 243.

3. Jonathan Scott, *Commonwealth Principles* (Cambridge: Cambridge University Press, 2004), 42.

4. Michael Walzer, *The Revolution of the Saints: A Study in the Origin of Radical Politics* (Cambridge, MA: Harvard University Press, 1982).

5. Diane Purkiss, 'Producing the Voice, Consuming the Body: Women Prophets of the Seventeenth Century', in *Women, Writing, History: 1640–1740*, ed. Isobel Grundy and Susan Wiseman (Athens: University of Georgia Press, 1992), 139–58.

6. Esther S. Cope, *Handmaid of the Holy Spirit: Dame Eleanor Davies, Never Soe Mad a Ladie* (Ann Arbor: University of Michigan Press, 1992).

7. Lady Eleanor Davies, *A Warning to the Dragon and All his Angels* (1625), in *Prophetic Writings of Lady Eleanor Davies*, ed. Esther S. Cope (New York: Oxford University Press, 1995), 1–56.

8. Lady Eleanor Davies, *Given to the Elector Prince Charles of the Rhyne* (1633), in *Prophetic Writings*, ed. Cope, 59–69.

9. Ibid., 69.

10. Lady Eleanor Davies, *Spirituall Antheme* (1636), in *Prophetic Writings*, ed. Cope, 73–74, quote from 73.

11. Lady Eleanor Davies, *Samsons Legacie* (1643), in *Prophetic Writings*, ed. Cope, 85–100, quote from 95. Subsequent references are cited parenthetically in the text.

12. Lady Eleanor Davies, *Excommunication out of Paradice* (1647), in *Prophetic Writings*, ed. Cope, 225–33, quotes from 226, 233.

13. See Lady Eleanor Davies, *Hells Destruction* (1651), in *Prophetic Writings*, ed. Cope, 333–39, and *The Restitution of Prophecy* (1651), in *Prophetic Writings*, ed. Cope, 343–68. Also, in *The New Jerusalem at Hand* (*Prophetic Writings*, ed. Cope, 259–69), Davies claims that her second husband, Douglass, was Charles's eldest son and hence as worthy as his other children of a share of the dead king's estate, including, for Douglass, the throne itself.

14. Lady Eleanor Davies, *A Sign Given Them Being Entred Into The Day of Judgement to Set their House in Order*, in *Prophetic Writings*, ed. Cope, 277–83, quote from 278. See also *The Everlasting Gospel* (1649) (*Prophetic Writings*, ed. Cope, 285–91); *The Appearance or Presence of the Son of Man* (1650) (*Prophetic Writings*, ed. Cope, 309–15); and *Before the Lords Second Coming* (1650) (*Prophetic Writings*, ed. Cope, 317–23).

15. Nigel Smith, *Perfection Proclaimed: Language and Literature in English Radical Religion, 1650–1660* (Oxford: Clarendon Press, 1989), 230. See also Christopher Hill, *The English Bible in the Seventeenth-Century Revolution* (London: Penguin, 1993), 301–04.

16. Katharine Gillespie, ed., *Katherine Chidley* (Aldershot: Ashgate, 2009); Dorothy P. Ludlow, '"Arise and Be Doing": English "Preaching" Women, 1640–1660', Diss. Indiana University, 1978; Katharine Gillespie, 'A Hammer in Her Hand: The Separation of Church from State and the Early Feminist Writings of Katherine Chidley', *Tulsa Studies in Women's Literature* 17.2 (Fall 1998): 213–33; Melissa Mowry, review of Marcus Nevitt, *Women and the Pamphlet Culture of Revolutionary England, 1640–1660*, *The Journal of British Studies* 46.3 (2007): 662–64.

17. Ian Gentles, 'Chidley, Katherine (fl. 1616–1653), religious controversialist and Leveller', *Oxford Dictionary of National Biography* (Oxford: Oxford University Press, 2004–07); Ian Gentles, 'London Levellers in the English Revolution: The Chidleys and Their Circle', *Journal of Ecclesiastical History* 29.3 (1978): 281–309.

18. Thomas Edwards, *Reasons against the Independent Government of Particular Congregations* (London: Printed by Richard Cotes for Jo. Bellamie & Ralph Smith, 1641); Katherine Chidley, *The Justification of the Independent Churches of Christ, being an answer to Mr. Edwards his booke* (London: Printed for William Larnar, 1641), *2. Subsequent references are cited parenthetically in the text.

19. Thomas Edwards, *Antapologia* (London: Printed by G.M. for John Bellamie, 1644); Katherine Chidley, *A new-yeares-gift, or A brief exhortation to Mr. Thomas Edwards* (S.l.: s.n., 1644), A2.

20. Chidley, *A new-yeares-gift*, A2.

21. Katherine Chidley, *Good counsell, to the petitioners for Presbyterian government, that they may declare their faith before they build their church* (London: s.n., 1645).

22. Phyllis Mack, *Visionary Women: Ecstatic Prophecy in Seventeenth-Century England* (Berkeley: University of California Press, 1992); Ethyn Morgan Williams, 'Women Preachers in the Civil War', *Journal of Modern History* 1.4 (1929): 561–79; Dorothy Ludlow, 'Shaking Patriarchy's Foundations: Sectarian Women in England, 1641–1700', in *Triumph Over Silence: Women in Protestant History*, ed. Richard L. Greaves (Westport, CT: Greenwood Press, 1985), 93–123.

23. Anon., *Tub-preachers overturn'd or Independency to be abandon'd and abhor'd as destructive to the majestracy and ministery, of the church and common-wealth of England* (London: George Lindsey, 1647), 15.

24. Sarah Jones, *To Sions Lovers, Being a Golden Egge, to avoide Infection* (London: s.n., 1644), B1–B3. See also her *The Relation of a Gentlewoman Long Under Persecution by the Bishops* (1642) published under the initials S.J., and *This is Lights Appearance in the Truth* (London?: s.n., 1650).

25. Barbara Ritter Dailey, 'The Visitation of Sarah Wight: Holy Carnival and the Revolution of the Saints in Civil War London', *Church History* 55.4 (1986): 438–55.

26. Henry Jessey, *The Exceeding Riches of Grace Advanced By the Spirit of Grace, In an Empty Nothing Creature (viz) Mris. Sarah Wight* (London: Printed by Matthew Simmons for Henry Overton, and Hannah Allen, 1647). See also Sarah Wight, *A Wonderful Pleasant Profitable Letter* (1656).

27. Jessey, *Exceeding Riches*, 17.

28. Manfred Brod, 'Politics and Prophecy in Seventeenth-Century England: The Case of Elizabeth Poole', *Albion* 31.3 (1999): 395–412.

29. Elizabeth Poole, *A Vision Wherein is Manifested the Disease and Cure of the Kingdome* (London: [s.n.], 1648 [1649]). Subsequent references are cited parenthetically in the text.

30. Rachel Trubowitz, 'Female Preachers and Male Wives', in *Pamphlet Wars: Prose in the English Revolution*, ed. James Holstun (London: Frank Cass, 1992), 112–33; Brian Patton, 'Revolution, Regicide, and Divorce: Elizabeth Poole's Advice to the Army', in *Place and Displacement in the Renaissance*, ed. Alvin Vos (Binghamton: Medieval & Renaissance Texts & Studies, 1995), 133–45.

31. Henry Ferne, *Conscience Satisfied: That there is no warrant for the Armes now taken up by Subjects* (Oxford [i.e. London]: Printed by Leonard Lichfield Printer to the Vniversity, 1643), 81.
32. Herbert Palmer, *Scripture and Reason Pleaded for Defensive Armes* (London: Printed for Iohn Bellamy and Ralph Smith, 1643), 35–36.
33. Elizabeth Poole, *An Alarum of War, given to the Army, and to their High Court of Justice (so called)* (London, 1649); Elizabeth Poole, *An(other) Alarum of War* (London, 1649).
34. Jane Baston, 'History, Prophecy, and Interpretation: Mary Cary and Fifth Monarchism', *Prose Studies* 21.3 (1988): 1–18; David Loewenstein, 'Scriptural Exegesis, Female Prophecy, and Radical Politics in Mary Cary', *Studies in English Literature, 1500–1900* 46.1 (Winter, 2006): 133–53.
35. Louise Fargo Brown, *The Political Activities of the Baptists and Fifth Monarchymen* (Washington: American Historical Association, 1912).
36. B. S. Capp, *The Fifth Monarchy Men* (London: Faber, 1972).
37. Mary Cary, *The little horns doom & dovvnfall or A scripture-prophesie of King James, and King Charles, and of this present Parliament, unfolded* (London, 1651).
38. Mary Cary, *A New and More Exact Mappe*, published with *The Little Horns Doom & Downfall*, A3.
39. Mary Cary, *A Word in Season* (London: Printed by R.W. for Giles Calvert, 1647), 3.
40. Mary Cary, *The Resurrection of the Witness* (London: Printed by D.M. for Giles Calvert, 1648), 169.
41. Mary Cary, *Twelve humble proposals to the supreme governours of the three nations now assembled at Westminster* (London: Henry Hills, for R.C., 1653).
42. Anne Bradstreet, *The Tenth Muse Lately Sprung up in America* (London: for Stephen Bowtell, 1650). Subsequent references are cited parenthetically in the text.
43. Mihoko Suzuki, 'What's Political in Seventeenth-Century Women's Political Writing?' *Literature Compass* 6 (2009): 1111/j. 1741-4113.2009.00641.x.
44. Wiseman, *Conspiracy and Virtue*, 192–93.
45. Megan Matchinske, 'Holy Hatred: Formations of the Gendered Subject in English Apocalyptic Writing, 1625–1651', *ELH* 60 (1993): 349–77; Sue Wiseman, 'Unsilent Instruments and the Devil's Cushions: Authority', in *New Feminist Discourses*, ed. Isobel Armstrong (London: Routledge, 1992), 176–96; Kate Chedgzoy, 'Female Prophecy in the Seventeenth Century: The Instance of Anna Trapnel', in *Writing and the English Renaissance*, ed. William Zunder and Suzanne Trill (London: Longman, 1996), 238–54; James Holstun, *Ehud's Dagger: Class Struggle in the English Revolution* (London: Verso, 2000).
46. Anna Trapnel, *Strange and wonderful newves from VVhite-Hall* (London: Robert Sale, 1654); Anna Trapnel, *The Cry of a Stone* (London: [s.n.], 1654). Subsequent references are cited parenthetically in the text.
47. Anna Trapnel, *Anna Trapnel's Report and Plea* (London: Thomas Brewster, 1654), 14–15.
48. Ibid., 18.
49. Anna Trapnel, *A Legacy for Saints* (London: T. Brewster, 1654).
50. Anna Trapnel, *[A] voice for the king of saints and nations* (S.l.: s.n., 1657; untitled, 990-page folio).

51. Trapnell, *Report and Plea*, 55.
52. John Rogers, preface to John Canne, *The Time of the End* (London: Livewel Chapman, 1657), A2–2v.
53. Anne Venn, *A Wise Virgin's Lamp Burning* (London: Printed for E. Cole, 1658), A3. Subsequent references are cited parenthetically in the text.
54. Thomas Goodwin, *An apologeticall narration humbly submitted to the honourable Houses of Parliament* (London: Robert Dawlman, 1643); John Owen, *A declaration of the faith ... agreed upon ... in their meeting at the Savoy, October 12, 1658* (London: Printed by John Field, 1659).
55. *An Hvmble remonstrance to the Kings most excellent Majesty in vindication of the honourable Isaak Pennington, lord major of the honourable city of London, Alderman Foulkes, Captaine Venne, Captaine Manswaring: whom His Majeste desires to be delivered to custody, to answer an accusation of treason against them: desiring that His Majesty would make them no let to his returne to his Parliament nor hinder the accomodation of peace* (London: Printed for T. Wright, 1643), 6; Anon., *A Most famous Victory Obtained by that valiant religious Gentleman, Colonel Venn* (London: Printed for J. Rich, 1642), 3–4.
56. Thomas Goodwin, *A glimpse of Sions glory* (London: Printed for William Larnar, 1641); *A child of light walking in darkness* (London: Printed by J.G. for R. Dawlman, 1659).
57. Henry Neville, *Plato Redivivus or, A Dialogue Concerning Government* (London: Printed for S.I., 1680), 119.
58. Scott, *Commonwealth Principles*, 61.

Part II
Modes and Sites

5
Seventeenth-Century Women's Manuscript Writing

Victoria E. Burke

Among the letterbooks of Mary Evelyn, wife of the diarist John Evelyn, is an epistle intended for Ralph Bohun, their son's tutor at Oxford (British Library MS Add. 78438, fols 1r–2r).[1] In this letter, Evelyn sends her commiserations that Margaret Cavendish, the Duchess of Newcastle has come to town. Evelyn writes, 'I was surprised to finde so much extrauagancy and vanity in any person not confined within four walls', and that Cavendish's physical gestures 'shew what may be expected from her discource which is as Ayery Empty whimsicall and rambling as her books, ayming at science difficulties high Notions, terminating com*m*only in nonsence Oathes and obsenity' (fol. 1r).[2] Evelyn contrasts 'This Lady and Mrs Philips the one transported with the shadow of reason the other possessed of the substance and insensible of her treasure' (fol. 2r). Evelyn's targets are multiple: Cavendish's demeanor, the subjects of her writing (science, religion, philosophy, romance), and, although it is not directly stated, the means by which she disseminated her work.[3] Cavendish had her works printed, usually in large folio format.[4] A handful of Philips's poems were printed individually before 1664, but much of the circulation of her verse took place in manuscript among her coterie, comprising friends and social contacts to whom she gave pastoral sobriquets.[5] Philips's horrified response to the unauthorized printing of her verse in 1664 sealed the image of Philips as a retiring poet avoiding the public realm. In a poem to the Archbishop of Canterbury she uses the striking image of her retired, humble muse 'dragg'd malitiously into the Light; / (Which makes her like the Hebrew Virgin mourn, / When from her face, her vaile was rudely torn.)'.[6] The biblical story to which Philips refers is that of Tamar, raped by her brother Amnon (2 Samuel 13:1–20).[7]

But to assume that by choosing manuscript Philips is shunning a public space for her poetry is not accurate, given what scholarship of the last twenty years has taught us about manuscript culture.[8] No simple answer exists for why a woman would choose to circulate her work in manuscript. The so-called 'stigma of print' may be in operation here, the notion that it was rather vulgar to seek an audience through print, though this attitude was by no means uniformly held.[9] Prescriptive literature is full of exhortations against women speaking publicly, and by extension bringing their writing into the public realm through print,[10] so Philips may indeed be tapping into cultural prescriptions against women seeking a wide audience. Writers sometimes chose manuscript dissemination of their work for its elitism or to evade censorship, potentially allowing greater control over the reception of their work. On the other hand, poets who chose to circulate their work in handwritten form could reach a very wide audience indeed. John Donne's verse famously survives in hundreds of exemplars in dozens of manuscript volumes, demonstrating the way circles might start small but open onto wider networks, progressively more distant from their originator.[11]

Philips did not simply shun the limelight; instead we know she wrote numerous poems to members of the royal family, and she sought the help of her ally Sir Charles Cotterell to sanction and distribute her work to the correct people. Thus her publicized disowning of the unauthorized printing of her poetry was due more to the imperfections of the text and her loss of control over her self-presentation than to a perceived affront to her feminine modesty. The posthumous publication of her collected works in 1667, approved and corrected, clinched her status as a major writer of the period, indicating that manuscript and print were not always in opposition, and indeed not always used in contrasting ways.

Two further accomplished poets, Lady Mary Wroth and Lucy Hutchinson, used manuscript and print in different combinations to both evade censure and publicize their work. Wroth is most famous for writing a Petrarchan sonnet sequence from the perspective of a female speaker, which was appended to her lengthy prose romance *The Countess of Montgomery's Urania*, printed in 1621. But an autograph manuscript of the sonnet sequence survives as Folger Shakespeare Library MS V.a.104. The manuscript's sonnets and songs are arranged in several disparate groups, and it contains additional poems which do not appear in the printed version.[12] No evidence of its circulation has been found, except for the fact that writers seeking patronage referred to Wroth's abilities as a poet from 1613 on.[13] The printed edition ends with the poem 'My muse now hapy, lay thy self to rest', a fitting moment of satisfaction with the constancy that the muse has helped the poet celebrate.

The poem also includes a call for the muse to inspire other poets with not merely the 'discource of Venus' but 'storys of great love' (possibly divine).[14] This poem is not given such a significant position in the Folger manuscript, however, suggesting that the complacency of the speaker is not where Wroth wanted to end her manuscript version – or indeed that in the process of revising her poems for print, she chose to impose more order on the sequence(s) than the manuscript allowed. Wroth chose manuscript much more often than print: her continuation of the *Urania* is extant in only one manuscript copy, and her verse drama *Loves Victorie* survives in two copies.[15] Born into the famous literary family of the Sidneys, for whom the manuscript production and circulation of writing was a well-established mode of disseminating literary work, it is not surprising that Wroth favored this format also.

Lucy Hutchinson's lineage was more modest, and yet manuscript was a similarly conducive format for her to write a variety of prose and verse works. She is best known today among historians for her biography of her husband, John Hutchinson, the regicide whose reputation she tried to restore after his death in 1664. This biography, based on her earlier writing about his actions during the Civil Wars, remained in manuscript until its first publication in 1806; even though she did not seek a printer she must have wished a readership for her vindication.[16] Her first major work was a translation of Lucretius's *De Rerum Natura*, which she worked on during the 1650s but presented to Arthur Annesley, Earl of Anglesey in 1675. She implies a readership of the potentially atheist text in her dedication, saying that it had 'by misfortune ... gone out of my hands in one lost copie'.[17] Hutchinson's additional surviving manuscripts testify to the scope of her literary activity: she produced a commonplace book, a collection of twenty-four elegies celebrating her husband as a republican hero, a religious notebook, and a religious treatise for her daughter called 'On the principles of the Christian religion'.[18] She also wrote a version of the Book of Genesis in rhyming couplets which survives in manuscript (Beinecke Library MS Osborn Shelves fb.100); part of it was printed anonymously in 1679 as *Order and Disorder*. Its anonymity can be explained by its pro-republican sentiments; to attach her name as the wife of a regicide would have only courted trouble.[19]

In her elegy 'The Night' Hutchinson laments the woe and dread that come to 'Orena' (a pastoral name for Hutchinson herself) at night.[20] In a series of questions Hutchinson remembers her husband in physical terms: 'his kind and constant breast' on which she laid her head, his hand that dried her tears, his 'kind Ensircling arme' that held her up, his 'Soft powerfull breath' that inspired her (lines 22–32). This sequential bodily description recalls the blazon. But the potential sensuality of these images is undercut by her acknowledgment that his lips and hands are now cold (line 33), and she turns to his spirit which, Christ-like, was sent from heaven and then returned at his death. Hutchinson's description now turns from the earthly to the qualities which are his 'soaring wings' and his 'Crowne of glorie' (lines 42–43) – again, physical attributes but which now indicate his spiritual essence – wishing she could commune again with him 'through pure Intelligence' (line 51). Her final image is one of union: she wishes that their streams could join back at their source (presumably, in their spiritual essence), and become so refined that their lines 'Would both in one Just centure fix' (lines 53–56). Interestingly, the image she uses to communicate her desire for their spiritual union is one of a centure, waist-belt or girdle (*OED*), which might actually bring us back to the body and the site of sensuality.[21]

While Philips's, Wroth's, and Hutchinson's writing appeared in both manuscript and print, the verse of two skilled contemporary writers, Hester Pulter and Anne Southwell, appeared only in manuscript.[22] Hester Pulter's work is known only through the evidence of one remarkable extant manuscript, Leeds University Library, Brotherton Collection MS Lt q 32. This manuscript consists of three sections: poems (fols 1r–89v), emblems (fols 90r–130v), and an incomplete prose romance entitled 'The unfortunate Florinda' (foliated in reverse from the back of the volume, fols 1r–36v). Most of Pulter's poetry was written during the 1640s and 1650s, probably at her husband's family seat at Broadfield, Hertfordshire.[23] Though her work seems not to have circulated, it is evidently the result of wide reading and learning in fields such as alchemy, and of political engagement in the royalist cause.[24] One poem, written while she was in childbed with her fifteenth child, imagines her spirit visiting all the planets. The combination of up-to-date scientific knowledge and personal comment is striking: she refers to the newly discovered four moons of Jupiter ('Next Jupiter that Mild Auspicious Starr / I did perceive about his Blazing Carr / Four bright Attendents alwayes hurrid Round', lines 41–43), then two lines later to Saturn ('whose Aspects Soe Sads my Soul'). This is probably a reference to Saturn's malign influence contributing to the deaths of children (thirteen of Pulter's fifteen children died).[25]

An elegy on her daughter Jane begins with the following phrase, 'Tell mee noe more ...', which she repeats a further six times in the poem.[26] Scott Nixon has suggested that this may be a variation of the popular poem attributed to Thomas Carew, 'Aske me no more', which is extant in more than forty manuscripts.[27] Carew's poem celebrates the beauty of his mistress, claiming that the rose, the sun's rays, the nightingale, the stars, and the phoenix have all found refuge in his beloved's beauty, hair, voice, eyes, and bosom. Pulter develops this blazon in interesting ways, reframing the potentially erotic components of her daughter's body (her hair, shoulders, eyes, cheeks, nose, lips, and breasts) into signs of her virginity and her cosmic power to offer comfort to her mother. In Carew's final stanza the image of a phoenix dying in his mistress's breast suggests the common early modern association of death with orgasm. Pulter chooses the end of her poem as the place to use Carew's phrase for the first time ('aske mee noe more') but to reconfigure a union in divine terms: that of mother and daughter as dust, rising at Judgment Day to praise God in Heaven (lines 41–44). Like Hutchinson, Pulter takes a well-known device from Petrarchan poetry, the blazon, and adapts it as a tool for spiritual comfort. Pulter's rewriting of a popular poem circulating in manuscript suggests her access to circles of manuscript exchange of verse. Elizabeth Clarke and Peter Davidson have suggested that Pulter might have read Marvell's verse in manuscript, given allusions in her verse to 'Upon Appleton House' and 'The Nymph Complaining for the Death of her Fawn'.[28]

A separate section in Pulter's manuscript consists of fifty-four poems which fit the emblem genre in some ways (the poems often use a description of a scene from which to draw a moral) but not in others (there is no accompanying picture or proverbial tag). Margaret Ezell notes that in the emblems in particular Pulter engages with classically derived natural history and philosophy, as well as contemporary science. Pulter does not give her readers a visual image to decode but instead uses stories of animal and plant life to reflect upon contemporary events.[29] The popular emblem writer Geoffrey Whitney moralizes an emblem depicting an oyster trapping a mouse as a caution against gluttony. Pulter's version describes the tides ultimately freeing the mouse, making her poem a comment on the unjust imprisonment of royalists who will be freed by the powers of God and nature.[30] Pulter's manuscript indicates a writer testing the capacities of several genres to write inventively of religious, political, domestic, and scientific matters.

Anne Southwell's poetry shows more evidence of an audience, and of several different types of scribal publication of her work. In Folger Shakespeare Library MS V.b.198, her original lyric poetry appears alongside longer digressive poetry on the Decalogue, and other apparently much more random material such as copies of letters, rental receipts, notes from sermons, extracts from a bestiary, and a library list. Scribal publication seems to have been a joint project with her second husband, Henry Sibthorpe, whose hand appears on many pages in the volume, sometimes in an editing capacity; Jean Klene has noted that he wrote 'wyf lyfe to ofte' beside what he felt was an overused rhyme.[31] Some of her lyrics are bitingly funny, including lines such as 'All.maried.men. desire.to.haue good wifes: / but.few.giue good example. by thir liues', others more poignant (such as these opening lines: 'Nature, Mistris off affection / gaue my loue to thy protection / Wher it hath receiued infection / and is dying').[32] Her verse on the Ten Commandments is not confined to theological matters; typically she uses a commandment as the occasion to reflect widely on a theme. In her poem on the seventh commandment, she uses vitriolic language against adulterers, comparing them to sodomites and hermaphrodites, and seems to relish images of infection and disease which can only be healed by 'the surgion christ' (line 17), soon turning the poem into partly a defense of women and partly a set of instructions about marriage aimed at men.[33]

Southwell's, or her husband's, desire to connect with well-born acquaintances is reflected in letters to Cicely, Lady Ridgeway, Countess of Londonderry and Henry Cary, Viscount Falkland, Lord Deputy of Ireland, prominently transcribed near the front of the volume, as well as in poetry celebrating the kings of Bohemia and Sweden, among others. A second manuscript, British Library MS Lansdowne 740, fols 142r–167v, consists of scribal copies of two lengthy Decalogue poems prefaced by a dedication to the King, and a commendatory poem on Southwell by 'H', presumably her husband, Henry. While intended at one stage for a royal audience this particular manuscript seems unlikely to have reached the King, given its increasingly rough appearance and frequent corrections. Neither of the Southwell manuscripts are straightforward presentation copies. Sibthorpe's closing verses in both manuscripts pay tribute to his wife's skills, and try perhaps to assert order on what can appear, at least in the case of the Folger manuscript, to be rather random compilations. But both manuscripts unveil a woman's engagement with popular poetry in manuscript, her reading of particular printed books, and her own strategies to create a distinct poetic voice.

Prose writings of all types are also well represented in extant manuscripts, and some of the best represented of these are life writing. Noting the variety of circumstances that help account for this outpouring of life writings (such as Protestant exhortations for self-examination and the turmoil of the Civil Wars), Michelle Dowd and Julie Eckerle suggest that autobiographical writing in this period experimented with many different generic forms, from 'diaries, letters, and memoirs' to 'religious treatises, fictional romances, and even cookbooks'.[34] Lady Anne Clifford experimented with different forms of life writing.[35] When she was ten years old a servant began an account book for her (which she signed at several points), recording gifts and disbursements in several categories (Beinecke Library MS Osborn Shelves b.27). Clifford wrote a retrospective memoir for the year 1603, summarizing the events of the year (including her reactions to Queen Elizabeth's death). A more daily form of diary survives for the years 1616, 1617, and 1619, charting her legal battles trying to gain her father's inheritance and recording social details, in addition to fascinating insights into her reading practices. Both of these, the memoir and the diary, survive only in much later copies compiled by Clifford's descendants, one from the mid-eighteenth century and the other from the mid-nineteenth century, indicating a female family readership for Clifford's words.[36] Another type of life writing survives: the *Great Book of the Clifford Family*, which consists of three large volumes of family history, legal documentation for Clifford's suit, and also yearly summaries of her life for the years 1650–75 (this last in volume three). An autobiography, headed 'The Life of Me', written in 1652–53, summarizing her early life to 1650, also survives in the *Great Book*. Three copies of these books survive, produced in several scribal hands, testament to Clifford's desire to record the progress of her claim for herself and for posterity. Finally, a daily diary from 1676 records the last months of her life. Mihoko Suzuki and Aaron Kunin have argued convincingly that Clifford portrays herself as a historian through this voluminous writing.[37] Even those documents written by amanuenses, and by later descendants of Clifford, show a writer directing exactly how her works should be read.

Clifford's life writing is striking in that it is primarily secular in focus. Much autobiographical writing by women engaged directly with their spiritual lives. Elizabeth Isham wrote an account of her life from her early childhood to about age 30, which makes frequent reference to her own spiritual development (Princeton University Library, Robert H. Taylor Collection RTC01 no.62).[38] The stated purpose for Isham's autobiography, which she calls 'My Booke of Rememberance' (fol. 2v), is to praise God: the volume opens and closes with a prayer, the first prayer stating her desire to 'tell of thy wonderous workes, that the memoriall of thine abundant Kindnes may never be forgotten' (fol. 2r).[39] Her intended audience is herself and her family, and ultimately her motherless nieces: she writes in a marginal note 'not that I intend to have th[is] published. but to this end I have it in praise a than[k]fullnes to God. and for my owne benefit. which if it may doe my Brother or his children any pleasure I think to leave it them' (fol. 2r). The autobiography follows a kind of narrative arc in which major events of her life are recorded: her education, her skills at needlework, the illnesses and deaths of family members (including a kind of spiritual depression suffered by her mother), her father's marriage negotiations for Elizabeth with three different men (all of which came to naught since she chose a single life), and her reading practices, among other topics. In much of her narrative, Isham almost seems to speak through the key book in her life, the Bible, seeing what happens to herself and her family via its lens, and internalizing its language. For example, after a vivid description of the suffering of her sister Judith due to her many broken bones, some of which had to be rebroken and reset (as soon as Judith saw the bonesetter 'her teeth would chatter in her head for very feare', fol. 6r), Isham writes of her own bitterness in recalling these things since she suffered with her sister and mother. But she records also her hope and consolation, 'more fully calling to mind these comforttable places of Scripture', such as 2 Corinthians 1:7 which she cites in the margin beside lines that are almost a direct quotation: 'but my hope is stedfast that as I have ben partakers of the\ir/ sufferings so I shall be also of the consolation' (fol. 6v). The final pages of the manuscript build up to a climax, leaving aside narrative in favor of repentant self-flagellation, culminating in a final prayer which begins, 'Whatsoever is here good. and may be acceptable to thee I offer' (fol. 38r). She asks God to receive this gift just as he received the offering of the women who spun goat's hairs for the Tabernacle (Exodus 35:26), placing her work in a tradition of humble but heartfelt female labor, and her choice of image suggests a link between her writing and her embroidery, both as fitting tributes.

A second manuscript compiled by Elizabeth Isham is very different: it is a single sheet folded to form 36 square sections, six across and three down, making a total of 18 squares on each page (Northamptonshire Record Office IL 3365).[40] The first three squares contain cryptic details about her life up to age eight; after that she numbers each square with her age, continuing until age 40 in 1648. These tiny notes record events in her life, such as her needlework, her reading material, domestic events, interesting happenings (e.g. in 1621: 'I delighted in a sun diall'), and with increasing frequency political news from 1639 on, the period of the Civil Wars. The relation between the longer autobiography and this more schematic diary is not direct; Millman suggests that Isham began writing this diary retrospectively from rough notes while writing the autobiography in 1638. This account of her life in chart form nevertheless allows for poignant commentary; for 1638, the year of her sister's death, she wrote 'my foolishnes of too much sorrow for my S[ister] Judeth'. The purpose and audience of both of Isham's forms of life writing can be uncovered only through careful attention to material features, genre, and other manuscripts written by her and her family (such as rough notes and letters). Autobiographical writing in manuscript did not fit neatly into one category for either women or men in this period.

Anne, Lady Halkett also compiled very different autobiographical and devotional writings during her life. She is the author and scribe of fifteen extant manuscripts: an autobiography (British Library MS Additional 32376) and fourteen volumes of religious meditations (National Library of Scotland MSS 6489 to 6502).[41] The extant meditations span the early 1650s to her death in 1699, recording her voluminous 'select' or biblical and 'occasional' meditations; the autobiography records events from her early life to her marriage to Sir James Halkett in 1656. But the autobiography was written retrospectively, between finishing one book of meditations on 10 September 1677 and starting another on 22 April 1678. At the beginning of the latter manuscript she explains her break:

> yett the occation of itt may bee of some aduantage to mee if ye Lord sees fitt to giue a Seasonable opertunity to devulge itt. [B]y representing my vnparaleld misfortunes & the wonderfull power and mercy of God in Suporting mee vnder them; wch beeing an euidence of the Lords Compasion may incline others to the greater Charity whose Seueare Censare of mee occationed an interruption to ye Conclusion of this booke to relate a True accountt of my life. What effects itt may produce I Leaue to him to whom I resigne the intire disposall of all that Concernes mee.[42]

This masculine figure is no doubt God, but it is significant that Halkett's avowed motivation for writing this account of her life is to defend herself publicly, challenging any reading of this text as a private, confessional document.

Indeed the autobiography's varied generic debts suggest a keen awareness of audience. The young Halkett experiences three romantic relationships: first with Thomas Howard, later second Baron of Escrick, a match of which both families disapproved, second with Colonel Joseph Bampfield, a royalist spy who concealed an existing wife (with a digression on a deceitful chaplain who tried to drive a wedge between Halkett and her hostess, Anne Howard, by implying that her host, Sir Charles Howard, had fallen in love with Halkett), and third with her future husband, Sir James Halkett. Politically, Halkett vividly chronicles her royalist actions, including how she and Bampfield helped James, Duke of York escape from St James Palace on 20 April 1648, which involved disguising him as a woman. Mary Ellen Lamb has argued persuasively that Halkett negotiates the spiritual and secular in her memoirs, envisaging two audiences simultaneously for this work: God (requiring that she examine her conscience and repent of her sins) and posthumous readers (who may remember the scandal of her dealings with Bampfield).[43] The text can be read as partaking of the genres of 'devotional treatise, family history, and romance' and also as 'a cautionary tale about male duplicity and inconstancy'.[44]

Halkett's select meditations explicate and contemplate individual biblical verses (such as Philippians 4:11, on learning to be content [MS 6500, pp. 238–68]), groups of chapters from scripture (such as 'Josephs Trialls & Triumph', Genesis 37–50, MS 6495, pp. 1–506, which is the whole manuscript), entire books of the Bible (such as the book of Esther in MS 6501, pp. 186–200), and topics such as Christ's Passion for every day of the week (MS 6497, pp. 123–273). Her occasional meditations use incidents in her household, her community, and her native and adopted countries (England and Scotland) as subjects for contemplation. The topics in her occasional meditations in MS 6497 for 1687–88, for example, range from events in her personal life (relating mainly to her son, her medical practice, her reading, and taking children into her household), wider political events (the anniversary of the Restoration, the pregnancy of the queen), and her spiritual life (preparing for the sacrament, the activities of Presbyterians in her parish). A meditation on beating sugar becomes a wish that the strokes she meets with might refine her and bring her higher toward God's calling (MS 6500, p. 187). The final meditation of MS 6494, dated 26 November 1678, gives thanks for Charles II's preservation after the Popish Plot (pp. 371–80). Though in 1661 Halkett wrote that '[I]n fundementalls both agree Episcopall and presbeterian' (MS 6491, p. 78), later in the century many of her meditations detail her efforts to help her Episcopalian ministers regain their positions after their ejection by the Presbyterian establishment.[45]

Generically, Halkett distinguishes between occasional and select meditations, but she also wishes to highlight when a personal reflection in a select meditation is worthy of note. Her first extant volume, MS 6489, contains a meditation on 1 John 5:4, which she has titled 'The great Conquest or the power of faith' (pp. 7–39). Her table of contents notes 'a remarkable accident' which she keys to specific pages within the meditation (pp. 36–37; Halkett numbers these 30–31). Halkett refers to seeing a flock of sheep when she was sad and unable to find comfort in religious duties. One sheep was apart from the flock on a slippery bank, eating from bushes of thorn, yet content. She drew a moral that a true sheep of Christ's fold should not lament severe circumstances. At the beginning of a meditation on Leviticus 19:2 Halkett explains that she has been attaching papers to the spine of each of her volumes of meditations with her dates of composition and that she resolves to transcribe the tables of contents of all of them, to help her find a subject she would like to read and to be more useful to any who should see her manuscripts after her death (MS 6500, p. 146). She refers at several points to her desire to keep her manuscripts private, unless they could ultimately be used for the honor of God, but Margaret Ezell has shown that in borrowing so many elements from print culture (tables of contents, titles, pagination, and marginal glosses), Halkett is consciously shaping her manuscripts for not just a manuscript readership but a specifically print readership.[46] In her varied writings Halkett constructs herself as both a pious, searching Christian, eager to find meaning in the trials of her life and times, and as a writer seeking an audience.

Scholars have long recognized the need to consider works produced, circulated, and read in manuscript culture alongside those which were part of print culture in order to gain an accurate picture of literary practice during the seventeenth century. When we are attentive to the genres favored by women in manuscript, such as life writing, devotional verse, and domestic and religious account keeping, we can move beyond what were assumed to be the appropriate literary genres and consider what women actually wrote.[47] Margaret Ezell has noted that if we ask what were the 'sites of writing' and 'scenarios of authorship' for early modern women we can help to understand why women wrote what they did.[48] Women, like men, used both manuscript and print in multiple ways to authorize their own work. Women's writing in manuscript in the seventeenth century was rarely a private concern, and in order to gain a full picture of literate life in this period one must take account of handwritten material.

Notes

1. Frances Harris, 'The Letterbooks of Mary Evelyn', *English Manuscript Studies, 1100–1700* 7 (1998): 202–15 (211).
2. In transcriptions from manuscript raised letters are lowered and supplied letters italicized.
3. Marie-Louise Coolahan has also analyzed this letter as evidence of the significance of Philips's manuscript circulation of her verse: '"We live by chance, and slip into Events": Occasionality and the Manuscript Verse of Katherine Philips', *Eighteenth-Century Ireland* 18 (2003): 9–23 (10).

4. The only first edition of her works not printed in folio was *Philosophicall fancies* (1653), printed in a small octavo format (Donald Wing, *Short-Title Catalogue ... 1641–1700*, 2nd edn, vol. 2 [New York: MLA, 1982], 617–18).
5. For a description of the major extant manuscripts see Marie-Louise Coolahan, introduction to 'Presentation volume of Katherine Philips's verse', in *Early Modern Women's Manuscript Poetry*, ed. Jill Seal Millman and Gillian Wright (Manchester: Manchester University Press, 2005), 128–30.
6. *Early Modern Women's Manuscript Poetry*, ed. Jill Seal Millman and Gillian Wright; contributing eds: Victoria E. Burke, Elizabeth Clarke, Marie-Louise Coolahan, and Jonathan Gibson (Manchester: Manchester University Press, 2005), 146–47, lines 8–10.
7. Ibid., 257 n. 9.
8. Key overviews of manuscript culture include Harold Love, *Scribal Publication in Seventeenth-Century England* (Oxford: Clarendon Press, 1993); Arthur F. Marotti, *Manuscript, Print, and the English Renaissance Lyric* (Ithaca: Cornell University Press, 1995); H. R. Woudhuysen, *Sir Philip Sidney and the Circulation of Manuscripts, 1558–1640* (Oxford: Clarendon Press, 1996); Noel J. Kinnamon, 'Recent Studies in Renaissance English Manuscripts', *English Literary Renaissance* 27 (1997): 281–326 and 'Recent Studies in Renaissance English Manuscripts (1996–2006)', *English Literary Renaissance* 38 (2008): 356–83; George L. Justice and Nathan Tinker, eds, *Women's Writing and the Circulation of Ideas: Manuscript Publication in England, 1550–1800* (Cambridge: Cambridge University Press, 2002); Victoria E. Burke and Jonathan Gibson, eds, *Early Modern Women's Manuscript Writing: Selected Papers from the Trinity/ Trent Colloquium* (Aldershot: Ashgate, 2004).
9. Steven W. May, 'Tudor Aristocrats and the Mythical "Stigma of Print"', *Renaissance Papers* (1980): 11–18.
10. Kate Aughterson, ed., *Renaissance Woman: A Sourcebook. Constructions of Femininity in England* (London: Routledge, 1995), 229–32.
11. Peter Beal, 'John Donne and the Circulation of Manuscripts', in *The Cambridge History of the Book in Britain: Volume IV: 1557–1695*, ed. John Barnard and D. F. McKenzie, with the assistance of Maureen Bell (Cambridge: Cambridge University Press, 2002), 122–26. On manuscript networks see Jason Scott-Warren, 'Reconstructing Manuscript Networks: The Textual Transactions of Sir Stephen Powle', in *Communities in Early Modern England: Networks, Place, Rhetoric*, ed. Alexandra Shepard and Phil Whithington (Manchester: Manchester University Press, 2000), 18–37.
12. For descriptions and analysis of the physical structure of the manuscript see Jonathan Gibson, introduction to 'Lady Mary Wroth *Pamphilia to Amphilanthus*', in *Early Modern Women's Manuscript Poetry*, ed. Millman and Wright, 35–38; Gavin Alexander, 'Constant Works: A Framework for Reading Mary Wroth', *Sidney Newsletter and Journal* 14 (1996–97): 5–32; Heather Dubrow, '"And Thus Leave Off": Reevaluating Mary Wroth's Folger Manuscript V.a.104', *Tulsa Studies in Women's Literature* 22 (2003): 273–91.
13. Josephine A. Roberts, introduction to *The Poems of Lady Mary Wroth* (Baton Rouge: Louisiana State University Press, 1983), 18–19, 44.
14. Roberts, *The Poems of Lady Mary Wroth*, 142 (P 103).
15. These are now Newberry Library Case MS fY 1565.W95, Huntington Library MS HM 600 (an incomplete version), and the privately owned Penshurst

manuscript. For editions see Lady Mary Wroth, *The Second Part of the Countess of Montgomery's Urania*, ed. Josephine A. Roberts, completed by Suzanne Gossett and Janel Mueller (Tempe, Arizona: Renaissance English Text Society in conjunction with Arizona Center for Medieval and Renaissance Studies, 1999) and S. P. Cerasano and Marion Wynne-Davies, eds, *Renaissance Drama by Women: Texts and Documents* (London: Routledge, 1996), 91–126.

16. David Norbrook, 'Hutchinson, Lucy (1620–1681)', in *Oxford Dictionary of National Biography* (Oxford University Press, September 2004); online edn, January 2008, http://www.oxforddnb.com/view/article/14285 [accessed 24 September 2008]. The memoirs are Nottinghamshire Archives DD/Hu4.

17. Hugh de Quehen, introduction to *Lucy Hutchinson's Translation of Lucretius: De rerum natura* (Ann Arbor: University of Michigan Press, 1996), 10–11, 17; Lucy Hutchinson, 'To the Right Honorable Arthur Earle of Anglesey', in de Quehen, *Lucy Hutchinson's Translation*, 23.

18. Nottinghamshire Archives, DD/HU1-3 and Northamptonshire Record Office, Fitzwilliam Collection Misc. vol. 793. David Norbrook lists the extant manuscripts, later printed editions, and missing manuscripts in his edition of *Order and Disorder* (Oxford: Blackwell, 2001), 265–66. See also Jill Seal Millman, introduction to 'Lucy Hutchinson's "Elegies"', in *Early Modern Women's Manuscript Poetry*, ed. Millman and Wright, 98.

19. Norbrook, introduction to *Order and Disorder*, xiv.

20. *Early Modern Women's Manuscript Poetry*, ed. Millman and Wright, 104–05.

21. For a fascinating reading of another blazon on her husband in Hutchinson's 'On the Picture in Armour', see Pamela Hammons, 'Polluted Palaces: Gender, Sexuality and Property in Lucy Hutchinson's "Elegies"', *Women's Writing* 13 (2006): 392–415 (404–07). See also Erica Longfellow's chapter on Hutchinson in *Women and Religious Writing in Early Modern England* (Cambridge: Cambridge University Press, 2004).

22. But Southwell was probably the 'A.S.' whose prose 'answers' appeared in *A wife Now the Widow of Sir Thomas Overburye* in response to Overbury's and John Donne's 'news'; see Jean Klene, introduction to *The Southwell-Sibthorpe Commonplace Book: Folger MS V.b.198* (Tempe, Arizona: Medieval and Renaissance Texts and Studies, 1997), xxviii–xxxi and Donald Beecher, ed., *Characters, Together with Poems, News, Edicts, and Paradoxes Based on the Eleventh Edition of A Wife Now the Widow of Sir Thomas Overbury* (Ottawa: Dovehouse, 2003), 298–305.

23. Elizabeth Clarke, introduction to 'Hester Pulter's "Poems Breathed forth By The Nobel Hadassas"', in *Early Modern Women's Manuscript Poetry*, ed. Millman and Wright, 111–13.

24. Jayne Archer, 'A "Perfect Circle": Alchemy in the Poetry of Hester Pulter', *Literature Compass* 2.1 (2005): 1–14, <DOI: 10.1111/j.1741-4113.2005.00160. x>; Sarah Ross, 'Tears, Bezoars and Blazing Comets: Gender and Politics in Hester Pulter's Civil War Lyrics', *Literature Compass* 2.1 (2005): 1–14, <DOI: 10.1111/j.1741-4113.2005.00161.x>.

25. *Early Modern Women's Manuscript Poetry*, ed. Millman and Wright, 117–18, 251.

26. Ibid., 114–15.

27. Scott Nixon, '"Aske me no more" and the Manuscript Verse Miscellany', *English Literary Renaissance* 29 (1999): 97–130 (129–30 n. 66).

28. Elizabeth Clarke, notes to 'The Larke' in 'Hester Pulter's "Poems Breathed forth By The Nobel Hadassas"', in *Early Modern Women's Manuscript Poetry*, ed. Millman and Wright, 251. Peter Davidson, 'Green Thoughts: Marvell's Gardens: Clues to Two Curious Puzzles', *Times Literary Supplement*, 3 December 1999, 14–15.

29. Margaret J. M. Ezell, 'The Laughing Tortoise: Speculations on Manuscript Sources and Women's Book History', *English Literary Renaissance* 38 (2008): 331–55 (344–47).

30. *Early Modern Women's Manuscript Poetry*, ed. Millman and Wright, 126–27, 253–54.

31. Klene, *The Southwell-Sibthorpe Commonplace Book*, 79; Jean Klene, '"Monument of an Endless affection": Folger MS V.b.198 and Lady Anne Southwell', *English Manuscript Studies 1100–1700* 9 (2000): 165–86 (177). For a discussion of Sibthorpe's and Southwell's joint bid for social preferment see Erica Longfellow, 'Lady Anne Southwell's Indictment of Adam', in *Early Modern Women's Manuscript Writing*, ed. Burke and Gibson, 111–33.

32. Klene, *The Southwell-Sibthorpe Commonplace Book*, 20, 16.

33. Ibid., 76–84.

34. Michelle M. Dowd and Julie A. Eckerle, introduction to *Genre and Women's Life Writing in Early Modern England* (Aldershot: Ashgate, 2007), 1.

35. For the best overview of the extant manuscripts see Katherine O. Acheson, introduction to *The Diary of Anne Clifford, 1616–1619: A Critical Edition* (New York: Garland, 1995), 14–29. See also D. J. H. Clifford, introduction to *The Diaries of Lady Anne Clifford* (Stroud: Sutton, 1990), x–xv.

36. For identifications of the hands see Acheson, *The Diary of Anne Clifford*, 17–23.

37. Mihoko Suzuki, 'Anne Clifford and the Gendering of History', *Clio* 30 (2001): 195–229; Aaron Kunin, 'From the Desk of Anne Clifford', *ELH* 71 (2004): 587–608.

38. This manuscript and the Northamptonshire manuscript described below are the subjects of the 'Constructing Elizabeth Isham 1608–1654' project at the University of Warwick (http://www2.warwick.ac.uk/fac/arts/ren/projects/isham/). See their website for articles by the project team on the two manuscripts, and for abstracts of papers given at a recent workshop. See also Isaac Stephens, 'The Courtship and Singlehood of Elizabeth Isham, 1630–1634', *The Historical Journal* 51 (2008): 1–25.

39. All citations are from Alice Eardley's transcription of the Princeton manuscript, mounted on the 'Constructing Elizabeth Isham' website.

40. All citations are from Jill Millman's transcription of the Northamptonshire manuscript.

41. For an edition of the autobiography, selections from the meditations, and an excellent introduction, see Suzanne Trill, ed., *Lady Anne Halkett: Selected Self-Writings* (Aldershot: Ashgate, 2007). An additional seven manuscripts, plus about 30 more 'stitched Books' of 10–12 sheets each, are now lost (S[imon] C[ouper], *The Life of the Lady Halket* [Edinburgh, 1701], sigs H2r–H4v ['Books written by the Lady Halket']). But not all of the lost manuscripts are completely lost, since SC arranged for the publication of extracts from a number of them in 1701 and 1702. These are *Meditations on the twentieth and fifth Psalm; Meditations and prayers, upon the first week; Instructions for youth*; and *Meditations upon the seven gifts of the Holy Spirit*.

42. MS 6494, p. 294; my transcription is from Trill, *Lady Anne Halkett*, xxxvi, who suggests the occasion as gossip about Halkett's previous affair with Colonel Joseph Bampfield (xxxvii).

43. Mary Ellen Lamb, 'Merging the Secular and the Spiritual in Lady Anne Halkett's Memoirs', in *Genre and Women's Life Writing in Early Modern England*, ed. Dowd and Eckerle, 93.

44. Sharon Cadman Seelig, *Autobiography and Gender in Early Modern Literature: Reading Women's Lives, 1600–1680* (Cambridge: Cambridge University Press, 2006), 110 and Trill, introduction to *Lady Anne Halkett*, xxi.

45. My transcription is from Trill, *Lady Anne Halkett*, 24.

46. Margaret J. M. Ezell, 'Ann Halkett's Morning Devotions: Posthumous Publication and the Culture of Writing in Late Seventeenth-Century Britain', in *Print, Manuscript, and Performance: The Changing Relations of the Media in Early Modern England*, ed. Arthur F. Marotti and Michael D. Bristol (Columbus: Ohio State University Press, 2000), 215–31 (217–20).

47. Alice Eardley has noted that the Perdita Project database (http://human. ntu.ac.uk/perdita) lists the following genres as significant categories in women's manuscript writing: advice, autobiography, commentary, culinary writing, dialogue, dream, letters, meditation, memorandum, prayer, sentential, and vision ('Recreating the Canon: Women Writers and Anthologies of Early Modern Verse', in *Still Kissing the Rod?*, ed. Elizabeth Clarke and Lynn Robson, special issue of *Women's Writing* 14 [2007]: 270–89 [284]). For women's participation in the important genre of letter writing see Susan Wiseman's eassy in this volume.

48. Margaret J. M. Ezell, 'Women and Writing', in *A Companion to Early Modern Women's Writing*, ed. Anita Pacheco (Oxford: Blackwell, 2002), 77–94 (79).

6

Reading Seventeenth-Century Women's Letters

Susan Wiseman

Feminist work of the last three decades has made it clear that women had complex and gendered relations to genre and textual circulation in the sixteenth and seventeenth centuries. Accordingly, the importance of particular genres and modes including spiritual autobiography, various forms of life-writing, and circulated manuscripts, has received increasing attention. This essay explores one such single, if internally diverse, genre from the period: the letter. Seventeenth-century women's letters are at the crossroads of two sets of critical debates, one on the status and genres of women's writing and how we should approach the specific forms used by early modern women, the other on the nature of the letter as a genre. As Margaret Ezell reminds us, the ways in which women's writing has been transmitted and anthologized plays a crucial role in shaping readers' apprehension of how and what women wrote.[1] At the same time, the letter's ambiguous status as both self-consciously literary and quotidian prompts us to consider the nature of specifically 'literary' value, and value more widely. Seventeenth-century women's letters, then, raise questions about the nature and reception, or transmission, of texts by women. 'Actual' letters are both, simultaneously, an important aspect of women's written production and ambiguously placed in terms of literary value. Comparing the letters of Brilliana Harley with those of Susan Fielding and the published, fictional, *Sociable Letters* of Margaret Cavendish this essay briefly explores the status of women's letters in mid-seventeenth-century England, and how they have come to us.

Historians and literary critics habitually use letters as evidence of how people experienced the Civil War, and women feature substantially as correspondents.[2] The reasons for the acknowledged importance of letters in the specific period 1640–1660 are uncertain. It may be because there are more of them – families are separated, news is more pressing – or for other reasons, such as that families have valued (and so kept) them because, for instance, they show the interaction of 'personal', 'family', and 'political' experience. Certainly, what is meant by 'letters' in this period is various, embracing the letters between Henrietta Maria and Charles I captured and published in *The King's Cabinet Opened*, the state letters reaching back to the previous century included in the *Cabala* (1653) (which was to be immensely influential), and the published letters of James Howell, as well as a huge range of manuscript materials. Each of these publications prompts us to consider the different, though perhaps overlapping, implications of the reading of letters by a much wider 'public' than their chosen recipients.

In terms of 'actual' letters, letters designed to be sent and received (itself not always a clear category), James Daybell's path-breaking research on the period 1540–1642 finds more than 10,000 manuscript letters substantially under-used by scholars.[3] In this field Brilliana Harley is relatively well known, in part, perhaps, because the troubled and exciting times in and of which she wrote brought her to the attention of historians but also because Thomas Taylor Lewis, vicar of Bridstowe in Herefordshire, transcribed the letters from Brilliana to her son, Edward or Ned Harley (who seems to have kept them) and they were published by the Camden Society in 1854. Lewis found the previously 'neglected' manuscripts at the Harleys' seat at Eywood and his transcription may have been at the behest or at least invitation of Lady Frances Vernon Harcourt, who had put them in order. In giving her correspondence with her son Lewis's volume presents Harley as a loving and inventive mother caught up in the Civil Wars. Lewis was unaware of letters to her husband and to the royalist besiegers of her home.[4] However, even the letters in his volume allow us to see her active political and religious interests as the letters fly up and down the west of England by courier, carrier, and messenger charting her reaction to events and, above all, to reports and writings on subjects dear to her – and subjects now, at last, being debated by a wider public. Later, the Historical Manuscripts Commission transcribed her correspondence with the royalist army commanders who besieged her at Brampton Bryan and we can see her political rhetoric. A third, very substantial, tranche of papers by her and related to her is in the British Library. The publication of each batch of material has reshaped Harley's presence for her modern readers and as we will see, the nature of transmission shapes who reads letters and how they are analyzed.

In the 1630s and 1640s, as political turmoil in England and Scotland intensified and religious and political views became increasingly polarized, Harley wrote letters. Harley wrote to her son, Ned, who set off to take his degree in Oxford but soon migrated to the exciting scenes of turmoil near the Commons in London. She wrote to her husband, the MP Sir Robert Harley, in London. When the Civil War came to royalist Herefordshire and her parliamentarian stronghold at Brampton Bryan was besieged, she wrote to the commanders besieging her and, in the end, addressed herself to their highest commander, Charles I. Additionally, we have a commonplace book from before her marriage and some meditations. Jacqueline Eales thinks that it is possible that letters to Harley don't survive because she destroyed potentially incriminating correspondence when her house was besieged in 1643.[5] It is at least possible that Harley had a wider, even substantially wider, range of correspondents.

The 'evidence' Harley's letters offer is often quite complex and raises questions about how to read them. Amongst the most recently edited letters we find that, on 28 March 1641, Brilliana Harley wrote to Richard Sancky (or Sankey), servant to her husband Sir Robert Harley.

> Richard Sancky
>
> I must pray you to rwite to me every weake how thinges goo in the Parlament I heare so many rumors in the Cuntry but I heare no surtainty I had no letter from Ned Harley this weeke which make me [] that I did not heare from him, but I heare he is well which gives me Content.
>
> Heare inclosed I have sent a letter to my sister Conway I pray you take care to send it with much care and by a safe hand and let me know wheather it be sent,
>
> I pray you be carefull of your Master, I thanke you for writing to me every weake how your Master does.
>
> I pray God prosper the Endevors of the parlament and guide them in all threare counsells, and I pray God keep you. B.H.[6]

Not often discussed by critics, this letter suggests a number of things about early modern gender, politics, and society. It indicates that Harley had many more correspondents than merely her son and husband. Sir Robert's servant monitored his doings weekly and passed them on. Someone else has been able to inform her (by letter? in person?) that her son is well though he has not himself written this week (an omission worthy of comment in itself). Harley has written to her sister and Sankey is to pass on that letter. It may be possible to track Sankey's correspondence through the Harley archive but, of course, we know of him as a letter writer because of the preservation of Harley's correspondence. The term 'network' almost understates the sense of Harley's constant use of, but also her testing and checking of, channels of communication. At the start and end of a letter to a servant she mentions Parliament and, as she is in the country, beset by 'so many rumours' but 'no surtainty', she asks him for news of 'the Parlament'. Any reader of Harley's correspondence more generally must notice how skeptical she is of the information she gets from those around her and how desperate to exchange truthful information with her correspondents. As she tells Sir Robert in March 1641, 'I was never less satisfied in a weakes inteligence then in this many rumors theare are in the Cuntry' and she does '[e]xceedingly long to heare the truth of thinges'.[7] She regards herself not as isolated from words but as in a mire of misinformation and royalist propaganda. Here we have just a glimpse of her sense that in Herefordshire, one of the most strongly and consistently royalist counties, she is alone, uninformed, and in her isolation vulnerable to manipulation and violence. The letter to Sankey confirms much of what we know about Harley. In disclosing her good relations with servants, and her trust in this one, it also suggests the way in which how we see a letter writer is dominated by what survives and adds to our understanding of the dynamic relations of the household. Harley writes to Sankey about family, religion, and politics but also about letters and communication. At the same time it reminds us that we can rely on letters to get lost and mislaid and that, perhaps, the further down the social scale correspondents are the more potentially vulnerable their caches of letters might be.

If Harley's motivations as a letter writer are clear even in the fragmentary correspondence we have with Sankey, she is explicit about why she writes to her son. Although letters to Sir Robert Harley exist from the earlier 1630s, the major section of correspondence we have seems to begin on 25 October 1638 when she was also separated from her son, Edward Harley, writing 'I hope thease lines will finde you well at Oxford. I longe to reseaue the ashurance of your comeing well to your journeys end.'[8] In this letter she worries about how Edward will keep his head amidst the exciting distractions of Oxford, and hopes that his tutor will be a good influence. By 17 February 1641 her concerns are overlappingly personal and political. She wants to know what has happened to a royalist petition in support of bishops, but also 'I more longe,' she writes, 'to heare the kings ansure to the petetion to take away the bis: vots in parlament.' In exchange she can offer local news of the struggle to right the innovations of the Laudian church – '[i]n Hariford, they haue turned the tabell in the cathedroll, and taken away the cops and bassons and all such things. I hope they begine to see that the Lord is about to purg His church of all such.'[9] On 10 January 1641 (1642) she wrote to Robert Harley of the King's attempt to arrest five members of the Commons – 'I was in many feares for on Saturday night I hard that many of the howes of Commons weare acused of treson.' Charles, abandoning a conciliatory initiative, had unexpectedly instructed the attorney-general to bring charges of treason against Pym, Hampden, Hazelrig, Holles, Strode (in the Commons), and Lord Mandeville.[10] This happened on 3 January and within a week Harley is responding to its significance – 'I feare great trubells are aproaching. But I hope the Lord will put forth his power to rescue his servants from all the plots of theare Enimyes.'

The letter of 25 March 1641 includes information on the trouble she has collecting rents in the difficult circumstances of war, and a crucial postscript:

> Deare Sir Let me desire you to send me word how you thinke thinges stand for if I heare should be any stirs Brompton in respect of worldly help is very weake. Now theare is not any that is watchfull my howis is very nacked, I doo not say this out of feare.

Harley's sense of being isolated in a sea of royalist rumor translated into a sharp and accurate awareness of physical vulnerability. The threat to Brampton is something to which she returns again and again, as the possibility of attack intensifies. That she does not want to be thought afraid again suggests her awareness of the perils of communication – she attempts to convey urgency and emphasize her own clear-sighted understanding of the situation.

As we know, her fears were justified and Brampton was besieged. Besieged, Harley wrote to the royalist commanders of her determination to preserve her house for her husband and family. Just after the siege ended, in September 1643, Brilliana wrote quite a long letter to her husband, Sir Robert Harley.[11] 'On []day last the 23 of this month I received your letter by fisher[] in which you advised me to come away from Brampton' and the letter is her response. First, she reminds her husband:

> Dear Sir [] heatherto God has made me (though an unworthy one) an instrument to keepe possession of your howes that it has not fallen into the hands of spoilers, and to keepe to geather a handful of [] such as feared the Lord together so that his word has yet had [] in theas parts

She reminds him that 'in this worke I have not thought my life deare' and, rather than leave at a critical juncture she reiterates a demand made fairly often:

> Sir Could Ned Harley come downe I should thinke meselfe to have much comfort and I think he would doo his country sarvis and himselfe good in helping to keepe what I hope shall be his and in maintaining the [Ghispell] in this place o let me begg of you to take poor Hearifordshir into consideration and commissiration

Harley binds together her keen mission to retain family property and insistence that, at the most dangerous of times, the gospel in Herefordshire must be preserved. She struggles against a situation where 'faithfull Ministers' are leaving hostile, royalist, Herefordshire, 'carried up to Londoun'. In a postscript she continues:

> If my sonne could come downe I should hope we might comforta-bely keepe what we have left, if that cannot be then I pray you thinke how some comistion may be granted that some strength may be []
>   Sr the man you write of to intrust your howes with if I should have foolowed his counsel it had bin goun. Thearefore I doo not thinke he would keepe it. Mr Ba[rryhe] is of an opinion that if pleas God I goo away it will not be [longe] [keepe] not that I doo any great matter but I have something more [authority] and I should have more care then any other.
>   My deare Sr I pray you consider all thinges and doo not looke upon me as if I weare afraid but what you would have me doo in that which may be best for you, and that I shall most gladly doo, all my pleasures are in you and then I must be most pleased when you are pleased and thearfore deare Sr thinke what you would have me doe and let me know it and I shall be best pleased to doo that. This bearer can relate all paseges to you and I hope you will hasten him out of towne.

Mixing main text and passionate postscript, Harley's letter offers the reader roughly the same information in two moods. In the main body of the letter she seems to be negotiating to stay at Brampton and to have Ned with her. The postscript tells the same story, but clarifies the reasoning behind it – the man chosen by Sir Robert to defend his prop-erty would have let it go. There is implicit, if restrained, criticism of her husband's choice of steward and an assertion of her status as Brampton's protector. She ends the letter with a third variation on the theme, 'I might begin a newe letter in letting you know how good God has bine to me in all thinges he has exceedingly bllesed the provistions of my howes so that it has held out beyond expectation.' Although Brilliana, Mr Barry, and, it seems, God agree that the house is best protected by Sir Robert's wife, the letter does seem marked by anxiety about the best way to convey this. If the first version is tactful perhaps it does not make her point clearly. If the postscript is too literal and, potentially, assertive then it can be reinforced by an account of God's providences, though she seems to feel that these belong in another letter.

Harley's letters respond to the circumstances in which she finds herself and are an index of her active reactions to them. They suggest, too, the nuances of authority, politics, affection, coercion, ritual, and practicality in a marriage, household, and county. Besides the obvious point that the letters mix pies and politics, they also show more significant areas of overlap. Strongly interested in national politics, Harley is also deeply concerned with the politics of Herefordshire – its royalist complexion both impacted on national affairs and, increasingly, influenced her daily life. At the same time, though, she worries about the money Robert Harley needs for himself and for the war effort, and, correspondingly, she worries about the difficulty she has in getting rent out of his tenants – something which is related to national, local, and immediately personal connections. In terms of style, Harley is both apparently highly spontaneous, or rather pressed by circumstances, often appending urgent, interesting or desperate postscripts, and, as her letters written to the commanders besieging her home in 1643 demonstrate, sharply aware of generic protocols. Like other correspondence found and discussed by James Daybell, Harley's letters tell us about 'female education and literacy; family, gender and other social relations; and the role of early modern women in patronage and politics'. Yet, if such letters are indeed a much-needed corrective to 'traditional' assumptions that letters are 'private, elite and non-political, they also beg the question of how contemporaries thought of them as reading experiences, and how we might consider our roles as readers'.[12]

For a non-recipient reader, the Harley archive is a complicated rhetorical and evidentiary resource. Its guides are the ascertainable purpose and content of each letter, use of the genre, context of sender, recipient and cast, and sequence. Unlike letters designed to be read (whether political or amatory laments like Ovid's *Heroides*) the letters don't necessarily give the reader all the information she needs. Complicating, too, is the way that while they are not crafted for a public yet, as we see in this last letter, they are made to persuade. They also bear traces of the fast pace of events (as in the multiplication of postscripts), and suggest family as well as political and religious dynamics. These do direct the reader. However, where fictional, or even published, letters often endeavor to supply some kind of coherence and clarity for a reader who is not the addressee, such clues are noticeably missing from Harley's letters. Although the texts are crafted, that shaping seems to be oriented toward their purposes – how far we can read them in relation to literary texts remains a question. Thus, Harley's letters provide a wonderful source of material – factual, topical, and stylistic – for a woman supporter of the Commons struggling in a position of power (as member of an elite) and weakness (in being alone, unguarded, and covertly active in the war effort while living amongst the royalists of Hertfordshire). Although there is a strong sense of Harley's persona as a letter writer – these epistolary characteristics and voice add up to the letter-subject 'Brilliana Harley' – and that is one key aspect of literary value, many questions remain, however, concerning the relationship between her vocabulary, even style, and her political and religious convictions, and how we can we investigate the questions of literary value in such texts.

The question of how we can evaluate the literary, political, and aesthetic status of Harley's letters is illuminated by comparison with a contemporary letter writer, Susan Fielding, sister of James I's favorite and Charles I's counselor, the Duke of Buckingham, and wife of the first Earl of Denbigh. Fielding wrote thus to her son, Basil:

> My Dear Son,
>   I was very glad to receive a letter from you, but when I found how little my persuasions had wrought upon you I was much afflicted. Methinks you spoke Mr Pym's language, and I do long to hear my dear son Fielding speak once again to me in the duty he owes to his Master and dread sovereign, the master of your poor afflicted mother, banished from the sight of you I do so dearly love.[13]

Just as Brilliana Harley's life was gradually transformed by the intensifying conflict of the early 1640s, so was Susan Fielding's. Where Harley's letters to family members are based on shared religious and political values which precipitate an eager exchange of information, Fielding's family was split. Accordingly, here, Susan Fielding's focus is the distinct languages of politics. Regarding her son as possessed by the vocabulary of John Pym, she longs to hear him once again speak as a true son and royalist. She begs him to join those journeying to York to support the king, and promises, 'If you will come hither I know the Queen will make your peace with the King.'[14]

Like Harley, Susan Villiers was separated from her husband, William, and her son, Basil, by the Civil Wars. William was a royalist, Basil served the Parliament, and when William was killed at the battle of Edgehill, his son was on the field on the opposite side. Susan herself was close to Henrietta Maria. However, although it is not inappropriate to present Susan Fielding as a victim of the wars, her political commitment was overriding and it may be that the way royalist and familial rhetoric overlap tends for us, as it might not for contemporaries, to locate the writing subject in patterns of familial loyalty alone. She followed Henrietta Maria into France, became a Catholic, and seems to have been involved in political plans.[15] Her loyalty to the Stuarts at least arguably implies a political understanding which embraces hierarchy and family as intertwined political values – that she attended Henrietta Maria's person can be conceived of as a loyalty to the person, even body, of the queen but that very commitment may also express a conception of the nature of politics.[16] And that conception would imply a political discourse in which we would not expect her to construct herself as a political subject in relation to concepts such as public good – so important for Harley. So, when she traveled with Henrietta Maria to The Hague we find her once again writing to her son. Commencing with tactful assertion that 'none in the world should be more joyed at an accommodation of the King and Parliament than myself' she continues, 'so that they would humble themselves to the King, and acknowledge their errors'. Before long she asserts:

> If you will believe me as I am a tender and loving mother, it is time for you to run to the King upon your knees and crave his pardon. I dare not write to you what I would, and I really tell you that I do believe your party does not deal fairly with you, to tell you the truth, for they know they are not so well as they have been, but you think that I shall be the last to know of the disorder they are in at this time, believe me this is true.[17]

Vividly, perhaps punitively, evoking a longed-for scene in which her son begs pardon of her monarch, Fielding insists on her own political insight and knowledge.

Brilliana Harley sustained a commitment to family and politics that made her an active, and targeted, Puritan activist in Hereford. Susan Fielding was sufficiently committed to the Stuarts, and so to Stuart politics, to allow her own life to be permanently swept up into that of Henrietta Maria. However, Fielding's letters come to us very differently from Harley's and her words seem to mean very different things, inflected as they are by the genre of aristocratic family memoir as opposed to Camden Society edition. The letters of Susan Fielding have not yet been edited in full. Rather, they live as snippets of color in Cecilia Countess of Denbigh's *Memories of the First and Second Earls of Denbigh*. The 1915 volume presents her as the poignant victim of war and crisis and the loyal servant of Henrietta Maria who followed her into exile, converted to Roman Catholicism, and 'died an exile in Paris – died without ever seeing again her beloved son'.[18] Two points are significant here. First, the familial nature of royalist political language may have served to emphasize the 'personal' nature of Susan Fielding's letters, yet there is also evidence that she was just as committed a Roman Catholic and royalist as Harley was Puritan and parliamentarian. Second, Harley's letters have been edited where Fielding's have been used to illuminate a striking narrative of aristocratic Civil War adventure. Admittedly, Harley was a prolific writer. Nevertheless, the transmission of the two casts Harley, increasingly, as a serious religious, political, and familial commentator, Fielding as disclosing a tragic personal, and political, story.

We can see that, as writers, Fielding and Harley have been differently shaped as religious and political commentators, and in ways that partly register the nature of their writing and partly suggest nineteenth- and twentieth-century assumptions about what to do with women's letters and with Puritan versus royalist lives and letters. Yet, as the increasing study of 'actual' letters has grown substantially and their significance as a form of early modern women's writing has increasingly been recognized, that leaves us with the question of how to approach them as texts. While for many years such texts were not studied seriously, it is not clear how far recognition of their importance brings a need to evaluate them aesthetically or, at least, to consider how 'actual', transitive letters relate to questions of literary value as we study them.

Harley and Fielding write vividly about the cultural and political events of the 1630s and 1640s and that writing has been transmitted to us on distinct terms. But how should we think of Harley's or Fielding's 'writing', indeed, of either woman as a 'writer'? Are these appropriate and helpful terms? This question brings in its wake the wider issue of how we can conjugate the complex relationships between the writing of letters and other forms of writing.

We have both 'actual' and fictional letters by Margaret Cavendish. In her *CCXI Sociable Letters Written by the Thrice Noble, Illustrious, and*

Excellent Princess, the Lady Marchioness of Newcastle Cavendish writes remembering criticism of her earlier works and wonders, '[a]s for the Present Book of Letters, I know not as yet what aspersion they will lay upon it', but:

> I fear they'l say, they are not written in a Mode-style, that is, in a Complementing and romantical way, with High Words, and Mystical Expressions, as most of our Modern Letter-writers use to do; But, *Noble Readers*, I do not intend to Present you here with Long Complements in Short Letters, but with Short Descriptions in Long Letters; the truth is, they are rather Scenes than Letters, for I have Endeavoured under the Cover of Letters to Express the Humors of Mankind, and the Actions of Man's Life by the Correspondence of two Ladies, living at home some Short Distance from each other[.][19]

As in other locations, Cavendish is critical of the 'romantical' style which she sees as what her detractors value and asserts instead the letter as 'scene'. The point of these letters is not the style and use of rhetoric, but the expression of 'Humors' and 'Actions' as well as the – again 'unromantical' – relationship between the two writers. Apparently aware of her departure from what she sees as the standard reason for the use of the letter form – the display of the rhetoric of the letter – she defends what she has claimed as her use of the form:

> But the reason why I have set them forth in the form of Letters, and not of Playes, is, first, that I have put forth Twenty Playes already, which number I thought to be Sufficient, next, I saw that Variety of Forms did Please the Readers best, and that lastly they would be more taken with the Brevity of Letters, than the Formality of Scenes ...[20]

While the defense that readers have had enough plays is in itself a weak one, it does show clearly Cavendish's thinking; the letter, like the scene of a play, can quickly and adroitly show the reader 'Humor' and 'Action' – life.

There is much more to be said about the *Sociable Letters* but, even from the outset, Cavendish invites the reader to consider genre and the power of specific genres to convey 'life'. She does not claim that the letters are like what we have called 'actual' letters, though there seems to be some implication that just as a person might use a letter to convey an event succinctly, so that is what makes them suitable for the same task as a literary genre. At the same time, she sees her own letters as contrasting in this with other explicitly literary genres. Cavendish has then, both a clear (even perhaps strategically overstated) view of the nature of the literary genre and, to a limited extent, implies an understanding of actual letters as designed to convey events. At the same time, there is a literary theory of authorship at work here and the framing of letters for publication – as at times, too, for manuscript circulation – illuminates the difference between letters which, though saved and treasured, were not edited by contemporaries or, as far as we can tell, written with desired third-party readers in the frame.

In mid-seventeenth-century Europe there were many different kinds of letters. Looking closely at women's letters, in England, in the mid-seventeenth century this essay has mainly discussed 'actual' letters with senders and recipients (Harley, Fielding), and set against these Cavendish's (mainly) fictional *Sociable Letters*.[21] We can see these in the context of the growing published genres of letters as disclosure – *The King's Cabinet Opened* (1645), later the many-editioned *Cabala* – and letters as a representation of the experiences of politics such as Howell's *Familiar Letters*. The 'actual' letter emerges as a key component in the genres used by women (though obviously men used them as well) and as one mid-seventeenth-century writers and readers distinguished in several ways – only some of them that we would call aesthetic – from circulated, published, and fictional texts. That it is, James Daybell notes, no longer the dominant view that letters are significant when they reveal issues of state politics – which meant that the letters of statesmen were important and led to the neglect of other letters (and women's letters particularly) – allows us to ask other questions of these texts.[22]

Shifts in historical values have changed the status of women's letters within historical writing. In the literary study of women's letters we can return to the question of the 'literary' and consider how it is influenced by the significance of the 'actual' letter amongst women's genres. The status of the letter has been changed by the growth in the study of manuscripts, and by the much greater range of texts being recognized as important genres for women. In the early 1990s Margaret Ezell wrote a path-breaking book on the question of writing women's literary history.[23] As she wrote, indeed, attitudes to women's writing were changing. The growth of scholarship on early modern women has fulfilled many of the changes that she called for. Thus, through careful investigation of the evidence scholars have begun to establish approaches to modes of authorship, circulation, and the complex relationship between private and public (to name but a few topics) that respond to the texts and circumstances we have for seventeenth-century writers.

In responding to the evidence of the period a substantial range of genres in which women wrote have come to the fore – manuscript miscellanies (poetic and general), family books, letters, and so on. These very changes in the approach of historians and literary scholars invite us to return to the question of how particular forms of writing might have been understood by contemporaries and how we, now, might approach them. The category of the 'woman writer' – arguably itself one of those categories from nineteenth-century studies that lives on in critical studies – invites examination in relation to seventeenth-century writing. The status of the letter as 'writing', and of the writer of letters in relation to if not exactly aesthetic concerns then, at least, questions of publication, invite us to investigate afresh the concerns of writers and readers. In considering the nature and purpose of letters, it is helpful to consider their place within literary studies.

Without returning to a position where letters are not considered objects of study for literary scholars, we can ask what kind of objects of study they offer. Thus, one group of Harley's contemporaries, including Margaret Cavendish, Katherine Philips, Anne Bradstreet, and Lucy Hutchinson wrote letters but they also wrote in genres now recognized as 'literary' – each wrote poems and some participated in other literary genres. Should we consider engagement with specifically literary kinds of writing as a crucial distinction between them and Harley, or as an incidental effect of long-dominant yet unhelpful understandings of what are 'literary' genres? If we approach Brilliana Harley with the category of the 'woman writer' (rough-and-ready, present at hand, but also, of course, value-laden) it becomes immediately apparent that the nature of her writings invites us to question that category. Other writers that we read now wrote only letters – to take just one example, Dorothy Osborne wrote a series of letters to her future husband, Sir William Temple.[24]

Given that Patricia Crawford found that most published writing by women did not fall into literary genres, and the letter clearly forms a significant genre in the writings of early modern women, non-literary forms are clearly important in evaluation of the writing in this period.[25] Do we need to decide on what terms? Is it necessary to see 'actual' letters in relationship to literary genres at all? In the context of Crawford's quantitative analysis (most of women's published literary productions are non-literary) and the work of Ezell and others on the need to look at the specific cultures of writing in early modern England and Scotland rather than impose on them nineteenth-century models it seems timely to reconsider the status of both the letter and the letter-writer.

Moreover, if manuscript genres were in fact often carefully prepared and circulated, there is no need to emphasize a chasm of 'crafted' versus 'actual' in imagining the relationship between the transitive letter (written to act on the world) and literary genres bound up with the question of literary value.

Other possible responses, if not answers, to how we can think about women's 'actual' letters include: comparison with literary and published genres; rethinking of assumptions concerning men's letters which perhaps still tend to be more mined for political evidence in the mode James Daybell discusses; consideration, as by O'Day and Daybell, of the aesthetic and rhetorical crafting of letters and discussion of meditation on them; consideration of the way the personae of the writers and the implications and contexts of the letters have been shaped by transmission and by assumptions about contrasting forms of vocabulary – like the royalist versus Puritan vocabularies of Fielding and Harley.

Such research, now emerging, is likely to invite revision of another assumption. The question of the literary or aesthetic value of seventeenth-century women's letters has at times been 'answered' by being transferred to the adequately literary genre of the late seventeenth century and the later feminocentric epistolary genre from Aphra Behn's *Love Letters Between a Nobleman and his Sister* (1684–87) or Samuel Richardson's *Pamela*. This deferred 'answer' to the question of the literary value of women's letters suggests a traffic between the transitive, crafted, letter; the shaping of letter writing; and the building of a fictional world. While such an articulation is likely and convincing, it is also worth returning to these 'actual' letters on terms outwith the narrative which binds them to a narrative of the rise of the novel. Shifts in historical method made more, and different, letters visible and different things visible within the letters. Similarly, perhaps, shifts in the understanding of the relationship between publication and manuscript, studies in the effects of transmission, and more closely and theoretically inflected studies of rhetoric and style allow a renewed engagement with the complicated question of the 'actual' letter and the even more complicated question of the possible relationships of such texts to aesthetic and rhetorical, as well as evidentiary, dynamics.

Notes

1. Margaret Ezell, *Writing Women's Literary History* (Baltimore and London: Johns Hopkins University Press, 1993), 1–13, 104–31.
2. For an evaluation of letters as a source see Rosemary O'Day, 'Tudor and Stuart Women: Their Lives through their Letters', in *Early Modern Women's Letter Writing, 1450–1700*, ed. James Daybell (Basingstoke: Palgrave Macmillan, 2001), 127–42.

3. James Daybell, *Women Letter Writers in Tudor England* (Oxford: Oxford University Press, 2006), 11.

4. See Jacqueline Eales, 'Patriarchy, Puritanism and Politics: The Letters of Lady Brilliana Harley (1598–1643)', in *Early Modern Women's Letter Writing*, ed. Daybell, 143–58 (145–46).

5. Ibid., 145.

6. Brilliana Harley to Richard Sancky, 28 March 1641. BL Add MSS 70003 f. 80; see also *Women's Political Writings, 1610–1725*, ed. Hilda L. Smith, Mihoko Suzuki, and Susan Wiseman (London: Pickering & Chatto, 2007), I: 153.

7. Brilliana Harley to Robert Harley, 25 March 1641, Add MSS 70003, f. 78. See also *Women's Political Writings*, ed. Smith et al., I: 152.

8. Thomas Taylor Lewis, *Letters of Brilliana Harley* (London: Camden Society, 1854), 7.

9. Brilliana Harley to Edward Harley, 16 February 1641, in ibid., 148–49.

10. See Richard Cust, *Charles I: A Political Life* (London: Longman, 2005), 320–25.

11. Brilliana Harley to Sir Robert Harley, [24?] September 1643; BL Add MSS 70110; *Women's Political Writings*, ed. Smith et al., I: 195–96.

12. Daybell, *Women Letter Writers*, 1.

13. Susan Fielding to Basil Fielding, ?1640, quoted in Cecilia Mary Clifford Fielding, Countess of Denbigh, *Royalist Father and Roundhead Son* (London: Methuen, 1915), 164–65.

14. Ibid.

15. Fielding, *Royalist Father*, 286.

16. Ibid., e.g., 36–37, 185, 193.

17. Susan Fielding to Basil Fielding, 1642, quoted in ibid., 167–68.

18. Fielding, *Royalist Father*, 287.

19. Margaret Cavendish, *CCXI Sociable Letters Written by the Thrice Noble, Illustrious, and Excellent Princess, the Lady Marchioness of Newcastle* (London, 1664), C2r–v.

20. Ibid., C2v.

21. *The King's Cabinet Opened* (London, 1645); James Howell, *Familiar Letters* (London, 1645); *Cabala*, e.g., *Cabala, Mysteries of State* (London, 1654).

22. Daybell, *Women Letter Writers*, 7–11.

23. Ezell, *Writing Women's Literary History*.

24. Kenneth Parker, ed., *Dorothy Osborne: Letters to Sir William Temple, 1652–54* (Aldershot: Ashgate, 2002).

25. Patricia Crawford, 'Women's Published Writings, 1600–1700', in *Women in English Society, 1500–1800*, ed. Mary Prior (London: Methuen, 1985), 211–74.

7
'Herselfe livinge, to be pictured': 'Monumental Circles' and Women's Self-Portraiture

Patricia Phillippy

I

In his funeral sermon for Alice Leigh, Duchess Dudley, *A Mirror of Christianity*, Robert Boreman promotes the 'Zealous Imitation … of the Graces and Virtues which Shined in the Life and Death of the Renowned Duchess', particularly by female auditors.[1] This printed monument advances its subject as an ideal of femininity in terms often rehearsed on sculptural monuments erected for women by men in the seventeenth century, where the image of the 'christal glasse'[2] is ubiquitous. John Davies of Hereford, for example, used the figure on his wife's tomb (1612) in St Dustan-in-the-West, London: 'And to those Wives that glory most doe gaine, / She was a mirror that no breath could staine'.[3] Although Boreman's sermon commemorates a widow who died at age 90, and who had lived as if single for 65 years,[4] the hyperbolic praise shared by these textual and monumental portraits belies the shared assumption of their male authors; that the celebration of exemplary feminine virtues also congratulates the domestic or parochial government of the men to whom these women are subordinate.

Confronted with this idealization and the domesticating force attending it, could early modern women make use of funeral monuments to record their own perceptions of their life's work and meaning and to transmit these self-authored images to contemporaries and posterity? Peter Sherlock's assertion that women 'used tombs to improve their place in the social order or to secure their family's honour within it, without fundamentally threatening the patriarchal basis of early modern society'[5] suggests that women's voices could do no more than harmonize with men's. Margaret Talbot's (d. 1620) incised brass monument, also in St Dustan-in-the-West (Figure 1), seems to prove Sherlock's point when

Figure 1   Unknown artist, Monument for Margaret Talbot, St Dustan-in-the-West, London (1620). Photo: Patricia Phillippy.

the author, probably Talbot herself, adapts the commonplaces of masculine praise to her self-portrait: her 'Chaste widow-hood ... / Was so imaculate, she deserves to be / The christall *mirror* to Posteritie'. Yet as a childless widow, Talbot directs her epitaph toward preserving her own reputation rather than honoring her family. 'Both *Veres* and *Windsors* best blood fil'd her veines', we're told, 'yet their noble straines / Were farre below her Vertue'. Indeed, the presence of her corpse raises the stature of the church itself: 'More honour hast thou by her buriall here, / *Dunston,* than to thee chanc'd this many a yeere'.[6]

While funeral monuments share a spectrum of strategies for gender construction with other cultural forms in seventeenth-century England, they also offer a unique site for women's writing and a means for women to represent themselves and to forge and preserve female alliances. As composite forms, funeral monuments required their patrons to attend to both literary and artistic features, and critics must do the same. Women's monumental 'writing', then, includes not only inscriptions and epitaphs, but also architectural, sculptural, and heraldic components of monumental programs, scripted by women and executed by tomb sculptors. Although one can sometimes attribute only a single tomb or epitaph to an individual woman, and authorship is often uncertain, a surprising number of seventeenth-century women created multiple tombs for friends, family members, and themselves. Moreover, a significant number of women authored both monuments and texts and, in some cases, their immediate female relations and descendants undertook similar activities. This group, whose membership will most likely grow as critical attention to this convergence of texts and monuments increases, includes: Elizabeth Russell (d. 1609), Anne Clifford (d. 1676), Mary Penington (d. 1682), Frances Matthew (d. 1629), Elizabeth Tanfield (d. 1629) and her daughter, Elizabeth Cary (d. 1639), Alice Spenser, Countess of Derby (d. 1637), Alice Lucy (d. 1648), Constance Lucy (d. 1637) and her daughter, Elizabeth (d. 1690), Elizabeth Ashburnham Richardson (d.1651), and Elizabeth Bassett (d. 1643), her mother, Judith (d. 1640), and daughters, Jane Cavendish (d. 1669) and Elizabeth Brackley (d. 1663).

The number and prominence of funeral monuments in seventeenth-century England meant that they offered major sites for self-representation, particularly for women, who often erected tombs following their husbands' deaths.[7] Setting funeral monuments in relation to specific circles of women who created them, however, sheds light on the many female portraits and alliances displayed in these works. These representations suggest motives for memorial projects that extend beyond the advancement of dynastic reputation – a goal that subordinates women's monumental writings to the interests of fathers or husbands. This chapter identifies and explores two 'monumental circles', communities of women who approached monuments as sites for writing and used them to represent themselves and others. First, I survey the prevalent monumental forms available to women in seventeenth-century England. Next, I consider the monumental circle surrounding Constance Lucy in detail, and touch upon that surrounding Alice Dudley, locating within them versions of female self-authorship that enable seventeenth-century women to challenge the inflexible ideals of femininity which would reduce their memories to mere reflections; silent mirrors of insensible glass.

II

Seventeenth-century funeral monuments offer performances of gender, enacted in a theatrical space bounded on one side by the deathbed and on the other by the historical afterlife. Within this theater, women of the middle and upper classes, from noblewomen to merchants' wives, play various roles, partially, but not fully, scripted by the cultural expectations within which they lived.

Perhaps the most frequent role assumed by women who created funeral monuments was that of widow. Nicholas Stone's notebook records that, 'I mad a tombe for Ser Charles Moreson and his lady and sett it up in the Chencell of Wattford in Harfordshear, for the which I had well payed unto me 400£.'[8] The contract between Stone and Mary Morison made after her husband's death in 1628 sets forth the structural design, decoration, and heraldry of the tomb, and provides for Stone to 'grave and guild such inscriptions as shall in due tyme be delivered unto him'. The effigies of husband and wife, daughter, Elizabeth, and 'two sons deceased' are also described:

> The statue or picture of the said Sir Charles Morrison ... is to be royally and artificially carved ... and made of good and pure white marble, in compleat armour, with sword and spurs, according to the life ... [and] a statue or picture, for and of the said worthy Lady ... to consist of good and pure white marble ... made according to life, in such abillaments, ornaments, and jewells as he shall receave direction for.

As the contract details the 'portraighture'[9] of Lady Morison's family, it also shows her creating her own self-portrait. 'In the higher social ranks,' Nigel Llewellyn explains, 'monuments usually marked the death of the first spouse (usually male) but were nevertheless designed to commemorate both parties. So it was that tomb patrons were so often engaged in a kind of self-portraiture.'[10] Since Lady Morison survived her husband by thirty-two years, she and her portrait 'made according to life' coexisted for three decades. Many women lived out their lives with similar *memento mori*, created according to their designs, before their eyes. As Charity Leche recorded on the tomb she erected for her husband, Richard (d. 1596), and herself in Ss. Mary and Andrew, Fletching (Figure 2), 'she, of her own accorde, caused this monument to be made, and herselfe living, to be pictured lying by him, as you see'.[11] Charity remarried within a year of Richard's death, and survived him by twenty-two years.

Often widows or single women, like Margaret Talbot, commemorated themselves in separate monuments, where they negotiated the strictures of their domestic or dynastic roles.[12] Anne Clifford commissioned her own tomb in 1655, which she placed in St Lawrence, Appleby, near the

Figure 2 Unknown artist, Monument for Richard and Charity Leche (detail), Ss Mary and Andrew, Fletching (1596). Photo: Patricia Phillippy.

tomb she erected for her mother, Margaret, Countess of Cumberland, in 1617. Devoid of effigy, the simple chest tomb replaces the intimacy of her mother's monument with the sterile dynastic concerns that characterize her father's memorial. As a commentary on Clifford's protracted struggle to recover her inheritance, the tomb confirms her role as her father's rightful heir and commemorates her ascension as head of her family, a place ordinarily reserved for men.[13] Mary Lusher (d. 1623), on her incised ledger stone in St Mary's, Putney, addresses her second husband in the first person, orchestrating from beyond the grave the domestic relations in which she participated in life:

> That you have laid my body here,
> By that first side I lov'd so deere,
> I thanke you Husband ...
> But yet I have another Boone ...
> That you would close my other side ...
> You once were second to my bed;
> Why may you not like title have,

> To this my second bed, the Grave?
> This Stone will cover us all three,
> And under it we shall be free
> From Love, or Hate, or least distrust
> Of Jealousie to vexe our dust:
> For here our bodies doe but wait
> The summons for their glorious state.[14]

Imagining an assembly of tombs to counter those common in early modern churches, where effigies of patriarchs rest accompanied by two (or more) wives, Mary constructs a vision of the afterlife in which multiple domestic arrangements can coexist without the cumbersome emotions attending these relationships in life.

Grieving mothers and grandmothers often erected monuments for lost children.[15] On a small mural tomb in St Margaret's Westminster, Hugh Haughton and his wife, Frances, kneel side by side, accompanied by daughters Frances and Elizabeth, the latter holding a skull. The inscription tells us that Hugh, 'departed this life ye 17th day of / October 1616 aged 50 years & Elizabeth departed this life ye 28th day / of August 1615 aged 7 years and lyeth here also interred'.[16] In St Matthew's, Salford Priors, the diminutive effigy of a child decorates the mural tomb of Margaret Clark, who died aged three and a half in 1640. A simple but beautiful inscription reads: 'As carefull nurses to their bed doe lay / Their children, which too long would wantons play: / So to prevent all my insuing crimes, / Nature my nurse laid me to bed betimes'. 'In memory of [w]home,' it concludes, 'ye Lady Dorothie Clarke her / loving Grandmother erected this'.[17]

Women sometimes built tombs for their mothers, or chose to be interred near them, despite later bonds of marriage. At her death at the age of 71, Anne Woollocke (d. 1657) was buried next to her mother, Katherine Agard (d. 1628) in St Werburgh, Hanbury. Near-identical effigies of mother and daughter adorn their tombs.[18] Anne Clifford's epitaph for her mother's tomb in Appleby faces her own, and recalls her mother's 'Fayth, Love, Mercy, Noble Constancie / To God, to virtue, to Distress, to Right'.[19] Clifford's famous 'Countess Pillar' commemorates the exact place and moment where she last saw her mother before her death. 'This Pillar', the inscription reads, 'was Erected Anno 1656 by the R. Honorable Anne Countess of Pembrook, &tc. ... For a memorial of her last Parting in this place with her good and Pious Mother ... ye 2nd of April 1616'.[20]

Sisters commemorated sisters. When Katherine Blount died at the age of 27 in 1617, 'she left her estate to her four sisters, viz. Elizabeth,

Anne, Martha, and Jane'; the inscription on her mural tomb in St Peter, Slinford, reads, 'to whose pious and sacred memory they erected this monument'.[21] A beautiful and dynamic portrait of Mary Brocas attends her tomb in St Margaret's, Westminster (Figure 3), which tells us, simply, 'Here lyeth the body of Mrs. Mary Brocas one / of the Daughters and Coheirs of William Brocas ... / who departed this life the third day of / December in the yeare of our Lord God 1654 / For whose memory her loving sister Mrs. Frances Staresmore / Erected this Monument'.[22]

Women sometimes memorialized servants and maids and, less frequently, built monuments for female friends or requested interment

Figure 3   Joshua Marshall, Monument for Mary Brocas, St Margaret's Westminster (1654). © Dean and Chapter of Westminster.

near them.[23] In Stratford-upon-Avon, a small mural tomb is placed near the free-standing monument of the Earl and Countess of Totnes. The inscription explains:

> Here lyeth interred the body of Mrs. Amy / Smyth, who (being ebout the age of 60 yeares & a maide) / departed this life at Nonsuch in Surrey the 13 day of Sep / Ao Dni. 1626. She attended upon the Right No[ble] Joyce Lady / Carew Countesse of Totnes, as her waiting gentlewoman, the space / of forty years together, being very desirous in her life / time, that after her death she might be laid in this church / of Stratford where her lady ... also her / self intended to be buried.

The countess, 'for [Amy's] so long trew & faithfull service [and] as an evident toaken of her', had the body transported and buried, and 'did cause this monument / and superscription to be erected in grateful memory of / her whom she had found so good a servant'.[24] On the tomb of Mary Barber (d. 1606) in St James, Bury, an inscription tell us that, 'Henry her sonn her body here did place / next to her friend [Ann Chitting] whose soules in heav'n imbrace'.[25] Although Mary's husband, Roger, is buried nearby, her son commemorates her love for her female friend. When in 1612, Frances Bourchier died at the age of 26, Anne Clifford built her tomb in the Bedford Chapel at Chenies, adding that she erected the monument, 'at her owne costes & charges', as the last duty of a 'deare cosen'.[26]

   Seventeenth-century women utilized monuments, as they did manuscripts and printed texts, to announce and preserve significant relationships, within their families and beyond. How sure can we be, though, that the voices speaking for women on these monuments are their own? Without explicit claims of authorship, attributions are necessarily uncertain, and even when women take responsibility for erecting tombs, the collaborative nature of monumental projects allows for the possibility that they turned to male relatives, advisors, or poets for hire for inscriptions. Nicholas Stone's contract with Mary Morison, however, suggests that female patrons often had detailed designs in mind for the tombs they commissioned and were responsible for providing decorative details, heraldic designs, and texts for inscription. Moreover, the long-standing critical assumption that seventeenth-century women generally lacked an adequate education to produce these written works has obscured women's contributions in favor of likely male candidates for authorship, particularly of Greek and Latin texts. The case of Elizabeth Ashburnham Richardson, Baroness Cramond, provides a salient example. This author of *A Ladies Legacie to her Daughters* (1645) also created a series of tombs for her parents, mother, grandparents, uncle, daughter, and husband.[27] Despite an inscription on her mother's monument in St Botolph Aldersgate, stating that 'This Table was set up out of Love and true Affection of Elizabeth, Lady Ashburnham, Widdow, her eldest Daughter, Anno. 1622', Stephen Porter has recently claimed that Richardson's inscription was 'assembled by her brother-in-law, Sir Wingfield Bodenham'.[28] Porter bases this view on eighteenth-century accounts of the tomb which credit Bodenham – a Cambridge-educated Member of Parliament and part-time antiquarian – with compiling the genealogy it records.[29] Yet, the inscription itself indicates that Bodenham was not Richardson's brother-in-law, but her grandson-in-law, and further investigation shows that he, born in 1615, was seven years old when the tomb was erected.[30] His manuscript account of the Beaumont genealogy is probably based upon the inscribed version of his grandmother, whose literary and monumental products affirm her ability to author all elements of the monument's design, including its text. Although this example cannot guarantee the female authorship of other tombs, it offers a compelling argument against dismissing that possibility out of hand. Rather, our willingness to recognize women's voices as their own may reward us with a newly enriched history of women's writing.

III

When Anne Suthes erected her husband's tomb 'as a loyall Testimony of her love' in Lambeth Church in 1625, she concluded, 'herein the Reader may see exprest the goodnesse of the deceased Husband, and the thank-fulnesse of a surviving Wife'.[31] Her understanding of the visitor to the monument as a 'reader' underscores the cooperation of seventeenth-century texts and monuments as sites for writing and life-writing.[32] In *Peplum Modestiae, the Vaile of Modesty* (1621), a printed memorial for Anne Bill (wife of the King's Printer, John Bill), Anne's eulogist imagines her death as an attack on the textual, rather than sculptural, tomb:

> O That each good thing should be soonest tooke
>   Out of the world; as in a Booke
> Of goodly Monuments, or faire Manuscript,
>   If the gilt letters should be clipt,
> From the rich parchment, by some unlettred hand,
>   How maimedly the rest would stand.
> Now here is torne by Death, not worne by Age,

The frontispiece, or title page
Of Natures booke.[33]

This textual iconoclasm, in which the unlettered hand of Death rips
the frontispiece, Anne, from the book of Nature (Figure 4), has a monumental parallel in the complaint of Alice Dudley's daughter, Katherine
Leveson, that 'the Tombs of her noble Ancestors [have been] much
blemished by consuming time, but more by the rude hands of impi-
ous people'.[34] The affinities between text and monument apparent in

Figure 4   Simon van de Passe, portrait of Anne Bill from Martin Day (?), *Peplem
Modestiae, The Vaile of Modesty* (London: John Hodgett, 1621). © The British
Library Board (C.122.b.8).

Anne Bill's eulogy also inform Duchess Dudley's funeral sermon, which offers, 'a lively and true Portraiture', of its subject, albeit lacking 'lively Colours ... being drawn after her death (and so not to the Life)'.[35]

Duchess Dudley's effigial self-portrait, unlike Boreman's textual portraiture, was drawn 'to the Life'. The duchess lived out her long life in the parish of St Giles-in-the-Fields, London, where Boreman was rector, but had her corpse transported to St Mary's, Stoneleigh, where 'a Noble Monument long since prepar'd by Her self' awaited her.[36] Her tomb includes effigies of herself and her eldest daughter, Alicia, who died, aged 24, in 1621. Both figures lie shrouded, with eyes closed. Latin inscriptions describe her lineage and marriage, her advancement to the rank of duchess, the marriage alliances of her daughters, and her charitable bequests.[37] If works such as *Peplum Modestiae* and *A Mirror of Christianity* offer male-authored portraits of seventeenth-century women, these female objects of praise become subjects by displacing portraiture with self-portraiture in their monumental programs.

Constance Lucy, wife of Sir Thomas Lucy II, traced this self-authored passage from object to subject in several monuments, where she portrayed herself in various roles. She participated in the creation of her father's tomb, and erected her husband's monument, thereby fulfilling her duties as a daughter and wife. She also authored monuments for a daughter and two granddaughters, where her epitaphs recall the affective bonds between herself and the girls, displacing the pragmatic concern of dynastic continuity with a more intimate sense of a mother's and grandmother's grief at the loss of beloved children. She stands at the center of a monumental circle comprised of the alliances commemorated in these projects; a circle which expands after her death to include her female descendants.

Although Lady Lucy was probably instrumental in creating a monument for her father, Richard Kingsmill, in St Michael's, Highclere, the contract for the tomb, dated 1 June 1601, is between Thomas Lucy and sculptors Bartholomew Ayte and Isaac James.[38] A wife, rather than widow, Constance yielded to her husband in this transaction, despite the fact that, as Kingsmill's sole heir, she brought to her marriage the means to finance the project. In the monument's program, too, wives are subordinate to husbands: Constance's mother, Alice (d. 1575), is not portrayed (nor is her stepmother, Elizabeth). Although the relationship between father and daughter is emphasized visually by the placement of Constance's effigy in front of her husband's (Figure 5), the tomb's theme and structure cast Constance as a means for the transfer of property from father to husband, and as the commodity traded between them. Moreover, the terms of the contract indicate another kind of

Figure 5 Bartholomew Ayte and Isaac James, Monument for Richard Kingsmill (detail), St Michael's, Highclere (1601). Photo courtesy of Jane Malcolm-Davies (http://www.tudoreffigies.co.uk).

subordination: while Thomas requires that his own effigy be carved of alabaster, he chooses the cost-saving option of having the remaining two effigies be made of inferior local stone.[39]

Lady Lucy places herself front and center on the tomb she erected for her husband in St Leonard's, Charlecote in 1605 (Figure 6).[40] On a platform projecting from the monument's base, she kneels in the attitude of a pious widow before her husband's recumbent figure, accompanied by the effigies of fourteen children (ten of whom survived to adulthood). The monument is unusually devoid of text: although joint tombs commonly carry blank panels where heirs failed to provide inscriptions following the death of a second spouse (usually the widow), such an oversight concerning the first is rare.[41] This tomb, however, is not technically, 'joint'. Although Constance had her corpse returned to Charlecote for burial from the parish of St Giles Cripplegate, where she lived for the last decade of her life,[42] her effigy does not lie peacefully

Figure 6   Bartholomew Ayte and Isaac James, Monument for Sir Thomas Lucy II, St Leonard's, Charlecote (1605). Photo: Phil Draper (http://www.churchcrawler. co.uk).

beside her husband's, but rises eternally before and above him. She has 'herselfe living, to be pictured', forever a widow, not a wife. As such, she controls her destiny and her self-image.

If Constance remains silent in the face of her husband's death, she is vocal and eloquent in commemorating her daughter and namesake, Constance, who died at the age of 10 on 14 February 1596. On 'a Faire Marble stone in the Chancell', of Holy Trinity in Minories, a Latin elegy of ten lines accompanies 'the Effigy of a Woman in Brass, praying':

> ... flos formosissimus aret:
> Optima praetereunt, deteriora manent.
> Rapta immature fato, CONSTANTIA LUCY,
> Nunc jacet: & quondam lucida, luce caret.[43]
> [the most beautiful flower withers: the best passes away, and the worse remains. Constance Lucy, carried away unripe, now lies scattered; and shining once, now no longer shines.]

Playing on the Latin translations of her own and her daughter's name, Lady Lucy recalls the girl as 'Ante annos Constans, / humilis, mansueta, modesta' (Constant, humble, gentle, and modest beyond her years). While the inscription describes Constance as the first-born daughter of 'D. Thomae Lucy Iuni=/oris, Militis Aurati, & D. Constantiae / Uxoris' (the illustrious knight, Sir Thomas Lucy the younger and Lady Constance, his wife), the effigy of her mother kneeling in prayer casts the poem in the maternal voice and argues that Lady Lucy is its author. A daughter's death is imagined chiefly as a maternal loss, and a daughter's value in the family is registered in affective, rather than economic, terms.

In her widowhood, Lady Lucy authored two mural tombs in St Giles Cripplegate for two granddaughters. The first was another namesake, Constance Whitney (Figure 7), who died in 1628 at her grandmother's London home. In a remarkable image adorning the tomb, Constance rises from her coffin, throwing off her shroud. The inscription gives the pedigrees of both Constances:

> In Memory of *Constance Whitney,* eldest daughter to Sir *Robert Whitney,* of *Whitney,* the proper possession of him and his Ancestors ... for above 500. yeeres past. Her Mother was the fourth daughter of Sir *Thomas Lucy* ... by *Constance Kingsmell,* daughter and Heire of *Richard Kingsmell* ... This Lady *Lucy,* her Grandmother, so bred her since she was eight yeeres of age.

A second inscription describes the young woman's qualities and manners, and praises her good death:

> As she excel'd in all noble qualities, becomming a Virgin of so sweet proportion of beauty and harmony of parts, she had all sweetnesse of maners answerable:
> A delightfull sharpnesse of Wit;
> An offencelesse modesty of conversation;
> A singular respect and piety to her Parents; but Religious even to example.
> She departed this life most Christianly, at seventeene; dying, the griefe of all; but to her Grandmother an unrecoverable losse, save in her expectation, shee shall not stay long after her, and the comfort of knowing whose she is, and where in the Resurrection to meet her.[44]

The image of Constance Whitney emerging from her winding sheet participates in a vogue in women's monuments which developed in the first half of the seventeenth century. Shrouded effigies from this

Figure 7 Unknown artist, Monument for Constance Whitney, St Giles Cripplegate, London (1628). Destroyed in World War Two. Photo: Catherine Weed Ward. Courtesy of George Eastman House, International Museum of Photography and Film.

period, nearly all of which are women, reflect a reformed idea of death and resurrection that sees death as the peaceful sleep in which the Christian life naturally culminates. These tombs tend to contain greater expressions of grief on the part of survivors, evidence, as Judith Hurtig argues, of an increased value placed upon women and children within the family, and a new understanding of the function of tombs as markers of affective loss, rather than records of dynastic identity.[45] These are, clearly, the chief features of Constance Whitney's monument. As the tomb rehearses the emotional toll exacted by Constance's death on her

Figure 8   Unknown artist, Monument for Margaret Lucy, St Giles Cripplegate (1634). Photo: Patricia Phillippy.

grandmother, it looks forward to a time when the two women, united by their shared name in life, may also be reunited in resurrection.

A simple marble plaque in the same church (Figure 8) commemorates a second granddaughter, Margaret Lucy, who died in 1634 at the age of 19. Lady Lucy's eulogy describes Margaret in more generic terms than those employed on Constance Whitney's memorial, suggesting, as does the simplicity of the monument's sculptural form, less intimacy between author and subject:

> For discretion and sweetness of Conversa=/ tion not many excelled, and for Piety and Patience, / in her Sickness and Death, few equalled her: which/ is the Comfort of her neerest Friends … but especiallie to / her old Grandmother, the Lady Constance Lucy, / under whose Governement shee died.[46]

Once again, Lady Lucy imagines that she is 'shortly / to follow after' her granddaughter, and will be reunited with her in the afterlife. Constance Lucy died three years later, at the age of 71.

The memorials for Constance Lucy's granddaughters carry traces of the social practices underlying and enabling alliances between female relations. The presence of these girls in the London household of their widowed grandmother reminds us that most upper-class girls grew to marriageable age away from their parents, 'under [the] Governement' of noblewomen or female relatives. Their burial from Lady Lucy's household may have been a matter of expedience, but also reflects the sense that daughters held a more tenuous, temporal connection to the paternal household than did sons. While the tombs of Constance Whitney and Margaret Lucy recall their subjects' dynastic identities, the most powerful and resilient relationship to which they testify is the affective bond between a grandmother and her granddaughters.

The alliances of the Lucy women across two generations did not end here. Constance Lucy's monumental projects find their textual complement in the 'Account of the Lady Lucy, write[n] to a pertickular friend of hers, Mrs Moore', a manuscript biography by Lady Lucy's daughter-in-law, Elizabeth, and later transcribed by her granddaughter, Martha Eyre. To this copy, Martha appended a biography of her own mother, Elizabeth.[47]

The production of the manuscript at the request of Lady Lucy's friend, Mrs Moore, joins these two women for posterity, as they were joined by friendship in life. Although the text's addressee has not been identified, Elizabeth gives details of her role in her mother's last years:

> [She] would praise God that / when she cold not indure to Read herself, she had those yt did, Read/ to her ... and Chiefly / yt she had ye Love and Friendship / of so many Worthy and Religious Fr-/ eindes; and ... / yt now in her declining Time (as / she Called it) she had found your Ex-cellent self ^ Mrs Moor, A Freind, whom she did/ realy call the Friend, / as such // she has published her Estemation / of you: in her Will. (10–11)

The publication of Lady Lucy's friendship with Mrs Moore in her will is a textual counterpart of her publication of relationships with female kin on her monuments. In response to this commemorative gesture, Elizabeth publishes the friendship once again in her account of her mother's life.

The manuscript begins at the end of Lady Lucy's life with details of her good death: 'From the Time of her Sickness / to the Time of her Death, they yt /were Constantly aboute her ne-/ ver heard her desire Health, / but Ease' (1). Thus the text shares with Lady Lucy's monuments the sense that death is the crowning achievement of life. The manuscript hearkens back, as memorial inscriptions do, to the events of Lady Lucy's life, from her girlhood in the house of Francis Walsingham, to her role as 'A Phenex Mother' following her husband's death, 'as if [her children] / had had no other Parent', to the manner in which 'she di-/ rected and provided for [her sons], in / thaire severall Courses ... or how she Ma-/rryed her Daughters, and what she did for ym after Marriage' (8, 22–23). The manuscript reiterates the roles Lady Lucy assumes in her monumental self-portraits, congratulating her for being 'as / Excellent A Child ... as / Wife and Mother ... endeavour[ing] to procure/ A thankfull remembrance of her / Father, whose only Child she was, / to after Ages' (23–24). Finally, the text offers a valuable piece of evidence toward affirming her authorship of the Latin elegy on her daughter's tomb: 'She was most / Kind and Bountyfull to her Child-/ ren', Elizabeth writes, 'and perfectly Obayed by them, / According to A saying she would of-/ten use in Laten, to this purpose;/ So Long Old Age is to be Reverenc-/ed, as it holds its ones Right, and / to ye Last Exercises its Atherity / over its Own' (11).

Constance Lucy's monumental projects and her descendants' manuscript biographies underscore a perceived alignment of texts and monuments as commemorative forms which is characteristic of their period. Anne Clifford's monuments 'are expressions of the same motivation that drives her diary', her 'desire to reproduce her own authoritative presence'.[48] A similar perception underlies the antiquarian project of Ann Chitting's son, whose written record of the proximity of his mother's and Mary Barber's tombs and their inscriptions are all that remain of these monuments.[49] The transience of these commemorative forms was often noted: members of the London Society of Antiquaries, founded in 1600, were motivated to 'seek out and record epitaphs to ensure their preservation and distribution in print, a medium which would outlast monuments'.[50] If the fleeting flesh is preserved in and displaced by the durable material of the effigy,[51] the Lucy women counted on the complementarity of text and monument to preserve the fragile contents of each of these ephemeral forms.

IV

Alice Dudley's daughters followed her example in life and death. A mural tablet erected in the Beauchamps Chapel following Katherine Leveson's death (1673) recalls her matrilineal heritage by reminding the reader that her mother was 'created Duchess Dudley by King Charles I, in regard that her said husband leaving this Realm had the title of a Duke confer'd upon him by Ferdinand II, Emperor of Germany'.[52]

The tomb of Frances Kniveton, erected by her sister, Anne Holbourne, in the Dudley's London parish, recalls the duchess in similar terms: 'the said Honour & Title of Duchess Dudley, was by the Letters Patents of his late Majesty/ of Glorious memory King Charles [ye] 1st allowed ... and She died worthy of that Honour'.[53] The tomb alludes to the Duchess visually as well, since Frances's shrouded effigy (Figure 9) mirrors those of her mother and sister at Stoneleigh. Anne's will requests that her sister's tomb should be 'set up in St. Gyles church, as I have agreed with one Mr. Marshall, a stone cutter in Shoe Lane [and] pay him £120 for it', near the spot where Frances was buried; that Anne herself 'be buried ... as near the body of her sister Lady Frances Kniveton as can be'; and that 'mine own figure be added to hers in a winding sheet as my deare sister's is'.[54]

Anne's effigy was never added to the tomb. Her sister's shrouded form rests alone, eyes closed, awaiting the resurrection, as her mother's and sister's do. As Boreman writes, 'Death was no more to this *Illustrious Duchess* then a sleep. Her body after many Toils, Troubles, and Disquiets in this world shall sleep or rest for a while in ... it's Dormitory

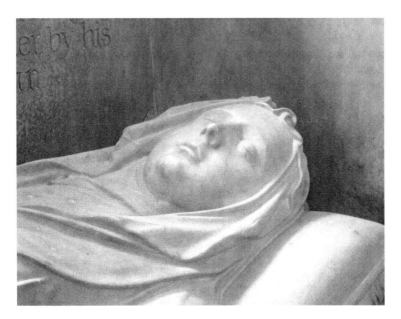

Figure 9   Edward or Joshua Marshall, Monument for Frances Kniveton (detail), St Giles-in-the-Fields, London (1663). Photo: Patricia Phillippy.

the Grave.'[55] The figures of the Dudley women sleeping calmly in their winding sheets recall Constance Whitney's awakening effigy and her grandmother's mingling of sorrow at her loss with hope for a reunion in the afterlife. The Dudley tombs give visual form to the metaphor of death as a protracted sleep – a metaphor interpreted in tomb sculpture as especially relevant to women, probably due to the period's frequent depiction of women who died in childbirth on tombs which represented the deathbed itself.[56] It may be, too, that the popularity of shrouded effigies – particularly in tombs built by women for women – reflects women's intimacy with the body in death: these images revisit in monumental form the female work of attending the dying and washing and winding the corpse. They place their female authors in immediate proximity to their female subjects at the moment of death, and imagine this intimacy as a feature of the afterlife.

The authors of the Dudley tombs, however, stop short of expressing their grief at their subjects' loss, or their hopes for resurrection: unlike Lady Lucy, they rely upon images instead of words to convey these sentiments. They share a visual, rather than textual, language that preserves the ties that bound them to each other throughout their lives. As the suite of monuments erected by the Dudley women celebrates the persistence and power of women's alliances before and after death, it manages, almost accidentally,[57] to evade its subjects' subordination to men's government and to the silencing force of their posthumous praise. Our attention to the quiet presence of these women licenses their awakening into the evolving narrative of early modern women's writing.

Notes

1. Robert Boreman, *A Mirrour of Christianity, and a Miracle of Charity* (London: E.C. for R. Royston, 1669), 2.
2. Philip Stubbes, *A Christal Glasse for Christian Women* (London: Richard Jhones, 1592).
3. See John Stowe, *Survey of London* (London: Nicholas Bourne, 1633), 881. The monument is not extant.
4. Married in 1595 to Sir Robert Dudley, Alice Leigh was abandoned by her husband in 1605 when his claim to legitimacy was denied and he left England permanently. See Simon Adams, 'Dudley, Sir Robert (1574–1649)', *Oxford Dictionary of National Biography* (Oxford University Press, September 2004; online edition, January 2008: http://www.oxforddnb.com/view/article/8161
5. Peter M. Sherlock, *Monuments and Memory in Early Modern England* (Aldershot: Ashgate, 2008), 12.
6. Stowe, *Survey*, 681. She was the second wife of John Talbot of Grafton (d. 1610), by whom she had no children. Her stepson, who survived her, was George Talbot, 9th Earl of Shrewsbury.

7. Nigel Llewellyn, *Funeral Monuments in Post-Reformation England* (Cambridge: Cambridge University Press, 2000), 7, estimates that 5,000 sculptural monuments were erected in England between 1530 and 1660; about 4,000 survive.

8. Walter Lewis Spiers, ed., *The Notebook and Account Book of Nicholas Stone* (Oxford: Walpole Society, 1919), 61.

9. Ibid., 61–62.

10. Llewellyn, *Funeral Monuments*, 279.

11. H. R. Mosse, *The Monumental Effigies of Sussex (1250–1650)* (Hove: Combridges, 1933), 91.

12. Llewellyn, *Funeral Monuments*, 151, explains that surviving widows often built separate tombs since their husbands were buried in family chapels or on dynastic lands, usually accompanied by previous wives.

13. See Jean Wilson, 'Patronage and Pietas: The Monuments of Lady Anne Clifford', *Transactions of the Cumberland and Westmorland Antiquarian and Archaeological Society* 97 (1997): 122–25, and Anne M. Myers, 'Construction Sites: The Architecture of Anne Clifford's Diaries', *ELH* 73 (2006): 591–92.

14. See Stowe, *Survey*, 784–86. Mary also wrote the epitaph for Richard Lusher's monument, near her own. Her ledger stone and another memorial, with Latin verses by her second husband, Thomas Knyvet, were rediscovered when the church was excavated in 1973. Knyvet apparently did not acquiesce to Mary's 'boone'.

15. Fathers, too, authored monuments for children, often commemorating them alongside wives who died in childbirth. See, for example, Stowe, *Survey*, 782, 789–90, 872.

16. Stowe, *Survey*, 809.

17. Philip B. Chatwin, 'The Later Monumental Effigies of the County of Warwick', *Transactions of the Birmingham Archaeological Society* 57 (1933), 146.

18. Katherine's father was buried nearby, but his tomb has not survived. See S. A. Jeavons, 'The Monumental Effigies of Staffordshire, Part III', *Transactions of the Birmingham Archaeological Society* 71 (1953), 21, 31. See also Peter Sherlock, 'Monuments, Reputation and Clerical Marriage in Reformation England: Bishop Barlow's Daughters', *Gender and History* 16.1 (2004): 57–82, on Frances Matthew's monument for her mother.

19. Quoted in George C. Williamson, *Lady Anne Clifford* (Kendal: Titus Wilson and Son, 1922), 408.

20. Ibid., 389.

21. Mosse, *Monumental Effigies*, 161.

22. Transcribed from the monument. See Adam White, *Biographical Dictionary of London Tomb Sculptors, c. 1560–1660*, Walpole Society 61 (London: W. S. Maney & Son, 1999), 99, for attribution.

23. Six of Elizabeth I's maids of honor were commemorated in Westminster Abbey and the adjacent St Margaret's, which established a compelling precedent for later memorials for servants.

24. Chatwin 'Later Monumental Effigies', 133–34.

25. Alan Bray, *The Friend* (Chicago: University of Chicago Press, 2003), 223–24.

26. Quoted in Williamson, *Lady Anne*, 70. Anne's diary recalls a night when, 'my Cousin Frances got the Key of my Chamber & lay with me which was the first time I loved her so well'. See D. J. H. Clifford, ed., *The Diaries of Lady Anne Clifford* (Stroud: Alan Sutton, 1992), 25. Both tombs have been seen as

commemorating lesbian relationships. See Bray, *The Friend*, 223–24, on Barber; Jonathan Goldberg, *Desiring Women's Writing: Renaissance Examples* (Palo Alto: Stanford University Press, 1997), 200 n. 27, on Bourchier; and Paul Salzman, *Reading Early Modern Women's Writing* (Oxford: Oxford University Press, 2008), 7–8, for an opposing view. Valerie Traub, *The Renaissance of Lesbianism in Early Modern England* (Cambridge: Cambridge University Press, 2002), 77–79, sees the Westminster Abbey tombs of Katherine Bovey (d. 1727) and Mary Kendall (d. 1710) as reflecting lesbian alliances.

27. Elizabeth Richardson, *A Ladies Legacie to her Daughters* (London: Thomas Harper, 1645). On Richardson's monuments, see Stephen Porter, 'Francis Beaumont's Monument in Charterhouse Chapel and Elizabeth Baroness Cramond as Patroness of Memorials in Early Stuart London', *Transactions of the London and Middlesex Archaeological Society*, 54 (2003): 111–20.

28. See John Stowe, *Survey of the Cities of London and Westminster*, ed. John Strype (London: A. Churchill et al., 1720), I: 3: 251, and Porter, 'Francis Beaumont', 116.

29. See John Nichols, *History and Antiquities of the County of Leicester* (London: J. Nichols, 1795–1815), II: 859.

30. See C. H. Cooper, 'Inventory of the Plate sent to King Charles I by Queens' College Cambridge', in *Antiquarian Communications* (MacMillan, 1859), 246–47 n. 6.

31. See Stowe, *Survey*, 792. The monument has not survived.

32. See Sherlock, *Monuments and Memory*, 197–230, for an excellent discussion.

33. Martin Day (?), *Peplum Modestiae, The Vaile of Modesty* (London: John Hodgetts, 1621), A2v.

34. George Adlard, *Amye Robsart and the Earl of Leycester* (London: John Russell Smith, 1870), 332–33.

35. Boreman, *Mirrour*, A2–A3.

36. Ibid., 26. The tomb was erected around 1650. See White, *Biographical Dictionary*, 101, 105, for attribution.

37. See Chatwin, 'Later Monumental Effigies', 151–52.

38. TNA SP Suppl. 45/23, f.137.

39. Mary E. Hazard, *Elizabethan Silent Language* (Lincoln: University of Nebraska Press, 2000), 133.

40. Chatwin, 'Later Monumental Effigies', 112–13. See also William Dugdale, *Antiquities of Warwickshire* (London: John Osborne and Thomas Longman, 1730), I: 261, and White, *Biographical Dictionary*, 8, for attribution.

41. Llewellyn, *Funeral Monuments*, 119.

42. *Calendar of State Papers, Domestic, of the Reign of James I* (London: Longman's, 1859), 392.

43. Stowe, *Survey*, 888. The monument has not survived.

44. Ibid., 779.

45. Judith W. Hurtig, 'Seventeenth-Century Shroud Tombs: Classical Revival and Anglican Context', *Art Bulletin* 64 (1982): 217–28.

46. See Stowe, *Survey*, ed. Strype, I: 86.

47. Folger MS V.a. 166, 'Biographies of Constance, Lady Lucy and her daughter-in-law, Elizabeth Lucy'. Subsequent references are cited parenthetically in the text. Another copy, dated 1637, is in the Warwickshire Country Record Office, L6/1246.

48. Myers, 'Construction', 592.
49. Bray, *The Friend*, 232.
50. Sherlock, *Monuments and Memory*, 203. See also Myers, 'Construction', 594.
51. Llewellyn, *Funeral Monuments*, argues post-Reformation monuments ensured social continuity by providing substitutes for bodies lost in death. Sherlock, *Monuments and Memory*, 41–70, greatly refines this thesis.
52. Adlard, *Amye Robsart*, 332–33.
53. TNA PROB 11/312/108, transcribed in Joseph Jackson Howard, *Miscellanea Genealogica et Heraldica* (Cambridge, MA: Harvard University Press, 1904), 131–32.
54. Chatwin, 'Later Monumental Effigies', 150–52.
55. Boreman, *Mirrour*, 15–16.
56. Judith Hurtig, 'Death in Childbirth: Seventeenth Century English Tombs and their Place in Contemporary Thought', *Art Bulletin* 65 (1983): 603–15.
57. This evasion is partially enabled by the duchess's abandonment, and by the fact that three of her daughters survived their husbands.

Part III

New Perspectives on Literary Genres

8
'More lively, parfett, lasting, and more true': Mary Wroth's Indefensible Apologies for Poesy

Clare R. Kinney

The publication of *The Countess of Montgomery's Urania* in 1621 introduced readers not only to the first romance written by an Englishwoman but also, in the appended *Pamphilia to Amphilanthus*, to the first female-authored sonnet sequence. Given the novelty of Mary Wroth's literary productions, the volume is also remarkable for what it does *not* offer: no prefatory material defends its author's potentially transgressive venture into print or explains her choice to write in such emphatically secular and erotic genres. The absence of any paratexts – the volume contains no epistles to particular readers or to the readers in general, no lyric panegyrics written by friends of the author – might suggest that Wroth had no hand in its publication. Indeed, Wroth herself would claim, in a letter written to the Duke of Buckingham ostensibly seeking his aid to suppress the edition and gather in its copies, that she had never desired it to be published.[1] But as Barbara Lewalski has argued, there is a distinctly disingenuous air about that letter (which also reveals that Wroth had sent Buckingham a copy of the work) and a fair amount of evidence that she may have supervised the *Urania's* printing. Lewalski notes that the title page of the graceful folio not only prominently proclaims the author's relationship to her literary Sidney relatives but also presents a superbly detailed engraving accurately illustrating an important episode in the first book of the romance; she also points out that there is no surviving evidence that the edition was, in fact, officially suppressed.[2]

Whatever Wroth's actual intentions, we are left with the material fact of a female-authored text that seems to be strikingly unapologetic about its own fiction-making. *Within* the idiosyncratic literary hybrid created by Wroth's splicing together of romance and sonnet sequence, however, matters are rather different. The work contains some suggestive discussions of poetic practice – with an emphasis upon the particularly

155

troubled relationship between artful mimesis and the representation of authentic feeling in women's writing – which are all the more striking because they share so little common ground with the various self-authorizing strategies one finds in the work of earlier women writers. My intention here is to discuss the articulation of Wroth's singular poetics in the composite text of 1621 in the light of both the defensive moves of her female predecessors and the more canonical apologetics of her uncle Philip Sidney. Wroth's published work does not, to be sure, offer her final word on the matter, and I shall offer a coda addressing the unpublished manuscript continuation of the *Urania*. *Urania* II offers a striking assault on transgressive female authorship that suggests Wroth's inability to leave behind her anxieties about the 'indefensibility' of her art.

When the women writers who circulated their work in the decades before the publication of the *Urania* address their own practice, they tend to erase or obfuscate their identity as artists. Isabella Whitney's writings encompass both a form of 'translation' (she versifies the sententious writings of Hugh Plat) and original poetry, but in so far as she addresses her own role as writer, she emphasizes her didactic agenda; her putative identity as a poet, an imaginative maker, is rendered almost invisible. Her *Copy of a Letter* to a faithless lover (1567) is written as 'an Admonition to al yong Gentilwomen and to all other Mayds in general to beware of mennes flattery'.[3] In the prefatory epistle to her *Nosegay* of Plat's aphorisms (1573) she does insist that 'though [the rhetorical 'flowers' it contains] be of an others growing', they are 'of my owne gathering and makeing', but she will later inform her readers that they are not to expect aesthetic beguilement from her verses: '... for thy health, not for thy eye / did I this Posye frame'.[4] In one of the verse epistles directed to members of her family that follow the versified *sententiae*, she presents her self, as much as any of her poems, as a model for her sisters in domestic service: 'Henceefoorth my lyfe as well as Pen / shall your examples frame'; in another poem, directed to her sister A.B., she represents her writing as a kind of substitute for more practical and conventional duties: 'til som household cares me tye / My bookes and Pen I will apply'.[5] One has the impression throughout of a kind of artless *copia*.

A woman writer may also deflect attention from her own act of 'making' (or, more troublingly, feigning) by insisting, as Margaret Tyler does in the prefatory epistle to her translation of the Spanish romance *A mirrour of princely deedes and knighthood* (1578), that she is simply obeying her superiors and that her project was 'put upon me by others' (145).[6]

Tyler plays down the work's literary and imaginative craft – 'The invention, disposition, trimming ... is wholy an other mans' (145) – and insists that literary translation itself is 'a matter of more heede then of deep invention or exquisite learning' (145). She finesses the issue of the dubious edification offered by chivalric romance by arguing that if men are able to write such fictions and present them to women readers, then 'it is all one for a woman to pen a story, as for a man to addresse his story to a woman' (145–46), even as she offers her translation to the male reader in the hope that its tales of noble deeds may encourage him to 'hazard [his] person' for ruler or country (145).

A rather different version of Tyler's displacement of agency is evident in the original poetry of Mary Sidney Herbert, Countess of Pembroke. Kim Walker observes that in her dedicatory poems to the 1599 Tixall manuscript of the co-authored translation of the Psalms completed after Philip Sidney's death (one addressed to Elizabeth I, the other to her late brother), Pembroke locates the project's origins outside herself: 'in the queen, in God, in Philip Sidney'.[7] In 'Even now that Care', imagining the translation as a 'liverie robe' (34) presented to the queen and woven jointly by the siblings, Pembroke emphasizes that this is a rendering of another, divinely inspired author's work and downplays the formal virtuosity of the translators' multifarious experiments in prosody: 'the stuffe not ours, our worke no curious thing' (28). Given that Elizabeth is herself the 'the shrine' where 'Wit, where Art, where all that is divine' resides (45; 47), the gift is otiose: 'what bring wee but thine owne?' (41). Meditating upon the volume rather differently in her elegy to Philip, 'To The Angell spirit', the Countess declares she has merely 'peec't' (24) – eked out, roughly completed – what was by 'thy Matchlesse Muse begunne' (23); it is at once a memorial tribute to the lost brother, a partial witness to his own 'rare workes' (68) and a testimony of 'simple love / not Art nor skill which abler wits doe prove' (82–83).

Mary Sidney presents herself as a devoted handmaid to her queen, her brother, and her God. In the poems dedicated to various influential women that preface the largely devotional poetry of *Salve Deus Rex Judaeorum* (1611), Aemilia Lanyer focuses upon her identity as an artless vessel moved by various inspiring forces rather than an autonomous artist.[8] On the one hand, God's 'powre hath given me powre to write' ('To the Ladie Katherine Countesse of Suffolk' [13]) and her text is '[b]lest by our Saviours merits, not my skil' ('To the Ladie Anne, Countesse of Dorcet' [9]); on the other, she is uplifted by the virtues of her imaginary court of female patronesses, wishing, for example, that in the light of Queen Anne's beneficence 'these rude unpollisht lines of mine, / Graced by you, may seeme the more divine' ('To the Queenes most Excellent Majestie' [35–36]). She explicitly refuses to 'compare with any man' and rejects scholarly 'Art' (148–49); instead, she asks a motherly Nature to 'grace my barren Muse / And in a Woman all defects excuse' (155–56). Finally, in the prose epistle to the 'Vertuous Reader' that concludes the prefatory material, Lanyer calls upon 'Good Christians and honourable minded men' to 'increase the least sparke of virtue' they may find in her work (55; 59–60). Inspired by God, supported by Nature, moved by the examples of idealized earthly women and relying on her readers to 'cherish' and 'nourish' any incipient skill she may possess, Lanyer never quite presents herself as an artist in her own right.

Turning to the *Urania* and its appended sonnet sequence after reading among Wroth's predecessors, one discovers that Wroth allows a woman poet – her romance heroine Pamphilia, who also 'shadows' Wroth in the manner of Sidney's Astrophil – to address her literary practice rather differently.[9] If other early modern women writers authorize their writing by insisting (however artfully) upon its artlessness, by deferring to higher powers, or by privileging didactic content above the aesthetic framing of that content, Wroth's unprecedented ventures into the emphatically secular territory of erotic fiction and lyric interrogate, by contrast, the very adequacy of *conscious* artistry to the representation of authentic feeling. In *Pamphilia to Amphilanthus*, the speaker rarely meditates upon her own poetic practice and in the sonnet which perhaps offers the most sustained consideration of her art in relation to that of others, she cannot bring herself to offer a defense of poesy. Robbed of her 'chiefest joy', all too 'us'd to sorrow' (P45 2, 4), she declares:

> Nor can I as those pleasant witts enjoy
>> My owne fram'd words, which I account the dross
>> Of purer thoughts, or recken them as moss
>> While they (witt sick) them selves to breath imploy,
> Alas, think I, your plenty shewes your want,
>> For wher most feeling is, words are more scant … (P45:5–10)

In an earlier poem she has already proposed that 'griefe is nott cur'd by art' (P9:4). Here she suggests that the framing of sorrow in poetry too easily produces either dross or moss: either the impure remainder of something nobler and of a higher temper or a mere overgrowth of something more substantial. 'Pleasant witts' may relish the overproduction of verse as a courtly pastime, but for Pamphilia, the more abundant the words, the less authentic the feeling. 'Your plenty shewes your want': the dismissal echoes Ovid's Narcissus who laments, as he contemplates his own reflection, 'inopem me copia fecit' – my plenty makes me poor.[10] Pamphilia rejects solipsistic and empty *copia*.

To be sure, her attempt to distinguish herself from these prolific writers is a little disingenuous: after all, this is only the 45th lyric in a sequence of 103 poems. Her oblique self-positioning, if only through critique, among a community of *artists* (she is, after all 'framing' poetry; consciously putting feeling into poetic measure) produces a variation on two very familiar Petrarchan *topoi*: the inadequacy of art to the task at hand and the writer's attempt to distinguish his or her efforts from the inferior artifice of other versifiers. We see a more aggressive version of this thematic in her uncle's *Astrophil and Stella* 6, in which Astrophil rapidly dismisses Petrarchism, Ovidian love poetry, and pastoral exercises in order to announce that his noblest and most authentic words are offered 'When trembling voice brings forth, that I do Stella love'.[11] The ambiguous syntax of Wroth's speaker in fact permits us an alternative reading in which it is the poet's own words, as opposed to those of the busy versifiers, which are to be dismissed as 'wit sick'. Astrophil, by contrast, imperially asserts that he can 'map' his 'state' in those putatively 'trembling' (but perfectly pitched) alexandrines (6:13) – and Astrophil has also, in the very first sonnet of his sequence, and even as he canvasses the shortcomings of his own art, represented his Muse's energetic and authorizing intervention. '"Fool," said my muse to me; "look in thy heart and write"' (1:14). The Muse's command licenses a heartfelt art: demands, at the very outset of the project, that the poet write and write and write.[12]

Pamphilia's Muse, by contrast, makes her first appearance at the opposite end of her sequence, invoked in its last lyric only to be commanded to silence: 'My Muse, now hapy, lay thy self to rest' (P103:1). But if Wroth's sequence does not offer the kind of extended meditations on the art of poesy that recur throughout *Astrophil and Stella* – meditations in which Astrophil ultimately has rather more to say about the tricky business of figuring forth passion *persuasively* than about the tensions between art and true feeling – its creator has not been entirely silent on the matter. Wroth's sequence is self-protectively presented as the literary production of a fictional character in the romance which precedes it.[13] Her readers would encounter *Pamphilia to Amphilanthus* after having spent a very long time in an imaginative universe full of people writing poems, a universe in which the art of poetry is on occasion an object for discussion. The *Urania* preaddresses what seems to be sidestepped in *Pamphilia to Amphilanthus*: both the uneasy situation of the woman artist and the vexed relationship between conscious artistry and the representation of authentic feeling. Rereading *Pamphilia to Amphilanthus* by way of the 1621 romance, it is possible, moreover, to identify an alternative poetics lurking in the sequence, a poetics that is both bolder and more 'indefensible'.

In an uneasy confrontation in Book I of the *Urania* between Pamphilia and Antissia, both of whom love the philandering Amphilanthus, Antissia hears Pamphilia's love complaints and spies a poem she has carved into the bark of an ash tree. Pamphilia will not at first admit that she loves, but jealous Antissia, fearful that Pamphilia is her rival for Amphilanthus's affections, declares that '"your owne hand in yonder faire Ash will witnes against you"' – to which Pamphilia evasively answers, '"Not so … for many Poets write as well by imitation as by sence of passion; therefore this is no proofe against me."'[14] Pamphilia invokes the notion that the writing of love poetry may simply be an act of *imitatio*, an intellectual exercise, and Maureen Quilligan argues that her words may speak to 'different literary risks for the different genders in Petrarchan poetry … a woman disguises her tabooed desire as conventional artistry, while a man masquerades verbal mastery as petitioning passion'.[15] Pamphilia never names her lover in her poems and the whole issue of whether their discourse is in any way mimetic continues to be an object of speculation for other characters in the romance.

Much later in the *Urania*, Pamphilia undertakes a sea journey in the company of the princess Orilena, and both women pass the time by writing love poetry. Orilena's subject is her beloved and absent husband, but Pamphilia is still concealing her love for Amphilanthus; the object of her passion remains unnamed. We are told that

> Pamphilia … so sister-like condoled with [Orilena], as she exceld her in passion, which   made some eroniously say, that counterfeting was more excellent then true suffering, because judgment governs where passions are free, when fully possest they master beyond, and so expresse not so well, as if ruld with discretion; for an Actor knowes when to speake, when to sigh, when to end: a true feeler is as wrapped in distempers, and only can know how to beare. (364)

Wroth here wrestles with the paradox to which Astrophil surrenders when he instructs Stella to read the representations of his woes as if they were solely the product of art: 'I am not I, pity the tale of me' (45:13). The critics who insist that Pamphilia's verses are too well made to reflect 'true suffering' speak 'eroniously'; Wroth wants to distinguish Pamphilia's poems (and by extension, of course, her own) from merely persuasive acts of feigning. Even as she testifies to the condition of the 'true feeler' who 'only can know how to beare', she wishes to advance the very special case of Pamphilia's poetry, which unites art with felt experience, and in which lyric agency is not just a matter of plausibly staging the self, not just a case of 'acting naturally'. Pamphilia the poet may elsewhere deplore the inadequacy of 'fram'd words' to deep feeling; the poet who creates Pamphilia insists on a poetics of presence.

The narrative action of the *Urania* has in fact already preempted the criticisms Wroth here addresses in an episode which foregrounds the mimetic capacity of Pamphilia's poems. Amphilanthus has persuaded Pamphilia to show him her poems, and after rather patronizingly telling her that they are the best he has seen '"made by woman"', he continues, '"But one thing ... I must find fault with, that you counterfeit loving so well, as if you were a lover, and as we are, yet you are free; pitie it is you suffer not, that can faigne so well"' (320). Amphilanthus is being disingenuous; he wants to provoke an admission of love. He is not interested in the poems as literary artifacts, but as documentary records. Pamphilia quietly concedes, '"my Lord, you are deceived in this for I doe love"'; he at once embraces her, and 'she chid him not, nor did so much as frowne, which shewed she was betrayd' (320). One might emphasize that word 'betrayd': the true feeler who only knows how to bear has ended up bearing – carrying – to Amphilanthus the words that also lay bare her feelings. One might also contrast this unmasking with the testimony of the *Pamphilia to Amphilanthus* sequence (if we embrace the fiction's implied fiction that its lyric appendix represents the poems that Amphilanthus has scanned). Those poems are in fact remarkably hermetic in their 'aporetic ambiguity of reference'[16] – and in the preceding romance, even as she admits that she is a lover, Pamphilia does not say 'I love *you*'. The narrative framing of the fram'd words, however, permits Amphilanthus to constitute himself as the object of Pamphilia's careful utterances; it also insists that their copia *signifies*. For once, Pamphilia's plenty has not made her poor.

This separation of Pamphilia's art from any notion of mere imitation, counterfeiting, or feigning is particularly interesting in light of a later episode in the *Urania*. Toward the end of the romance, we find the Dukes of Brunswick and Wertenberg enjoying the hospitality of a noble family. The young daughter of the house falls in love with

Brunswick; after a brief dalliance the Duke goes on his way, present-ing his lady, as a parting gift, with a manuscript copy of an *aubade*. He offers the poem to her as his own composition, but the narrator informs us it was in fact written at a different time by the *other* Duke: 'great pitty is was not his owne worke, but as it was, it was liker a Lovers present, counterfeite as his vowes, and protestations, yet true beguilers of welbeleeving women' (606). Wroth suggests that both the protesta-tions of the lover and his poetic tributes are equally (and oxymoroni-cally) 'true beguilers'; by contrast, the only readers who will be beguiled by Pamphilia's poems are those who will not concede that they might speak the truth.

The Duke's borrowed gift evokes a world like Wroth's own, where a still thriving manuscript culture produced poem-commodities that were not necessarily closed texts fixing unique and individualized feelings or the private property of their supposed addressees, but were eminently recyclable. An encomium of an ostensibly peerless woman might thus be pragmatically borrowed to praise another as lyrics circu-lated in multiple contexts.[17] But the women poets of the *Urania* would risk accusations of immodesty if they applied their poetry to the task of overt courtship, and even when their poems are shared with others to perform an *instrumental* function, it is in contexts rather different from that of the Brunswick episode. It is true that the romance at times depicts women somewhat incontinently putting angry poetry into cir-culation (as when a lady recites a quasi-Ovidian complaint against her false lover before mixed company [492–95]);[18] such a gesture becomes more loaded, however, when it is carried out obliquely by Pamphilia. Wroth's heroine, made wretched by Amphilanthus's infidelity, tells her attendant Dorolina the sad tale of Lindamira which, as Josephine Roberts notes, closely 'shadows' incidents from both Wroth's and Pamphilia's own histories.[19] She ends by rehearsing Lindamira's own 'complaint' which, according to Pamphilia, '"because I lik'd it, or rather found her estate so neere agree with mine, I put into Sonnets"' (502). It is not entirely clear whether Lindamira's 'complaint' is sup-posed to have been a verse complaint, now reframed as a miniature seven-part sonnet sequence by Pamphilia, but it is clear that it is a fac-tual fiction deployed for Pamphilia's own purposes: when Pamphilia, speaking of Lindamira's faithless beloved, declares '"I will with the story conclude my rage against him"' (502) the 'him' might as eas-ily be Amphilanthus – or for that matter, Wroth's own philandering lover, William Herbert.[20] Pamphilia's feigning or counterfeiting of Lindamira's distress sets in circulation the history of a true beguiler that its hearer, Dorolina (not coincidentally, perhaps, the author of the Ovidian complaint mentioned previously), perceives to be 'more exactly related than a fixion' (505).

At moments like these the *Urania* both interrogates and exploits the act of 'counterfeiting', both puts it in suspicion *and* deploys a poetic that can copiously reorder the dross and moss of strong feeling. To arrive at the *Pamphilia to Amphilanthus* sonnet sequence after perusing the romance can feel like a retrenchment for the reader who has been confronted not only with lyrics that can be so visibly instrumental within a very fully fleshed-out narrative context but also with a narrative that can speak so acerbically to the merely cynical recycling of unfelt woe. That retrenchment is indeed made quite visible within the sonnet with which I started, for, unlike Sidney's urbane Astrophil, Wroth's speaker backtracks before her poem is done:

> Alas, think I, your plenty shewes your want,
> For wher most feeling is, words are more scant,
> Yett pardon mee, Live, and your pleasure take,
>
> Grudg nott,, if I neglected, envy show
> 'T'is nott to you that I dislike doe owe
> Butt crost my self, wish some like mee to make. (45:9–14)

Pamphilia apologizes: in her abjection she has been unfairly venting her own frustration upon other poets. They are to continue with business as usual. But this is not quite the end of the matter: elsewhere in her sonnet sequence, Pamphilia offers a less skeptical account of what one's 'own fram'd words' might actually empower one to do, proffering an alternative *modus operandi* which attempts to transcend the anti-aesthetic insistence that 'wher most feeling is, words are more scant'.

In the most formally ambitious sub-sequence of *Pamphilia to Amphilanthus*, the 'Crowne of Sonetts dedicated to Love' (P77–P90), Pamphilia asks 'In this strang labourinth how shall I turne?' and then, following the 'thread' of a higher and more idealizing love (P77:1, 14), proceeds to imagine how one might 'turn' – or trope – quite differently. Her *corona* celebrates a noble passion that

> ... doth inrich the witts, and make you see
> That in your self, which you knew nott before,
> Forcing you to admire such guifts showld bee
> Hid from your knowledg, yett in you the store. (P82:9–12)

No longer 'witt-sick', the poet's words may ultimately transcend the 'constant art' (P3:8) that testifies to constant abjection:

> Love will a painter make you, such, as you
>   Shall able bee to drawe your only deere
>   More lively, parfett, lasting, and more true
>   Then rarest woorkman, and to you more neere (P83:9–12)

On the surface, the words testify to a kind of neo-Platonic power surge: the Heavenly Cupid celebrated in the *corona* will allow the poet to outdo the finest craftsman in making a true picture of the one she loves. But the briefly suspended syntax before 'more true' is enjambed with 'Then rarest woorkman', hinting at an alternative prospect. The artist may not only represent the beloved in a more lifelike way, but also perfect him, make him more true to the speaker, and more lasting in his affections. If one recalls the romance's portrayal of the less than heavenly Amphilanthus, the Platonic Idea collapses into a testimony to art's beguiling power to refashion lived experience – not, as in Sidney's *Defence of Poesy*, to offer elevated, didactic and moving exemplars, but rather to energize a kind of wish fulfillment.[21] In the hypothetical future imagined by the crown of sonnets, love poetry would no longer be the discourse where excellent 'feigning' testifies to true suffering; it would be the discourse where fantasy might trump reality.

Pamphilia cannot sustain this vision. The last sonnet of the *corona* re-imprisons its maker in her 'strang labourinth' (P90) of jealous frustration. Wroth herself will never be able to unite Pamphilia conclusively with Amphilanthus, either in the printed portion of the *Urania* or in its manuscript continuation. One might compare the *corona*'s shattered vision with a climactic moment in *Astrophil and Stella*, the 8th Song's third-person narration of an encounter in a pleasant grove between Astrophil and Stella. Astrophil wants to seize the hour, but Stella, while passionately reconfirming her love for him, invokes the weight of social and cultural imperatives: 'Tyrant honour thus doth use thee; / Stella's self might not refuse thee' (l.95). The poet cannot bring Stella any 'more neere' to Astrophil and this impasse derails Astrophil's creator's lyric project: '… therewith my song is broken' (l. 104). The 'tale of me' in fact turns out to be the same old story: the sequence's final sonnet recycles the 'living deaths, dear wounds, fair storms, and freezing fires' Astrophil so roundly rejected in Sonnet 6 in its closing declaration to Stella that 'in my woes for thee thou art my joy, / And in my joys for thee my only annoy' (108:13–14). As Ronald Levao suggests, it is as if Sonnet 108 shows Astrophil looking in his heart and finding only the absolutely conventional image of the Petrarchan lover caught in 'an inescapable cycle of joy and despair'.[22]

Wroth's Pamphilia reaches a different impasse in her own concluding sonnet:

> My muse now hapy, lay thy self to rest,
> Sleepe in the quiett of a faithfull love,
> Write you noe more, butt lett thes phant'sies move
> Some other harts, wake nott to new unrest. (P103:1–4)

As so often, Pamphilia's ambiguous syntax bears a double interpretation. On the one hand, the muse is to silence herself in quiet recognition of the speaker's own constancy, a constancy that requires no more words: 'what's past showes you can love, / Now let your constancy your honor prove' (P103:13–14). Further writing is indefensible, the constant art is merely otiose, just dross and moss compared to the lived testimony of the constant heart. But the line might also be read as 'Sleep in the quiet knowledge of your beloved's faithfulness'. This is of course a much more problematic assertion, already put in question for the reader of the hybrid text of 1621 by the inconclusive, supplementary word that undercuts the reunion between Pamphilia and Amphilanthus celebrated at the end of the prose romance, a teasing, dangling 'And ...' (661). Is the speaker consoling herself with the powers promised by the *corona*'s flight of fancy, drawing her only dear as if he were indeed truer and closer to hand than in reality? If this is indeed the case, she has (albeit fleetingly and obscurely) embraced a very different poetic as she takes her leave. If she is now enacting Touchstone's suggestion that the truest poetry is the most feigning, her concomitant dismissal of her Muse may be complicated by her willingness to let '*these* phant'sies move / Some other hearts'.[23] Her Muse may speak no more, but Pamphilia's fantasies, Wroth's fantasies, may energize those other hearts to re-weave the thread of love. The poet-lover counterfeits a retreat; in reality she is passing on the flame of fancy.

The final sonnet of *Pamphilia to Amphilanthus* is not, however, Wroth's last word on the uses of the poetic imagination, and in the manuscript continuation of the *Urania* she comes near to delegitimizing female authorship and to confirming Pamphilia's skepticism about her own art. In *Urania* II, Antissia, whose unrestrained and publicly indecorous passion for Amphilanthus is presented as a foil to Pamphilia's private pain in the published portion of the romance, emerges as a grotesque exemplar of an overreaching female poet. The extravagant artifice of Antissia's speech and writings are mocked by Pamphilia's brother Rosindy, who also declares roundly that all poetry '"att the best is butt a frency"' before complicating his own pronouncement:

> 'And yet in Lovers itt is a most commendable and fine qualitie, bee-ing a way most excellent to express their pretious thoughts in a rare and covert way (butt they are meere Poetts that I spake of when I condemned poetry), this way I adore it. Butt my Aunts raging, raving ... language is most aparantly ... flatt madness. Such Jestures and such brutish demeanor, fittinger for a man in woeman's clothing acting a sibilla ... '[24]

Rosindy seeks to distinguish between the poet-lovers whose art properly gives voice to 'pretious' feeling and Antissia's practice of unrestrained 'phantisy' (33). His reference to 'meere Poets' evokes the wordsmiths whose verbal 'dross' and 'moss' Pamphilia's own poetry condemns, but his final indictment of Antissia also introduces the notion of gendered transgression: he has previously criticized her 'stage-like-acting taulke' (35) and he now imagines her impersonating a male actor impersonating a sibyl as she usurps the vatic voice. It is as if he not only voices a suspicion of poetry's capacity for non-mimetic world-building ('phantisy') but also deplores an act of spectacular transvestitism that renders the woman who aspires to vatic power the imitator of a male imitator of a crazed oracle. Wroth's own anxieties about the mixed reception of the 1621 *Urania* may inform this passage: Rosindy's words (and Antissia's own husband's criticism of 'poetical furies ... that in raving rime bury truth of modestie' [51]) recall Sir Edward Denny's description of Wroth as 'Hermophradite in show, in deed a monster', a woman whose 'witt runns madd', a woman who has made herself 'a lying wonder'.[25] Antissia may function in both parts of the *Urania*, as Mary Ellen Lamb has argued, as a 'kind of lightning rod' to preempt and absorb criticisms of its female author, but I would suggest, furthermore, that the opprobrium she arouses in the continu-ation also contaminates Wroth's exemplary female poet and alter-ego, Pamphilia.[26]

Antissia is eventually chastened and 'cured' of her versifying on the isle of Delos by the enchantress Melissea – but that same chastening seems to extend to Pamphilia herself: *Urania* II contains not one poem written by its heroine. We do, however, read a tellingly censored scene of poetry-making. Very shortly after Pamphilia has wedded the King of Tartaria, thus confirming a separation from Amphilanthus already set in motion by his marriage to another woman, she traverses the same 'secrett waulkes' whose trees she decorated with her poems in the published portion of the romance. Here she breaks down and acts with unprecedented extravagance: 'she wept, she cride, nay she allmost roared out her complaints'. Eventually she recovers enough to 'wring her conseites ... into some od and unusuall (as her fortunes were turned) sort of verce: a thing she had nott in a pretty space dunn ... They were extreame sad and dolefull, and sertainly such as would have moved too farr in Amphilanthus, had hee then seene them' (279). But neither Amphilanthus nor the reader sees the verses. Wroth's text does not quote them – and indeed the narrator's remark that they might have 'moved' Amphilanthus *too* greatly hints that there is something excessive about their unrecorded content. The manuscript continuation does not reaffirm Pamphilia's ability to unite art and felt experience but rather speaks to a suspicion of poetic excess, as if even *her* creations may partake too much of the dangers identified by the contrite Antissia, when she eventually declares herself to have been the promulgator of dangerous 'raptures and fixions' (251).

Did Pamphilia's untranscribed verses testify to her desire to 'drawe [her] only deere' into a universe where he was 'more neere', unestranged by the marriages both lovers have entered into? If so, Wroth chooses to silence her own Muse rather than disclose them. Pamphilia's poetry has, it seems, become truly indefensible. At the same time, Wroth's heroine seems, in *Urania* II, to participate in – or to have regressed to – the courtly world of 'counterfeiting' that was viewed with such suspicion in the 1621 *Urania*. On the single occasion Pamphilia gives public voice to a lyric, it is a sung performance of one of Amphilanthus's poems, 'Had I but loved at such a rate' – a poem that is not of Wroth's own making but was written by her own lover, William Herbert.[27] We are told that the poem was composed when Amphilanthus 'made a shew of love to Antissia' and was originally presented to her 'although ment to a higher beauty' (30). But the rather Donneian song is far from complimentary: its speaker disingenuously offers a lady his regrets for unfairly overwhelming her with his wholehearted love since it was 'more, / Then againe thou cowldst restore, / And woeman bee' (31). He misogynistically excuses her failure to return his affection adequately by claiming she wouldn't have been a 'real woman' if she could love

at his own 'rate'. Amphilanthus sees no irony in Pamphilia's performance of his verses, pronouncing them 'delicately sung' and reading
her courtly recycling of his wit as a compliment to the maker. But for
all his complacency, the poem testifies to a series of duplicities: it was
originally presented to a woman for whom it was not 'meant'; it was
actually meant as a gift to a preternaturally constant woman – but
nevertheless doubts its addressee's capacity to love constantly; it masks
as the work of Amphilanthus within the larger fiction while reproduc-
ing what may have been a less than felicitous offering to Wroth herself.
Urania II's oddly palinodic narrative has as thoroughly evacuated the
1621 *Urania*'s dream of a poetics of presence as it has undone *Pamphilia
to Amphilanthus*'s fantasy that poetry might reorder (and improve) lived
experience: the unpublished continuation suggests, after all, the anti-
aesthetic conclusion that 'wher most feeling is' words are – and should
be – 'more scant'.[28]

Notes

1. Wroth's letter to Buckingham is reprinted in *The Poems of Lady Mary Wroth*,
    ed. Josephine A. Roberts (Baton Rouge: Louisiana State University Press,
    1983), 236. Rosalind Smith offers an interesting complication of received
    opinion about Wroth's putatively 'defensive' agendas in the letter in 'Lady
    Mary Wroth's *Pamphilia to Amphilanthus*: The Politics of Withdrawal', *ELR*
    30 (2000): 408–31; 407–12.
2. Barbara K. Lewalski, *Writing Women in Jacobean England* (Cambridge, MA:
    Harvard University Press, 1993), 264.
3. Isabella Whitney, *The Copy of a Letter, lately written in meeter, by a Yonge
    Gentilwoman: to her unconstant Lover* (London, 1567), A1r.
4. Isabella Whitney, *A Sweet Nosgay, or pleasant posye: contayning a hundred and
    ten phylosophicall flowers* (London, 1573), A4v; A7r.
5. Ibid., D1r; D2r.
6. Tyler's preface is reprinted in Betty Travitsky, ed., *The Paradise of Women:
    Writings by Englishwomen of the Renaissance* (New York: Columbia University
    Press, 1989), 144–46. Further citations are given parenthetically in the
    text.
7. Kim Walker, *Women Writers of the English Renaissance* (New York: Twayne,
    1996), p. 76. For the two poems, hereafter cited parenthetically, see *The
    Collected Works of Mary Sidney Herbert, Countess of Pembroke*, vol. 1, ed.
    Margaret P. Hannay, Noel J. Kinnamon, and Michael G. Brennan (Oxford:
    Clarendon Press, 1998), 102–04, 109–12.
8. *The Poems of Aemilia Lanyer: Salve Deus Rex Judaeorum*, ed. Susanne Woods
    (New York: Oxford University Press, 1993). Line references to the dedicatory
    material are noted parenthetically.
9. References to *Pamphilia and Amphilanthus* are from Roberts's edition, with
    sonnet and line numbers noted parenthetically.
10. Ovid, *Metamorphoses*, trans. Frank Justus Miller, 3rd edn, vol. 1 (Cambridge,
    MA: Harvard University Press, 1977), III:466.

11. *Astrophil and Stella* in *Sir Philip Sidney: A Critical Edition of the Major Works*, ed. Katherine Duncan-Jones (Oxford: Oxford University Press, 1989), 6:14. Further references are cited parenthetically in the text.

12. I share Neil Rudenstine's sense that the last line of the sonnet does not merely invoke the Petrarchan topos of the lady's image held within the poet-lover's heart but allows for some reference to the speaker's own emotion in its most immediate sense; see *Sidney's Poetic Development* (Cambridge, MA: Harvard University Press, 1967), 200.

13. On the implications of Pamphilia's lyrics being presented as the 'makings' of a fictional character, see Wendy Wall, *The Imprint of Gender: Authorship and Publication in the English Renaissance* (Ithaca: Cornell University Press, 1993), 336, and Danielle Clarke, *The Politics of Early Modern Women's Writing* (Harlow: Longman, 2001), 215.

14. Lady Mary Wroth, *The First Part of the Countess of Montgomery's Urania*, ed. Josephine A. Roberts, MRTS 140 (Binghamton: MRTS, 1995), 94. Further references are cited parenthetically in the text.

15. Maureen Quilligan, 'The Constant Subject: Instability and Female Authority in Wroth's *Urania* Poems', in *Soliciting Interpretation: Literary Theory and Seventeenth-Century English Poetry*, ed. Elizabeth D. Harvey and Katharine Eisaman Maus (Chicago: University of Chicago Press, 1990), 307–35; 315.

16. Walker, *Women Writers,* 189.

17. For an interesting representation of and meditation upon the recycling of love poems within the context of another early modern prose fiction, see George Gascoigne, *The Adventures of Master F.J.*, in *An Anthology of Elizabethan Prose Fiction*, ed. Paul Salzman (Oxford: Oxford University Press, 1987), 39. On manuscript and coterie culture see Wall, *Imprint of Gender*, and Arthur F. Marotti, *Manuscript, Print, and the English Renaissance Lyric* (Ithaca: Cornell University Press, 1995).

18. Mary Ellen Lamb, *Gender and Authorship in the Sidney Circle* (Madison: University of Wisconsin Press, 1990), 165.

19. Introduction to *The First Part of the Countess of Montgomery's Urania*, lxxii.

20. On the *Urania*'s topicality and autobiographical 'shadowing', see Roberts's introduction (lxix–lxxi), Jennifer Lee Carrell, 'A Pack of Lies in a Looking Glass: Lady Mary Wroth's *Urania* and the Magic Mirror of Romance', *SEL* 34 (1994): 79–107, and Lamb, *Gender and Authorship,*185–88.

21. Sir Philip Sidney, *The Defence of Poesy*, in *Sir Philip Sidney*, ed. Duncan-Jones, 217–18.

22. Ronald Levao, *Renaissance Minds and their Fictions* (Berkeley and Los Angeles: University of California Press, 1985), 178.

23. The mixed messages of the final sonnet in the 1621 text are particularly interesting in the light of Vicki Burke's observation in this volume that it does not play the same conclusive role in the manuscript form of the lyric sequence as it does in the printed version (pp. 100–01).

24. Lady Mary Wroth, *The Second Part of the Countess of Montgomery's Urania*, ed. Josephine A. Roberts, completed by Suzanne Gossett and Janel Mueller, MRTS 211 (Tempe: University of Arizona Press, 1999), 41. Further references are cited parenthetically in the text.

25. For Denny's verses, see *The Poems of Lady Mary Wroth*, ed. Roberts, 32–33.

26. Lamb, *Gender and Authorship*, 162; see also 168.

27. For the ascription of the poem to William Herbert, see the editors' note on this lyric in *Urania* II, 481.

28. For a more extended consideration of the 'undoing' of romance in *Urania* II, see Clare R. Kinney, '"Beleeve this butt a fiction": Female Authorship, Narrative Undoing and the Limits of Romance in *The Second Part of the Countess of Montgomery's Urania*', *Spenser Studies* 17 (2003): 239–50.

9
Valuing Early Modern Women's Verse in the Twenty-First Century

Pamela Hammons

Early modern women poets, in the last two decades, have undergone a second renaissance. From the 1988 publication of *Kissing the Rod: An Anthology of Seventeenth-Century Women's Verse*, to the production of editions of individual women's verse, to the development of electronic databases of women's writing such as the Brown University Women Writers Project and the Perdita Project, seventeenth-century women's poetry has become increasingly available to a wide audience.[1] Scholarship in the last twenty years has been enabled – indeed, radically reconfigured – by the emergence of these important resources, which have provided substantial introductory essays, glosses, and notes to accompany their accessible copies of the poems. Much of this scholarship, not surprisingly, is grounded in various feminisms and gender theories; however, there tends to be a divide between scholars performing archival work and those focusing their analyses upon the best known, most accessible – and by now, effectively canonical – women poets (e.g., Isabella Whitney, Mary Sidney, Aemilia Lanyer, Mary Wroth, Katherine Philips, Lucy Hutchinson, and Aphra Behn).

While all of this scholarship is extremely valuable, and it all wrestles, even if only implicitly, with questions concerning how best to value early modern women's poetry today, in this essay I highlight the particular importance of putting archival work on lesser-known women poets into productive dialogue with recent theoretical concerns in Renaissance studies. The recovery of early modern women's poetry is inherently valuable for the rich literary, historical, and cultural information it provides about women's lives and creative practices. However, it is also crucial that we make the study of early modern women's verse central to the scholarly understanding of Renaissance literature by highlighting explicitly how our discoveries about women's poetry contribute significantly to ongoing conversations about the period. In this chapter, I detail resources especially useful for the study of lesser-known early modern women's verse and survey a few recent approaches to it, particularly those calling attention to its value in relation to Renaissance studies. Finally, by discussing a rarely examined sonnet by Jane Cavendish, I suggest how the careful analysis of manuscript poetry intersects productively with current interests in Renaissance material culture and constructions of sexuality.

Those of us who study seventeenth-century women's poetry are deeply indebted to Germaine Greer, Susan Hastings, Jeslyn Medoff, and Melinda Sansone's groundbreaking edition, *Kissing the Rod*, which remains an important resource because of its impressive assembly of diverse poems – love lyrics, songs, dedicatory verse, country house poetry, elegies, dream visions, patronage verse, religious poetry, etc. – by a wide variety of ordinary and elite women who circulated their verse in both print and manuscript. However, in using this volume today, one must also be aware that more recent editions and scholarship have corrected some misleading theoretical assumptions underpinning its organization and contextual apparatus. In particular, while the editors admit the 'shock reaction' to their chosen title and insist upon its appropriateness because 'women have always been obliged for their own survival to humble themselves before' the rod, the universalizing and ahistorical assumptions behind this idea are among the least helpful aspects of the collection, and they regrettably influence its Introduction and selection of poems.[2] One need only read 'Eve's Apologie' from Lanyer's *Salve Deus Rex Judaeorum* – rather tellingly omitted from *Kissing the Rod* but included in Susanne Woods's influential edition of Lanyer's works – to realize that writing poetry created striking opportunities for seventeenth-century women's bold resistance to the patriarchal expectations theoretically constraining them.[3] More recent editions and studies have also refuted Greer's assertion in her Introduction that seventeenth-century women poets were 'untrained, ill-equipped, isolated and vulnerable'.[4]

Perhaps the most important corrective to distorted assumptions about early modern women's writing – including their verse – is Margaret J. M. Ezell's landmark *Writing Women's Literary History*, which exposes and challenges 'the theoretical model of women's literary history and the construction of women's literary studies as a field [that] rest[s] upon the assumption that women before 1700 either were effectively silenced or constituted in an evolutionary model of "female literature" an early "imitative" phase, contained and co-opted in patriarchal discourse'.[5]

Ezell also critiques the universalizing, ahistorical thinking underpinning some of *Kissing the Rod*'s claims about women poets when she points out how women's literary histories 'have ... tended to assert that emotional responses to landmark human experiences such as giving birth and psychological responses to social stress such as isolation or injustice have remained constant. Loneliness is loneliness, and anger is anger, we have assumed, whether it was felt by a thirteenth-century nun or a twentieth-century professor.'[6] Most importantly, Ezell argues powerfully against the 'view ... that all authors wish to be in print, and therefore something must be preventing these women from publishing their writings' and emphasizes that, before the eighteenth century, 'to publish was the exception for both men and women, and the most common practice was the circulation of manuscript copies'.[7]

Marion Wynne-Davies's edition *Women Poets of the Renaissance*, Jane Stevenson and Peter Davidson's *Early Modern Women Poets: An Anthology (1520–1700)*, and Jill Seal Millman and Gillian Wright's *Early Modern Women's Manuscript Poetry* are very important verse anthologies that pursue the path blazed by *Kissing the Rod*; the latter two also respond to Ezell's call for work in the field that resists literary theoretical assumptions grounded in the study of women's nineteenth-century literature (especially novels) transmitted in print for a competitive, capitalist literary market.[8] Wynne-Davies's anthology makes an early gesture toward canonizing a select group of women's verse by including substantial selections by twelve key poets rather than attempting to delineate the widest possible range of authors and works. Yet it relies on the notions that translation was a second-rate form of literary activity, that many 'women of the period chose to allow their works to exist *only* in manuscript form' (my italics), and that we can safely assume that women's poetry was mostly autobiographical, which tends to undermine the idea that women deliberately crafted their verse as art in response to poetic traditions.[9] Wynne-Davies nevertheless argues very effectively against the vision of the isolated woman poet by emphasizing the familial and artistic coteries surrounding women such as Sidney, Lanyer, and Jane, Elizabeth, and Margaret Cavendish, and by highlighting ways in which women's verse engaged with important political issues of the day.[10] In fact, she develops these crucial ideas in further detail in her recent book, *Women Writers and Familial Discourse in the English Renaissance: Relative Values*, where she also explains the methodological imperative of analyzing women's writing in relation to men's 'because it is essential that women writers are not ghettoised into a gender-specific unit and because it ensures that their work remains valued within the wider remit of Early Modern textual productivity'.[11]

Like *Kissing the Rod*, *Early Modern Women Poets* represents a monumental collaborative achievement in its illustration of 'the sheer energy and diversity of women's cultural activity in the British islands and in the communities of exiles from those islands': it is especially commendable because it includes poems written at life stages ranging from childhood to old age by 'working-class women, middle-class women, citizens (i.e., members of the mercantile élite), country gentlefolk, nuns, and courtiers' and queens in multiple languages (English, Latin, Greek, Irish, French, Scottish Gaelic, Lowland Scots, and Welsh), and because it highlights women's verse production and transmission in overlapping oral, manuscript, and print cultures.[12] Challenging the idea that 'women wrote primarily about their personal emotions, their religion, perhaps, their husbands and children', Stevenson and Davidson call attention to poems about 'the Plague, the Great Fire of London, the "Popish Plot", and the "Glorious Revolution" of 1688', and addressing issues of work.[13] Perusing this collection may afford the most expansive and historically accurate means readily available to gain an overview of the sheer complexity and variety of early modern women's verse. Although the anthology contains some inevitable errors in transcription and biographical detail because it represents such a massive endeavor, it serves as an excellent starting point for pursuing research in the field.

While Millman and Wright's *Early Modern Women's Manuscript Poetry* does not demonstrate the range of *Early Modern Women Poets*, it nonetheless does important literary historical work by thoroughly contextualizing and effectively highlighting the cultural centrality of women's manuscript circulation of poetry. Like Wynne-Davies's edition, this one presents just a few poets – fourteen – to include more poems by each; since the manuscript verse of women such as Jane Seager and Anna Ley is not widely available, it is especially valuable to have a substantial group of their poems in print. As Elizabeth Clarke and Jonathan Gibson explain in their Introduction, *Early Modern Women's Manuscript Poetry* has its roots in the Perdita Project, which seeks to catalogue early modern women's manuscript writing, and which 'has been driven by the conviction that printed works by women between 1500 and 1700, on which most teaching, and attempts at early modern women's literary history, have tended to be based, represent the efforts of a minority of early modern women writers' and that 'a greater volume of writing activity took place in manuscript'.[14] Agreeing with Ezell's earlier warnings against imposing modern assumptions about print publication upon early modern writing practices, Clarke and Gibson assert that 'texts written in manuscript enjoyed at least as much and often far more prestige with their early modern readers than printed books'.[15] Anyone wishing to gain a rich, detailed, historicized understanding of the material production and circulation of early modern women's verse should study this crucial volume.

Resources such as these key anthologies have enabled the energetic scholarship on early modern women's verse that has emerged in the last few years. A survey of collections of essays and books published in the last decade and dedicated entirely or mostly to Renaissance women's poetry will highlight recent efforts to call attention to the importance of women poets as a group (as opposed to individual, effectively canonical women poets). Barbara Smith and Ursula Appelt's *Write or Be Written: Early Modern Women Poets and Cultural Constraints* represents an important early collection of essays upon a diverse range of women poets, mixing together lesser-known and well-known writers (e.g., Katherine Austen, Behn, Damaris Masham, Wroth, Lanyer, Anne Finch, Anne Askew, Sidney, and Philips), and it also notably insists upon treating together women's poems circulated in print and manuscript. Ultimately, *Write or Be Written* provides not only a useful analytical overview of a variety of women poets, but it also foregrounds how they deployed their verse strategically 'to cope with or to change their cultural contexts', how they '[intervened] in male-dominated or patriarchal genres (Petrarchan love poetry and country house poetry)' and the Psalms, and how they 'fashion a gendered, writerly persona'.[16]

Eugene R. Cunnar and Jeffrey Johnson's collection *Discovering and (Re)Covering the Seventeenth-Century Religious Lyric* merits comment because half of its essays focus on women poets, including Lanyer, Elizabeth Middleton, Eliza, An Collins, Elizabeth Major, and Mary Carey. As Cunnar and Johnson explain, this book is both useful and unusual in its project of revising our understanding of 'seventeenth century religious lyrics, especially those written by lesser-known or minor writers ... as both indicators of the political/religious conflicts, and of gender conflicts, and as influences on those conflicts'.[17] The editors include essays foregrounding 'Anglo-Catholic, High Anglican, and women writers'; thus, the collection contextualizes women writers in relation to 'the hegemonic emphasis upon Protestant/Puritan aesthetics and culture that has long dominated scholarship'.[18] Furthermore, particular contributions implicitly illustrate how attention to lesser-known women poets relates to recent concerns in Renaissance studies. Kari Boyd McBride, for instance, reads male- and female-authored verse accounts of Christ's passion together to 'reveal a spectrum of attitudes about nationality, religion, gender, and sexuality' and criticizes Elizabeth

Middleton's anti-Semitic versification of the Passion as a 'textbook case illustrating the way in which dominant identity is produced through the othering of the Jews'.[19] Meanwhile, in a rare feminist psychoanalytic reading of little-known women poets, Patricia Demers uses Julia Kristeva's theories to analyze the 'religious melancholy' characteristic of the verse of Collins, Eliza, and Major in contrast to the many 'explorations of melancholia as figured by male artists in the early modern period'.[20] Erica Longfellow's *Women and Religious Writing in Early Modern England* similarly shows how the study of diverse women poets – Anne Southwell, Lanyer, Eliza, Anna Trapnel, and Hutchinson – revises our knowledge about religious issues central to Renaissance culture and also 'uncovers some of the historical nuances of those overarching categories of "public" and "private" that mediate and polarise our understanding of gender, print, and manuscript culture'.[21]

Sidney L. Sondergard's *Sharpening Her Pen: Strategies of Rhetorical Violence by Early Modern English Women Writers* is among the first book-length studies to offer a sustained analysis of women's verse, among other texts, without centering exclusively upon now-canonical women writers; instead, it discusses the writings of Elizabeth Colville, Askew, Anne Dowriche, Elizabeth Tudor, Lanyer, Wroth, and Southwell. Emphasizing these writers' diversity, rather than assuming a homogeneity guaranteed by gender, Sondergard seeks 'to demonstrate how discrete women authors exploit, or evade, the use of a rhetorical discourse common in the work of early modern male authors', thereby inserting his analyses into a larger discussion about Renaissance rhetoric.[22]

Likewise, my own *Poetic Resistance: English Women Writers and the Early Modern Lyric* shows how women poets as varied in rank, religion, education, personal experiences, and poetic style as Gertrude Aston Thimelby, Anne Bradstreet, Philips, Carey, Trapnel, Lanyer, and Austen revise multiple lyric traditions (e.g., elegies, Psalms, ballads, country house verse) to change or to reconceive damaging, restrictive conventions shaping their social lives and to add their own creative innovations to the history of the Renaissance lyric.[23]

Victoria E. Burke and Jonathan Gibson's collection, *Early Modern Women's Manuscript Writing: Selected Papers from the Trinity/Trent Colloquium*, expands upon the archival work of the Perdita Project and builds upon Ezell's observations about writing women's literary history to offer studies of rarely examined women's manuscript writing, including poetry. As the editors explain, '[t]he essays in this volume celebrate the heterogeneity of women's writing in manuscript, complicating any simple identifications that can be made between "public" versus "private" writing or between genres frequented by men versus those by women.'[24] Elizabeth Heale's contribution, which analyzes the Devonshire Manuscript (BL Add MS 17492), deserves special mention because it models how scrupulous attention to the materiality of manuscript verse combined with an engagement with concerns in Renaissance studies at large generate especially valuable results. In particular, Heale's research serves as a potent corrective to Jonathan Goldberg's *Desiring Women Writing* by foregrounding the complexity and malleability of the eroticized subject positions available to male and female poets, compilers, and readers in courtly manuscript verse.[25] Burke's essay emphasizes the significance of 'not just gender but class' in her study of how 'women could tap into the manuscript transmission of poetry' originating in male-dominated spaces.[26] Marie-Louise Coolahan, meanwhile, in her analysis of the keens of early modern Irish poet, Caitlín Dubh, reveals how her elegies 'skilfully negotiate the demands of competing allegiances; they appropriate the military achievements and English alliances of the Irish patron to Gaelic ideological tradition; and they rewrite the tropes by which an Irish noble is traditionally mourned by a male poet'.[27] Finally, essays about Southwell, Austen, and a female member of the Feilding family further our understanding of these lesser-known women poets.

Kate Chedgzoy's *Women's Writing in the British Atlantic World: Memory, Place and History, 1550–1700* represents an example of how to make the ongoing project of recovering women poets central to cutting-edge concerns – in this case, questions of transatlantic cultural production – within literary and historical studies. Chedgzoy engages with a striking variety of early modern American, English, Irish, Scottish, and Welsh women's poetry (including songs, charms, elegies, laments, dream visions, love lyrics, verse translations, and dialogues), in addition to their letters and other forms of life writing. She discusses verse by Martha Moulsworth, Rachel Speght, Katherine Thomas, Isobel Gowdie, Angharad James, Grisell Baillie, Caitlín Dubh, Elizabeth Melville, Anna Hume, Màiri nighean Alasdair Ruaidh, Diorbhail Nic a' Bhriuthainn, Philips, Jane Vaughan, Catherin Owen, Bradstreet, Elizabeth Brackley, Jane Cavendish, Hester Pulter, and Hutchinson. Noting that the 'relative absence of gender as an analytical category from work in the disciplines of both history and literature on the "British problem" has been paired with a metropolitan and anglocentric bias in much feminist literary scholarship on the period', Chedgzoy explains that her 'book situates women's writing of the early modern period in relation to the historic changes that refashioned the political and cultural relations among the four constituent nations of the British Isles, and that also changed the meanings of those islands' location in a wider Atlantic cultural and political world'.[28] Her project on women's cultural production and memory – which serves as a logical extension of and literary historical/ critical companion to *Early Modern Women Poets: An Anthology*, for which she served as a contributor – successfully meets its goal of 'offer[ing] a more capacious, diverse and inclusive history of early modern British women's writing than has previously been attempted'.[29]

As we have seen, the recent trajectory of scholarship on lesser-known early modern women poets increasingly puts archival work into dialogue with ongoing conversations in Renaissance studies about constructions of gender, notions of sexuality, rank and class distinctions, religious differences, and questions of geographical and cultural location with respect to the British Isles and broader transatlantic contexts. As I suggest below, analyzing a sonnet of thanks written by Jane Cavendish during the mid-1640s to her exiled royalist father, William, Marquis (later Duke) of Newcastle and preserved in a presentation copy by her father's secretary can exemplify how early modern women's manuscript verse opens new perspectives on the last decade's focus upon relations between Renaissance subjects and objects, and notions of sexuality.

Margreta de Grazia, Maureen Quilligan, and Peter Stallybrass foreground mutual relations between subjects and objects in their groundbreaking collection, *Subject and Object in Renaissance Culture*. Revisiting Jacob Burckhardt's *The Civilization of the Renaissance in Italy*, which associates the dawning of the Renaissance with the emergence of an individual subject possessing a secular self-consciousness and a masterful relation to subordinated objects firmly separate from the self, de Grazia, Quilligan, and Stallybrass critique Burckhardt and ask, 'in the period that has from its inception been identified with the emergence of the subject, *where is the object?*'[30] These scholars note a similarly strict separation between subject and object, and privileging of one term over the other in Marx's historical narrative of the development of capitalism, where 'the object comes to overpower the subject'.[31] Analyzing Burckhardt's and Marx's assertions allows de Grazia, Quilligan, and Stallybrass to expose a tendency underpinning much Renaissance scholarship to treat relations between subjects and objects in negative, overly simplified terms. In other words, they suggest that scholars have collectively succumbed to streamlining, binary assumptions about a crucial set of terms relevant to understanding Renaissance art, literature, culture, and history. They thus propose that others join them in focusing deliberately upon how subjects and objects relate to each other during the period – instead of assuming subjects to be fundamentally separate and distinct from objects, as has tended to be the case.

A number of materialist studies have appeared answering *Subject and Object in Renaissance Culture*'s call to inquiry.[32] Several of these studies focus upon how gender inflects relations between subjects and objects, and some even specifically address women's relation to material objects during a period in which men were prone to treat women (especially wives, who were theoretically subject to the legal and economic constraints of coverture) as if they were passive objects in which fathers and husbands had property rights of ownership and exclusion. However, most of these studies also foreground men's texts, especially drama and portraiture, to make their claims about people and material culture.[33]

I suggest that we cannot fully understand gendered relations among people, things, subjects, and objects unless we analyze women's writing, in addition to men's, and unless we attend specifically to poetry. Because the lyric typically represents the first-person perspective of its speaker and foregrounds his or her emotions and thoughts, the genre serves as an especially rich site for examining how Renaissance poets imagined mutual influences between people and things, between human and non-human subjects and objects. Furthermore, women's lyrics are particularly key to this kind of investigation because many women poets created female speakers explicitly asserting themselves as active subjects while simultaneously conforming to poetic and cultural conventions conflating women with objects: women poets might have seemed – from some patriarchal perspectives of the time – to be talking things according to the terms Lorraine Daston introduces in *Things That Talk*.[34] Even a cursory analysis of Jane Cavendish's sonnet to her father challenges the traditional Burckhardtian master narrative concerning the so-called emerging Renaissance (male) subject who is independent from and master over objects by exposing one woman's strategies for resisting the sexualized objectification of the female beloved typical of male-authored Renaissance verse; by revealing ways in which she imagined herself as a subject dominating (via possession) objects; and by highlighting the possibility of women's objectification of men.

The sonnet's focus upon specific material objects – tokens of affection from her father – partially rewrites gifts conventionally exchanged between lovers in Renaissance poetry to downplay their potentially bawdy resonances; thus, for Jane Cavendish, centering her poem upon paternal love tokens enables her to deflect away from herself, at least in part, the tendency for male-authored gift poems to render women's bodies sexual objects:

> My Lord
>> Your present to mee was soe justly kind
>> Th'interpretation comfortable find
>> The curious Fan, was sent to stand betweene
>> To shadowe mee from Traytors as a Screene
>> Thy fyner Combes sweete teeth, lookes speaking say
>> Counsaileing mee to combe sad thoughts away
>> Thy neater Brasletts bids of Joyes to thinke
>> And not betray my selfe to malencholly winke
>> Thy dainty Twises say steale away tyme
>> Let workes of silke bee a true Captives signe
>> The Maskes & Chinclothes hopes I am not tan'd
>> Promiseing againe my ffather will here land
>> All these in Choros sings this songe to mee
>> Of comfort; That my Father I shall see.[35]

Cavendish's poem foregrounds the active process of interpreting love tokens and attempts to fix the significance of her father's presents: ultimately, in 'Choros', these animated gifts together sing 'this songe … / Of comfort; That my Father I shall see' (14). 'Fan', 'Combes', 'Brasletts', 'Maskes & Chinclothes' point to William's abundant love for his daughter, offer material comfort in his absence, and promise his return from exile; in fact, these possessions physically foreshadow the moment when this daughter will make her father the passive object of her active gaze (3, 5, 7, 11). While many other poets, male and female, wrote lyrics focused upon the exchange of a single love token, Jane's sonnet details a cornucopia of luxurious paternal gifts: this creative choice advertises her father's power and status, despite his exile as a defeated royalist, and suggests the superiority of his love to any young wooer's.

As Marion Wynne-Davies has suggested, in the wartime verse and drama of sisters Jane and Elizabeth Cavendish, 'sexual dalliance, even if within the bounds of courtship and marriage, becomes a "toy" that cannot be admitted while male family members are exiled and homes threatened by opposition troops'.[36] Jane thus depicts William's gifts as if they protect her both politically and sexually. In men's verse, love tokens – especially circular adornments that can evoke female genitalia – typically become conflated with the female beloved's body, reinforcing her status as a passive object of the male lover's sexual desire. For instance, in Shakespeare's 'A Lover's Complaint', broken rings represent violated virginity; Silvia's bracelet of pearl that Robert Herrick's speaker breaks similarly points to sexual penetration; Edmund Waller's girdle enables the speaker to imagine embracing the area of his beloved's body – her waist – where she used to wear it.[37] However, certain of Cavendish's personified love tokens instead absorb the active attributes of her father or his servants; they shield her from dangerous persons and bad thoughts. William's fan becomes 'a Screene', for example, 'to stand betweene' the female speaker and 'Traytors' (4, 3). This has quite different connotations from a similar gift in 'On Aurelia's Fan', in which the motion of the fan is provocatively sensual: 'Look how the panting Winds obey / The Swelling Fan, and airs convey / Which o're her curled Tresses play'.[38] Here, the token – 'The Swelling Fan' – might obliquely suggest an animated phallic substitution for the male lover or foreshadow associatively an impregnated female body. By contrast, Cavendish portrays the fan from her father as physically shielding her from the gaze of male suitors. As a material reminder of William, the fan also serves as a symbolic barrier – ultimately protecting her from her own fears – between her and the political and military dangers of the civil wars.[39] As Marie-Louise Coolahan explains, 'Upon her father's and brothers' exile in July 1644, Jane was left in charge of the family estates at Welbeck and Bolsover in Derbyshire. Welbeck was besieged and taken by parliamentary forces in August 1644, retaken by the royalists in July 1645, and finally ceded to Parliament in November 1645, by which point, at the latest, Jane and her sister Frances ... must have decamped to Bolsover.'[40] Jane thus assigns her father's fan multiple meanings surpassing the usual symbolism of a sexualized love token. Similarly, while a lover's gift of a comb in a different poem might 'speakeing say' that her beautiful hairs are wires entrapping her captive wooer against his will, the 'sweete teeth' of William's lively material ambassador specifically advise her 'to combe sad thoughts away' – sad thoughts related to missing her father and dreading the military conflict surrounding her (5, 6).

Cavendish's sonnet, however, arguably does not escape altogether the pervasive sexualized connotations of round, open love tokens in Renaissance verse; for example, in lines 7–8, she writes, 'Thy neater Brasletts bids of Joyes to thinke / And not betray my selfe to malencholly winke'. If one reads these lines out of context – given the commonplace association of rings, bracelets, and necklaces with female genitalia – one might assume that these bracelets help the female beloved to fight her 'malencholly' not only by symbolizing the emotional ties binding her to her lover, but also by encouraging her 'to thinke' of sexual 'Joyes' in the near future, when they are reunited. Ezell similarly observes that Jane's 'series of "Passion" poems, if read out of context, would naturally be assumed to refer to a lover'.[41] Considered in context with Jane's many poems celebrating William and declaring undying loyalty and love to him, the portrait of bracelets in this sonnet might at first seem like one more articulation of the daughter's profound sorrow in missing her father: in this view, the bracelets merely recall her father's binding love for her, his ability to protect and to provide for her, even at a great distance. As Wynne-Davies observes, '[i]f there is one overriding element in the joint and individual compositions of Jane and Elizabeth during their captivity at Welbeck, it is the overwhelming sense of loss at the exile of their father'.[42]

Yet, I would propose that this connotation does not simply replace or expunge the potential eroticism the lines invoke in relation to the commonplace poetic deployment of bracelets as particularly sexualized love tokens, despite Jane's choice of a familial context for her gift poem. In fact, her sonnet extends into the seventeenth century what Quilligan, in *Incest and Agency in Elizabeth's England*, calls 'the remarkable presence in the Renaissance of what we may call incest schemes' in relation to Elizabethan women writers' ability 'to claim an active female authority'.[43] Jane's many pledges of love to her father (and to her brothers, Henry and Charles, and her uncle, Charles) throughout Bod. Rawlinson Poet. 16 literally form much of her verse (see, for instance, pages 1–4). Thus, while her sonnet neatly frames certain love tokens, such as her fan and comb, to avoid invoking the often bawdy objectification of a female beloved, her efforts to reinforce her father's prestige and the intimacy of their connection still manifest themselves, if obliquely, in an incestuous eroticism. This eroticism has significantly different effects and implications from that common to male-authored heteroerotic lyrics. Rather than rendering a female figure passive and silent, Jane's 'incest scheme' (to borrow Quilligan's useful phrase) – her expression of active, passionate devotion to her father – displaces any articulation of desire for (or from) a young male suitor, while it also enables and expands her poetic range. Provocatively, it also suggests a compelling link – deserving of further study – between Jane Cavendish and some of her female Elizabethan predecessors, who employed similar writing strategies in very different historical circumstances.

Recognizing the innovation with which Cavendish rewrites her love tokens as signs of paternal affection, material substitutions for William's fatherly protection, and objects through which she demonstrates her agency as a possessing subject inevitably changes our perception of male-authored verse – such as Shakespeare's, Herrick's, and Waller's – that invokes love tokens to enable masculinist fantasies about passive female beloveds open to sexual penetration. Cavendish's sonnet answers back to such verse: it resists the conflation of women with static objects; it constructs the poet as an active subject who bestows the valuable gift of her verse upon her father; and it assigns new, creative, personalized meanings to the everyday domestic items making up her world. Careful attention to the historical context of her verse and its contrast to male-authored Renaissance love lyrics focused upon material gifts reveals that Jane Cavendish did not humbly submit without question to the patriarchal expectations for women that *Kissing the Rod* assumed, in 1988, to delimit seventeenth-century women's poetic efforts. As we have seen, analyzing the significance of material gifts in Cavendish's verse reveals important dimensions to her writing that would otherwise be overlooked; seeking additional strategies for bringing lesser-known women poets' writing into ongoing conversations central to Renaissance scholarship will further highlight the crucial importance of early modern women's verse today.

Notes

I am grateful to Mihoko Suzuki and Gema Pérez-Sánchez for their insightful feedback on this essay. I would also like to thank the United States National Endowment for the Humanities (NEH) for the Faculty Research Award that helped to make this work possible; the views and conclusions expressed in this essay do not necessarily reflect those of the NEH.

1. Along with Danielle Clarke's *Isabella Whitney, Mary Sidney, and Aemilia Lanyer: Renaissance Women Poets* (New York: Penguin, 2000) and David Norbrook's edition of Lucy Hutchinson's epic *Order and Disorder* (Malden, MA: Blackwell, 2001), there are several book series that have published many editions of individual women's poems or miscellanies containing women's verse (e.g., Ashgate Publishing's *The Early Modern Englishwoman: A Facsimile Library of Essential Works*; Oxford University Press's *Women Writers in English 1350–1850*; and Medieval and Renaissance Texts and Studies).
2. Germaine Greer et al., eds, *Kissing the Rod: An Anthology of Seventeenth-Century Women's Verse* (New York: Noonday Press, 1988), xvi.
3. Susanne Woods, ed., *The Poems of Aemilia Lanyer: Salve Deus Rex Judaeorum* (New York: Oxford University Press, 1993).
4. Greer, *Kissing the Rod*, 1.
5. Margaret J. M. Ezell, *Writing Women's Literary History* (Baltimore: Johns Hopkins University Press, 1993), 4; for Ezell's critiques of *Kissing the Rod*, see *Writing Women's Literary History*, 42–43, 51–54. Also see Ezell's '"To Be Your Daughter in Your Pen": The Social Functions of Literature in the Writings of Lady Elizabeth Brackley and Lady Jane Cavendish', in *Readings in Renaissance Women's Drama: Criticism, History, and Performance, 1594–1998*, ed. S. P. Cerasano and Marion Wynne-Davies (New York: Routledge, 1998),

246–58 and *The Patriarch's Wife: Literary Evidence and the History of the Family* (Chapel Hill: University of North Carolina Press, 1987), esp. 62–126.

6. Ezell, *Writing Women's Literary History*, 26–27.
7. Ibid., 37, 34.
8. Ibid., 2–4.
9. Marion Wynne-Davies, introduction to *Women Poets of the Renaissance* (New York: Routledge, 1999), xviv, xxvi, xxii–xxiii.
10. Ibid., xxii, xxii, xxiv–xxv.
11. Marion Wynne-Davies, *Women Writers and Familial Discourse in the English Renaissance: Relative Values* (New York: Palgrave Macmillan, 2007), 9.
12. Jane Stevenson and Peter Davidson, introduction to *Early Modern Women Poets: An Anthology (1520–1700)* (New York: Oxford University Press, 2001), xxix, xxx.
13. Ibid., xxxvii, xxxviii, xxxix.
14. Elizabeth Clarke and Jonathan Gibson, introduction to *Early Modern Women's Manuscript Poetry*, ed. Jill Seal Millman and Gillian Wright (New York: Manchester University Press, 2005), 1.
15. Ibid.
16. Ursula Appelt, introduction to *Write or Be Written: Early Modern Women Poets and Cultural Constraints*, ed. Barbara Smith and Ursula Appelt (Aldershot: Ashgate, 2001), xv, xvi, xix.
17. Eugene R. Cunnar and Jeffrey Johnson, introduction to *Discovering and (Re)Covering the Seventeenth Century Religious Lyric* (Pittsburgh: Duquesne University Press, 2001), 5.
18. Ibid., 3, 15.
19. Kari Boyd McBride, 'Gender and Judaism in Meditations on the Passion: Middleton, Southwell, Lanyer, and Fletcher', in *Discovering and (Re)Covering the Seventeenth Century Religious Lyric*, ed. Cunnar and Johnson, 40, 25.
20. Patricia Demers, '*Penseroso* Triptych: "Eliza," An Collins, Elizabeth Major', in *Discovering and (Re)Covering the Seventeenth Century Religious Lyric*, ed. Cunnar and Johnson, 188, 189. Also see Lynette McGrath's use of feminist psycho-analytic theories to explicate the now well-known works of Whitney, Lanyer, and Elizabeth Cary in *Subjectivity and Women's Poetry in Early Modern England: 'Why on the Ridge Should She Desire to Go?'* (Aldershot: Ashgate, 2002).
21. Erica Longfellow, *Women and Religious Writing in Early Modern England* (New York: Cambridge University Press, 2004), 11.
22. Sidney L. Sondergard, *Sharpening Her Pen: Strategies of Rhetorical Violence by Early Modern English Women Writers* (Selinsgrove, PA: Susquehanna University Press, 2002), 14–15.
23. Pamela S. Hammons, *Poetic Resistance: English Women Writers and the Early Modern Lyric* (Aldershot: Ashgate, 2002).
24. Victoria E. Burke and Jonathan Gibson, introduction to *Early Modern Women's Manuscript Writing: Selected Papers from the Trinity/Trent Colloquium* (Aldershot: Ashgate, 2004), 2.
25. Elizabeth Heale, '"Desiring Women Writing": Female Voices and Courtly Balets in some Early Tudor Manuscript Albums', in *Early Modern Women's Manuscript Writing: Selected Papers from the Trinity/Trent Colloquium*, ed. Burke and Gibson, 9–31; Jonathan Goldberg, *Desiring Women Writing: English Renaissance Examples* (Stanford: Stanford University Press, 1997).

26. Victoria E. Burke, 'Reading Friends: Women's Participating in "Masculine" Literary Culture', in *Early Modern Women's Manuscript Writing: Selected Papers from the Trinity/Trent Colloquium*, ed. Burke and Gibson, 75.

27. Marie-Louise Coolahan, 'Caitlín Dubh's Keens: Literary Negotiations in Early Modern Ireland', in *Early Modern Women's Manuscript Writing: Selected Papers from the Trinity/Trent Colloquium*, ed. Burke and Gibson, 91.

28. Kate Chedgzoy, *Women's Writing in the British Atlantic World: Memory, Place and History, 1550–1700* (New York: Cambridge University Press, 2007), 4.

29. Ibid., 14.

30. Margreta de Grazia, Maureen Quilligan, and Peter Stallybrass, introduction to *Subject and Object in Renaissance Culture* (New York: Cambridge University Press, 1996), 3, 2.

31. Ibid., 3.

32. Especially important recent works following this trajectory of thought include Ann Rosalind Jones and Peter Stallybrass, *Renaissance Clothing and the Materials of Memory* (New York: Cambridge University Press, 2000); Natasha Korda, *Shakespeare's Domestic Economies: Gender and Property in Early Modern England* (Philadelphia: University of Pennsylvania Press, 2002); Jonathan Gil Harris and Natasha Korda, eds, *Staged Properties in Early Modern English Drama* (New York: Cambridge University Press, 2002); Julian Yates, *Error, Misuse, Failure: Object Lessons from the English Renaissance* (Minneapolis: University of Minnesota Press, 2003); Nancy E. Wright, Margaret W. Ferguson, and A.R. Buck, eds, *Women, Property, and the Letters of the Law* (Buffalo: University of Toronto Press, 2004); Will Fisher, *Materializing Gender in Early Modern English Literature and Culture* (New York: Cambridge University Press, 2006); and Elizabeth Mazzola, *Women's Wealth and Women's Writing in Early Modern England: 'Little Legacies' and the Materials of Motherhood* (Farnham: Ashgate Press, 2009).

33. Mazzola's *Women's Wealth and Women's Writing in Early Modern England* and Wright, Ferguson, and Buck's *Women, Property, and the Letters of the Law*, in particular, are important exceptions because of their strong emphasis upon women's texts. I regret that I have not been able to engage in this chapter with Mazzola's book, which includes sustained analyses of women's verse, due to matters of timing in the publication process.

34. Lorraine Daston, 'Speechless', in *Things That Talk: Object Lessons from Art and Science* (New York: Zone Books, 2004), 9–24.

35. Jane Cavendish, 'Thankes [Lettre?]', in Bod. MS Rawlinson Poet. 16, 15; my transcription. References to Cavendish's lyric are hereafter cited parenthetically by line number. On the dating and material features of the writings of Jane and Elizabeth Cavendish, see Alexandra G. Bennett, '"Now let my language speake": The Authorship, Rewriting, and Audience(s) of Jane Cavendish and Elizabeth Brackley', *Early Modern Literary Studies* 11.2 (September 2005): 1–13; Wynne-Davies, *Women Writers*, 151–53 and '"My Fine Delitive Tomb": Liberating "Sisterly" Voices During the Civil War', in *Female Communities 1600–1800: Literary Visions and Cultural Realities*, ed. Rebecca D'Monté and Nicole Pohl (New York: St. Martin's Press, 2000), 113–14; and Ezell, '"To Be Your Daughter in Your Pen"', 247, 250.

36. Wynne-Davies, *Women Writers*, 141.

37. William Shakespeare, *A Lover's Complaint*, in *The Norton Shakespeare: Based on the Oxford Edition*, ed. Stephen Greenblatt et al. (New York:

W.W. Norton & Company, 1997), 1977–84; Robert Herrick, *The Complete Poetry of Robert Herrick*, ed. J. Max Patrick (Garden City, NY: Anchor Books, 1963); Edmund Waller, 'On a Girdle', in *Ben Jonson and the Cavalier Poets*, ed. Hugh Maclean (New York: Norton, 1974), 242–43.

38. 'On Aurelia's Fan', in Bod. MS Rawlinson Poet. 94, fols. 89–90, lines 1–3; my transcription.

39. Also see Chedgzoy, *Women's Writing*, 139.

40. Marie-Louise Coolahan, 'Presentation Volume of Jane Cavendish's Poetry', in *Early Modern Women's Manuscript Poetry*, ed. Millman and Wright, 88. On Jane's management of Welbeck and Bolsover, also see Lucy Worsley, *Cavalier: A Tale of Chivalry, Passion, and Great Houses* (New York: Bloomsbury, 2007), 187–90; Wynne-Davies, '"My Fine Delitive Tomb"', 112–13; and Chedgzoy, *Women's Writing*, 135–36.

41. Ezell, '"To Be Your Daughter in Your Pen"', 253.

42. Wynne-Davies, *Women Writers*, 155; also see Chedgzoy, *Women's Writing*, 136–37.

43. Maureen Quilligan, *Incest and Agency in Elizabeth's England* (Philadelphia: University of Pennsylvania Press, 2005), 7.

10
Early Modern English Women Dramatists (1610–1690): New Perspectives

Marion Wynne-Davies

Introduction

In 1991 I applied for a lectureship at one of the UK's leading universities; during the interview I was asked, by a staunch feminist critic, to name the English women dramatists from the early modern period. Before I could reply, she hastily corrected herself, 'Oh, but of course there aren't any, are there,' choosing instead to ask about early modern women poets. Had I thought out an answer, I would have referred to two women, Elizabeth Cary and Mary Sidney, both of whose dramatic works had already been published.[1] Still, I was forced to reconsider: the question had been well-intentioned and the questioner's afterthought arose, not from a lack of commitment to women's writing, but from the almost total lack of existing printed material – editorial and critical – devoted to early modern women dramatists. It was this casual comment that fueled my own interest and led me to trace plays by sixteenth- and seventeenth-century English women, culminating in the collection, *Renaissance Drama by Women: Texts and Documents* (1996) that I edited with S. P. Cerasano.[2] This chapter sets out to follow some of that editorial and critical history, building upon the strengths of previous scholarship in order to suggest possible initiatives for the present and future. The study is divided into four sections: the first offers an overview of who the early modern women dramatists were and what they wrote; the second focuses on the availability of primary material and criticism; and the third looks at the perennial question of performance and performability. The fourth section consists of three 'case studies' that focus upon thematic issues raised in the previous sections: Innovation: Elizabeth Cary's *Edward II*; Performability: Margaret Cavendish's *The Sociable Companions*; and Continuity: Frances Boothby's *Marcelia*. Through this discursive process I intend to locate and highlight areas where new perspectives are being, and need to be, generated. Oh, and just in case you were wondering, I didn't get the job.

Dramas, fragments, and fifteen women

Between 1610 and 1690 around fifteen women chose to write texts that may roughly be described as 'plays'. The origins of this dramatic output may be identified in sixteenth-century translations: Jane Lumley's *Iphigeneia* (c.1553); Elizabeth I's fragment of *Hercules Oetaeus* (late sixteenth century); and Mary Sidney's *The Tragedy of Antonie* (c.1590).[3] These texts were not intended for the public stage, although stage directions in *Iphigeneia* suggest that a private performance might have been envisaged, while the exposition of closet drama in Mary Sidney's cultural circle demands that *The Tragedy of Antonie* be considered as a play to be read aloud by the coterie at Wilton House. The seventeenth century, however, saw two significant shifts in the way that women conceptualized their production of dramatic texts: translation was eschewed for original writing and performance gradually became intrinsic to the text. The first change is evidenced by Elizabeth Cary's *The Tragedy of Mariam* (published 1613), which was the first original tragedy to be written by an English woman, and Mary Wroth's *Love's Victory* (c.1615), which was the first original comedy.[4] Both plays demonstrate a sharp awareness of generic traditions and contemporary dramatic activity on the public stage: for example, *Mariam* may be compared productively with Shakespeare's *Othello*, while Wroth's play participates in the politicization of pastoral tragicomedy. Although *Mariam* is the best-known of Cary's oeuvre, being the most anthologized – or 'Nortonized' – of all plays by early modern Englishwomen, her other quasi-dramatic work, *The History of the Life, Reign, and Death of Edward II* (c.1627) is emblematic of another recurrent element in women's dramatic writing of this period – it is innovative.[5] Cary was not alone in her radical manipulation of form, so that when developing new perspectives on early modern women's dramatic writing, the challenging use of genre and undercutting of cultural expectation should be used to suggest new ways of interpreting the plays.

The second development in the seventeenth century was the trend toward performability, where a transitional phase was followed by the first professional women dramatists. The first stage of this shift – envisioning a performance that was never realized – is demonstrated by the works of three women of the Cavendish family.

The two plays by Jane Cavendish and her sister, Elizabeth Brackley, *The Concealed Fancies* and *A Pastoral* (*c.*1644), were written while they were imprisoned and/or besieged at their home, Welbeck Abbey, and focus on, understandably, a sense of mourning for the lost certainties of the pre-Civil War period.[6] The plays of Margaret Cavendish, the sisters' stepmother, are too numerous to list; they were published in two collections, *Plays Written by the Thrice Noble, Illustrious and Excellent Princess, the Lady Marchioness of Newcastle* (1662) and *Plays Never Before Printed* (1668).[7] Although these works were not performed at the time, all three Cavendish women demonstrate an awareness of staging, with theatrical devices, such as an angel descending from above (*The Concealed Fancies*) and a consanguinity between language and action (for example, the bawdy 'midwife' in Margaret Cavendish's *The Sociable Companions*).[8] There are two immediate influences on the Cavendish women that allow for such material evocations: first, the role of William Cavendish (Jane and Elizabeth's father and Margaret's husband) was essential in supporting their writing and providing a secure space in which dramatic activity was normalized for women. Without William's collusion Jane and Elizabeth would never have prepared plays that were set up as productions to celebrate his triumphant return from the wars – a homecoming which, of course, never happened – and Margaret could not have pursued publication of her many creative and philosophical works.

But I think there is a deeper trend than such patriarchal support suggests and this second influence may be identified in the pre-Civil War court's flirtation with female performance, in particular, the fact that, as Karen Britland notes in her comprehensive account, *Drama at the Courts of Queen Henrietta Maria* (2006), 'Henrietta Maria, herself, became the first recorded English queen to take a speaking and singing role in dramatic production.'[9] The impact of the Queen's performance in court dramas, in particular *The Shepherd's Paradise* (1632–33) was considerable, controversial, and well-recorded, perhaps the verbal highlight being William Prynne's indirect attack upon the aristocratic actors as 'notorious whores'.[10] While Britland accurately locates the importance of European theatrical traditions in Henrietta Maria's engagement with female performance, the influence of these productions on the subsequent generation of women writers has not been fully explored. Moreover, the link between women writing for performance and women performing may be traced as a continuing line of influence from the early-seventeenth to mid-eighteenth century. Currently there has been no overarching analysis of this interface, although research on certain elements has begun to emerge. Marguerite Corporaal has undertaken an analysis of the trend as seen in the earlier part of the period; she points out, 'The analogy between the prostitute, the actress and the female playwright was reinforced by the fact that, like the prostitute, the actress and the female playwright were engaged in a process of offering pleasure in exchange for money.'[11] In parallel, Elizabeth Howe's *The First English Actresses: Women and Drama, 1660–1700* provides a solid historical base for increased textual analysis.[12] The characteristics of the plays by Cary, Wroth, and the Cavendish women may be identified as: a familiarity with staging, the use of European as well as British dramatic conventions, an acute awareness of political issues that encompass ideas beyond gender, and, perhaps above all, a readiness to embrace innovation.

Change, of course, never happens overnight, so that earlier traditions, such as translation and closet drama, recur in post-Civil War plays written by women. Katherine Philips's translation of Corneille's *Pompey* (1663) and part of his *Horace* (1668; the final scenes were completed after her death by John Denham) offered careful versions of the originals, while self-fashioning an authorial identity as 'the matchless Orinda' that located her writings securely within the frame of femininity and domesticity.[13] Similarly, Anne Finch's two plays, *The Triumphs of Love and Innocence* (1688) and *Aristoemes, or the Royal Shepherd* (1690), were closet dramas in which she dextrously evaded the personal censure public productions necessarily entailed, while simultaneously engaging with Jacobite politics and a proto-feminist valorization of women.[14] Finally, Anne Lee Wharton claimed that her tragedy, *Love's Martyr, or Witt above Crowns* (1685), 'never deserved nor was ever designed to be publick'.[15] Still, despite the reservations a present-day focus upon originality and performability might entail, the combination of apparent compliance with patriarchally determined codes of female behavior and political, and therefore public, content, suggests that women's drama, even when overtly submissive, engaged with issues that were considered unsuitable for women writers. The thread of political and public subtexts is one that recurs persistently in early modern women's dramatic writing: Lumley's *Iphigeneia* includes a self-aware focus upon the betrayal and execution of Lady Jane Grey; Sidney's writings encode careful Protestant allegories; Wroth draws telling parallels between the heroine of *Love's Victory* and the plight of Elizabeth of Bohemia; the Cavendish sisters' Civil War plays engage with the suffering and loss caused by the conflict; while Margaret Cavendish's plays demonstrate knowledge of a wide range of political issues. Restoration and eighteenth-century closet theatre and country house productions need to be read not as contained discourses, but as texts containing material that it might not have been prudent – or possible – to enact upon the public stage.

The most significant change in the way that women's drama was perceived during this period was a result of the Drury Lane production of Frances Boothby's tragicomedy, *Marcelia, or the Treacherous Friend* (1669), which was the first original play by an English woman to be commercially staged and the only known play by Boothby.[16] There has been little critical analysis of Boothby's play, but the work deserves further exploration since it serves – through its generic division – as a fulcrum between the earlier, unperformed dramas and the Restoration, and the output of early eighteenth-century women playwrights. *Marcelia* combines an almost Jacobean main plot replete with dark intrigues and an idealized heroine – the eponymous Marcelia – together with the witty, independent female characters of the sub-plot. This division lends a disjointed air to the whole production, since the scenes from the main plot are more effective read than acted, while the fast-paced comic sub-plot demonstrates a sharp awareness of theatrical production. The distinction between tragedy that relies upon text and comedy that depends upon action might seem a generic one, but the differences are underscored by comparisons with plays that both precede and postdate Boothby's work. The tragedies of Cary, Sidney, and Margaret Cavendish, which were not intended for performance, demonstrate exactly the same ponderous language as seen in *Marcelia*. More significantly, exactly the same reliance upon excessive linguistic embellishment and overbearing morality occurs in the tragic plays written by women at the end of the seventeenth and beginning of the eighteenth centuries. In contrast, the deft manipulation of comedy to question gender stereotypes and valorize independent witty heroines is replicated in the earlier plays by Wroth and all Cavendish women, as well as on the post-Restoration stage. *Marcelia* is interesting, therefore, not only because it is the first play written by an English woman to be performed on the stage, but also because it demonstrates that women dramatists cannot be neatly categorized into unperformed/performed and pre-/post-Restoration. Alongside innovation, we need to begin exploring how the links between women dramatists were developed and how themes, genres, and linguistic patterns reemerge throughout the seventeenth and eighteenth centuries.

The demarcation between tragedy and comedy may also be seen in the works of Elizabeth Polwhele who, by her own account, wrote three plays: *The Faithful Virgins* (*c.*1670) that was performed at Lincoln's Inn Fields; what was apparently an unperformed play, *The Frolick's,* *or The Lawyer Cheated* (c.1671); and the third play, *Elysium*, which is referred to in the dedication to *The Frolick's* but, unlike the former two that exist in manuscript form, is currently lost.[17] Both of Polwhele's extant plays are self-evidently meant for performance; for example, drawing on a series of devices such as dumb shows, costuming, and metatheater, that demonstrate her awareness of staging. More significantly, she engages with contemporary politics and challenges female stereotypes; as Alison Findlay astutely notes, 'Polwhele explores the performative quality of gender and the power of women to "master" events.'[18] Nevertheless, the distinctions between Polwhele's plays show an inclination toward static declamation and overly sentimentalized heroines in her tragedy, *The Faithful Virgins*, and the adroit employment of cross-dressing and farce in the tour-de-force comedy, *The Frolick's*.

The question of lost texts is still an area for scholarly investigation; we may identify fifteen women writing plays between 1610 and 1690, but we also know that not all of their works are extant. Indeed, another woman dramatist, who was known only by the pen name 'Ephelia' wrote a play called *The Pair-Royal of Coxcombs* that was produced c.1678.[19] Although the whole work seems to have been lost, excerpts were included by Ephelia in *Female Poems on Several Occasions. Written by Ephelia* (1679). The play was a racy comedy, the political sub-text of which might provide an explanation as to why, in Ephelia's own words, the work was 'damn'd', that is, unlicensed and performed only once. Maureen E. Mulvihill has posited a reason for this limitation, arguing that 'The play's male principals, represented under the cover of fictitious, silly names, must have been the two most recognizable of royal coxcombs at the Restoration court: Charles II and his brother, James, Duke of York.'[20] Increasingly, critics are beginning to investigate a wider cultural, social, and political remit within early modern women's dramatic writing than the earlier focus on gender politics, autobiographical representation, and moral issues allowed. It can no longer be questioned that female-authored plays dealt with the same public discourses as those of their male counterparts. Ephelia's acidic commentary upon the royal brothers should be identified as a common attack that appeared both in print and on stage. Aphra Behn is one of the few female dramatists whose work has attracted a wider analysis of this sort and, perhaps predictably, her plays are considered in more depth by Theodora Jankowski's chapter in this volume. Behn's inclusion here serves simply to note the divide between women who wrote plays and the professional women dramatists who relied on economic recompense for their textual production.[21] By 1690, however, women dramatists had become more commonplace with dramatists such as Delarivier Manley, Catherine Trotter, and Mary Pix having plays produced on the public stage.

Anthologies, editions, and criticism

The availability of dramatic texts written by early modern women was, as the questioner at my interview demonstrated, until the 1990s a serious obstacle to research and teaching. Some excerpts were included in pioneering anthologies, such as *The Female Spectator: English Women Writers Before 1800* (1977), edited by Mary R. Mahl and Helen Koon, which includes small sections from Cary's *Mariam* and Aphra Behn's *The Unfortunate Bride*.[22] Cary's *Mariam* is supplemented with an extract from *The History of the Life, Reign, and Death of Edward II* by Betty Travitsky in *The Paradise of Women: Writings by Englishwomen of the Renaissance* (1981).[23] Given the lack of availability of dramatic texts some anthologies notably eschewed drama altogether and concentrated upon poetry and prose. Gradually, however, individual works and collections of plays became more readily available; for example, my own edition, with S. P. Cerasano, *Renaissance Drama by Women: Texts and Documents* (1996), Diane Purkiss's *Three Tragedies by Renaissance Women* (1998), and Stephanie Hodgson-Wright's *Women's Writing of the Early Modern Period, 1588–1688: An Anthology* (2002). Today, scholars, students, and practitioners have available in modern editions the plays (or fragments) of: Lumley, Elizabeth I, Sidney, Cary, Wroth, the Cavendish sisters, Margaret Cavendish, Katherine Philips, Anne Finch, Boothby, Polwhele, Ephelia, Anne Wharton, and Aphra Behn. It is unfortunate that not all of these works are readily available. Even more disturbing is the fact that there has been the tendency to anthologize increasingly short extracts. For example, Helen Ostovich and Elizabeth Sauer's *Reading Early Modern Women: An Anthology of Texts in Manuscript and Print, 1550–1700* (2004) is an excellent resource that includes a whole section on 'Plays' covering the period dealt with in this chapter (Cary, Wroth, all three Cavendish women, Polwhele, Behn, and Ephelia); yet it reproduces very brief excerpts.[24] Internet resources, such as the comprehensive Brown University Women Writers Project, are essential for academic scholarship, but are not yet able to provide a specific focus on women's dramatic writing that allows for continuities and consanguinities to be made evident.[25] In considering what immediate new resource would enable expanded performance, in-depth scholarly analyses, and imaginative classroom activities, the production of full-text, readily available, and reasonably priced single editions of plays by seventeenth- and eighteenth-century women dramatists must be prioritized.

Since the 1980s, criticism, both of women's plays in general and, increasingly, of individual women dramatists have become more available. One of the earliest books – and still a source of inspirational material – was Nancy Cotton's *Women Playwrights in England ca. 1363–1750* (1980).[26] By the 1990s critical collections focusing on early modern women writers had become commonplace and occasionally some essays were devoted to female dramatists, although these were often the most well known; for example, Anita Pacheco's collection for Longman includes Margaret Cavendish and Aphra Behn.[27] My edited collection of essays, with S. P. Cerasano, *Readings in Renaissance Women's Drama* (1998), had a specific generic focus, but did not extend beyond Margaret Cavendish, while Margaret Rubik's detailed account in *Early Women Dramatists, 1550–1800* (1998) focuses almost entirely upon Behn and later dramatists such as Susanna Centlivre and Hannah Cowley.[28] In parallel with the need for more editorial endeavor, drama by early modern English women demands more detailed and sustained critical scholarship that extends beyond conventional periodization.

Performance history

By the beginning of the twenty-first century the known corpus of plays written by early modern English women was considerable. But this availability of text has not translated into dramatic productions, either on the public or the private stage. Intriguingly, contemporary awareness and use of the plays replicates their initial reception. First, plays written by women were acknowledged to exist, but could hardly be claimed to be part of the canon. Second, the few performances or readings that took place were mainly private events in academic environments, mirroring the early modern coterie performances and closet theater. Third, stagings in public arenas were seen as experimental and confined primarily to the later plays, especially those of Aphra Behn. There is an acute lack of stage and performance history of any of the plays written by early modern women dramatists, but it is worth undertaking a limited survey here because evidence of successful production is essential to engaging with the key question – are plays by early modern dramatists performable?

A path-breaking project in the 1990s, *Women and Dramatic Production 1550–1670*, by Alison Findlay, Stephanie Hodgson-Wright, and Gweno Williams, involved practical performances, and demonstrated categorically that works by early modern women dramatists were readily adaptable to modern stage productions.[29] A useful teaching DVD was one of the outcomes; it introduces and discusses extracts from four plays (Jane Lumley's *Iphigenia at Aulis*, Elizabeth Cary's *The Tragedy of Mariam*, Jane Cavendish and Elizabeth Brackley's *The Concealed Fancies*, and Margaret Cavendish's *The Convent of Pleasure*). A subsequent project undertaken by Gweno Williams, The Margaret Cavendish Performance Project, aimed to investigate the performability of Cavendish's plays and resulted in a DVD, *Margaret Cavendish: Plays in Performance* (2004).[30] A number of other productions of whole plays and scenes have been initiated by universities as part of the curriculum or in a conference venue. In terms of performance on the public stage, one of the most important projects was *First Hundred Years: The Professional Female Playwright* (2002–03) undertaken by the Juggernaut Theatre Company, although of the earlier playwrights, only Behn is listed as part of the reading and discussion series. There have, of course, been other individual productions such as the path-breaking RSC version of Behn's *The Rover* in 1986, but gathering information on them requires intensive searches that often produce inadequate information. From the small amount of material we have, there can be no doubt that plays by early women dramatists are performable in both private and public spaces, but there can be no tradition of performance, no chance of building upon earlier productions, if no stage history exists. Just as the plays themselves became lost or muted after their composition, so the lack of investment in scholarly projects based on the field of early women's dramatic writing prevents the development of a repository of previous production experience and, as such, hinders future stagings. If we cannot prove that these plays were performable, how can we ensure that in the future they will be performed?

Three case studies

In the preceding sections on female dramatists, editorial and critical work, and performability, some key issues have emerged, offering a series of new loci for critical perspectives. Although this final section cannot do justice to the range of possibilities opening up in the field of drama by early modern English women, it aims to foreground three areas in which immediate work is possible: innovation, performability, and continuity. Since the late 1990s women dramatists have been increasingly integrated into the canon; this movement is clearly shown by the inclusion of their plays in major anthologies of English literature. However, while there can no longer be any question that women did negotiate the same cultural, economic, and political discourses as their male counterparts, we are left with elements that do not quite *fit* the dominant forms of expression. These incongruities become more obvious if we trace the history of scholarship: first, the plays were located and published in modern editions; subsequently, criticism tended to focus on so-called women's issues such as private identity, autobiography, spirituality, and domesticity; then, by the end of the twentieth century it became apparent that female dramatists were interested in public concerns – the political, economic, international, militaristic, and social agendas that intrigued their male counterparts. The consequent integration was an essential step, but there, on occasion, remain certain elements in plays by early modern women – discourse, genre, form, theme, language, and character – which do not correspond neatly with the categories of either 'women's issues' or 'the canon'. There are no set patterns for these, often acutely individualistic, explorations, but in order to offer a new perspective on the plays, such dislocations, negations, and innovations need to be explored more carefully, avoiding the presuppositions generated by either a feminist or canonical agenda. In the second case study, the idea of performability is addressed through an analysis of Margaret Cavendish's *The Sociable Companions*. Work on performance is, perhaps, the area that needs to be addressed most urgently; here we need to move beyond the debate about whether or not it's possible to perform successfully plays written by sixteenth- and seventeenth-century English women – the performances we know of already confound the opinion that they are texts merely for erudite study. Instead, we need to recognize that female performance had a persistent influence on the way women wrote for the stage and that this history needs to extend back to the court of Henrietta Maria so that continuities and influences may be recognized. The importance of recognizing consanguinities between early modern women dramatists is the focus of the final case study which explores Frances Boothby's *Marcelia*.

Innovation: Elizabeth Cary's *Edward II*

The interpolation of dramatic passages into the prose narrative of *Edward II* challenges the way conventional tragedy negotiates the divide between history and literature, demanding a focus upon how play texts are gendered and engendered. Diane Purkiss in the introduction to her edition of the work suggests that this collage indicates an unfinished text, 'the work may not be the finished piece as Cary intended, and we must bear this in mind especially when talking about its mixture of genres'.[31] On the other hand, Tina Krontiris identified Cary's predisposition to blur generic boundaries as a more complex interplay between forms, pointing in particular to the autobiographical elements in the prose history: 'The queen's [Isabel, Edward's wife] condition as described in this part [of *Edward II*] parallels that of Lady Falkland shortly after her conversion to Catholicism in 1626.'[32]

Krontiris's argument may be evidenced from the way in which Cary translates her escape from her husband in Ireland to pursue the Catholic faith into Isabel's flight from England:

> Thus did our pilgrims scape the pride and malice
> Of him which little dreamed of this adventure.
> His craft and care, that taught him all those lessons of cunning greatness, here fell apparent short of all discretion, to be thus over-reached by one weak woman ... when the glorious power of heaven is pleased to punish man for his transgression, he takes away the sense and proper power by which he should foresee and stop his danger. (168–69)

Autobiographical narrative merges with historical account and then is transformed into a providential homily on true faith. These elisions are welded together in a seamless transition from verse – 'this adventure' – to prose – 'His craft' – and subsequently into dramatic dialogue, as Isabel addresses her brother, the King of France:

> Behold in me (dear sir) your most unhappy sister,
> The true picture of a dejected greatness,
> That bears the grief of a despised wedlock ... (173)

To fix the 'intention' of the author in relation to their text is neither possible nor desirable; it is more productive to explore the way in which Cary experiments with dramatic form precisely because she can and precisely because she was not writing for public performance. We need to avoid accepting performability as the dominant purpose of a play text or fragment and, consequently, judging those works as failures or 'unfinished' that do not offer a neat generic fit.

Performability: Margaret Cavendish's *The Sociable Companions*

At the same time, one of the most common accusations directed at seventeenth-century women dramatists is that their plays are unperformable. The previous section of this chapter has demonstrated the limitations of such a condemnation; however, a more challenging test may be made by analyzing and working with an individual scene that was not written for the public stage.

Margaret Cavendish's works were not performed during her lifetime, nor is there any indication that she intended them for production, yet they are surprisingly successful when acted. Take the mock trial scene in *The Sociable Companions* in which Get-all the usurer is conned into marrying Peg Valorosa with fake evidence that he has impregnated her. The key witness is Mistress Informer who pretends to be a midwife and explains how she was summoned to aid 'the Labouring Woman'.[33] Informer recounts a tale replete with sexual innuendo; she is woken by a man who 'raps' on her 'rotten Door' and she fails to tie her undergarments 'fast enough' so that they 'fell quite down from my hips ... [when] I was striding over the broad Kennel, in which posture I stood a great time, until the man helpt me over; but my Coats [petticoats] were all wet' (46–47). The imagery provides a humorous scene in which Informer's morals are shown to be as loose as her petticoats and it serves to introduce an illicit sexual encounter into a narrative in which Get-all must be accused of illicit sex in order to be coerced into marrying the virginal Peg. At the same time, when performed, the scene is a comic extravaganza in which Informer disrupts the court with a graphic, action-packed narrative. The clue – and cue – to the performance occurs in the first line of her 'evidence' when she explains how the man, 'raps, and raps, and — raps at the Door', allowing her to act out the subsequent events, from dropping her petticoats to standing, legs apart, in front of the audience both in the fake court room and on stage.

The false trial serves to underline the necessity of performance in that it offers a play within a play and, significantly, allows a female dramatist to underscore comic power not only through innuendo, but also through material action. Simultaneously, Cavendish challenges the male domination of legal and dramatic discourse, as well as disturbing the settings in which these discourses operated – the courtroom and stage. In assessing the performability of plays by early modern women it not sufficient to test the works out on stage, we also need to interrogate the texts for evidence that there is a self-referential awareness of the potential destabilization of patriarchal discourses that the scenes could engender when performed.

Continuities: Frances Boothby's *Marcelia*

The first play by an English woman to be performed on the public stage was Frances Boothby's *Marcelia* and, as has already been noted, this is often used as evidence of a watershed, dividing female dramatists who remained closeted in the world of text and coterie, and those who were to occupy a theatrical milieu dominated by male managers, directors, playwrights, and actors. It is worth exploring Boothby's play more closely, however, since it may be excavated for precisely the opposite evidence, since it links earlier plays with later ones, demonstrating continuities between the first female dramatists, such as Cary and the Cavendish sisters, and the successful public playwrights of the Restoration period, such as Behn and the Female Wits.

Marcelia is a tragicomedy that combines a plot centering upon the virtuous and seemingly spurned Marcelia and a comic sub-plot that follows the escapades of the rich widow, Perilla, as she thwarts her would-be lovers. The shifts between the two narratives are often read as evidence of a disjointed play and an inexperienced dramatist, but the paralleling of two women, one idealized and virtuous and the other sexually liberated and independent, was an entrenched dialectic of European culture and early modern drama. In-depth editing and analysis of *Marcelia* is certainly needed to explore the ways in which Boothby engages with works written by her male contemporaries and to excavate issues that might be pertinent to a feminist criticism of the play. Here, I would like simply to point to the connections between Boothby's play and those written by women who precede and postdate her through a focus upon Marcelia and Perilla. The titular protagonist's speeches are romantic and self-torturing; for example, toward the beginning of the play she bewails that she must conceal her true love:

> I cannot promise I shall e're be free,
> But I will colours wear of Victory;
> And my sad thoughts dress up in such disguise,
> As shall deceive the most informing eyes.
> Thus I an inward Martyr must become,
> And seem to triumph, when I'm most undone.
>
> (Boothby, *Marcelia*, fol. E.r.)

The need for women to conceal their feelings is a common device and one that was particularly appealing to early modern women dramatists; for example, at the beginning of Cary's *Mariam*, the titular protagonist also hides her grief: 'My passion now is far from being feigned. / But tears fly back and hide in your own banks' (50). Wroth in *Love's Victory* allows the main female protagonist, Musella, to confide her love to a female friend but admits that she cannot speak of her desire: 'Sometimes

I fain would speak, then straight forbear, / Knowing it most unfit; thus woe I bear' (108). Marcelia, Mariam, and Musella are, however, set against independent, articulate women who are perfectly capable of arranging to obtain their own desire. Cary provides us with the vibrant character of Salome who declares that if men can obtain a divorce then 'why [is it] barred from women then?' (53). Correspondingly, in *Love's Victory* the witty Dalina persuades Rustic to marry her (125). There is a subtle shift in the way that such female independence is contextualized: in the early seventeenth century Cary balances an ideal, chaste, and silent Mariam, with the wicked and sexually rapacious Salome, who in time-honored tradition gets all the best lines; writing in the pre-Civil War period Wroth does not condemn Dalina, but such freedom bars her from the role of central protagonist. For Boothby, composing her play in post-Restoration London, the role of the independent woman had shifted to one of comic power as Perilla proves. The widow is wooed by Moriphanus, 'a proud, silly, rich fellow', and, seeking to discourage him, she predicts death for any future husband:

> *Per.* It was told for certain by my Nativity, that my second Husband should be kill'd.
> *Mor.* But are you to have no more?
> *Per.* O, yes, yes!
> *Mor.* Why then I'le be the third; I'le tarry with all my heart for you, till the danger be over, that is to come upon the second.
> *Per.* There's a far worse, and more un-gentleman-like death that threatens the third and fourth, then all the rest; for the one will be hang'd, and the other —
>
> (*Marcelia*, n.p.)

While the stage directions require Perilla to laugh somewhat frequently and excessively, her ability to wield wit in order to secure her own ends, in this case to elude Moriphanus in order to marry the play's rake, Lucidore, allies her to a host of Restoration heroines constructed by male and female dramatists alike. If Boothby's play is allocated a place in the history of early modern drama, it should not occupy a space defined only by its peculiarity as the first drama by an English woman to be produced on the public stage. A Johnsonian sub-text lurks beneath this definition, tempting us to produce a revised version of the infamous quotation: 'Sir, a woman writing a play for public performance is like a dog walking on his hind legs. It is not done well; but you are surprised to find it done at all.' Instead, by locating Boothby in a tradition of female dramatists, it becomes evident that women were adept at writing plays, envisaging staged productions, and dealing with contemporary issues of genre, language, politics, and culture.

Conclusion

This chapter began with a memory of the early 1990s and went on to trace the ways in which the study of early modern English women dramatists has developed since then. So, to move to the present and another – this time hypothetical – interview: should I now ask a candidate about sixteenth- and seventeenth-century women dramatists what answer would the candidate supply? She or he might name the dramatists, they might refer to the many editions and critical works now available, and they might also suggest new ways of thinking about the plays. These new perspectives could include: investigating political and public discourses; changing our assumptions about how we judge texts to be un/performable; the need for modern editions, dedicated critical analyses, and a stage history; the recognition of innovation and challenging discontinuities; and the location of a female dramatic tradition that extends from the sixteenth into the eighteenth century. Oh, and just in case you were wondering, I would give that candidate a job.

Notes

1. Elizabeth Cary, *The Tragedie of Mariam, The Faire Queene of Jewry* (1613), in *Renaissance Drama by Women*, ed. S. P. Cerasano and Marion Wynne-Davies (London: Routledge, 1996), 43–75; citations from the works edited in this collection are made parenthetically. Mary Sidney, *The Tragedie of Antonie*, in *Renaissance Drama by Women*, ed. Cerasano and Wynne-Davies, 13–42.
2. Cerasano and Wynne-Davies, eds, *Renaissance Drama by Women*.
3. Jane Lumley, *The Tragedie of Iphigeneia*, in *Three Tragedies by Renaissance Women*, ed. Diane Purkiss (Harmondsworth: Penguin, 1998), 1–35. Elizabeth I, *Hercules Oetaeus* in Cerasano and Wynne-Davies, *Renaissance Drama by Women*, 6–12. Sidney, *The Tragedie of Antonie*, in *Renaissance Drama by Women*, ed. Cerasano and Wynne-Davies.
4. Cary, *The Tragedie of Mariam*, in *Renaissance Drama by Women*, ed. Cerasano and Wynne-Davies. Mary Wroth, *Love's Victory*, in *Renaissance Drama by Women*, ed. Cerasano and Wynne-Davies, 90–126.
5. Elizabeth Cary, *The History of the Life, Reign, and Death of Edward II* is a complex text since there are two versions: the longer folio, *The History of the Life, Reign, and Death of Edward II...Written by E.F. in the Year 1627* (1680) and the shorter octavo, *The History of the Most Unfortunate Prince King Edward II* (1680). For a modern edition see Diane Purkiss, ed., *Renaissance Women: The Plays of Elizabeth Cary. The Poems of Aemilia Lanyer* (London: Pickering & Chatto, 1994), 79–237.

6. Jane Cavendish and Elizabeth Brackley, *The Concealed Fancies*, in *Renaissance Drama by Women*, ed. Cerasano and Wynne-Davies, 127–54. *A Pastoral* in 'Poems, Songs, a Pastorall and a Play', Bodleian Library Rawlinson MS Poet 16 and in Germaine Greer et al., eds, *Kissing the Rod: An Anthology of Seventeenth-Century Women's Verse* (London: Virago, 1988), 106–15.

7. For an up-to-date list of editions and critical works see the homepage of the international Margaret Cavendish Society: http://jan.ucc.nau.edu/~jbf/CavBiblio.html#eds

8. Cerasano and Wynne-Davies, eds, *Renaissance Drama by Women*, 152–53; Margaret Cavendish, *The Sociable Companions or, the Female Wits*, ed. Amanda Holton (Oxford: Seventeenth Century Press, 1996), 46–47.

9. Karen Britland, *Drama at the Courts of Queen Henrietta Maria* (Cambridge: Cambridge University Press, 2006), 6.

10. William Prynne, *Histrio-Mastix: The Players Scourge or Actors Tragedies* (1633), Index.

11. Marguerite Corporaal, 'Wicked Words and Virtuous Voices: The Reconstruction of Tragic Subjectivity By Renaissance and Early Restoration Women Dramatists' (PhD Thesis, University of Groningen, 2003), 230.

12. Elizabeth Howe, *The First English Actresses: Women and Drama, 1660–1700* (Cambridge: Cambridge University Press, 1992).

13. Katherine Philips, *Pompey* and *Horace*, in *Poems by Orinda. To which is added Pompey and Horace* (1667), in G. Greer and R. Little, eds, *The Collected Works of Katherine Philips*, vol. 3 (Essex: Stump Cross, 1993).

14. Anne Finch, *The Triumphs of Love and Innocence* (1688) and *Aristoemes, or the Royal Shepherd* (1690) are both collected in *Miscellany Poems with Two Plays by Ardelia* (Folger Shakespeare Library, MS N. b.3). *Aristoemes* is available from the Brown Women Writers Project (on subscription: http://www.wwp.brown.edu/). In addition, M. Reynolds prints *The Triumphs of Love and Innocence* and *Aristomenes* in her edition, *The Poems of Anne, Countess of Winchilsea* (Chicago: University of Chicago Press, 1903).

15. Anne Wharton, *Love's Martyr, or Witt above Crowns* (BL Add MS 28, 693), A1v. See also G. Greer and S. Hastings, eds, *The Surviving Works of Ann Wharton* (Essex: Stump Cross, 1997).

16. Frances Boothby, *Marcelia, or the Treacherous Friend* (1670); available from the Brown Women Writers Project. Further references are cited parenthetically in the text.

17. Elizabeth Polwhele, *The Faythfull Virgins*, Bodelian Library MS. Rawlinson Poet. 195; and *The Frolick's: or, The Lawyer Cheated An New Comedy, the first Coppy written by Mrs E.P.*, Cornell University Library Rare Manuscript Collection, Kroch Library 4600Bd. MS/43 MRC. See also Judith Milhous and Robert Hume, eds, *The Frolick's: or, The Lawyer Cheated* (Ithaca: Cornell University Press, 1977).

18. Alison Findlay, 'Elizabeth Polwhele, "The Frolick's: or The Lawyer Cheated"', in *Reading Early Modern Women: An Anthology of Texts in Manuscript and Print, 1550–1700*, ed. Helen Ostovich and Elizabeth Sauer (London: Routledge, 2004), 441.

19. Ephelia, *Female Poems on Several Occasions* (1679). See also Maureen Mulvihill, *Ephelia* (Aldershot: Ashgate, 2003).

20. Maureen Mulvihill, 'Ephelia Epilogue, *The Pair-Royal of Coxcombs, Performed at a Dancing School'*, in *Reading Early Modern Women*, ed. Ostovich and Sauer, 447.
21. Janet Todd, ed., *The Collected Works of Aphra Behn* (Columbus: Ohio State University Press, 1992).
22. Mary R. Mahl and Helen Koon, eds, *The Female Spectator: English Women Writers Before 1800* (Bloomimgton: Indiana University Press 1977), 99–114, 165–78.
23. Betty Travitsky, ed., *The Paradise of Women: Writings by Englishwomen of the Renaissance* (London: Greenwood, 1981), 209–34.
24. Ostovich and Sauer, eds, *Reading Early Modern Women*, 420–69. While I have referred only to those playwrights who wrote within the timeframe of this volume (1610–90), the following women dramatists are also included in Ostovich and Sauer: Ariadne, Delarivier Manley, Mary Pix, Catharine Trotter and Susanna Centlivre.
25. http://www.wwp.brown.edu/
26. Nancy Cotton, *Women Playwrights in England ca. 1363–1750* (Lewisburg: Bucknell University Press, 1980).
27. Anita Pacheco, ed., *Early Women Writers, 1600–1720* (London: Longman, 1998), 109–222.
28. Wynne-Davies and S. P. Cerasano, eds, *Readings in Renaissance Women's Drama* (London: Routledge, 1998); Margaret Rubik, *Early Women Dramatists, 1550–1800* (London: St. Martin's Press, 1998).
29. On this project, see Alison Findlay, Stephanie Hodgson-Wright, and Gweno Williams, '"The Play is Ready to be Acted": Women and Dramatic Production 1550–1670', *Women's Writing* 6.1 (1999): 129–48. A video of the project is also available: Findlay, Hodgson-Wright, and Williams, *Women Dramatists, 1550–1670: Plays in Performance* (Lancaster: Women and Dramatic Production with Lancaster University Television, 1999). Copies of the DVD are available from stephanie.hodgson-wright @sunderland.ac.uk
30. Copies of the DVD are available at www.margaret-cavendish.net
31. Purkiss, *Renaissance Women*, xxviii. Further references are cited parenthetically in the text.
32. Tina Krontiris, 'Style and Gender in Elizabeth Cary's *Edward II*', in *The Renaissance Englishwoman in Print: Counterbalancing the Canon*, ed. Anne M. Haselkorn and Betty S. Travitsky (Amherst: University of Massachusetts Press, 1990), 138.
33. Cavendish, *The Sociable Companions*, ed. Holton, 46. Further references are cited parenthetically in the text.

11
History, Satire, and Fiction by British Women Writers in the Seventeenth Century

Margaret Reeves

Seventeenth-century women's prose fictional narrative is often addressed within one of two generic frameworks. The first is that of romance, and the second, that of the novel. Although a consensus among literary historians assumes that romance was eventually overtaken and displaced by the eighteenth-century novel, romance remained a vibrant and dynamic form of writing in the seventeenth century. Links between romance narrative and women's culture, moreover, are well recognized, not only because of the prevalence of women as writers and patrons of prose romance, but also because of the emphasis on female subjectivity within the narratives themselves.[1] Feminist literary historians have had less success in integrating seventeenth-century women's narrative into the story of the rise of the novel. Amatory fictional narratives written toward the end of the century have recently been recognized as key contributors to the evolution of the novel, but they are usually seen to anticipate rather than exemplify novelistic prose.[2] Other fictions written by women in the seventeenth century are often read in similarly teleological fashion, of interest only as rudimentary versions of the later, more sophisticated narrative form of the novel.[3] Whereas a novel-centered approach to early modern fiction is often limited by its preoccupation with the problem of realism as a factor in the trajectory of the rise of the novel, other approaches to the larger question of the history of fiction remain open to us. Ian Watt's category of formal realism – with its emphasis on 'particular people in particular circumstances' – explains how the eighteenth-century novel came to provide sufficient referential adequacy to count as realistic,[4] but an examination of seventeenth-century fiction suggests alternative means to explore relationships between truth, fiction, and historical narrative. This chapter steps outside of a romance/novel binary, tracing intersections between historical, satiric, and fictional modes of writing in women's prose narratives written between 1610 and 1689, and taking as specific examples prose narratives written by Elizabeth Cary and Aphra Behn. Cary's *The History of the Life, Reign, and Death of Edward II* and Behn's longest and most celebrated narratives, *Love-Letters Between a Nobleman and his Sister* and *Oroonoko: or, The Royal Slave. A True History*, illustrate the need to explore seventeenth-century fiction on its own historical ground rather than positioning it as mere precursor to a literary form that did not come into its own until the next century.[5]

Moving away from the literary and historical framework of 'declining romance' and 'rising novel' enables an analysis of Cary's and Behn's works through an alternative critical lens grounded in seventeenth-century narrative conventions. Shifting the interpretative framework in this direction will reveal how Cary and Behn exploit for satiric purposes the blurring of boundaries between fiction and history typical of seventeenth-century prose narratives. This approach is well suited to fictional prose of this period given its refusal, as Michael McKeon observes, to make clear distinctions between fictional and factual narrative.[6] D. R. Woolf notes a related phenomenon in his study of early modern historical writing, explaining that 'history in the seventeenth century was conceived of as a form of literature'. During the early modern period, Woolf shows, the movement of the discipline of history toward a scientific model, which would entail claims to greater objectivity, had not yet occurred, so the line dividing the falsehoods of fiction from the truth-telling aims of history remained intriguingly blurred during the seventeenth century.[7] Even toward the end of the century, booksellers' quarterly lists or 'term catalogues' (which were produced by London booksellers to show titles of books currently in production) placed prose fictional narratives in the same category as historical works. For example, the Michaelmas Term Catalogue of 1677 includes under the category 'History' the following books: 'The English Princess, or The Duchess Queen; being English and French Adventures. A Novel'; '*Zayde*. An excellent new Romance'; and '*Capello* and *Bianca*. A Novel. Written in French; and now Englished by L. N., Gent'. Moreover, these term catalogues reinforce an alliance between fiction and history by excluding imaginative prose from the category 'Poetry', which was reserved for poems and dramatic works.[8] This refusal to separate fictional from historical narratives in the seventeenth century frees us from the constraints that arise in a novel-centered approach to literary history, in which fiction must be realistic but *not* true, as Watt contends in defining formal realism, the novel's distinguishing feature.[9] The value placed upon plausibility and referential adequacy within formal realism is necessary precisely because the characters, circumstances, and events are invented.

Woolf demonstrates that prior to the seventeenth century, historical writing underwent significant changes, when a 'moribund medieval chronicle tradition [that] lingered through the sixteenth century ... breathe[d] its last in the seventeenth'.[10] The chronicle, with its temporal record of events, had produced factual knowledge without the texture of analytic interpretation now intrinsic to historical writing. Nevertheless, interest in documentary evidence for its own sake was preserved in another form, for as J. G. A. Pocock explains, the sixteenth and seventeenth centuries witnessed 'a great divorce between the scholars and antiquarians on the one hand, and the literary historians on the other'. According to Pocock, antiquarians would ultimately provide the necessary factual resources upon which the new analytically oriented literary historians would still need to rely.[11] In the seventeenth century, however, the interest of those in the first camp lay in the erudite accumulation of material evidence as manifestations of historical fact; those in the second camp – the more *literary* historians – focused instead on telling their stories in an engaging narrative form.

It is this latter approach – the one taken by literary historians – that Cary self-consciously adopts in *History of Edward II*, as she indicates in her preface: 'I have not herein followed the dull Character of our Historians, nor amplified more than they infer, by Circumstance'.[12] Although it is unclear here whether Cary is characterizing as dull an older chronicle style or the more recent antiquarian approach, her declaration nevertheless aligns her writing with the more literary approach to which Pocock refers. Moreover, her promise not to amplify beyond conventional patterns of inference is sufficiently vague to provide ample scope for a livelier style of narration. Histories written in this more literary style, according to Malcolm Smuts, constituted a new form of 'analytic' historiography emergent during the late Elizabethan and early Stuart period. These narratives explore contemporary political issues through analysis of analogous historical examples.[13] As Smuts shows, this approach has its origins in two sources: the classical historical writings of Tacitus and the neo-classical satires popular in the 1590s: 'Both genres were characterized by efforts at greater realism and insightfulness and by a pervasive cynicism concerning the behavior of the rich and powerful. Both were often seen as vehicles for cryptic references to living individuals, including prominent members of the court'.[14] Ronald Syme comments on the imaginative nature of Tacitus's history, especially his 'artifice and ingenuity and soaring eloquence. Perhaps to excess ... the products being not always congruous with the persons and events'.[15] Cary's historical narrative aligns with this new mode of writing because its critical commentary on the political turbulence leading up to Edward II's deposition and death during the early fourteenth century applies remarkably well to the contemporary political situation in England during the 1620s. The emphasis on motive and cause in *History of Edward II*, as Barbara Lewalski and F. J. Levy show, provides insistent parallels to present-day concerns, and the commentary itself, expressed frequently in the form of maxims, aligns Cary's style with this new 'politic history'.[16] Moreover, her use of dialogue to dramatize interactions between the historical characters she depicts is consistent with Cary's Tacitean model. Tacitus includes speeches in *The Histories*, almost all of which are invented, according to Syme. In effect, Syme argues, the use of invented speech 'takes Tacitus a long way in the direction of drama or prose fiction', a claim that applies equally well to *History of Edward II*.[17]

This is not to say that early modern writers were unaware of differences between historical and imaginative literature. Yet it is imaginative writing that is placed in closer proximity to truth than history in Philip Sidney's *An Apologie for Poetrie* (1595). Sidney argues that 'the historian, wanting the precept, is so tied, not to what should be but to what is, to the particular truth of things and not to the general reason of things, that his example draweth no necessary consequence, and therefore a less fruitful doctrine'.[18] History's alignment with particular representations, then, puts it at a disadvantage in comparison to literature, the latter having more direct access to higher moral truths because it is not grounded in particulars. Sidney's rationale can be used to explain a further prefatory comment in *History of Edward II*. Having asserted the distinctiveness of her livelier narrative style, Cary explains that 'I strive to please the truth not time'.[19] Despite these claims to singularity, the preface to *History of Edward II* thus situates Cary's work within early modern debates about the nature of historical writing and the form within which writers can best convey truth.

Cary's approach to truth-telling relies on a considerable amount of 'amplification', despite the above-noted claim to the contrary, to the extent that her deployment of literary strategies has occasioned considerable debate among modern scholars over the narrative's generic status. Louise Schleiner, for example, suggests that rather than a history, Cary's narrative should be defined as 'fictionalized history or historical fiction' because of its affinity with the modern historical novel.[20]

The story is told through the voice of an omniscient narrator who is relentlessly intrusive in her moral evaluations of character. The narrator claims she will demonstrate the difference between appearance and reality by showing that 'the visible Calendar is not the true Character of inward Perfection; evidently proved in the Life, Raign, and Death of this unfortunate Monarch'.[21] Dialogue and action reveal Edward's and others' motivations, yet it is the narrator's insights into the thoughts and behaviors of Edward, his two favorites, Gaveston and Spencer, and his wife, Queen Isabel, that demonstrate the underlying corruption motivating their decisions. For example, Edward's desire to recall Gaveston from exile is represented through a comment on the King's state of mind:

> He dares not Communicate the depth of his Resolution, being a secret of too great weight to be divulged; he thinks intreaty an act too much beneath him; and to attempt at random, full of hazard. In these his restless passions, he out-runs the Honey-month of his Empire; looking asquint upon the necessary Actions of State, that requir'd his more vigilant care and foresight.[22]

Whereas Edward's passions are strong, his rule is weak, because the collective strength of the barons places limits on his power, and he lacks the wherewithal to manage or circumvent these limitations. Edward's numerous errors become an object lesson in the perils of irresponsible rule, with his failures as a monarch deriving from flaws in his moral character. The narrator's analysis of behavior and motivation is the principal method through which characterization is achieved throughout the narrative, yet as Schleiner observes, dramatizations of dialogue and action as well as the reported thoughts and motives of characters are entirely invented.[23] The representation itself of narrative omniscience, underscored by the narrator's confidence in her own judgment and authority, contributes to the narrative's distinctively literary nature, thereby enabling a seamless blurring of boundaries between fiction and history within this narrative.

Other scholars have had more difficulty in coming to terms with the literary amplifications in *History of Edward II*. Donald Stauffer styles it as a 'wedding ... of verse and prose, of biography and the drama'. Attempting to demonstrate that the narrative 'has been shaped by metrical drama', Stauffer reproduces several passages of prose in lines of blank verse.[24] Not surprisingly, this works particularly well for sections taken from passages of dialogue, for many of them scan as iambic pentameter verse. Strongly influenced by Stauffer's argument, Betty S. Travitsky defines the narrative as an unfinished proto-drama, and Tina Krontiris, assuming that *History of Edward II* is 'closer to the form of a play', suggests it is '*written* predominantly in blank verse'.[25] Diane Purkiss applies this conception of form to her edition of the narrative by arranging all of the dialogue and some of the more rhythmical prose passages into verse paragraphs, although the folio volume used as copy text for Purkiss's edition is in fact printed entirely in prose form.[26] Building on these speculations, Donald Foster suggests 'verse biography' as an appropriate generic identification because the history is '*written* principally in end-stopped blank verse'.[27] Although Foster acknowledges that the folio is printed as prose, he further speculates that if the printer of the 1680 folio found the manuscript in prose form, it demonstrates Cary's need 'to conserve paper by printing her verse as prose'.[28] These critics swim energetically against the tide of available evidence in order to reconcile the formal properties of *History of Edward II* with those of Cary's published play, *The Tragedy of Mariam*.[29] These arguments are embedded in conflicted assumptions about what constitutes an historical as opposed to a literary narrative. Attempts to read beyond the materiality of the text at hand – the 1680 folio – in order to get at 'the truth' of an original copy text place us in pursuit of a literary pot of gold, for the text was printed long after Cary's death, and the printer's copy text does not survive. There is, however, a fair copy of Cary's history in an extant manuscript in the Fitzwilliam Museum, and this document is composed entirely in prose. Even more to the point, there is no evidence that its prose form rather than verse has been chosen to conserve paper, for there are ample double-ruled margins along the top, bottom, and outer edges of every page of the manuscript, and the paragraph breaks, while marked by an oblique line, are also indicated with the use of end-stopped lines.[30] It could be that these debates over form and genre illustrate the extent to which the narrative's literary features invite us to read it as imaginative literature, but more importantly, they also exemplify the interpretative problems that arise when we impose a modern conception of history onto an early modern historical narrative.

Like Cary, Behn plays self-consciously with the idea of the historian's role in *Love-Letters*, explicitly declaring an historical orientation, yet using fictional strategies of narration to produce larger truths that move beyond mere facticity. Interestingly, both writers position their writing as a departure from an imagined norm of historical narrative. The 1680 printer of *History of Edward II*, picking up on Cary's self-conscious distinction between her own and other historians' styles, remarks that 'we are apt to believe those days produced very few who were able to express their Conceptions in so Masculine a Stile'.[31] These 'Conceptions', evident in the narrator's intrusive commentary and analytical reflections on the theory and practice of kingship, suggest a level of authority in the narrative voice that the printer evidently associates with masculinity. As with Cary, Behn distinguishes between her approach to historical writing and that of an inferred historiographical norm:

> But as it is not the Business of this little History to treat of War, but altogether Love; leaving those rougher Relations to the Chronicles and Historiographers of those Times, I will only hint on such things in this Enterprize as are most proper for my purpose, and tell you that Cesario omitted nothing for the carrying on his great Design.[32]

Whereas style marks the difference between *History of Edward II* and its contemporaries for both Cary and her printer, subject matter is singled out here as the distinguishing feature of Behn's narrative, although both texts articulate their differences from projected historiographical norms through the same two registers of gender and genre. Behn's claim that she focuses primarily on love is obviously disingenuous, however, for that 'great Design', the 1685 rebellion against James II led by James Scott, Duke of Monmouth, depicted as Cesario here, is the climactic event of the third volume of *Love-Letters*. Indeed, the narrator's promise to limit her focus to love is contradicted by the extent to which she portrays the events leading up to, during, and following the rebellion. Nor is this 'little History' as brief as she implies, for the above passage appears toward the end of the third of three substantial volumes. Granted, *Love-Letters* offers little statistical or other 'hard' data on the rebellion, but the roles played by Monmouth and his political ally, Ford Lord Grey, are dramatized in considerable detail throughout all three volumes, the first two focusing on the amours of Philander and Sylvia, who are meant to represent Grey and his wife's sister, Henrietta Berkeley, with whom he had an affair. An additional level of irony in the above-quoted denial of the text's historical status arises from the uncertain truth status of the narrative, for most of the details Behn incorporates are invented. She goes far beyond Cary's Tacitean amplifications, creating a richly satiric imaginative gloss overlaying the bare framework of historical events – Grey's escape with Berkeley to the continent, the planning of the rebellion by a group of radical Whigs led by Monmouth and Grey, and the failed rebellion itself. Like Cary, Behn dramatizes the thoughts, private conversations, and sexual preoccupations of her main characters, but the extent to which Behn embellishes history with fictional letters, imagined dialogue, and depictions of intimate relations between Sylvia and a range of male lovers are deliberately extravagant as is appropriate for a work that satirizes the figures whose follies it depicts. Behn's readers, of course, would recognize the considerable degree of invention as an additional layer of irony lending humor as well as color to her much amplified version of recent political history.

For both Cary and Behn, satire is the impetus for and result of the 'amplifications' that shape their narratives, and both *History of Edward II* and *Love-Letters* function as satiric interventions in politically volatile situations. *History of Edward II* is positioned to avert an incipient crisis that nevertheless culminates in two historically significant events – the assassination of the Duke of Buckingham in 1628 a few months after Cary completed the narrative, and Charles I's subsequent, ill-fated decision to prorogue Parliament and initiate his eleven-year term of personal rule. Cary's narrative offers a satiric corrective in its illustration of the fatal consequences of a king's excessive reliance on unpopular favorites, and his resulting inability to negotiate or manipulate to his own advantage the powerful factions among the barons whose collective strength, when united, overpowered his own.[33] Edward II's reign encodes telling parallels with that of James I and Charles I up to 1628, and Cary's commentary includes critical analysis of kingship and royal patronage in ways that gesture insistently to contemporary problems in the early Stuart courts. In dramatizing Edward II's emotional attachments to Piers Gaveston, his first favorite, and Hugh Spencer, his second and more powerful favorite, Cary exploits a parallel situation in James I's relations first with Robert Carr, the Earl of Somerset, and subsequently with George Villiers, the Duke of Buckingham. By the time Charles I succeeded his father in 1625, Buckingham had become the most powerful man in England next to the King, despite considerable dissatisfaction with Buckingham expressed by opposing factions in Parliament. As Curtis Perry shows, the parallel between the fourteenth- and seventeenth-century English King and his favored administrators had been the subject of a hotly contested speech in Parliament during the early 1620s, in which a Member of Parliament had publicly compared Buckingham to Spencer.[34] Three hundred years earlier, both Gaveston and Spencer had been put to death by the barons for perceived abuses of power, and Edward II's dependence on his favorites played a key role in his eventual deposition and execution. A narrative written during the late 1620s at the height of parliamentary hostility towards

Buckingham would, then, inevitably recall the historical parallel of the fourteenth-century series of events. Cary positions as disastrous Edward's 'natural vicious inclination' for Gaveston and Spencer, suggesting that these intimate relations produce an unhealthy dependency that undermines this king's ability to rule.[35] Yet Cary is equally critical of Isabel for neglecting her duties as queen, wife, and mother by helping to bring about Edward's deposition and death. Despite its strong satire on corruption within the court, *History of Edward II* ultimately lends support for a monarchy whose theoretical underpinnings Cary so thoroughly interrogates in her analytical commentary on Edward II's failures as a ruler.

The political significance of *Love-Letters* is less stable, shifting as the narrative progresses because the events under scrutiny are still unfolding, their outcome not yet fully evident even as Behn completes the second of three volumes shortly after Monmouth's rebellion.[36] The political motivations at work in the first volume, published in 1684 before the rebellion, are served by undermining the credibility of both Grey and Monmouth as political leaders. The narrative advocates public abhorrence for the group of radical Whigs who opposed James Stuart's succession, and who had indicated by 1684 that they were prepared to use violence to achieve this end. By the time Behn completed the second volume in 1685, Monmouth had been executed, whereas Grey was in the process of negotiating a pardon from the King. Grey would escape execution because his great wealth made him useful to the King and his courtiers, and his confession a source of information for prosecution of other rebels. Grey began writing his confession on 21 July 1685, completed it on 16 October, and was pardoned on 12 November 1685.[37] The publication of the second volume of *Love-Letters* in the interim situated Grey's republican rhetoric of liberty within a licentious context as immoral and unprincipled as it was treasonous. As an attempt to intervene in the legal process through which Grey was obtaining his pardon, the second volume of *Love-Letters* reminded readers that his reputation was well deserved. The political motivations of the third volume of *Love-Letters* are consistent with those shaping the first two volumes, for it satirizes in detail the rebels involved in the planning and execution of the rebellion, even though it is curiously out of step with developments current at the time of its publication in 1687. By this time, James II's appetite for retribution had diminished, for, as Melinda Zook observes, not only did James's policies undergo a notable shift in 1687 in opening up offices and granting favors to Whigs and dissenters, he also went further in giving clemency that year to several rebels still in hiding on the continent.[38] Throughout *Love-Letters*, history literally engenders Behn's fiction, and further animates it when the rebellious activities of the King's son, the Duke of Monmouth, and his radical Whig associates prove politically as well as sexually titillating.

Although both Behn and Cary blur the boundaries between fiction and history by deploying textual narrative to comment on extra-textual situations, important differences between Cary's 'politic history' and Behn's satirical treatment of political rebellion illustrate the versatility of seventeenth-century notions of history and fiction. Cary's narrative is a 'cryptohistory' that is suggestive primarily because the set of 300-year-old historical events it depicts align in recognizable ways with recent and current events, its imaginative amplifications serving to illuminate the historical parallels in order to remind its readers of the potential consequences should the King fail to intervene effectively in the growing hostility between his favorite and Parliament. Behn's parallel narrative is easily recognizable as a roman-à-clef because of the distinctiveness of the figures whose lives she depicts. Grey's incestuous affair with his wife's sister became widely known once her family took him to court. Monmouth was famous not only as the oldest and much loved illegitimate son of Charles II, but also as the man favored by the Whigs as the King's successor when they tried to pass a law excluding Charles II's brother, James, from the succession because of his Catholicism. Cesario's affair with Hermione alludes to the relationship between the Duke of Monmouth and his lover, Henrietta Wentworth, who accompanied Monmouth to Europe and helped to finance his 1685 rebellion. Behn satirizes Monmouth's ineptitude as a political leader by depicting him as a dupe of the much more intelligent but duplicitous Hermione. Although both narratives blur boundaries between fiction and history, Cary's *History of Edward II* negotiates this divide as a means to realize narrative's potential for truth-telling. The truths to which it alludes resonate through the parallel structures of historical allegory enabled by coincidental similarities between past and present relations of kings with their favorites. Behn's *Love-Letters*, however, destabilizes for its own satiric purposes such assumptions about the relationship between truth and historical representation. This effect is further complicated by the fact that the first two volumes of *Love-Letters* have the potential to shape the ultimate outcome of the events that constitute its own subject matter, should its readers be persuaded by its royalist, propagandist agenda. In this respect, Behn's narrative registers its capacity to construct both literally as well as figuratively its own truths.

Behn's most famous prose narrative, *Oroonoko*, published in 1688, also occupies the dual grounds of fiction and history as is evident in its titular assertion of its status as a *'True History'*. In the dedication, and in the narrator's insistence on her status as an 'eye-witness', the text asserts its authenticity with a vehemence that, paradoxically, invites a reconsideration of its truth claims.[39] Unlike *History of Edward II*, which can entertain readings of its past-to-present parallels because it rests on an historically verifiable set of events, the opposite has occurred with *Oroonoko*. This work has often been read as an authentic historical account, and until recently, most of Behn's biographers have accepted her claim that she traveled to Surinam as a young woman.[40]

Yet doubts exist as to whether the events portrayed in *Oroonoko* actually occurred, whether Behn traveled to Surinam, and even whether an African man named Oroonoko ever lived in either Coramantien or Surinam. Regardless of the veracity of these claims, however, Behn uses a set of known historical events – the transportation of Coramantien slaves to Surinam, the English occupation of Surinam, and its subsequent loss to the Dutch – to animate her story of an attractive, royal-blooded but tragically misguided rebel.[41] I have argued elsewhere that insisting on *Oroonoko*'s truth status shifts attention away from the text's resonance with the recent Monmouth rebellion and with political tensions on the rise during the summer of 1688 when *Oroonoko* was published.[42] Uncertainties about the text's truth status and its lead character's historical reality suggest a creative ambiguity in Behn's blurring of the fiction/history divide. Troubled by the text's inadequate establishment of its fictional or historical status, however, modern scholars feel compelled to take a stand on this question, as if we must prove its falsehood or veracity. Yet I would argue that such an approach refuses to engage with early modern fiction on its own ground, and views the text through a generic lens that is modern, or at least, novelistic. This is why *Oroonoko*'s status as a novel remains a vexed question. Within seventeenth-century prose narrative, however, the distinction between fiction and history is a matter of degree rather than kind. If we embrace the intersections between fiction and history in seventeenth-century narrative rather than see the convergence as suspect, we are better able to read early fiction on its own terms rather than lamenting its pre-novelistic inadequacies.

Blurring boundaries between fiction and history entails, then, a creative negotiation between past and present, text and context. Constance C. Relihan argues that such instances of signaling to the world outside the text constitute realism, but in explicating his influential concept of formal realism, Watt claims much more than that of signaling to an external reality.[43] The paradoxical premise of formal realism is that it is not true, nor does it stake truth claims. Rather, Watt's conception of formal realism makes claims for referential adequacy, presenting plausible plots and believable characters by adhering to laws of causality and probability. Formal realism is the term Watt applies to this collection of techniques when writers use them to fabricate a circumstantial view of life. Seventeenth-century verisimilitude, I would argue, occupies a different semantic terrain than the fully articulated theory of formal realism that Watt applies to the mid-eighteenth-century novel. For example, links between text and context are more relational than mimetic, dependent as they are on blurring such divisions between history and fiction, past and present, or truth and satire. This does not mean that we cannot discuss verisimilitude in relation to seventeenth-century fiction, but that such discussion should be undertaken on early modern terms and with reference to the specific features of seventeenth- rather than eighteenth-century fictions to avoid the teleology that inevitably arises in discussions of realism conducted within a novelistic epistemological framework.

Therefore, allegorical resonance, systematic allusion, and similar parallel narrative structures provide more useful models through which to theorize a reconfigured concept of verisimilitude in seventeenth-century fiction, because these earlier fictional narratives engage with reality through the versatile medium of historical narrative. The narratives by Behn and Cary that I examine illustrate that fiction and history converge readily in satiric narratives, as in cases where fictional (or fictionalized) characters portray the errors and vices of historical personages in ways that suggest correspondence with an extra-textual situation. Points of intersection between fictive and historical personages reveal their satiric meaning as the stories unfold, so that the activity of narration – of storytelling – remains an essential element of the satiric project. True, this relational interaction between fictive landscapes and an historicized reality is qualitatively different than the 'realism' that is considered the defining element of novelistic fiction, but then again, when we discuss seventeenth-century fiction, we are not, nor should we be, discussing the novel.

Notes

1. See, for example, Helen Hackett, *Women and Romance Fiction in the English Renaissance* (Cambridge: Cambridge University Press, 2000); and Mary Ellen Lamb, *Gender and Authorship in the Sidney Circle* (Madison: University of Wisconsin Press, 1990). I would like to thank Sean Lawrence and Mihoko Suzuki for their helpful comments on earlier drafts of this essay.

2. See Rosalind Ballaster, *Seductive Forms: Women's Amatory Fiction from 1684 to 1740* (Oxford: Clarendon Press, 1992); William Warner, 'Licensing Pleasure: Literary History and the Novel in Early Modern Britain', in *The Columbia History of the British Novel*, ed. John J. Richetti (New York: Columbia University Press, 1994), 1–22; John J. Richetti, '*Love Letters Between a Nobleman and His Sister*: Aphra Behn and Amatory Fiction', in *Augustan Subjects: Essays in Honour of Martin C. Battestin*, ed. Albert J. Rivero (Newark: University of Delaware Press, 1997), 13–28; and Toni Bowers, 'Seduction Narratives and Tory Experience in Augustan England', *The Eighteenth Century: Theory and Interpretation* 40.2 (1999): 128–54.

3. A consensus, although not unanimous, among feminist literary historians accords primacy of place to Aphra Behn in tracing women's contributions to the history of the novel. Some of the most influential are Jane Spencer, *The Rise of the Woman Novelist: From Aphra Behn to Jane Austen* (Oxford: Basil Blackwell, 1986); Janet Todd, *The Sign of Angellica: Women, Writing and Fiction, 1660–1800* (New York: Columbia University Press, 1989); and Deborah Ross, *The Excellence of Falsehood: Romance, Realism, and Women's Contribution to the Novel* (Lexington: University Press of Kentucky, 1991). A notable departure from this view appears in Josephine Donovan's *Women and the Rise of the Novel, 1405–1726* (New York: St. Martin's Press, 1999). Donovan identifies an emergent tradition of women's literary realism in English fiction beginning with some of Margaret Cavendish's prose fiction narratives, but insists that *Oroonoko* and *Love-Letters* lack sufficient realism to merit inclusion in this tradition. See Donovan, *Women and the Rise of the Novel*, 79 and 91.

4. Ian Watt, *The Rise of the Novel: Studies in Defoe, Richardson and Fielding* (London: Chatto & Windus, 1957), 15.

5. Aphra Behn, *Love-Letters Between a Nobleman and his Sister* (initially published in three separate volumes in 1684, 1685, and 1687), ed. Janet Todd (London: Penguin, 1996); Behn, *Oroonoko: or, The Royal Slave. A True History* (1688), in *Oroonoko and Other Writings*, ed. Paul Salzman (Oxford: Oxford University Press, 1998); and Elizabeth Cary, *The History of The Life, Reign, and Death of Edward II. King of England, And Lord of Ireland. With The Rise and Fall of his great Favourites, Gaveston and the Spencers. Written by E.F. in the year 1627. And Printed verbatim from the Original* (London: Printed by J.C. for Charles Harper, at the Flower-de-luce in Fleet-street; Samuel Crouch, at the Princes Arms in Popes-head-Alley in Cornhil; and Thomas Fox, at the Angel in Westminster-hall, 1680).

6. Michael McKeon, *The Origins of the English Novel 1600–1740* (Baltimore: Johns Hopkins University Press, 1987), 269.

7. D. R. Woolf, *The Idea of History in Early Stuart England: Erudition, Ideology, and 'The Light of Truth' from the Accession of James I to the Civil War* (Toronto: University of Toronto Press, 1990), xv. Woolf acknowledges that such debates about the nature of history continue without having reached unanimity on the question of the adoption of science as a model for history.

8. See Edward Arber, comp., *The Term Catalogues, 1668–1709 A.D.; with a number for Easter Term, 1711 A.D. A Contemporary Bibliography of English Literature in the reigns of Charles II, James II, William and Mary, and Ann* (London: Privately Printed, 1903), I:289.

9. Watt, *Rise of the Novel*, 34.

10. Woolf, *Idea of History*, 14.

11. J. G. A. Pocock, *The Ancient Constitution and the Feudal Law: A Study of English Historical Thought in the Seventeenth Century* (Cambridge: Cambridge University Press, 1987), quoted in Woolf, *Idea of History*, 15.

12. Cary, 'The Author's Preface to the Reader', sig. A2v.

13. Malcolm Smuts, 'Court-Centred Politics and the Uses of Roman Historians, *c*.1590–1630', in *Culture and Politics in Early Stuart England*, ed. Kevin Sharpe and Peter Lake (London: Macmillan, 1994), 22.

14. Malcolm Smuts, *Court Culture and the Origins of a Royalist Tradition in Early Stuart England* (Philadelphia: University of Pennsylvania Press, 1987), 79.

15. Ronald Syme, *Tacitus*, vol. 1 (Oxford: Clarendon Press, 1958), 192–93. See also Syme's discussion of Tacitus's treatment of motivation, 316.

16. Barbara Lewalski, *Writing Women in Jacobean England* (Cambridge, MA: Harvard University Press, 1993), 203; and F. J. Levy, *Tudor Historical Thought* (San Marino: Huntington Library, 1967), 270–71.

17. Syme, *Tacitus*, 192, 317.

18. Philip Sidney, *An Apologie for Poetrie* (London, 1595), reprinted in *An Apology for Poetry or The Defence of Poesy*, ed. Geoffrey Shepherd (Manchester: Manchester University Press, 1973), 107.

19. Cary, 'The Author's Preface to the Reader', sig. A2v.

20. Louise Schleiner, 'Lady Falkland's Reentry into Writing: Anglo-Catholic Consensual Discourse and Her *Edward II* as Historical Fiction', in *The Witness of Times: Manifestations of Ideology in Seventeenth-Century England*, ed. Katherine Z. Keller and Gerald J. Schiffhorst (Pittsburgh: Duquesne University Press, 1993), 210.

21. Cary, *History of Edward II*, 1–2.

22. Ibid., 8.

23. Schleiner, 'Lady Falkland's Reentry into Writing', 210.

24. Donald A. Stauffer, 'A Deep and Sad Passion', in *Essays in Dramatic Literature*, ed. Hardin Craig (Princeton: Princeton University Press, 1935), 314.

25. Betty S. Travitsky, 'Husband-Murder and Petty Treason in English Renaissance Tragedy', in *Disorder and the Drama*, ed. Mary Beth Rose, special issue of *Renaissance Drama*, new series 21 (1990), 183. Tina Krontiris, 'Style and Gender in Elizabeth Cary's *Edward II*', in *The Renaissance Englishwoman in Print: Counterbalancing the Canon*, ed. Anne M. Haselkorn and Betty S. Travitsky (Amherst, MA: University of Massachusetts Press, 1990), 137, emphasis added.

26. Diane Purkiss, ed., *Renaissance Women: The Plays of Elizabeth Cary, The Poems of Aemilia Lanyer* (London: William Pickering, 1994), 79–228, xxviii.

27. Donald Foster, 'Resurrecting the Author: Elizabeth Tanfield Cary', in *Privileging Gender in Early Modern England*, ed. Jean R. Brink, special issue of *Sixteenth Century Essays & Studies* 23 (1993), 166, n. 36, emphasis added.

28. Ibid.

29. Cary's play, *The Tragedy of Mariam, the Fair Queen of Jewry*, was published in London in 1613. Like *History of Edward II*, it addresses the problem of tyranny and offers representations of strong, rebellious women.

30. Cary, 'The Rainge and deathe off Edwarde the Seconde. The highe and Fall of his too great Favorites Gaveston and Spencer. February 2°. 1627. By E.F'. Ms 361. Fitzwilliam Museum, Cambridge. These remarks are based on my examination of the manuscript.

31. 'The Publisher to the Reader', in Cary, *History of Edward II*, sig. A2r.
32. Cary, *History of Edward II*, 426.
33. For detailed commentary on the political resonances of *History of Edward II*, see Lewalski, *Writing Women*; Curtis Perry, '"Royal Fever" and "The Giddy Commons"*: Cary's History of the Life, Reign, and Death of Edward II and the Buckingham Phenomenon'*, in *The Literary Career and Legacy of Elizabeth Cary, 1613–1680*, ed. Heather Wolfe (New York: Palgrave Macmillan, 2007), 71–88; and Mihoko Suzuki, '"Fortune is a Stepmother": Gender and Political Discourse in Elizabeth Cary's *History of Edward II*', in *Literary Career and Legacy*, ed. Wolfe, 89–105.
34. Perry, '"Royal Fever" and "The Giddy Commons"', 75. For extensive accounts of James I's relations with these two favorites, see Alastair Bellany, *The Politics of Court Scandal in Early Modern England: News Culture and the Overbury Affair, 1603–1660* (Cambridge: Cambridge University Press, 2002); and Roger Lockyer, *Buckingham: The Life and Political Career of George Villiers, First Duke of Buckingham, 1592–1628* (London: Longman, 1981).
35. Cary, *History of Edward II*, 3.
36. Behn's dedicatory remarks to the second volume, which refer to 'our late Victory', suggests that she completed it shortly after the July 1685 rebellion (119).
37. Cecil Price provides these details of Grey's restoration and the costs entailed. For his role in testifying against the rebels, Grey was granted a full pardon. After clearing his debts, contracting for payments in property, annuities, allowances to his wife, Mary, payments to Lord Rochester and other servants of the King, and entering into a bond of £140,000, Grey was restored to his former title on 7 June 1686. See Cecil Price, *Cold Caleb: The Scandalous Life of Ford Grey, First Earl of Tankerville, 1655–1701* (London: Andrew Melrose, 1956), 197–207.
38. Melinda Zook, *Radical Whigs and Conspiratorial Politics in Late Stuart England* (University Park: Pennsylvania State University Press, 1999), 145.
39. Behn, *Oroonoko*, 5, 6.
40. Maureen Duffy, *The Passionate Shepherdess: Aphra Behn, 1640–1689* (London: Jonathan Cape, 1977); Angeline Goreau, *Reconstructing Aphra: A Social Biography of Aphra Behn* (New York: Dial Press, 1980); and E[dmund] G[osse], 'Behn, Afra, Aphra, Aphara, or Ayfara 1640–1689'. *Oxford Dictionary of National Biography* CD Rom (Oxford University Press, 1995).
41. For alternative views, see Jane Jones, 'New Light on the Background and Early Life of Aphra Behn', in *Aphra Behn Studies*, ed. Janet Todd (Cambridge: Cambridge University Press, 1996), 310–20; and Derek Hughes, 'Race, Gender, and Scholarly Practice: Aphra Behn's *Oroonoko*', *Essays in Criticism* 52.1 (January 2002): 1–22.
42. See Margaret Reeves, 'History, Fiction, and Political Identity: Heroic Rebellion in Aphra Behn's *Love-Letters Between a Nobleman and His Sister* and *Oroonoko*', *1650–1850: Ideas, Æsthetics, and Inquiries in the Early Modern Era* 8 (2003): 269–94.
43. Constance C. Relihan, *Fashioning Authority: The Development of Elizabethan Novelistic Discourse* (Kent, OH: Kent State University Press, 1994), 140–43.

Part IV
Revisioning Contexts

12
Critiquing the Sexual Economies of Marriage

Theodora A. Jankowski

The portrait (1)

The cover of *The Cambridge Companion to Aphra Behn*, edited by Derek Hughes and Janet Todd, features the portrait of a luxuriously dressed European woman being offered pearls and coral by a young African slave/servant (Figure 10). The portrait splits the words of the book's title so that 'The Cambridge Companion to' appears above the portrait and 'Aphra Behn' below it, suggesting that the European woman is Behn and allowing the young African to conjure up images of the slaves that populate Behn's *Oroonoko*. It would be an elegant conceit, one that accords 'Behn' beauty, power, and the riches that come from involvement in a colonialist enterprise. But the conceit does not work, for the woman in the portrait is not Behn. She is Louise Renée de Kéroualle, maid of honor to the Queen of England and later Charles II's mistress. She bore him a son, was given many titles including duchess of Portsmouth, and remained a close friend and advisor until the monarch's death. But why does her portrait serve as an image of *Aphra Behn*? There was no confusion in the choice, for the book's back cover identifies Pierre Mignard's portrait as that of de Kéroualle.

Behn is often considered to be the first woman to earn a living by her pen. Is this portrait meant to suggest, incorrectly, the riches Behn's fame bought? Or is it meant to suggest that Behn was as open with her favors as was the King's mistress: an allusion to another kind or source of wealth? Or was this a random choice from a specific genre of portraits – white Europeans with black Africans – to suggest Behn's adventures in Surinam and her African hero?[1] This curious superimposition of Behn and de

221

Figure 10   Louise de Kéroualle, Duchess of Portsmouth by Pierre Mignard. National Portrait Gallery, London (497).

Kéroualle may indicate the hybridity of the sexual economy of the Restoration, which both replicated and challenged stage presentations of the early modern sexual economy during the first half of the seventeenth century. Though Behn and de Kéroualle can be seen to represent two now 'acceptable' kinds of 'public' work for women – author and courtesan – these employments contrast sharply with the traditional 'private' work of marriage always available to women.

Behn's 'work' as a writer is decidedly transgressive; crossing gender boundaries, it reinforces the threat *any* women poses to the sexual economy when she engages in any 'work' that is not that of 'wife'. Yet the position of early modern wife is not only a 'private' one, but one designed to deny her any sort of personal autonomy, such as that obtained by Behn through financially supporting herself. In this chapter, I want to consider some ways in which female characters in Restoration plays strive to attain autonomy within their economy. To do so, I will examine two plays by Behn – *The Feign'd Curtezans* (1679) and *The Dutch Lover* (1673) – and two by Margaret Cavendish – *The Bridals* and *The Convent of Pleasure* (both 1668). These plays can all be viewed as critiques of the sexual economy, specifically in terms of how early modern marriage is designed to deny women personal autonomy beginning with the choice of husband. Even though the plays were written for very different audiences – Behn's for the public theater and Cavendish's for a private audience – they consider radical ways in which women can reclaim their personal autonomy, even if that means living in deliberately confrontational ways: as whores, or virgins, or both.

Early modern marriage

In examining the relationship between women and the early modern sexual economy, I also want to consider women as working subjects whether or not they marry. I will be considering sex work in its broadest range, from marriage to prostitution. Claude Lévi-Strauss famously defined marriage as a 'total relationship of exchange ... not established between a man and a woman, but between two groups of men [in which] the woman figures only as one of the partners'.[2] Lévi-Strauss's definition of marriage corresponds to that of the 'dynastic marriage', contracted by aristocratic families from the medieval to the early modern periods. This type of marriage was usually brokered for political alliance or property increase, and rarely considered the wishes of either party to the union. Thus, the future wife became a proxy for her father and her family in a business deal. Since her primary function was to breed heirs who would inherit the increased wealth produced by the financial union, it was imperative for her to come to the marriage as a virgin, to produce an undisputed heir, and to take care of the household under her husband's orders. Even though only a proxy, the wife did have some control over the body she would use as a mother/worker to produce these heirs. She could invalidate a marriage contract by giving up her virginity, or undermine the legitimacy of any heirs if a man other than her husband fathered them. Consequently, early modern society recognized that safeguarding premarital virginity granted a woman power and autonomy beyond that of her gender.[3]

The development of a mercantile class as well as the predominance of Protestant theology in sixteenth-century England led to the development of what was called the 'companionate marriage'. While couples may still have been married to secure contracts or alliances – especially among the mercantile classes – the focus of the marriage became somewhat more personal. Protestant marriage theory suggested that partners be equal in class and age and described the three primary reasons for marriage as: companionship, *remedio fornicationis* (avoidance of fornication), and the raising of Christian children. While such a focus necessarily indicated an expanded role for wives, they were still perceived to need the support of a husband. Complete female autonomy was neither a condition nor a result of marriage.

Plays of the period, especially Shakespeare's comedies, accomplish the major cultural work of valorizing marriage and creating the expected image of the 'happy-ever-after' union. Focusing on middle- and upper-class couples, these plays seduce us into thinking that the concept of 'work' was completely divorced from members of these classes, especially women. Yet even if the wife was wealthy enough to afford servants, *she* was the one who provided sexual service to her husband and labored over the production of his heirs. I do not want this specific type of work to be forgotten – or argued away – just as I do not want to forget the specifics of sex work provided by prostitutes and courtesans.[4] What I specifically want to examine in Behn's and Cavendish's plays are the ways in which the women's jockeying for husbands differs from that of similarly classed women in Shakespeare's plays. In the latter, the women who desire autonomy in choosing husbands – such as Rosalind, Portia, or Viola – often disguise themselves as men and ultimately achieve a different, sometimes closer, relationship with the potential husband because of their sometime 'same' sex. However, various texts condemned crossdressing women as transgressive: the anti-theatrical tracts; the *Hic Mulier/Haec Vir* pamphlets; attacks on historical figures like Moll Cutpurse, etc. Both Behn and Cavendish use the trope of the crossdressed woman as a transgressive figure who challenges the role of women in early modern marriage. Yet while Behn uses the trope in a number of plays, she also introduces another 'disguise', that of the courtesan. In what follows, I will examine how both Cavendish and Behn use drama to radically critique early modern marriage and argue for greater female autonomy. In the plays I examine, even though Behn uses the 'disguise' of the courtesan in contrast to Cavendish's female-to-male crossdressing, both make similar points regarding the abject position of women in early modern marriage. I will begin this analysis with Cavendish's *The Bridals*, a 'baseline' text that does not make use of either disguise or crossdressing.

The Bridals

This play explores two marriages: that of Sir William Sage and Lady Vertue and that of Sir John Amorous and Lady Coy.[5] Lady Vertue and Lady Coy's attitudes toward marital sexuality make it seem as though the characters might have been misnamed. Lady Coy calls attention to her virginal state by refusing to be led to bed and expressing extreme embarrassment at the thought of either consummating her marriage or letting anyone know she has done so. In contrast, Lady Vertue follows what seems to be the expected behavior of a wife on her wedding night: being taken to her bed by the female guests and tucked in, then waiting for the male guests to bring her new husband to her.

It may initially seem odd that the lady named 'Vertue' is apparently willing to engage in sexual activity, while the lady named 'Coy' corresponds more closely to the stereotypical picture of the virgin bride unwilling to engage with her husband sexually. Were this character to succeed in remaining a virgin, however, she would completely subvert the union itself.[6] By presenting a character named Lady Vertue as willing to consummate her marriage, Cavendish is not being as counterintuitive it as might seem, for Lady Vertue models the actions of a compliant wife. While we may wonder that such virtuous characters as Lady Vertue and Sir William Sage exist in the bawdy world of Restoration drama, Cavendish's play can be viewed as a debate between the ideal, virtuous, companionate marriage and the looser, 'open' marriages of the period, those in which both parties satisfied their own sexual desires, as Sir John Amorous and Lady Coy eventually do.

Lady Vertue may be regarded as a conventionally compliant wife, willing to attend to her husband's guests or not, dress elaborately or not, according to her husband's wishes. Yet Cavendish saves her from being deadly boring by marrying her to a 'Sage' man. No man who is wise would expect – or command – his wife to do anything but that which is virtuous. No woman who is truly virtuous, it would seem, would marry a man who was not wise. Whoever arranged this marriage clearly took good account of the characters of its two parties. So while Cavendish's play may seem to be reinforcing early modern marriage tenets which demand that the wife obey her husband, it is simultaneously questioning them: there is no reason for a wife *not* to obey her husband if he is as wise as Sir William – most likely named after Cavendish's own husband – whose wisdom ensures that he treats his wife in a respectful manner.

This ideal and chaste companionate marriage is presented against a backdrop of the licentious and empty living of the Restoration period.

The bachelor Courtly spends his time chaperoning women wherever they wish to go. While his relationships with them are apparently non-sexual, he is certainly engaged in duties that would be more proper to their husbands. Sir John also takes leave of his wife to engage in entertainments without her. Again, we are uncertain whether or not they are sexual, but he defends his right to do so when his wife complains of being left alone. It is because of his frequent absences that Facil is able to court Lady Coy and tempt her into a sexual relationship. In the first scene, Facil was attracted to Lady Coy as a 'young Virgin' with a 'modest Countenance' (1.1, p. 171).[7] This impression is solidified by her modest, blushful reactions to the bawdy wedding jokes. Most of the men in the play, however, challenge Facil's reading of the lady's character. Take-Pleasure, for example, points out that

> Women have more modesty in their Countenance, than in their natures; ... Womens countenances, like false glasses, make their minds appear fairer than they are; for a modest countenance may have a wanton mind. (1.2, p. 171)

Mimick reinforces this position: 'Womens Countenances for the most part are as false as their faces; ... all Womens minds are as inconstant as the wind' (2.3, p. 186). This is, in fact, the case with Lady Coy, and apparently with all the other female characters. While Cavendish's play presents a very unflattering picture of the women of this society, it is the society as a whole that the play critiques, not simply its female members. Individuals, marriage as an institution, or society itself may, indeed, have serious flaws, and Cavendish reveals some of them in this play. But by accepting virtue and virtuous behavior, individuals can establish marriage as a moral ideal, the foundation of their society, in fact, and create a life that is virtuous even if lived in the midst of vice.

The courtesan

By the 1660s and 1670s, with a male monarch who accepted a courtly culture more sexually permissive than Elizabeth's, actual courtesans were considered not entirely transgressive, but women who could gain power at court through sex work. Louise de Kéroualle, discussed earlier as the subject of the 'portrait' of Behn, Barbara Palmer, Hortense Mancini, and Nell Gwyn are examples of actual women who gained wealth and power working as courtesans and mistresses to Charles II.[8] Thus, the power such Shakespearian characters as Rosalind, Portia, and Viola attained by impersonating the dominant gender, would later be claimed by dramatic characters who assumed the disguise of the courtesan. In this, they modeled actual women, members of a dominant – and dominating – female profession that granted women wealth and power enough to live without marriage, or to choose their own husbands if they did marry.

While 'courtesans' and 'whores' may seem to be interchangeable terms used to describe a sex worker, 'courtesans' in early modern drama are figured as European, usually Italian, versions of the plain English whore. These European/Italian sex workers look and behave like upper-class women. They are clearly different from the diseased whores or the lower-class sex workers who threatened the social order in the Vienna of *Measure for Measure*. I will acknowledge this distinction by referring to courtesans as 'higher-class' sex workers and the others as 'lower class', with the understanding that the 'class' I am calling attention to may not be the class to which the workers were born, but that which reflects the clients they can attract with their particular beauty, location, and skills. Examples of such European sex workers in early seventeenth-century English drama are Franceschina in John Marston's *The Dutch Courtesan* (1604–05) and Bellafront in Thomas Dekker and Thomas Middleton's *The Honest Whore* (1604). The two title characters live independently, devise the boundaries of their work – they control the clients they accept and the favors they will grant them – and pocket the payment themselves. While they may live with others who might be bawds, these dramatic courtesans seem to be hardly controlled by them.

The Feign'd Curtezans

Behn's play is set in Rome, again reinforcing the courtesan's European provenance. But the printed text of the play includes a significant preface that would not have been spoken in the theater. Behn dedicates her play to none other than Nell Gwyn. Born in a brothel, she became a successful actress on the Restoration stage, and crowned her career by becoming Charles II's mistress. Behn lauds her as 'so Excellent and perfect a Creature',[9] a model for all female wits. Now, granted, it would not be particularly prudent to cast aspersions upon a royal mistress, but this fulsome lauding of Gwyn certainly calls attention to the main plot of Behn's play, in which the young, upper-class women disguised as courtesans challenge a sexual economy that demands they be available for use by their families either to achieve important political/financial connections through marriage, or to save their families money by entering convents. Nell Gwyn becomes, like Behn, a 'type' of a woman who works to control her own life to suit her own wishes, whether that life is licit or not. Being aware of the economy – both sexual and financial – and how it works allows such women to achieve success rather than failure. Behn's play also looks at how issues of class inflect the sexual economy. What options exist for upper-class women who want to survive on their own? Is the life of a courtesan an economically viable one? How easy is it for an upper-class woman to become a courtesan?

As the play begins, Laura Lucretia – already 'reserv'd for' a man of her father's choosing as a wife, 'that unconcern'd Domestique Necessary' (2.1.162–63) – is attracted to Julio. Wishing to learn about him without disclosing her identity, she instructs her servant to tell him she is anything other than she is: even a courtesan. Observing the encounter, the Englishman Fillamour remarks to his friend Galliard: 'I see the trade of Love goes forward still' (1.1.20). Thus the play's first comment regarding love/sex is phrased in terms of its relationship to the economy. Neither character knows any specifics of the scene they have just witnessed, but a woman's meeting alone with an ardent man causes both to reflect upon trade. As the scene progresses, it becomes clear that Galliard's idea of 'trade' with a woman involves himself as a customer and the woman as a courtesan. Fillamour, by contrast, seems to be on the lookout for a wife rather than a mistress. Yet even though he seems to focus on 'true love' with a virgin bride, both friends openly acknowledge the aspects of trade that motivate and control *any* encounter with a woman. The sex trade still involves marriage, though the trade in courtesans is more acceptable as a theater plot than it was earlier in the century. Predictably, the two friends then argue over whether it is or is not a violation of 'natural law' to love a courtesan. Fillamore refuses to be seduced by a fancy name and bluntly demystifies the situation: 'And yet this rare piece is but a Curtizan, in coarse plain English, a very Whore! – Who filthily exposes all her Beautys to him can give her most, not Love her best' (1.1.56–58). Fillamore and Galliard are pacing off the turf of the major discussion of the play. Galliard is a lover of all women, one who accepts 'natural law' as that which allows – or even demands – that he engage in sexual intercourse with whichever woman he meets who pleases him. He can be seen as either the stereotypical 'cavalier' or simply someone whose passions are let loose to go where they will, to allow him to be 'merry' in the style of Charles II. Fillamour is, in one sense, a precursor of the new romantic heroes of eighteenth-century novels, or, in another, a throwback to the Romeos and Claudios of Shakespeare. The character is presented as viewing 'true love', rather than sexual gratification, as the motivating factor of an alliance with a woman, thus causing us to assume his interest is in marriage rather than dalliance. Yet both characters see whatever alliance they have with women as one that 'costs' something, that involves some form of commerce. For Fillamour, the definition of 'courtesan' – or 'whore' as he prefers – is a woman who parlays beauty to the one who pays most. For him, what determines love – and what should determine a woman's reaction to a man – is the question of who loves her most. This thinking, however, occludes the negotiations involving dowers and marriage contracts whereby a father with any foresight tries to get the best deal he can for his daughter (and himself). And, in fact, any woman contemplating marriage would be a fool to sell herself to the lowest bidder.

Those more particularly engaged in trade or commerce – merchants, adventurers, or a rising middle class – are not pictured in this play's society as they are in the city comedies involving courtesans of the earlier part of the century. Behn's play shows us a lower class primarily consisting of servants who do the bidding of their masters/mistresses and also engage in whatever additional commerce they can find, such as being re-hired by their masters' or mistresses' friends to perform additional services. The major players in the commercial enterprises presented in this play are the daughters (Laura Lucretia and Marcella), heiresses in their own right, destined to be married to those their fathers or brothers have chosen for them, those who will make a good political or financial match. If not destined for marriage, they are destined for the convent (Cornelia). So while these women have value as potential wives (or nuns), that value would be diminished should they lose their virginity and their consequent ability to produce undoubted heirs for their husbands. Ironically and unusually, all three women disguise themselves as courtesans. The fact that they succeed in hiding from their families so disguised, shows that there is a radical 'class' difference between various types of sex workers.

The more privileged sex workers, like Nell Gwyn or Louise de Kéroualle, make direct arrangements with upper-class or noble men. They own – in the sense of having complete control over – their own bodies. The men they entertain pay in luxurious gifts, rather than a set 'per act' fee in cash. In many cases the worker may eventually become a 'mistress' and be supported by one man, as Gwyn and others were by Charles II. Thus the 'class' difference between these kinds of sex workers is not simply one of the social stratum to which each was born, for the privileged worker, such as Gwyn, may have been born to the same social class as the abject one. The difference arises from commerce and the woman's place in the economy. Although she may live on the edges of respectable society, the 'upper-class' sex worker can control her life in a way that 'lower-class' ones cannot. While the privileged sex worker cannot refuse to accept 'customers' altogether – or she would not survive – she can refuse to accept those she does not wish to. As long as she is not under the protection of any man, her body is under her own control.

Desiring the ability to direct their own lives, Behn's virgin characters choose to disguise themselves as courtesans, probably the only example of truly autonomous women in their society. Yet the fact remains that a prosperous marriage cannot occur if a woman is known to have sacrificed her virginity. Though the women may seem naïve in choosing to disguise themselves as courtesans, they are thoroughly honest in defining themselves as virgins, much to the amazement of their suitors: 'a Curtizan! And a Zitella [virgin] too? a pretty contradiction!' (3.1.8). That the two states coexist boggles the minds of their suitors who encounter the seemingly impossible. In fact, a woman as a courtesan (or whore) is simply an extension of the actual social position of all women as sex workers who exist on a continuum of licit-to-illicit, virgin to whore.[10] Living as 'courtesans' allows Marcella and Cornelia to position themselves in the capitalist marketplace. Cornelia urges her sister to make a better financial deal for a husband than had been made for her. She states that 'Curtezan' is a 'Noble title and has more *Votaries than Religion*, there's no Merchandize like ours, that of Love, my sister!' (2.1.65–66). While I would suggest that it is her body she is 'merchandizing' and not love, Marcella also uses economic language to indicate that, for courtesans, 'there's no Rethorick like ready Money, nor Billet-Doux like Bill of Exchange' (2.1.264–66). Thus the women reflect their culture's complete commodification of love and pursue financial success where smart courtesans prefer bills of exchange to love letters. Smart wives would do well to prefer the same offerings.

The Dutch Lover

Behn's earlier play reveals women who find additional ways to take control of their unhappy love and marriage arrangements. Before the play begins, Hippolyta, who had been contracted to Alonzo, elopes with Antonio, the man she loves, and consummates that love. Euphemia has been promised to a dolt, and searches for an attractive and willing man to please herself. Cleonte finds herself desiring her brother, who returns her affection. Behn demonstrates that men, too, can be the victims of parental pressures, for Marcel has been contracted to Flavia so that he cannot marry his love Clarinda. The mismatched lovers are correctly paired at the end, but only because of the action taken by the women themselves, action that is not socially sanctioned. But this autonomy does not come without its consequences. Hippolyta's loss of virginity casts shame upon her family as well as herself, since Antonio refuses to marry her and considers her his whore. His rejection of her is even more painful once he reveals that he seduced her to punish her brother, Marcel, who was successfully courting Clarinda, the woman Antonio really wanted (3.3). These revelations force Hippolyta to reconsider the sexual economy of which she is a part, one that stipulates that a woman who bestows her virginity on a man without marriage becomes totally marginalized if that man repudiates her. For society provides her with no way to make a life for herself, except as a whore. Disowned also by her family, Hippolyta becomes an object lesson of what can happen to a woman who gives herself sexually without considering the social or familial cost of her actions.

But for women who desire autonomy within early modern society, the dangerous or difficult option appears to be the only one. When she discovers that her father has betrothed her to a wealthy dolt, Euphemia also discovers her lack of autonomy in making a marital choice. Unable to change her father's mind, she takes to the streets to find a stranger willing to be her husband. She finally settles on Alonzo who, suspecting she is a courtesan, is willing to play along with any of her plots in order to gain access to her bed. But Euphemia, who is not disguised as a courtesan, realizes that her bold actions alone make Alonzo think she is one. His perception does not bother her, though she is careful to identify herself correctly as 'the sole Daughter of a rich Parent, young, and as I am told not unhandsome; I am contracted to a man I never saw, ... and I had rather dye than marry him' (1.3.35–37; 30).

Behn's play presents a woman who tries and succeeds at arranging her own marriage, even though she is assumed to be a courtesan for dealing directly with the man, as a courtesan would. I will not further describe how the other women in this play end up with their true loves, since the plot convolutions are conventional and resemble a French farce. Rather, I will focus on how the play presents its audience with women who actively try to arrange their own marriages despite a social structure that does not allow them to do so. Hippolyta suffers social scorn by sacrificing her virginity without assurance (and insurance) that her integrity will be respected. Euphemia, feeling that any man is better than an idiot, negotiates a marriage with a wealthy man of character who is smitten both by her looks and her manner. While Alonzo initially takes her for a courtesan, his misidentification does not bother him. Once he realizes the advantages of matching with an heiress, and realizes that he will have to marry sooner or later, Alonzo allows himself to be persuaded. Thus the play demonstrates that women are intelligent enough to negotiate financially and emotionally successful marital arrangements on their own. Even Hippolyta seems to have done so, as Antonio reveals his true, but hidden, love for her.

The Convent of Pleasure

Behn's play demonstrates that some of the problems attached to courtship and marriage can be overcome or readjusted by women to make them acceptable to themselves. Marrying one's true love does not necessarily lead to disaster, but might lead to a more companionable marriage than 'dynastic' family arrangements. Yet while Behn's plays may critique the ways in which male family members arrange marriages, Cavendish's *The Convent of Pleasure* goes much further by critiquing virtually every aspect of early modern marriage. While the editor of this play wonders to what degree it may be considered a continuation of *The Bridals*,[11] I view *The Convent of Pleasure* not so much as a 'second part' in terms of plot, but rather a continuous – if more pointed – examination of the nature of early modern marriage as well as women's place within the estate.

The play begins with the report that Lord Fortunate has died leaving his daughter, Lady Happy, fabulously wealthy. The fact that the *daughter* has inherited shows that Cavendish is considering inheritance as *tail générale* rather than *tail male*, which immediately calls into question the patrilineal inheritance of medieval and early modern England.[12] However, given this situation in which the apparently sole daughter does inherit, she is pictured as the immediate target of male interest solely because of her fortune. The news of Lady Happy's riches reveals the three courtiers of *The Bridals* as even more distasteful than before. While initially shown as simply chasing after and seducing married women, they are pictured here as distinct predators on the lookout for rich wives.

If these are the only kinds of sexual partners women have to look forward to, it is not surprising that Lady Happy prefers to do without them. In fact, while *The Bridals* demonstrated that there may be positive aspects to marriage, Lady Happy defines 'Mary'd life' as having 'more crosses and sorrows then pleasure, freedom, or happiness; … Men are the only troublers of Women; … they cause their pains but, not their pleasures' (1.2, pp. 218, 220). Aware of her financial desirability, Lady

Happy informs Madam Mediator that she will use her wealth to escape marriage by creating a convent for women who cannot afford *not* to marry. Questioned whether she will live 'incloister'd and retired from the World' (1.2, p. 220), Lady Happy describes the luxurious convent she will create, one that will provide a completely pleasurable experience that is totally divorced from the extreme asceticism of the 'usual' Roman Catholic convent experience. But ultimately the convent is designed to remove women from 'Men, who make the Female sex their slaves' (1.2, p. 220) and allow them to 'live a single life, and vow Virginity: ... with all the delights and pleasures that are allowable and lawful' (1.2, p. 220).

While the title of the play seems to be an oxymoron, the actual situation it presents is not, unless one assumes that no pleasure of any kind can occur without men. Lady Happy and her companions are fortunate to reside in a beautiful, luxurious estate, with ample leisure to enjoy their surroundings. The absence of men in the convent enables the women to engage in whatever pleasurable activities they wish with members of their own sex. Thus the crossdressing and dalliance of these couples suggests same-sex activity as an acceptable, desirable substitute for immoral, unhealthy, and dangerous contact with men. Lady Happy and the Princess lead the way in this same-sex dalliance, and the images we are presented of happily paired female couples contrasts strongly with the tragic predicaments of the married women pictured in the play-within-the-play (Act 3, pp. 228–34).

These vignettes reveal the marital struggles of all classes of women. They indict husbands who run off with other women (3.4), beat their wives and children (3.2), spend all their money in ale-houses and allow their children to starve (3.4), gamble away their own wealth as well as their wives' jointures (3.4), or let their apprentices and journeymen run wild and steal from them (3.6). Even if husbands themselves are not an actual problem, the mere fact of engaging with men sexually is fraught with danger: pregnancy and childbirth bring pain in and of themselves and can result in the death of the mother and her child (3.7 and 9). If the child survives to adulthood, he may become involved in a capital offense and be executed (3.8). Simply living in the world can expose a woman to perpetual harassment by men and solicitation for sexual favors (3.10).

While Cavendish in *The Bridals* presents at least one loving couple whose morality and wisdom become the only saving grace of the patriarchal sexual economy, she proposes a much more radical alternative in *The Convent of Pleasure*. Not only does she call attention to the specificity of the often desperate lives of women, she dramatizes an

Edenic alternative: a female community organized around the various aspects of *female*, rather than male, pleasure. Its inhabitants do not need to work, are provided with luxurious living arrangements, and are secured from male incursions. These alone would make Lady Happy's convent an egregious threat to the patriarchal world. But the play poses an even greater threat: women pleasuring themselves sexually and romantically with other women. Despite the recuperative gesture of revealing the Princess as in fact a man, this play presents scene upon scene of apparently opposite-sex couples, who are in fact same-sex couples. Although her own marriage to a wealthy and prominent noble-man granted her an unusual degree of autonomy which allowed her to publish many folio volumes, Cavendish does not hesitate to make her readers aware of the actual condition of most women in Restoration England.

The portrait (2)

I want to conclude by briefly considering a portrait of Margaret Cavendish, an engraving by Pieter Louis van Schuppen (1627–1702) that appears on the cover of *The Convent of Pleasure and Other Plays*, and originally appeared as the frontispiece of *Playes* (1662), *The Blazing World* (1666), and *Plays Never Before Printed* (1668) (Figure 11). The placement of Cavendish's image in a classical architectural niche with Athena on one side and Apollo on the other suggests her noble estate, her female power, and her literary might. But another aspect of this image marks Cavendish's almost 'regal' power: she is pictured as stand-ing with her right hand on her hip and her elbow pointed toward, and looking over her right shoulder at the viewer. This particularly regal stance has a history. In about 1635, Anthony van Dyck (1599–1641) painted Charles I in hunting dress with two servants and his horse. While he wears a dress sword and carries a walking stick, there is noth-ing in the portrait ostensibly to mark him as monarch. Van Dyck solves this problem by positioning Charles with his left hand on his hip, elbow bent and pointed toward the viewer, looking superciliously over his shoulder at his audience. The painter's genius lies in establishing his subject as unquestionably regal without having to rely on the tradi-tional trappings of the royal portrait: crown, scepter, orb, etc. The pose was obviously copied by van Schuppen in his engraving of the woman who referred to herself as 'Margaret the First'.[13] Titled but not royal, female and not male, Cavendish appears to tread upon sovereign turf here in her chosen pose.

Figure 11 Margaret Cavendish (Lucas), Duchess of Newcastle by Pieter Louis van Schuppen (after Abraham Diepenbeeck). National Portrait Gallery, London (D 11111).

The editors of *The Convent of Pleasure and Other Plays* and *The Cambridge Companion to Aphra Behn* have chosen specific ways to present their female authors. Using one of Cavendish's own approved self-representations, the editor of that collection reinforced not only the personally regal nature but also the nobility of the author. This image thus prompts reflection on the way in which Cavendish's plays critique the nature of early modern marriage. While they do consider the negative effects marriage can have on lower-class women, Cavendish's position as critic is that of the noblewoman – whether 'disguised' as Lady Happy or Lady Vertue – who seeks ways to allow women autonomy even within a social system designed to deny them as much autonomy as possible. While Behn's heroines I have examined here are of the same class – though Italian – as Cavendish's, they are presented as willing to adopt the dress as well as the autonomous behavior of the European courtesan to achieve their desires: the power to choose their own husbands and the life they will subsequently lead. While they seem to be violating the sexual norms of their society, their appearance in the dress of courtesans actually serves a purpose similar to the male disguise often adopted by upper-class women in Shakespeare's plays: providing the ability to appear/act in public autonomously. Is this the reason why the editors of *The Cambridge Companion to Aphra Behn* chose to 'represent' Behn with a portrait of an empowered actual courtesan: Louise de Kéroualle? Does this portrait seek to call attention to the autonomy desired by the women characters in *The Feign'd Curtezans* and *The Dutch Lover*? Or does it suggest that the only autonomy available to the non-noble writer Aphra Behn was that of the courtesan, like Nell Gwyn, not that of the author? Do *all* women who write plays for the public stage themselves become a 'stage' upon which a public sexuality or sexual victimization is enacted? Or do these portraits tell us that even women who have the power of birth or wealth to cock their elbows at their inferiors cannot always avoid the public opprobrium of whore?

Notes

1. See Kim F. Hall, *Things of Darkness: Economies of Race and Gender in Early Modern England* (Ithaca and London: Cornell University Press, 1995), chapter 5, for more on this portrait and others of white Europeans and black Africans and how they comment on colonialism and the slave trade.
2. Claude Lévi-Strauss, *The Elementary Structures of Kinship* (Boston: Beacon Press, 1969), 115. For further discussion on the early modern marriage economy, see Theodora A. Jankowski, *Women in Power in the Early Modern Drama* (Urbana and Chicago: University of Illinois Press, 1992), chapter 2, and 'Hymeneal Blood, Interchangeable Women, and the Early Modern Marriage Economy in *Measure for Measure* and *All's Well That Ends Well*', in *A Companion to Shakespeare's Works. Volume IV: The Poems, Problem Comedies, Late Plays*, ed. Richard Dutton and Jean E. Howard (Malden, MA and Oxford: Blackwell, 2003), 89–105.
3. See Theodora A. Jankowski, *Pure Resistance: Queer Virginity in Early Modern English Drama* (Philadelphia: University of Pennsylvania Press, 2000), chapters 4–6, for an extended discussion of the power of virginity and how the drama of the period reflected it.
4. See Kay Stanton, '"Made to Write 'Whore' Upon?" Male and Female Use of the Word "Whore" in Shakespeare's Canon', in *A Feminist Companion to Shakespeare*, ed. Dympna Callaghan (Malden, MA and Oxford: Blackwell, 2000), 80–102.
5. Interestingly, despite Lady Coy's reference to the fact that she must change her name to 'Amorous' (an ominous change) now that she is married,

Cavendish refers to Coy and Lady Vertue continuously by their 'maiden' names. Cavendish also clearly indicates what her husband has contributed to this play, notably an Epithalamion. He is also identified as the author of the 'recuperative' section of *The Convent of Pleasure*; it is significant that the achievement of heteronormative marriages in both plays is attributed to him. See also Mihoko Suzuki, 'Margaret Cavendish and the Female Satirist', *Studies in English Literature, 1500–1900* 37.3 (1997): 483–500 on how Cavendish critiques marriage in other plays.

6. See Jankowski, *Pure Resistance*, chapter 1. Only a consummated marriage was considered to be valid.

7. Margaret Cavendish, *The Bridals*, *The Convent of Pleasure and Other Plays*, ed. Anne Shaver (Baltimore and London: Johns Hopkins University Press, 1999). Further citations to Cavendish's plays will be by act, scene, and page number.

8. Louise de Kéroualle's income, from various sources, became astronomical. In 1681 she reputedly received more than £136,000 from the secret service alone. Nancy Klein Maguire, 'The Duchess of Portsmith: English Royal Consort and French Politician, 1670–1685', in *The Stuart Court and Europe*, ed. R. Malcolm Smuts (Cambridge: Cambridge University Press, 1996), 247–73.

9. Aphra Behn, *The Feign'd Curtezans, The Works of Aphra Behn*, ed. Janet Todd (Columbus: Ohio State University Press, 1992), 5: 86–87. Further references are cited parenthetically in the text.

10. Among the many scholars who have called attention to Behn's focus on the mercantile aspects of marriage are Susan J. Owen, '"Suspect my loyalty when I lose my virtue": Sexual Politics and Party in Aphra Behn's Plays of the Exclusion Crisis' and Elin Diamond, 'Gestus and Signature in Aphra Behn's *The Rover*', both in *Aphra Behn*, ed. Janet Todd (New York: St. Martin's Press, 1999), 57–72; 32–56; and Robert Markley, 'Behn and the Unstable Traditions of Social Comedy', in *The Cambridge Companion to Aphra Behn*, ed. Derek Hughes and Janet Todd (Cambridge: Cambridge University Press, 2004), 98–117.

11. Anne Shaver, Introduction to Cavendish, *The Bridals*, 11–13.

12. See Jankowski, *Women in Power*, chapter 2, for further discussion on laws of inheritance, and *Pure Resistance*, chapter 6, for relationships between women in *The Convent of Pleasure*.

13. Margaret Cavendish, 'To the Reader', *The Description of a New World Called The Blazing World* (1666; 1668), in Kate Lilley, ed., *The Description of a New World Called The Blazing World And Other Writings* (New York: New York University Press, 1992), 124.

13
'The Empire of Man over the inferior Creatures': British Women, Race, and Seventeenth-Century Science

Cristina Malcolmson

Hans Sloane tells of 'a *Negro*' who healed him of a '*chego*' in his toe while he was a doctor in Jamaica. She was 'famous for her ability in such cases', yet Sloane finally concludes that 'Blacks ... are a very perverse Generation of People'.[1] Thus the Secretary of the Royal Society in 1707 provides a glimpse of a different kind of science that might have developed if non-Europeans and European women had been credited as producers of scientific knowledge.[2] According to feminist historians of science, a number of women practiced healing and wrote works on natural philosophy in seventeenth-century England, but these possibilities began to diminish. Londa Schiebinger argues that natural philosophy was more open to European women in the seventeenth and early eighteenth centuries than in later periods, and she traces the process by which women were marginalized as science emerged as an institution. Lynette Hunter, Sarah Hutton, and Patricia Fara have redefined the history of the 'scientific revolution' beyond a list of 'great men' or 'great women' to include domestic knowledge, technical know-how, medicine, midwifery, and family networks where natural philosophy was central. Ruth Watts contends that, whereas many women did participate in scientific activity and the networks associated with it, there was an increasing emphasis on the masculinity of natural philosophy, and its practice at exclusively masculine locations. In her book on *Cartesian Women*, Erica Harth argues that several seventeenth-century women interested in Descartes's theories wrote before the new norms of objectivity became universalized, and transformed women from observers into objects of study.[3]

Some work has been done to clarify how race influenced this process, but it remains unclear to what extent British women were marginalized in ways similar to other groups, like non-Europeans or the working classes, and to what extent women writers contributed to the marginalization of others.[4] If feminist writers are right to challenge modern assumptions that science is 'rational, objective, shared, reliable knowledge', and to argue instead that science is a construct 'based on relationships of power, with its content and processes dependent on cultural assumptions', then British women writers in the seventeenth century not only suffered from some damaging effects of this construct but were also able to enjoy some of its privileges.[5]

Healers and midwives

The all-male fellowship of the Royal Society that began in 1661 was accompanied by the rise of male professional groups that made it difficult for British women to participate in scientific activities. Schiebinger argues that women were eventually removed from the field of health care, and that such exclusion was then made to seem natural. Before this, the engagement of women in these activities cut across class lines. Upper-class women worked in the field of chemical technology by developing and collecting recipes for food and healing, and all women took the role of physician and surgeon within the household and the wider community. Women not in the upper classes attended at childbirth and worked as physicians and nurses in the towns. Cooking originally included both food and medicine, whereas during the eighteenth century, medical cookery was replaced by academic fields like botany and nutrition. The Royal College of Physicians, the Society of Apothecaries, the guilds for barber-surgeons, and the development of male midwives enforced a new division between professional and household duties.[6]

Medical societies attempted to weed out not only women but working men who had customarily provided health care. According to *An Act for the Appointing of Physicians an Surgeons* (1512), 'common Artificers, as smiths, weavers, and women boldly and accustomably take upon them great cures, and things of great difficulty'.[7] Midwives lobbied for a self-governing corporation in 1634 that could provide them with education about new birthing techniques, but the College of Physicians rejected their petition. Thus the new science of anatomy, books on midwifery by men, male midwives, and new childbirth practices that were not shared with women sped up the process that, by the nineteenth century, would produce the professional obstetrician and remove women from a practice that had been in their hands for centuries.[8] In *The Midwives Book or the Whole Art of Midwifery Discovered* (1670), Jane Sharp criticizes the lack of formal education for midwives, defends education through experience rather than university training, points out the ignorance of male physicians about female anatomy, and celebrates the sexual pleasure that Galenic theories taught was necessary for women to conceive.[9] In *A Scheme for the Foundation of a Royal Hospital ... for its Maintenance of a Corporation of Skillful Midwives* (1687), Elizabeth Cellier petitions James II for an educational institution for midwives similar to that in France. In *To Dr..... an answer to his queries concerning the Colledg of Midwives* (London, 1688), she defends the skill of midwives against a sharp rejection of her proposal by the College of Physicians.[10]

Upper-class women wrote collections of recipes, and a few were published between 1639 and 1655.[11] Lord Ruthven's *The Ladies Cabinet Opened* (1639), Elizabeth Grey's *A Choice Manual of Rare and Select Secrets* (1653), Alethea Talbot's *Natura Exenterata* (1655), and Queen Henrietta Maria's *The Queen's Closet Opened* (1655) make little distinction between medicine and food preparation. Grey and Talbot were sisters and granddaughters of the Countess of Shrewsbury, and both were friends of Lady Ruthven. Lynette Hunter argues that these texts provide evidence of an early scientific circle surrounding Queen Henrietta Maria which included these women as well as Sir Kenelm Digby, John Evelyn, and John Pell, who eventually became fellows of the Royal Society. *The Ladies Cabinet Opened* includes the following sub-title: *Wherein is found hidden severall Experiments in Preserving and Conserving, Physicke, and Surgery, Cookery, and Huswifery*. Hunter suggests that the authors of many of these collections were 'Lady Experimenters'.

Natural philosophers

Caroline Merchant and others have argued that new theories about astronomy and physics destroyed the traditional view of nature as organic, that institutionalized science emphasized mastery of the physical world to the detriment of the environment, and that this occurred partially because of the lack of women within these groups.[12] The new theories can be characterized by comparing Mary Herbert, Countess of Pembroke (1561–1621) to Aphra Behn, professional writer (1640–89). However, it is unclear to what extent either woman would have challenged the goal of mastering nature. Both were in favor of English control over the Americas, and would have promoted the Royal Society's interest in colonization.[13]

Herbert is an example of the 'scientific lady', who encountered natural philosophy through court culture, as Schiebinger and Patricia Phillips describe, and had the money and leisure to explore it.[14] She was a member of the famous Sidney-Herbert network, along with her brother Sir Philip Sidney and her son, William Herbert. Herbert set up a laboratory in Wilton House, her country estate, and brought in Adrian Gilbert to supervise it. Gilbert was one of the first organizers of the western planting movement, and Mary invested in overseas exploration along with several members of her family. Gilbert also laid out the garden at Wilton House in the shape of the Ptolemaic, geocentric universe. According to John Aubrey, both Herbert and Gilbert were 'great Chemists'. Knowledge of practical medicine was the norm for educated women, but Herbert seems to have sought out innovations in her experiments. As Mary Ellen Lamb puts it, 'Gilbert worked with his patron in her laboratory to produce medicines.' Margaret P. Hannay demonstrates that the same receipts, or recipes for medicine, were recorded as developed by Herbert and by Gilbert. Mary Sidney Herbert's patronage of a local man who studied the philosopher's stone suggests that she was engaged in alchemical experiments.[15]

In contrast, Aphra Behn's *A Discovery of New Worlds* (1688) taught the principles of the Copernican heliocentric universe and a mechanical natural philosophy derived from Descartes.[16] In this philosophy, the universe was governed by laws of motion controlling the planets as well as tiny particles which produced the effects of light, heat, and sound. In her translation of a work by Fontenelle, a dialogue between a natural philosopher and a young aristocratic woman entertains its reader with corpuscular philosophy, satires of contemporary society, and an account of the visit to the moon in *Orlando Furioso*. Fontenelle's purpose was to teach the tenets of the new science to as wide an audience as possible, including the 'ladies', and it was tremendously successful. The following passage provides a compelling image of a mechanistic universe:

> I fancy still to my self that Nature is a great Scene, or Representation, much like one of our *Opera's*; for, from the place where you sit to behold the *Opera*, you do not see the Stage, as really it is, Since every thing is disposed there for the representing agreeable Objects to your sight, from a large distance, while the wheels & weights, which move and counterpoise the Machines are all concealed from our view; nor do we trouble our selves so much to find out how all those Motions that we see there, are performed; and it may be among so vast a number of Spectators, there is not one Enginier in the whole Pit, that troubles himself with the consideration how those flights are managed that seem so new and so extraordinary to him, and who resolves at any rate to find out the contrivance of them. (9–10)

Fontenelle does not use the analogy of the opera to suggest that human life is simply a temporary drama that will give way before the realities of a spiritual eternity, the implication of earlier claims that 'all the world's a stage'. Rather the image of the opera implies that what we see with our eyes cannot explain how things work, and that only a natural philosopher will take the trouble to look 'backstage', to penetrate beyond the 'scenes' of nature to find the mechanisms by which planets and atomic particles move:

> You cannot but guess, Madam, that this Enginier is not unlike a Philosopher; but that which makes the difficulty incomparably greater to Philosophers, is, that the Ropes, Pullies, Wheels and Weights, which give motion to the different Scenes represented to us by Nature, are so well hid both from our sight and understanding, that it was a long time before mankind could so much as guess at the Causes that moved the vast Frame of the Universe. (10)

Ptolemy relied on his eyesight, and so was taken in by the stage-drama when he claimed that the sun and planets revolved around the earth, whereas Copernicus and Galileo were like Fontenelle's 'Enginier' who finds the 'pullies' and ropes behind the 'deus ex machina'. The new philosophy exposes the laws of motion that nature and the senses have kept secret, and reveals that the earth and other planets revolve around the sun.

In her introduction, Behn values the dialogue for passages like that printed above, but resists the constraints that the work places on its women readers. Behn recognizes that the narrator's interlocutor is a figment of the writer's imagination, 'for his Lady *Marquiese*, he makes her say a great many very silly things, tho sometimes she makes Observations so learned, that the greatest Philosophers in *Europe* could make no better' (A6v).[17] Behn objects to the *Marquiese* as either too stupid or too brilliant, perhaps because such unrealistic extremes obscure the capabilities of actual female natural philosophers, and fail to challenge the work's investment in its repeated notion of 'Learned men'. Margaret Cavendish's visit to the Royal Society in London has often been noted, but Behn reports in *Oroonoko* that she sent insects acquired in Surinam to the Royal Society, and she also shaped the description of Surinam according to the Society's 'General Heads'.[18] Her translation of Fontenelle may also have been addressed to the Royal Society, but it had no effect, whereas Fontenelle was awarded membership into the Académie française and the Académie des sciences for his work. Nevertheless, Behn challenges

Fontenelle's *Marquiese* by providing a model of a self-taught woman with a genuine interest in science who has the sense to see the linguistic and philosophical flaws of the book she translates.[19] She defends the Copernican view of the universe through an argument against religious opponents, but disagrees mightily with the claim that there are creatures on other planets.

However, her resistance to science as a construct 'based on relationships of power' disappears when Behn translates Fontenelle's words on non-Europeans. Fontenelle uses an analogy between inhabitants on other planets and non-Europeans which operated in all philosophical considerations of the plurality of worlds and in fictional voyages to the moon. Just as those on earth will be surprised by inhabitants on other planets, so Europeans did not expect to find people in a 'new world'. In the use of this analogy, wonder and curiosity accompany bigotry and Eurocentrism.[20] Fontenelle is far more racialized in his comments than earlier writers on the topic, such as Francis Godwin or Cyrano de Bergerac, and Behn follows Fontenelle, even at times increasing this racialization.[21] When Fontenelle's narrator divides European and African into separate 'families', Behn writes, 'All the Faces of Mankind are in general near the same Form. Yet the two great Nations of our Globe, the *Europeans* and *Africans*, seem to have been made after different Models. Nay, there is a certain resemblance and Air of the Countenance peculiar to every Family or Race of Men' (94). To Fontenelle's 'chaque famille', Behn adds 'Race', a word newly significant since François Bernier had used it for the first time in its modern meaning in 1684.[22] This explicitly racialized difference takes shape in the claim that the inhabitants of Mercury would 'have no more Memory, than the most part of our *Negroes*; they never think, and are void of Reflection' (99–100).[23] Although Behn tries to open up possibilities for European women in natural philosophy through her translation, she participates in shutting them down for others.

British women who wrote on atomism had a variety of responses to the developing belief in the scientific superiority of European men. Lucy Hutchinson opposed the arrogance of male natural philosophers, and Margaret Cavendish and Anne Conway countered the belief in a strict separation between matter and spirit, body and mind, important to the theories of Descartes. Cavendish called Eurocentrism into question, but she also celebrated English imperialism.

Lucy Hutchinson (1620–81) translated into English poetry Lucretius's *De Rerum Natura*, a major source for Epicurean atomism, newly popular because of the mechanistic philosophies emerging on the continent.

Although Hutchinson's translation was not published during this period, scholars have concluded that she translated the work in the 1650s, as atomism appeared in England through the work of Hobbes and Cavendish.[24] Following Lucretius and Epicurus, these writers challenged religious accounts of creation by claiming that the universe was entirely material, including the mind and soul.[25] Hutchinson translated Lucretius's work to consider it directly, 'to understand things I heard so much discourse of at second hand'.[26] She seems to have had a genuine interest in the theory originally. However, in her prefatory letter written in 1675, she joins in a widespread outcry against its dangerous atheism, which also led Gassendi, Walter Charleton, and Robert Boyle to seek out a reconciliation between atomism and Christianity. She criticizes Lucretius, who 'devized this Casuall, Irrational dance of Attomes', and she laments those in her own day who 'make the incorruptible God part of a corruptible world, and chaine up his absolute freedome of will to a fatal Necessity' (24).

Hutchinson may have withheld her manuscript from publication for reasons of religious humility, or because Sir Aston Cockayne in 1658 decried 'a Lady' working on a translation of *De Rerum Natura* who would never be able to put such a 'masculine' poem into 'womens rhimes'.[27] Her prefatory letter suggests, however, that Hutchinson hoped her translation would be published, partially to rebuke Cockayne's masculine pride. She wanted to teach others the humility she had learned: 'I could not but in charity sett up this seamarke, to warne incautious travellers' (26). The letter genders humility as female and arrogance as male. Hutchinson stresses the difference between her milieu and that of learned men: 'I turnd it into English in a roome where my children practized the severall quallities they were taught with their Tutors, and I numbred the sillables of my translation by the threds of the canvas I wrought in, and sett them down with a pen and inke that stood by me' (23–24). As an educated gentlewoman, Hutchinson had the leisure to write, but, in her letter, she emphasizes the gendered nature of her surroundings as an act of intellectual humility: she has maternal duties and no study of her own, and she translates Latin poetry into English couplets with the care taken in her embroidery. This allows her to rebuke the arrogance of male philosophers like Lucretius and another translator of his, John Evelyn, who, she implies, lack the humility to admit that their theories may be misguided. Hutchinson criticizes Lucretius's self-praise at the beginning of the fourth book ('I ... delight to crowne / My head with a fresh wreath of flowers new blowne, / Such as noe muse hath ever worne before') as well as Evelyn's publication of his translation of only the first book of *De Rerum Natura* in 1656: 'a masculine Witt hath thought it worth printing his head in a lawrel crowne for the version of one of these books'.[28] A family portrait painted of Hutchinson also associates her with the laurel, but she holds it in her lap, rather than placing it on her head.[29] Thus she warns 'poor vainglorious scholars' and natural philosophers to be cautious (26).

Hutchinson's interest in Lucretius may have been influenced by the publication of the philosophy of Margaret Cavendish, the Duchess of Newcastle (1623–73). Like Evelyn, Cavendish presents herself crowned with laurel, along with her husband, in the frontispiece to *Nature's Pictures* (1656). According to Robert Kargon, Cavendish was one of the principal philosophers who shocked Christian thinkers with materialistic theories in the 1650s.[30] She did not consider herself an atheist, and she defended herself against the charge in later works, but, like Bacon, she separated natural philosophy from theology.[31] Her husband William Cavendish, Duke of Newcastle, cultivated a scientific circle from the 1630s which continued on the continent during the commonwealth period, and included Hobbes, Descartes, Mersenne, and Gassendi. Margaret learned the basics of mechanical philosophy in this group, and she presented the universe as entirely material in her works written in the 1650s.

Cavendish did not reproduce the doctrine of Epicurus or Hobbes. Rejecting atomism in the 1650s, she constructed a view of motion significantly at odds with prevailing versions of atomism, evident in *Philosophical Letters* (1664), *Observations upon Experimental Philosophy* (1666), and *Grounds of Natural Philosophy* (1668).[32] Instead of a collision theory, in which inanimate particles hit and move each other by chance, Cavendish argued that matter was intelligent and self-moving. Her perspective has been called organicist, or vitalistic materialism.[33] This view disrupted Descartes's mind/body split, and placed humans squarely within the natural world rather than as observers outside of it.[34] In *Observations upon Experimental Philosophy*, Cavendish developed an account of a supremely intelligent nature which orchestrates all within it (84). Therefore man has no ability to master nature, since he is part of it: 'But I perceive man has a great spleen against self-moving corporeal nature, although himself is part of her, and the reason is his ambition; for he would fain be supreme, and above all creatures' (209). From this basis, Cavendish launched an attack on the experimentalism of the Royal Society. Although she had been part of her husband's scientific circle from 1645, the establishment of the all-male Royal Society in 1661 fixed Cavendish at the margins of the scientific community.

Cavendish kept up her side of the dialogue, however, and argued for the superiority of logical deduction, along with Hobbes, because experiment depended too greatly on the unreliable physical senses.[35] She recognized that the Royal Society sought to control nature:

> 'But', say they, 'it is no wonder that our power over natural causes and effects is so slowly improved, seeing ... the forces of our minds conspire to betray us ...' I do not understand what they mean by our power over natural causes and effects ... neither can natural causes or effects be overpowered by man so, as if man was a degree above nature, but they must be as nature is pleased to order them. (49)[36]

She took aim not only at Robert Hooke's celebration of the microscope in *Micrographia* (1665), but at Robert Boyle's defense of the experimental method in *Some Considerations touching the Usefulness of Experimental Natural Philosophy* (1663, 1671). She may have orchestrated her famous visit to the Royal Society in 1667 to call attention to her criticism of their method in her *Observations* published the year before. Although no mention of her views appears in the official record, the Royal Society arranged experiments for her visit intended to defend themselves from her attack.[37] It is remarkable that no other woman made an official visit to the Society until the twentieth century.[38]

Like Behn and Hutchinson, Cavendish recognized the value of poetry and imaginative literature in exploring natural philosophy. *The Description of a New World, called the Blazing World*, first published with her *Observations*, built on the model of the voyage to the moon written by Godwin and Cyrano. Cavendish links science and literature, but also seems to mark their ultimate division, since she writes of them as two quite separate ventures, and the *Blazing World* appeared separately in other editions.[39]

The Blazing World uses satire instead of argument to attack the Royal Society. Cavendish creates animal-people (for example, bears who walk upright) not only to present her view that all creatures have intelligence and knowledge, but also to make fun of Hooke and Boyle: the bear-men are her experimental philosophers.[40] Cavendish is far more respectful of her inhabitants of this 'new world' than Fontenelle or Behn; in fact, she satirizes the strange coupling of optics and skin color in Boyle's *Experiments and Considerations Touching Colours* (1664).[41] Nevertheless, the fiction ends with an imperialistic triumph of the nation most closely linked with England, in which the science of the Blazing World creatures is marshaled to defeat that nation's enemies.[42] As a member of the Royal Society, Cavendish would have vigorously opposed efforts to master nature, but she also would have celebrated the development of technology that could establish English dominance in the world.

Anne, Viscountess Conway (1631–78) wrote one of the most remarkable works of natural philosophy of the time. Like Cavendish, she opposed the mind/body split of Descartes and the collision theory of mechanical philosophers. She differed significantly from Cavendish, however, by claiming that spirit produced all movement, and that everybody and everything could eventually be transformed back into spirit.[43] Her vitalistic philosophy included the doctrine of universal salvation, and was explicitly developed to account for and appeal to 'Jews, Turks, or other Peoples'.[44] As an upper-class woman, she received a thorough education in natural philosophy, particularly Cartesianism, through her brother John Finch, and through the tutor that he provided for her, Henry More. More was a Cambridge Platonist committed to a refutation of the materialism of Hobbes and Cavendish, and he and Conway corresponded for several years about these questions.[45] He also argued that spirit was the source of movement, but retained a more traditional account of the distinction between spirit and body. Conway broke away from her teacher, partly through the influence of her doctor, Francis Mercury van Helmont, and their shared interest in the Jewish Lurianic Kabbaleh as well as Quakerism. Conway accepted the Kabbalistic view that the world could be restored to its perfect state before the Fall, and she eventually converted to Quakerism.[46] Her treatise *The Principles of the Most Ancient and Modern Philosophy* was published in Amsterdam in the original Latin in 1690, twelve years after her death, probably by van Helmont, and an English translation appeared in London in 1692. Her philosophy had a direct influence on Leibniz, who was also a vitalist, and he seems to have acquired the term 'monad' from Conway and van Helmont.[47]

Conway might have made a major difference in the Royal Society. Her interest in universal salvation could have countered the objectification of Africans and other non-Europeans developing through the Society's interest in skin color and questions about 'inhabitants' sent out to the colonies and other countries in the 'General Heads'. Quakers in the colonies fought against the racism of slave-owners (although not against slavery) and sought to bring enslaved peoples into Christianity through baptism.[48] However, her presence at Society meetings would have been unlikely, since she suffered from debilitating headaches throughout most of her life. Nevertheless, Conway was familiar with the experimental philosophy of the Royal Society through More and publications of

Robert Boyle.[49] A more consistent dialogue between Boyle and Conway on subjects of mutual interest – the refutation of atheism in the context of the new science and the relevance of Christianity to non-Europeans – might have moderated the Eurocentricism of the Royal Society.

'Sisters of the Royal Society'

Some women contributed to the scientific activities of male relatives through running the household, performing experiments, and discussion. These women have been called 'sisters of the Royal Society' because of their proximity to members of the group, which makes the exclusion of women from the Society even more noteworthy.[50] Katherine Jones (1615–91), Lady Ranelagh, provided a home for her brother Robert Boyle for the last thirty years of his life. As Boyle built and worked in his laboratory in Jones's house, she performed experiments in her kitchen and developed medicinal recipes collected in two notebooks, one of which explored chemistry, using alchemical symbols probably shared with her brother. Jones had been a member of Samuel Hartlib's circle of correspondents on various topics like natural philosophy in the 1640s and 1650s, a circle that included several in Gresham College and the Oxford Circle, groups influential in the founding of the Royal Society. Lady Barrington and Dorothy Moore also corresponded within Hartlib's group, and Jones visited the Oxford Circle once. According to Lynette Hunter, 'It was said of this circle, possibly caustically, "The Lords are the Lords and the Ladies the Commons", a comment which combines an implicit devaluing of the women.' It also demonstrates that women were directly involved in scientific conversations with those who founded the Society in 1661, and this suggests that all-male membership in the Society was a conscious decision.[51]

Fellows of the Society were also quite aware of the intelligence and education of Mary Evelyn (c.1635–1709), the wife of the naturalist John, since her letters were shared with them by the family tutor, Ralph Bohun.[52] Evelyn helped her husband in gardening experiments, the development of a recipe book, and her work in the still or distillation room, distinct from, yet very like her husband's 'elaboratorie'. Evelyn was far less interested in entering into scientific circles than Cavendish, and, in one of her letters, she wrote a sharp satire of the Duchess's social manner, writing style, and personal ambition.[53] Evelyn places the laurel on the head of her husband, since she designed the very frontispiece of his translation of the first book of Lucretius's *De Rerum Natura* which Hutchinson derides in the prefatory letter to her own complete translation.[54] Certainly the Society had models of both aggressive and more obedient women to consider when it chose to exclude all women from its membership.

If sisters and wives had been members of the Society, the 'Commons' may have questioned some of the assumptions of the 'Lords'. In a letter to her brother, Jones directly criticizes England's imperial ambitions. She wonders whether Boyle's goals for experimental science, what he calls the 'Empire of Man, as a Naturalist, over the Creatures', can solve the problems of political empire and colonization, 'Wheather the Domminion you are recommending to men wil take soe much with them to rayse their Ambitions towards its attainment [rather than that colonial domination] they most commonly persue with much more paines: I know not & much doubt the worst.'[55] She seems quite skeptical that Boyle's program will decrease in any way the use of 'swords & gunns' or the violent effects of the English empire: 'we dayly see that by that way of overcomeing we spoyle what we should governe'. She uses the generic term 'man' throughout the passage, and therefore never directly disputes the masculine emphasis in Boyle's project. However, she also suggests that men will continue to fail to produce an empire that is characterized by anything but greed and aggression. One could argue that Jones's response is gendered, but it is worth noting that Jones and Cavendish would not have supported each other on these points. Cavendish refutes the notion of the 'Empire of Man, as a Naturalist, over the Creatures' while Jones supports it; Jones refutes the belief that swords and guns can legitimately establish English domination, whereas Cavendish celebrates it.[56] It is clear, however, that the Royal Society would have benefited from their debate.

Conclusion

Rebecca Merrens argues that, in his 'Free Enquiry into the Vulgarly Receiv'd Notion of Nature' (1686), Robert Boyle answers Cavendish's *Observations* (1666), with its conception of nature as intelligently controlling humans and all else.[57] Just as feminist historians of science demonstrated Conway's influence on Leibniz, so Merrens suggests that the role of women in seventeenth-century science has yet to be fully discovered. As this project proceeds, however, it would be valuable to coordinate analyses of gender, race, and politics in order to avoid the suggestion that the participation of British women in the institutions of science would have solved all of its problems. Although Conway and Cavendish may have refuted the claim of Boyle and the Royal Society that they could step outside nature to create an 'Empire of Man over the inferior Creatures',[58] Herbert, Behn, and Cavendish would have promoted the goals of British nationalism, including colonization and slavery. Boyle's phrase is telling: although the inclusion of women in British science may have lessened the emphasis on 'Man', it is not clear that science would have had cooperated less with the project of 'Empire'.

Notes

1. Hans Sloane, M.D., *A Voyage to the Islands Madera, Barbados, Nieves, S. Christophers and Jamaica* (London: Printed by B.M. for the Author, 1707), cxxiv, lvi.
2. Sandra Harding, *Is Science Multicultural?* (Bloomington: Indiana University Press, 1998), esp. 39–72. Pamela Smith outlines fascinating new work on 'Creole epistemology' and local knowledge in 'Science on the Move: Recent Trends in the History of Early Modern Science', *Renaissance Quarterly* 62 (Summer 2009): 368–72.
3. Londa Schiebinger, *The Mind Has No Sex? Women in the Origins of Modern Science* (Cambridge, MA: Harvard University Press, 1989); Lynette Hunter and Sarah Hutton, eds, *Women, Science and Medicine, 1500–1700* (Phoenix Mill: Sutton, 1997); Patricia Fara, *Pandora's Breeches: Women, Science & Power in the Enlightenment* (London: Pimlico, 2004); Ruth Watts, *Women in Science: A Social and Cultural History* (London: Routledge, 2007); Erica Harth, *Cartesian Women: Versions and Subversions of Rational Discourse in the Old Regime* (Ithaca: Cornell University Press, 1992).
4. Harding, *Is Science Multicultural?*; Ania Loomba and Jonathan Burton, eds, *Race in Early Modern England: A Documentary Companion* (New York: Palgrave Macmillan, 2007); Sujata Iyengar, *Shades of Difference: Mythologies of Skin Color in Early Modern England* (Philadelphia: University of Pennsylvania Press, 2005); Londa Schiebinger, *Nature's Body* (Boston: Beacon Press, 1993); Watts, *Women in Science*, 7–8.
5. Watts, *Women in Science*, 3.
6. Lynette Hunter, 'Women and Domestic Medicine' (89–107), and Margaret Pelling, 'Thoroughly Resented? Older Women and the Medical Role' (63–88), in *Women, Science and Medicine*, ed. L. Hunter and Hutton. Pamela Smith discusses women's engagement in 'technoscience' in 'Science on the Move: Recent Trends in the History of Early Modern Science', 357–60.
7. Quoted in L. Hunter, 'Women and Domestic Medicine', 99.
8. A. Eccles, *Obstetrics and Gynaecology in Tudor and Stuart England* (London: Croom Helm, 1982; Schiebinger, *The Mind Has No Sex?*, 104–12; H. Marland, ed., *The Art of Midwifery: Early Modern Midwives in Europe* (London: Routledge, 1993); Watts, *Women in Science*, 47–49; Adrian Wilson, *The Making of Man-Midwifery: Childbirth in England, 1660–1770* (Cambridge, MA: Harvard University Press, 1995).
9. Elaine Hobby, introduction to Jane Sharp, *The Midwives Book Or the Whole Art of Midwifry Discovered* (New York: Oxford University Press, 1999).
10. Cellier's *Scheme* is reprinted in *Women's Political Writings, 1610–1725*, ed. Hilda L. Smith, Mihoko Suzuki, and Susan Wiseman (London: Pickering & Chatto, 2007), III: 150–57. On Cellier, see especially Mary Phillips, 'Midwives

versus Medics: A 17th-century Professional Turf War', *Management & Organizational History* 2.1 (2007): 27–44; Frances Dolan, *Whores of Babylon: Catholicism, Gender and Seventeenth-Century Print Culture* (Ithaca: Cornell University Press, 1999); Schiebinger, *The Mind Has No Sex?*, 104–12; and Watts, *Women in Science*, 47–49.

11. These texts were written some time before they were published, and there is skepticism about whether these women were directly involved in their production (L. Hunter, 'Women and Domestic Medicine', 89–90).

12. Caroline Merchant, *The Death of Nature: Women, Ecology, and the Scientific Revolution* (San Francisco: Harper & Row, 1980); Brian Easlea, *Fathering the Unthinkable: Masculinity, Scientists and the Nuclear Arms Race* (London: Pluto Press, 1983). Sarah Hutton also addresses this issue in *Anne Conway: A Woman Philosopher* (Cambridge: Cambridge University Press, 2004), 238–42.

13. On the Society's support for colonization, see Cristina Malcolmson, '"The Explication of Whiteness and Blackness": Skin Color and the Physics of Color in the Works of Robert Boyle and Margaret Cavendish', in *Fault Lines and Controversies in the Study of Seventeenth-Century Literature*, ed. Claude J. Summers and Ted-Larry Pebworth (Columbia: University of Missouri Press, 2002), 187–203; and Gary Taylor, *Buying Whiteness: Race, Culture, and Identity from Columbus to Hip Hop* (New York: Palgrave Macmillan, 2005). Also pertinent is Denise Albanese, *New Science, New World* (Durham: Duke University Press, 1996).

14. Schiebinger, *The Mind Has No Sex?*, 37–65. Patricia Phillips, *The Scientific Lady: A Social Theory of Women's Scientific Interests, 1520–1918* (New York: St. Martin's Press, 1990), 139–41, tells a story of unmitigated progress that the scholars listed in note 3 refute.

15. Alchemy was studied throughout this period, especially by chemists; see, for instance, William Newman and Lawrence Principe, *Alchemy Tried in the Fire* (Chicago: University of Chicago Press, 2003). On Herbert, see Margaret P. Hannay, '"How I These Studies Prize": The Countess of Pembroke and Elizabethan Science', in *Women, Science and Medicine*, ed. L. Hunter and Hutton, 108–21; Mary Ellen Lamb, 'The Countess of Pembroke's Patronage', unpublished PhD dissertation, Columbia University, 107; Cristina Malcolmson, 'William Herbert's Gardener, Adrian Gilbert', in *George Herbert's Pastoral* (Newark: University of Delaware Press, 2010), 113–33.

16. Fontenelle's work was published in 1686. Further citations in the text will refer to Behn's 1688 translation. Deborah Uman points out Behn's subtle change in the title in 'A World of Her Own: Aphra Behn's Translation of Bernard le Bovier de Fontenelle's *Entretiens sur La Pluralité des Mondes*', unpublished seminar paper, Shakespeare Association of America, 2006, 1.

17. Uman, 'A World of Her Own', 6–7.

18. Aphra Behn, *Oroonoko*, ed. Catherine Gallagher (Boston: Bedford/St. Martin's Press), 38; Judy Hayden, '"As Far as a Woman's Reasoning May go": Aphra Behn, *Oroonoko* and the New Science', ASECS conference, Montreal, 2006. Behn also translated the sixth book of Abraham Cowley's *Six Books of Plants* (1689). 'General Heads for a *Natural History of a Country*, Great or small', *Philosophical Transactions* I: 186–9 (no. 11, 2 April 1666); *The Works of Robert Boyle*, ed. Michael Hunter and Edward B. Davis (London: Pickering & Chatto, 1999), V: 508–11.

19. Uman, 'A World of Her Own', 7.
20. Mary Baines Campbell, *Wonder and Science* (Ithaca: Cornell University Press, 1999).
21. Francis Godwin, *The Man in the Moone* (London, 1638); Cyrano de Bergerac, *Selenarhia, or, The Government of the World in the Moon a Comical History*, trans. Thomas St. Serf (London: J. Cottrel, 1659). Line Cottegnies surprisingly argues that Behn lessens Fontenelle's racism in 'The Translator as Critic: Aphra Behn's Translation of Fontenelle's *Discovery of New Worlds* (1688)', *Restoration: Studies in English Literary Culture* 27 (2003), 32.
22. Ivan Hannaford discusses Bernier in *Race: The History of an Idea in the West* (Baltimore: Johns Hopkins University Press, 1996), 191, 203ff. For a different view, see Loomba and Burton, eds, *Race in Early Modern England*, 1–36, 272–74.
23. See Taylor, *Buying Whiteness*, 294–301, on the racialization of 'reflection' in early modern optics.
24. Reid Barbour, 'Lucy Hutchinson, Atomism and the Atheist Dog', in *Women, Science and Medicine*, ed. L. Hunter and Hutton, 136, n.1; Lucy Hutchinson, *Order and Disorder*, ed. David Norbrook (Oxford: Blackwell, 2001), xii–lii.
25. Robert Hugh Kargon, *Atomism in England from Hariot to Newton* (Oxford: Clarendon Press, 1966), 54–76. See also Jonathan Goldberg, *The Seeds of Things* (New York: Fordham University Press, 2009), 122–78.
26. *Lucy Hutchinson's Translation of Lucretius*, ed. Hugh de Quehen (Ann Arbor: University of Michigan Press, 1996), 23. Further references are cited parenthetically in the text.
27. Barbour, 'Lucy Hutchinson', 123–24.
28. Hutchinson translates the beginning of Lucretius's fourth book (p. 115 or 4: 1–8). She refers to his self-praise in 'The Argumente of the fourth booke', lines 1–2, p. 114. In her prefatory letter (p. 23), she comments on Evelyn's title page in *An Essay on the First Book of T. Lucretius Carus De Rerum Natura* (London, 1656). See also David Norbrook, 'Margaret Cavendish and Lucy Hutchinson: Identity, Ideology and Politics', *In-between: Essays and Studies in Literary Criticism* 9.1–2 (2000): 179–203.
29. *Order and Disorder*, ed. Norbrook, xv. Norbrook publishes the portrait on the cover.
30. Kargon, *Atomism in England*, 73–77.
31. Margaret Cavendish, *Observations upon Experimental Philosophy*, ed. Eileen O'Neill (Cambridge: Cambridge University Press, 2001), 219–20. Further references are cited parenthetically in the text. Sarah Hutton, 'Anne Conway, Margaret Cavendish, and Seventeenth-Century Scientific Thought', in *Women, Science and Medicine*, ed. L. Hunter and Hutton, 227–32 (225).
32. Line Cottegnies, 'Margaret Cavendish and Cyrano de Bergerac: A Libertine Subtext for Cavendish's *Blazing World*?' *Bulletin de la Société d'Etudes Anglo-Americaines des XVIIe and XVIIIe Siècles* 54 (2002): 179; for a different view, see O'Neill in Cavendish, *Observations*, xx–xxi.
33. O'Neill in Cavendish, *Observations*, xix.
34. Schiebinger, *The Mind Has No Sex?*, 52.
35. Elizabeth Spiller, *Science, Reading, and Renaissance Literature* (Cambridge: Cambridge University Press, 2004), 137–77.

36. For useful analyses of this issue, see Anna Battigelli, *Margaret Cavendish and the Exiles of the Mind* (Lexington: University Press of Kentucky, 1998), 85–113; Campbell, *Wonder and Science*, 180–223; John Rogers, *The Matter of Revolution* (Ithaca: Cornell University Press, 1996), 177–211.
37. Malcolmson, '"Explication"'; Battigelli, *Margaret Cavendish*, 110–13.
38. Watts, *Women in Science*, 50.
39. Spiller, *Science, Reading*, 137–77.
40. Margaret Cavendish, *The Blazing World and Other Writings*, ed. Kate Lilley (London: Penguin Books, 1992), 142.
41. Malcolmson, '"Explication"'; Robert Boyle, *Experiments and Considerations Touching Colours* (London: Herringman, 1664), 151; or in Boyle, *Works*, IV: xi–xvi, 84–93.
42. Cavendish, *The Blazing World*, 203–16.
43. Hutton, 'Anne Conway, Margaret Cavendish'; Stephen Clucas, 'The Duchess and the Viscountess: Negotiations between Mechanism and Vitalism in the Natural Philosophies of Margaret Cavendish and Anne Conway', *In-between: Essays and Studies in Literary Criticism* 9.1–2 (2000): 125–36. See also Hutton, *Anne Conway*, and Fara, *Pandora's Breeches*, 74–87.
44. Anne Conway, *The Principles of the Most Ancient and Modern Philosophy*, ed. Allison P. Coudert and Taylor Corse (Cambridge: Cambridge University Press, 1996), xi–xii.
45. *The Conway Letters: The Correspondence of Anne, Viscountess Conway, Henry More, and their Friends 1642–1682*, ed. Marjorie Hope Nicolson, rev. Sarah Hutton (Oxford: Clarendon Press, 1992).
46. Conway, *Principles*, xviii–xxix.
47. Ibid., xxxi.
48. Ibid., xxii–xxix; Alden T. Vaughan, *Roots of American Racism* (New York: Oxford University Press, 1995), 55–81.
49. Hutton, *Anne Conway*, 116–39.
50. Lynette Hunter, 'Sisters of the Royal Society: The Circle of Katherine Jones, Lady Ranelagh', in *Women, Science and Medicine*, ed. L. Hunter and Hutton, 178–97; Frances Harris, 'Living in the Neighbourhood of Science: Mary Evelyn, Margaret Cavendish, and the Greshamites', in *Women, Science and Medicine*, ed. Hunter and Hutton, 198–217.
51. L. Hunter, 'Sisters', 186.
52. Harris, 'Living in the Neighbourhood'.
53. Ibid., 198–99.
54. Ibid., 202.
55. *Correspondence of Robert Boyle, 1636–1691*, ed. Michael Hunter, Antonio Clericuzio, and Lawrence M. Principe (London: Pickering & Chatto, 2001), Lady Ranelagh to Boyle, 6 August 1665 (2: 503–04). Ranelagh responds to the 'Empire of Man' discussed in Boyle's *Usefulnesse of Natural Philosophy* (1663), *Works*, III: 212.
56. Cavendish considers Boyle's 'Empire of Man' in *Observations*, 203.
57. Rebecca Merrens, 'A Nature of "Infinite Sense and Reason": Margaret Cavendish's Natural Philosophy and the "Noise" of a Feminized Nature', *Women's Studies* 25 (1996): 421–38; Boyle, *Works*, X: 450, 548. Boyle's work was originally written in the 1660s (*Works*, X: li).
58. Robert Boyle, 'Free Inquiry', *Works*, X: 450.

14
Questioning Gender, War, and 'the Old Lie': The Military Expertise of Margaret Cavendish

Joanne Wright

In this chapter, I read Margaret Cavendish as a political theorist, devoting particular attention to her deliberations on the subject of war. Women have a long and rich history of war writing but are rarely perceived to be military experts in their own right, rarely understood to have political knowledge about war and military affairs. Indeed, just as war itself is a deeply gendered human activity, and ideas about natural male and female roles are central to our conceptions of its function and necessity, writing and thinking about war is also deeply gendered. In the discipline of political science, feminist critics of international relations discourse, or strategic studies, have begun to deconstruct the gender order that is central to militarist thinking.[1] Resisting simplistic assumptions about men's and women's proper roles in, and responses to war, they take issue with the militarization of society, militaristic definitions of leadership and masculinity, and the push for war at the expense of other, peaceful solutions.

Keeping these feminist critiques at the forefront, I suggest that Cavendish lays an important historical foundation for thinking through a critical stance on war. In *Orations of Divers Sorts* (1662), *Bell in Campo* (1662), and *Sociable Letters* (1664), she persistently draws our attention to the brutality as well as the futility of conflict as she undermines the much celebrated and time-worn notion of the honorable military death. In so doing, Cavendish de-centers traditional military expertise to include a new emphasis on women's specialized, but unrecognized, knowledge of military affairs and the experience of war. Coming to terms with Cavendish's political thought on war will allow us to position her both within the rich texture of Civil War political thought and on a larger trans-historical trajectory of women's critical writings on war and militarism.

Although Margaret Cavendish was vitally engaged with the political debates and issues of Civil War and Restoration England, as literary historians and others have shown,[2] her participation in, and contributions to political discourse, and especially the discourses of war and militarism, have not been properly recognized within the history of political thought. Her complete lack of recognition in the discipline of political science illuminates something of the differences between the literary and political canons, the former being far more receptive to revisions and alterations over time, but the problem goes deeper than the politics of canon creation. This resistance to including women's historical contributions to political discourse within the discipline of political science points to a larger inability to recognize women's perspectives on politics and war as epistemologically authoritative. Scholars of early modern political thought, as the field is presently defined, confine their inquiry to male theorists and operate on the unstated but tacitly held assumption that no women *theorized* about politics or war during the early modern period. The fact that, as Hilda Smith recently described, 'almost no attention has been given to women thinkers of the past',[3] indicates not just an oversight or omission but a failure, one that gives us a skewed impression of the character of political and intellectual discourse in early modern England.

As with women's political writings, so too with their perspectives on war: there are no great women war thinkers or military experts. Significantly, as feminist epistemologist Lorraine Code points out, women have long been subjects of male expertise, but are rarely viewed as experts about themselves or their own experiences.[4] Military expertise, then as now, is an area of knowledge production particularly closed to women since useful knowledge of war is thought to be gained from experience in battle, something few women have. Nevertheless, Cavendish demonstrates her conventional knowledge of war in her military biography of her husband, William Cavendish, the former general of the King's northern army, in *The Life of the (1ˢᵗ) Duke of Newcastle*. In addition to this, Cavendish uses a surprisingly diverse array of literary forms to deliberate on the hardships of conflict and to generate an alternative knowledge about war. Although the texts I will consider here are different stylistically, from orations and letters to drama, thematically they are mutually reinforcing and allow Cavendish to challenge the idea of war as something that can be neatly contained on the battlefield. Practically, war happens to communities, to families, to women left behind. Thus even when they are not soldiers women are very much *in the war* and their knowledge of it, as Cavendish demonstrates, is as germane to military expertise as that which is gained in direct conflict.

On gender, war, and 'the old lie'

In *Three Guineas*, Virginia Woolf lays bare the connection between gender and war: '… though many instincts are held more or less in common by both sexes, to fight has always been the man's habit, not the woman's … Scarcely a human being in the course of history has fallen to a woman's rifle; the vast majority of birds and beasts have been killed by you, not by us …'[5] Cavendish draws out the same connection when, in her 'Child-bed Womans Funeral Oration' she states plainly, women 'increase life when men for the most part destroy life'.[6] How do we contend with the unassailable fact that war has been a predominantly masculine endeavor?

In Cavendish's writing, we see the three possible responses to this statement: to accept and justify it as an empirical fact by drawing on traditional ideas about gender roles; to challenge it by declaring that women, too, can perform masculine tasks, thereby ruling out the notion that women are by nature unfit for combat; and finally, to challenge the whole enterprise of war by offering a critique of the masculine propensity to violence. Certainly, at many points in her writing, Cavendish leaves her readers with a sense of her own acceptance of, and complicity with, gender roles in war and elsewhere. In 'An Epistle to Souldiers', Cavendish relays her fearfulness and lack of courage as stemming from the 'constitution of my Sex':

> Great Heroicks, you may justly laugh at me, if I went about to censure, instruct, or advise in the valiant Art, and Discipline of Warre … these Armies I mention, were rais'd in my braine, fought in my fancy, and registered in my closet.[7]

Given the preponderance of evidence to this effect, it might be tempting to assume, as Roger Hudson does, that in Cavendish's war writings, 'the prevailing tone is one of submission'.[8] However, this first response is far from the whole story, and does not account for the risks Cavendish takes in challenging these gendered norms.

Cavendish's second response to the gender of war asserts women's capacity to 'hawk, hunt, race, and do the like exercises as men have' (Oration #132, p. 249). Contemporary scholars analyze what Mihoko Suzuki calls the 'Elizabeth effect' on Cavendish, that is, Cavendish's use of Elizabeth I (and Queen Henrietta Maria) to introduce notions of female agency into the masculinized culture of war and politics in early modern England.[9] In *A Description of a New World called the Blazing-World*

(1666), with its formidable Empress and her knowledgeable scribe, the Duchess of Newcastle, Cavendish demonstrates her enchantment with Amazonian imagery, female heroism, and power. In *Bell in Campo* (1662), Lady Victoria and her army outperform their masculine counterpart proving that women can be brave; they can be like men in war, and perhaps even superior – more skilled, more effectual, better trained and more highly disciplined, and potentially more vengeful and bloodthirsty. While some of her contemporaries turned to the Amazons to reaffirm the natural basis of the patriarchal order, Cavendish is more interested in exploring the complicated relationship of women to power, politics, and even aggression. The heroickesses of *Bell in Campo* are able to translate their military successes in the war into social and political gains in peacetime, bringing about a rebalancing of power relations in the political sphere.[10] Here we also begin to see the complexity of Cavendish's thinking on gender and war, as the agency she attributes to these characters also sends a message to men that women are not simply the hapless victims of war and that their relationship to power and conflict cannot be so neatly simplified. While Cavendish's experiments with female heroism constitute an important scholarly focus, we should not overlook a different – which is not to say necessarily competing – theme, that is her persistent and provocative disruptions of militarism itself. To properly assess Cavendish's range of thought on war we need to look not only to her assertions of how women can be *like men* in conflict, but to her challenge to the masculine endeavor of war itself. For Cynthia Enloe, a feminist critic of international relations theory, confronting militarism is potentially the most disruptive to the political status quo, more challenging than gender role reversals which leave intact a militaristic sensibility that war serves some higher purpose. Enloe regards militarism as a 'compilation of ideas, assumptions, and beliefs' that normalize and naturalize military solutions to political conflict. Included on her list of 'distinctively militaristic core beliefs' are the following ideas: that armed force is the ultimate resolver of tensions; that having enemies is a natural condition; that, in a time of national or political crisis, any man who refuses to engage in military conflict is 'jeopardizing his own status as a manly man'.[11] The absence of a fully elaborated proto-feminist anti-war discourse in Cavendish's period may cause us to overlook the extent to which Cavendish herself challenges these militarist lines of thinking. In what follows, I highlight some of the ways in which she variously subverts and disrupts militarism in her own distinctive manner.

How, then, does Cavendish take up the ideology of militarism? It is unlikely that Cavendish would have defined herself as a pacifist, as she praises intermittently an absolute, united, and imperial English nation, extols the virtues of foreign wars for their capacity to unify a nation against a common enemy, and even repeats the commonly held assumption that peace causes sluggishness and effeminacy within a nation. The repetition and acceptance of such ideas are central to the maintenance of a militarist ideology, and to any war effort, and given Cavendish's choice in marriage we should not be surprised that she enumerates them with rhetorical skill. At the same time, however, a careful reading suggests that as Cavendish rehearses some of these well-worn themes, they begin to take quite a different shape. In her preamble to her poems on war and peace in *Poems and Fancies* (1653), 'An Epistle to Souldiers', just as she attempts to position herself as an unreliable, feminine observer of war who fundamentally lacks the expertise required to comment on it, she nevertheless reveals herself as more than a benign spectator and offers her own subtle judgment: 'I never saw an Army together, nor any Incounters in my life ... neither have I the courage to looke on the cruell assaults, that Mankind (as I have heard) will make at each other ...'[12] In *The Worlds Olio* (1655), commenting on war in general and its capacity to bring out men's true natures, she concludes by listing all of its negative effects, including 'Envy, Faction, Revenge, Theft' and 'Death and Destruction to that Kingdom that is the weaker'.[13] From here she speculates in 'Of the Loss in Battels' on the unsettling question of how long it would take to slit the throats of fifty thousand men in battle, concluding that as the battle proceeds, 'dead Bodies of Horses and Men will hinder much their encounters', slowing their capacity to fight and slay the opponent (112).

Among the most powerful of the militaristic themes that Cavendish takes up is that of the triumphant military death. In her 'Oration for those that are Slain in the Wars and brought home to be Buried' Cavendish praises the virtues of men who serve their country, claiming that loved ones left behind have 'more cause to rejoice than to grieve'. For, she explains, 'it is an honour to their memory to die in the service of their country' (#11, p. 140). To serve one's country is to achieve manly honor such that 'all wise men will gladly quit a present, frail and uncertain life to live eternally in the memory of the present and future ages, in whose memories their actions live like glorified bodies and purified souls'. A superficially celebratory tone infuses Cavendish's oration, as she describes the soldiers whose 'deaths are their triumphs' and whose bodies are 'brought home as a witness of their victory'. This is to be a glorious occasion with 'music, bells and bonfires' as well as offerings to the gods (141). Yet, as much as Cavendish is prepared to recite and celebrate the timeless sentiment, *Dulce et decorum est pro patria mori* – it is sweet and right to die for one's country – she is frequently unable to do so without explicit reference to hearses, corpses, and the fate of bodily remains.[14]

A prime example of Cavendish reciting an idea only to recast its meaning can be found in 'A Soldier's Funeral Oration', in which her opening declaration of the soldier's profession as a noble one is eroded almost immediately by her references to Death as the soldier's friend and companion:

> all valiant soldiers are Honour's sons, Death's friends, and Life's enemies, for a soldier's profession is to destroy lives to get honour and fame, by which destruction, Death is a gainer. (#109, p. 227)

What starts out to mark a man's honorable service quickly becomes a stark description of his true fate, an assessment of his profession as destructive and his pursuits as shallow. Death is personified as perpetually hungry, with an insatiable appetite for soldiers. Death is,

> like some gluttons, the more they eat, the leaner they are; nay Death is so lean as to be only bare bones, and by his empty skull he may be thought a fool, having no brains, for he be rather a Knave than a fool, for he deceives or robs Nature and Time of many lives, taking them away before nature and Time had ordained them to die... (#109, p. 227)

She concludes:

> we must also leave him this dead soldier's body for to feed upon, for all heroic men are Death's most nourishing food, they make him strong and lusty; since there is no remedy, let us place this dead Hero on Death's table, which is to put him into the grave, and there leave him. (#11, p. 140)

The simple mandate to honor and celebrate, which is the very purpose of the funeral oration, is refused as the reader/listener is left to contemplate the physical consumption of the soldier's body.

It is evident that Cavendish aims to do more that merely restate and reaffirm the standard statements about the nature and purpose of war; she engages and confronts them. Just as her depiction of female warriors is not confined to mythical and heroic language but is, as Karen

Raber describes, 'redolent in the materiality of war',[15] Cavendish is not content to recite sentimental phrases attesting to the benefits of war without testing how they play out on the ground, examining how different our ideas about war can be when we shift our gaze away from the pageantry and the weapons to examine war's gritty underside. She effectively subverts military enthusiasm by getting into the trenches, as it were, to expose war's physical effects – bodies, wounds, blood, and all.

Sentimental phrases offer a short-lived comfort, but the experience of war teaches something quite different. And it is the experience of war – including her own – that she cannot contain. Since these orations deal with soldiers who die in war, we might assume their purpose is to recognize Cavendish's own brother's service. Charles Lucas was summarily shot by parliamentary soldiers after he had submitted to them, an execution Cavendish likens to cold-blooded murder. Cavendish records the trauma of this event both in her poetry and in her memoir, *A True Relation of my Birth, Breeding and Life*. Referring to Charles's death, as well as that of another brother, her sister and mother, all of whom died in a span of three years while she was in exile, Cavendish claims, 'I shall lament the loss so long as I live.'[16] Cavendish's evocation in the oration of bodily remains 'being brought home as a witness to their victory' raises the question of what happened to Charles's body, and neatly glosses over the fact that, under the circumstances – his execution by parliamentary forces, the absence of family members who would have mourned his death in England, along with the fact that Civil War soldiers were often so disfigured they were 'buried hastily, in unmarked graves'[17] – Lucas's body was initially not given a proper burial.[18] 'Having invariably been stripped of clothes and possessions, as well as being scarred by fatal wounds', military historian Charles Carleton explains, remains of the Civil War dead 'were extremely hard to recognize'.[19] Rather than being assured of fame in after ages, most soldiers, Cavendish recognizes, are buried in 'oblivion's grave', their 'slain bodies for the most part lie and rot above ground or are devoured by carrion-birds or ravenous beasts'.[20] Cavendish's writing exposes *Dulce et decorum est pro patria mori* for what it is, in Wilfred Owen's famous description, 'the old lie'.[21]

Cavendish is not content simply to mourn, nor to rally in support of the war effort. Instead she allows the ugliness of war to bubble through the surface of her seemingly non-judgmental, multi-sided orations as well as in her other more fanciful works. She returns again and again to the subject of bodies. At the opening of the second part of *The Blazing World*, the Empress has just learned from spirits that her homeland is besieged by war, news that is deeply troubling to her. At a loss as to how she can aid her home country, she consults the Emperor for advice and, in an elaborate passage, the two debate whether the same spirits who had informed her of the wars could not be called upon to inhabit some of the slain bodies in her native country to form an army to resist the destruction. The Empress concludes the impossibility of this plan, citing several practical difficulties: where would they get enough bodies to mount a sufficient resistance? And more importantly, before the bodies could be inhabited and put in a posture of war to make a great and formidable army, it is quite likely that 'they would stink and dissolve; and when they came to a fight, they would moulder into dust and ashes and so leave the purer immaterial spirits naked'.[22] In this unusual passage, Cavendish is barely disguising her own experience of living in exile and receiving news about the destruction of her native England and the loss of her family members – and relating a sense of her own powerlessness to respond. Whatever the lofty ideas being used to justify the war and the naïve optimism held that one's own side will prevail, the inevitable outcome, Cavendish illustrates, is dead and rotting bodies.

A persistent theme of Cavendish's treatment of the Civil War is summarized in Sociable Letter #185: 'those that never had the Sweetness of Peace, or have not known the Misery of War, cannot be truly and rightly Sensible of either' (p. 251). More than a pat phrase, this is an expression of Cavendish's epistemological frustration about political knowledge. Why are human beings, and perhaps particularly men in this case, unable to connect thought and action, to understand the consequences of their ideas?

> You imagine you shall be victorious, otherwise you would not make war, for imagination can easily and suddenly conquer all the world; yet you will not find it so in action as in thought. It is one thing to fight a battle in the brain and another thing to fight a battle in the field. (Oration #5, p. 135)

She reserves particular scorn for those who allowed trivial differences to escalate into full-blown conflict, the effects of which bring about the long-overdue realization that the petty faults ought to have been overlooked in the first place. In her 'Oration to a Dejected People Ruined by War', she berates citizens who, while enjoying the benefits of peace before the war, complained of unfair taxation and other inconveniences, which they came to regard later as minor in comparison to the destruction of their city. To these citizens, who were puffed up with pride and failed to see the tenuousness and precariousness of the peace they enjoyed, she asks in a distinctly Hobbesian tone,

> Where are your chargeable buildings, your stately palaces, your delightful theatres? All burnt to ashes. Where are your wise laws? All broken. Your ancestor's monuments? All pulled down, and your fathers' bones and ashes dispersed. Where are your beautiful wives, daughters, sisters and mistresses? The enemy enjoys them and your country is desolate, ruined and forlorn; and you that are left are miserable. (#28, p. 156)[23]

Like Hobbes, Cavendish fears disorder and criticizes both sides in the Civil War for their part in precipitating it. In this passage, Cavendish summons another occasion of Lucas family horror, in which the parliamentary forces, in 1648, with nothing left to loot, turned to the Lucas family tomb, where the recently interred bodies of Margaret's mother and sister lay. In Douglas Grant's description, 'finding the undecomposed bodies of both Elizabeth Lucas and her daughter, Mary Killigrew, they cut off their hair and wore it in their hats, scattering the other corpses' bones about "with profane jests"'.[24] Cavendish uses her own family's terrifying experiences, and that of many others, to generalize about civil war's destructive chaos: while 'a foreign war is but like an outward sore on the body … a civil war is as an inward disease even in the vital parts' (#154, p. 268).

While Hobbes's description of the absence of rule and order in the Civil War is most famous, as 'solitary, poore, nasty, brutish, and short',[25] Cavendish's references to the condition of war are even more unsettling. What are we to make of Cavendish's bleak realism? Do her musings about death on the battlefield reveal a morbid fascination or even an enthusiasm for the spectacle of battle? In an era not yet saturated with photographs, Cavendish's realism serves the political function of countering the glory of war by illuminating the destructiveness and brutality of battle. More than just reveling in the graphics and gore, Cavendish is working through a third possible response to the connection between gender and war, which involves eroding militaristic definitions of masculinity to confront militarism itself. Again, at points, Cavendish can be read as a proponent of a militarized masculinity; this is especially the case where in *The Worlds Olio* she describes the attributes of the Duke: 'A Gentleman ought to be skilful in the use of his Sword, in the Menage of Horses, to Vault, to Wrestle, to Dance' (129); 'It is more manly to be a Soldier, than a Clerk' (130); and 'A Valiant Man will sooner part with his Life, than part with his Sword, which he counts as his Mistress …' (117). In theory, war also provides an opportunity for men to raise themselves from 'low birth to a glorious renown', since even common soldiers who fight with courage will be remembered (Oration #1, p. 131).

On the one hand, then, Cavendish acknowledges that, for early modern English men, there was a strong imperative to prove themselves competitively through the use or threat of violence[26] and most particularly through the demonstration of courage in battle. On the other hand, she is also sensitive to the reality that 'it is neither courage nor conduct that gets fame in wars, but fortune that gives it' such that 'common soldiers are never mentioned, although they are the only fighters' (Oration #2, p. 132; #20, p. 148). Thus war is not the great status equalizer for men that it might be. Moreover, if, as Diane Purkiss posits, Civil War notions of masculinity are centered around an impenetrable, hard body, always ready to stand firm and resist attack,[27] Cavendish's descriptions of bodies mutilated, turned to ashes, literally consumed by the earth or voracious carrion birds, is a forceful counter to socially constructed ideas of manhood. Beyond her descriptions of the physical decay of the soldier's body is her psychological critique of men's reasons for going to war. 'Worthy men go to the Wars with Joy, hoping to gain Honour', she notes in *Sociable Letters* (#185, p. 251). Men go to war seeking more than victory; they go seeking affirmation and recognition of their courage, bravery, their willingness to serve and sacrifice and indeed, 'some love Honour more than Life' (*Worlds Olio*, 116).

Cavendish faults men for allowing themselves to be overcome by anger. War is a 'dangerous physic', she warns, for men whose 'minds are hot and ... spirits inflamed through an over-earnest desire to be in war' (Oration #3, pp. 132–33). Rather than have your enemy be your physician, she recommends that men should cure themselves with temperance and prudence. She takes a particularly dim view of soldiers who, 'to satisfy [their] bloody minds and furious rage' will unleash death and destruction on the vanquished, for to 'kill us after our submission' is murderous and will only blemish the historical record of their conquest (Oration #14, p. 143; #12. p. 142). In a well-known passage, she asks why women are thought cowardly and men brave when women risk and endanger their lives more than men, while leading more profitable lives: 'for they increase life when men for the most part destroy life, as witness wars, wherein thousands of lives are destroyed, men fighting and killing each other, and yet men think all women mere cowards' (Oration #108, p. 226). Emphasizing classical virtues, Cavendish implies that masculinity might be redefined, that the wise man will moderate his impulses, the honorable soldier will exercise just conduct, and the wise commonwealth will be governed with justice, fortitude, temperance, and prudence but also charity, love, and unity (Oration #6, p. 146).

Military expertise as a 'home-made article'

In calling traditional notions of masculine honor into question, Cavendish shows herself to be a political thinker who is prepared to take risks. Precisely because she did not have the opportunity to connect to a larger proto-feminist discourse that questioned competitive and war-like masculinity, her attempt to draw out some of the complicated connections between gender and war, and to critique militarism, is very much a 'home-made article'.[28] There would have been little rhetorical space for such questioning, very little receptive space for women's military knowledge more generally.[29] Cavendish, as we have seen, claims never to have so much as witnessed battle, much less participated in one, but she asserts her authority within this most gendered societal discourse of military affairs. Of course, she derived much of her knowledge of military matters from her own husband in preparation for writing his biography, which is still cited in military histories of the Civil War.[30] While William undoubtedly supported her in her writing about his military endeavors, and even shared her progressive views about women, he is less likely to have sympathized with her interrogation of war-like masculinity given the 'centrality of violence to assertions of male identity and authority'[31] in Civil War England. Thus, I am suggesting that Cavendish's subtle attempts to undermine military thinking are entirely of her own making, her 'home-made article', knowledge that she developed in isolation without the support or confirmation of receptive listeners.

For Cavendish, part of depicting what happens on the ground is accounting, not just for the aftermath on the battlefield, but also for what happens to the women who are left behind. Her analysis draws upon, but is not limited to her own family's losses; she gathers and assimilates the collective experience of the Civil War, of its cost to human life and to communities, and of a nation 'burie[d] ... in the Waves of Ruin' (*Worlds Olio*, p. 114). Cavendish interjects the grander narrative of peace and war with women's private travails. She points repeatedly to the need to include women's experiences of wartime as part of the bank of empirical evidence on which we should assess the merits of war. Once men leave for war, women

> never enjoy a minutes rest or quiet, for there is not only a war in the mind, as betwixt hope and doubt, but a Tyrant, which is fear, for fear is an absolute conqueror and a tyrannical possessor of the mind, plundering the mind of all content and happiness, banishing

all hopes, and then inhabiting it only with the worst of passions, as with grief, sorrow and impatience, making despair the governour thereof. (*Sociable Letters*, #185, p. 251)

Of course many English women recorded their participation, their courageous acts, and their fear and anxieties during the war. These accounts provide valuable documentary evidence of the events of the war and especially aid our understanding of how a large event like the Civil War was experienced by people and families.[32] 'Wars have their endings inside families', Cynthia Enloe points out, yet rarely do we consider the experience of widows, or of wives whose husbands returned from war permanently changed.[33] Cavendish synthesizes, with remarkable attention to diversity, the varied experiences of those left behind, some of it humorous and ironic, some of it devastating.

At the forefront of this collective experience is grief, and given her obsession with bodies in war, we should not be surprised that Cavendish devotes considerable attention to it. Throughout several of her works, Cavendish demonstrates a fascination, nearing an obsession with death and dying, and with how we will be remembered after our deaths. Her preoccupation is not entirely unusual since death 'was omnipresent in early modern England, its reminders everywhere'.[34] Here I am most interested in passages that not only document but also politicize grief. Her funeral orations stand out, the purpose of which, theoretically, is to pay homage to the dead and comfort the living. Yet, as we saw in 'A Soldier's Funeral Oration', Cavendish cannot keep the politics out of it. Not content to fall back on 'the old lie', Cavendish refuses to lament the death in the usual manner, and quickly draws our attention away from the immediacy of this one death to consider the larger events or circumstances in which it occurred and the unfortunate fate of this body and others like it. Cavendish's funeral orations, including those to recently deceased brides and child-bed women, constitute forms of protest elegy, or anti-consolatory elegy, terms Edna Longley uses to describe a style of Great War poetry. Rather than merely commemorating, this form of elegy 'politicizes mourning and keeps it alive'.[35] These orations acknowledge the significance of grief, but without the familiar comfort of tenderness or nostalgia.

A different tone infuses the treatment of grief in *Bell in Campo*. From the beginning, Cavendish gives us a sense of women's hardships during men's absence in war. Following the deaths of Seigneur Valeroso and Monsieur La Hardy, Madam Jantil and Madam Passionate in *Bell in Campo* liken their recently widowed state to an illness or dropsy.

Madam Jantil, afraid to lie in her bed for fear of the dreams that will haunt her, determines it best to 'lie down on this floor, and try if I can get a quiet sleep on the ground, for from earth I came, and to earth I would willingly return'.[36] In a striking passage that begins in a tone similar to the funeral orations – lamenting life as a curse and source of misery – Madam Jantil plans the monument that she wishes to erect to honor her husband's death. A grand marble monument will testify to his virtues and will be situated amidst ten or twenty acres of land, all of which will be surrounded with a brick wall. Inside, at one end of this enclosure, will be her own house of three rooms, a gallery, bed-chamber, and closet. A cloister will lead from her own small dwelling to her husband's tomb. Her bedroom will be hung with white, symbolizing chastity, whereas her closet will be dressed in black, 'to signify the darkness of death, wherein all things are forgotten and buried in oblivion' (Act IV, Scene 21, 67).

> I will live a signification, not as a real substance but as a shadow made betwixt life and death; from this house which shall be my living tomb, to the tomb of my dead husband, I would have a cloister made ... (Act IV, Scene 21, 67)

In the description of the living tomb, Cavendish circumscribes the publicity of Seigneur Valeroso's tomb with the privacy of Madam Jantil's grief: she will be tended by few servants; she will have no need of her many earthly possessions; her house and the tomb will be surrounded by a wall of 'a reasonable height', and even her passage from her chambers to his tomb will be 'encloistered'.

For Cavendish, the living tomb is about more than one woman's desire to honor her husband. It is a public testimonial that wars do have their endings in families. It is a monument, not merely to his death, but to her grief. The elaborate marble structure will commemorate his military endeavors, but the entire compound is a public symbol of *her mourning*; its imposing presence invites us to remember, this is what the war did to her. In this rendering, grief is not transient, but is rather permanent, like its stone marker, 'dull and heavy ... bringing but a cold advantage' (*Bell in Campo*, Act IV, Scene 21, 68). Cavendish's insertion of grief into the public discourse, an extension of her graphic imagery of bodies in war, challenges the boundaries of war to encompass life beyond the battlefield. Women are *in the war* in the fullest sense, and their knowledge of its effects constitutes its own form of military expertise. Expertise and knowledge about war cannot be limited to questions of arms and strategy; it must also include how human beings will cope with its aftermath.

While Cavendish's writings on war are diverse and wide-ranging and resist easy summary, *Orations of Divers Sorts, Bell in Campo* and *Sociable Letters* each reveal Cavendish as an insightful theorist of war, and as an early contributor to a larger critical discourse that probes the relationship of gender and militarism. By foregrounding the violence, death, and grief that accompany war, Cavendish politicizes it, forcing her readers to question the utility as well as the necessity of conflict. As important as her depictions of women soldiers saving men from defeat on the battlefield are her persistent efforts to question the relationship of masculinity to war and to cast military endeavor itself into question. In both cases, she asserts that women are political agents and citizens in their own right whose ideas about politics and war cannot continue to be marginalized in the master narrative of the English Civil War. Correspondingly, I am suggesting that a properly comprehensive study of Civil War political thought requires that we treat Cavendish as an epistemologically authoritative voice on this most masculine of political subjects.

Notes

1. See Cynthia Enloe, *The Curious Feminist: Searching for Women in a New Age of Empire* (Los Angeles: University of California Press, 2004); Christine Sylvester, *Feminist International Relations: An Unfinished Journey* (Cambridge: Cambridge University Press, 2002); and Brooke A. Ackerly, Maria Stern, and Jacqui True, eds, *Feminist Methodologies for International Relations* (Cambridge: Cambridge University Press, 2006).
2. For example, Mihoko Suzuki, *Subordinate Subjects: Gender, the Political Nation, and Literary Form in England, 1588–1688* (Burlington, VT: Ashgate, 2003); Susan Wiseman, *Conspiracy and Virtue: Women, Writing, and Politics in Seventeenth-Century England* (Oxford: Oxford University Press, 2007); Paul Salzman, *Reading Early Modern Women's Writing* (Oxford: Oxford University Press, 2006); and Victoria Kahn, *Wayward Contracts: The Crisis of Political Obligation in England, 1640–1674* (Princeton: Princeton University Press, 2004).
3. Hilda L. Smith, 'Women Intellectuals and Intellectual History: Their Paradigmatic Separation', *Women's History Review* 16.3 (July 2007): 353–68; quotation on 357.
4. Lorraine Code, *What Can She Know? Feminist Theory and the Construction of Knowledge* (Ithaca: Cornell University Press, 1991), 177.
5. Virginia Woolf, *Three Guineas*, in *A Room of One's Own and Three Guineas* (Toronto: Oxford University Press, 1998), 158.
6. Margaret Cavendish, *Orations of Divers Sorts*, in *Political Writings*, ed. Susan James (Cambridge: Cambridge University Press, 2003), Oration #108, p. 226. Further references are cited parenthetically in the text.

7. Margaret Cavendish, 'An Epistle to Souldiers', *Poems and Fancies* (London, 1653), 167.

8. Roger Hudson, ed., *The Grand Quarrel: Women's Memoirs of the English Civil War* (Phoenix Mill, UK: Sutton, 2000), xx.

9. Mihoko Suzuki, 'Elizabeth, Gender, and the Political Imaginary of Seventeenth-Century England', in *Debating Gender in Early Modern England, 1500–1700*, ed. Cristina Malcolmson and Mihoko Suzuki (New York: Palgrave Macmillan, 2002), 235.

10. See, for example, Mary Beth Rose, *Gender and Heroism in Early Modern Literature* (Chicago: University of Chicago Press, 2002); Suzuki, *Subordinate Subjects*; Claire Jowitt, 'Imperial Dreams? Margaret Cavendish and the Cult of Elizabeth', *Women's Writing* 4.3 (1997): 383–99; Karen L. Raber, 'Warrior Women in the Plays of Cavendish and Killigrew', *SEL* 40.3 (Summer 2000): 413–33.

11. Enloe, *The Curious Feminist*, 219.

12. Margaret Cavendish, *Poems and Fancies*, 167.

13. Margaret Cavendish, *The Worlds Olio* (London, 1655), 110. Further references are cited parenthetically in the text.

14. Wilfred Owen, 'Dulce Et Decorum Est', in *War Poems and Others*, ed. Dominic Hibberd (London: Chatto & Windus, 1973), 79.

15. Raber, 'Warrior Women', 428.

16. Margaret Cavendish, *A True Relation of my Birth, Breeding, and Life*, in *The Life of the (1st) Duke of Newcastle and Other Writings by Margaret Duchess* (London & Toronto: J. M. Dent, 1916), 198.

17. Diane Purkiss, 'Dismembering and Remembering: The English Civil War and Male Identity', in *The English Civil Wars in the Literary Imagination*, ed. Claude J. Summers and Ted Pebworth (Columbia, MO: University of Missouri Press, 1999), 221.

18. Charles Lucas was disinterred and reburied in the family tomb in 1661. Katie Whitaker, *Mad Madge* (New York: Basic Books, 2002), 146 and 237.

19. Charles Carleton, *Going to the Wars: The Experience of the British Civil Wars, 1638–1651* (New York: Routledge, 1992), 219.

20. Cavendish, *Divers Orations*, Oration #20, p. 148.

21. Owen, 'Dulce Et Decorum Est', 79.

22. Margaret Cavendish, *The Description of a New World, Called The Blazing World*, in *Political Writings*, ed. James, 90–91.

23. Margaret Cavendish, *Sociable Letters*, ed. James Fitzmaurice (Peterborough, ON: Broadview Press, 2004), #119, p. 174 and #187, p. 253. Further references are cited parenthetically in the text.

24. Douglas Grant, *Margaret the First* (Toronto: University of Toronto Press, 1957), 101.

25. Thomas Hobbes, *Leviathan*, ed. Richard Tuck (Cambridge: Cambridge University Press, 1991), ch. 13, p. 89.

26. Alexandra Shepard, *Meanings of Manhood in Early Modern England* (Toronto: Oxford University Press, 2003), 140.

27. Purkiss, 'Dismembering and Remembering', 224.

28. A term used by Carol Shields to describe the singular creativity of Jane Austen's novels and which aptly describes Cavendish's drive to forge her own ideas about war. Carol Shields, *Jane Austen: A Life* (Toronto: Penguin, 2001), p. 143.

29. See Lorraine Code, *Rhetorical Spaces: Essays on Gendered Locations* (New York and London: Routledge, 1995).

30. Malcolm Wanklyn, *Decisive Battles of the English Civil Wars: Myth and Reality* (Barnsley, UK: Pen and Sword, 2006).

31. Shepard, *Meanings of Manhood*, 149.

32. Diane Purkiss, *The English Civil War: A People's History* (London: HarperCollins, 2006). See also Sara Heller Mendelson, 'Stuart Women's Diaries and Occasional Memoirs', in *Women in English Society 1500–1800*, ed. Mary Prior (New York: Methuen, 1985).

33. Enloe, *The Curious Feminist*, 204.

34. David Cressy, *Birth, Marriage and Death: Ritual, Religion, and the Life-Cycle in Tudor and Stuart England* (Toronto: Oxford University Press, 1999), 380.

35. Edna Longley, 'The Great War, History and the English Lyric', in *The Cambridge Companion to the Literature of the First World War*, ed. Vincent Sherry (Cambridge: Cambridge University Press, 2005), 79.

36. Margaret Cavendish, *Bell in Campo*, in *Bell in Campo; The Sociable Companions*, ed. Alexandra G. Bennett (Peterborough, ON: Broadview Press, 2002, Act IV, Scene 21, p. 69. Further references are cited parenthetically in the text.

15
Women, Civil War, and Empire: The Politics of Translation in Katherine Philips's *Pompey* and *Horace*

Mihoko Suzuki

Scholarship on Katherine Philips has until recently focused primarily on her poetry circulated in manuscript among her coterie and her homoerotic relationship with her correspondents.[1] However, as Maureen Mulvihill points out, 'Philips initially made her mark in the Anglo-Irish theatre, not the poetic coteries of the Restoration court';[2] Hero Chalmers and Catharine Gray have begun to discuss this aspect of her career, turning their attention to the political import of Philips's translations of Corneille.[3] Chalmers foregrounds Philips's royalism and derives from it her desire for 'reconciliation' after the Civil Wars, and Gray argues for Philips's construction of an elite courtly community across the British Isles.[4] In this chapter, building on the work of Chalmers, I will discuss Philips's translations of *Pompey* and *Horace*, though produced after the Restoration, as examples of women's Civil War writings that Katharine Gillespie discusses in Chapter 5; they join works from the Restoration and later in the seventeenth century which take as their subject the mid-century Civil Wars, such as Lady Anne Halkett's *Memoirs* or Jane Barker's Jacobite poetry written in exile in France.

These translations also concern the political position of women under civil war as it intersects with the position of the colony in relation to the empire. Extending Gray's argument, I will discuss Philips's interest in the question of English colonialism in Ireland and Wales. The recent confluence of translation studies and postcolonial theory has posited the analogy of the translation and the colony, as copies of the original: for example, Tejaswini Niranjana has stated that the 'post-colonial "subject" ... lives always already "in translation"', suggesting that translation is an overarching metaphor for the unequal power relationship which defines the condition of the colonized.[5] Philips had lived in Wales since she was fifteen, and translated *Pompey* in Ireland; she calls Wales 'my Desart', 'so rude and darke a Retreat' and describes herself 'convers[ing] with Rocks and Mountains' in the colonial margins, repeatedly expressing her desire to visit London.[6] Despite this attraction to the metropole, her sympathy with the colonial subject position is expressed explicitly in her poem, 'On the Welch Language', published in the posthumous 1667 edition of her works.[7] While Corneille's plays concern Roman history, with, in the case of *Pompey*, topical correspondences to the French Fronde, Philips's translations suggest topical correspondences with the recently concluded English Civil Wars, which were also known as the War of the Three Kingdoms. Philips's *Pompey* and *Horace* thereby provide occasions for her to reflect more generally on the political position of women during civil war as they intersect with the position of the colony, making larger claims concerning women, civil war, and empire.

In presenting such a reading, I join recent scholars who have challenged the assumption by an earlier generation of scholars that women's translations were gender-appropriate and self-effacing in declining to assert authorship.[8] In fact, Corneille in his *Examen* of *Horace* indicates that his work is *already* a translation:

> S'il ne prend pas le procédé de France, il faut considérer qu'il est Romain et dans Rome, où il n'aurait pu entreprendre un duel contre un autre Romain et dans Rome, sans faire un crime d'État, et que j'en aurais fait un de théâtre, si j'avais habillé un Romain à la française. (249)

> (If he does not follow the procedure of France, it needs to be remembered that he is a Roman in Rome, where he could not have entered into a duel against another Roman in Rome without committing a crime against the state, and that I would have committed one in the theater, if I had dressed a Roman in the French style [my translation])

Here Corneille reflects upon the two senses of translation – the linguistic translation of a text and the cultural transfer from Rome to France in which Roman mores or dress would be transformed into French ones.

Philips's letters to Charles Cotterell – significantly a translator of Davila's *Storia della guerre civili di Francia* on the French religious wars – whom she calls 'Poliarchus', contain numerous discussions of Cotterell's own translations from the French as well as translations by Edmund Waller and other prominent literati of the day. In fact, Philips offers to send her own translation of *Pompey* as well as Abraham Cowley's Virgil in exchange for Cotterell's translations of *Le Temple de la Mort* (II: 48). Moreover, Philips's explicit rivalry with Waller and other 'Persons of Honour' concerning their translation of *Pompey*, which I will discuss in further detail below, indicates that Philips certainly did not regard translation as gender-appropriate and self-effacing.

As stated in the Introduction, placing women's writings in a context broader than the strictly national one can encourage a reexamination of translations as examples of cultural exchange. Translations from the French, for example by Mary Sidney and Anne Dowriche, arising from English Protestant interest in the French religious wars of the late sixteenth century, have already received attention from scholars of women's writing for their political implications.[9] The mid-seventeenth century civil wars on both sides of the channel certainly call for a comparative analysis, especially since Henrietta Maria, the sister of Louis XIII, fled England to establish the Stuart court in exile in her native country; such an analysis could include, for example, English women writers' interest in the Fronde, the French civil war that took place contemporaneously with the one in England.[10]

Philips translated Corneille's *La Mort de Pompée* (1642), as *Pompey* (1663), which was produced in Dublin's Theatre Royal with the backing of the Earl of Orrery. The subject matter of Corneille's play, the civil war between Caesar and Pompey, concluding with the victory of Caesar and the institution of the Pax Romana, certainly calls to mind the recently concluded English Civil War – which had far-reaching effects in both Ireland and Wales – and the Restoration of Charles II. Corneille began as a supporter of Mazarin but switched his allegiance to support the Frondeurs; Orrery initially supported Cromwell but by the Restoration had become a staunchly loyal colonial administrator for Charles II. Philips went on, of her own initiative, to translate Corneille's *Horace* (1640). She translated four of the five acts before her death in 1664 as a result of smallpox; Sir John Denham translated what remained and the play was produced in 1668 at Dublin's Theatre Royal as well as at the court of Charles II. Both *Pompey* and *Horace* were published in Dublin and London, and both editions were extremely successful.

Focusing on the context of Philips's composition of *Pompey*, Catherine Cole Mambretti has emphasized her royalist coterie and her desire to seek favor with Charles on behalf of her parliamentarian husband.[11] By contrast, Andrew Shifflet has argued that Philips criticizes Charles's clemency in *Pompey*, and draws on the play's republican sub-texts to argue for the opposite perspective.[12] This debate itself arises partly from the complex meanings accruing to the historical events as first transformed into a literary text by Lucan in his *Pharsalia* and most recently for Philips by Corneille's play. But the ambiguities concerning Philips's position derive also from the multi-voiced nature of dramatic discourse by contrast with the unambiguous praise of Charles II voiced in Philips's poems on the monarch, such as 'Arion to a Dolphin, on his Majesty's Passage into England'.[13] While Jacqueline Pearson is surely right to point to the topical suggestiveness of the beheading of a ruler and the eventual restoration of order, what Leah Marcus has called 'the unease of topicality' in her discussion of the problematics of correspondence between the historical antecedents and contemporary events in Shakespeare's plays complicates the deciphering of Philips's politics as either unequivocally royalist or republican.[14] In fact, Chalmers points out that Pompey, a republican leader, could be associated with both Charles I and Charles II.[15]

In what follows, I explore the possibility of a more ambiguous politics in Philips's translation of *Pompey*. As I have already mentioned, Corneille himself began as a royalist but later turned against Mazarin. He fulsomely dedicated his play to Mazarin, whom he called 'eminentissime', and compared Pompey, 'le plus grand personnage de l'ancienne Rome', to Mazarin, 'le plus illustre de la nouvelle'.[16] His praise of Mazarin suggests multiple layers of irony because Pompey, with whom he is compared, was the defender of the republic who has already been decapitated by the beginning of the play. As is well known, Philips was a royalist who was married to a parliamentarian and whose family included parliamentarian members; Sir Charles Cotterell, Charles's master of ceremonies and Philips's sponsor at court, intervened on her husband's behalf when he was accused of having signed the execution warrant of a royalist colonel. Philips's patron, who enjoined her to complete the translation of *Pompey*, as well as sponsored its production, was Roger Boyle, Lord Orrery, a confidential advisor of Oliver Cromwell who at the Restoration allied himself with Charles II. These contexts suggest that Philips's translation was a political act of mediation between two opposing forces.[17] Philips herself had addressed the issue of divided loyalties in 'To Antenor', where she writes as a wife who wishes to speak from a different position from her husband's, thus dramatizing the conflicting obligation to husband and to king.[18] Moreover, the name 'Antenor', by which Philips called her husband, is an ambiguous one, in that he is represented at times as one who sought to bring peace between Troy and Greece, and at others as one who betrayed Troy.

Philips's translation was also an act of political mediation in another sense: by playing Cotterell and Orrery off against each other, she successfully gained entry into the highest circles of Restoration society. She sought Cotterell's advice on her translation and when he made suggestions for revision, she showed them to Orrery who rejected them; finally she told Cotterell that she was compelled to go against his advice, though she agreed with him. Philips sent to Cotterell a copy of Orrery's poem celebrating 'Orinda's "Copy greater then th'Original"'; this poem was printed in the 1663 edition of her poems. Moreover, she playfully represents to Cotterell Orrery's request for the translation as an order to assassinate Pompey, in obeying which she takes on the role of his political agent: 'Lord ORRERY's Commands to me, have proved no less fatal to him, than the Orders that PTOLEMY gave to that Assassin' (II: 58).

Orrery sponsored the play's production in Dublin to the sum of £100, and Cotterell presented her play to the King and to Anne Hyde, the Duchess of York, both of whom reportedly received it with favor. Philips's strategic use of her translation as an object of exchange for her own benefit gives another lie to the notion of translation as an appropriately subservient form of writing for women; it also calls for a re-examination of the anthropological dictum that women serve as passive objects of exchange between men, first articulated by Claude Lévi-Strauss in *The Elementary Structures of Kinship* and elaborated by Gayle Rubin and Eve Sedgwick.[19]

It is in keeping with Philips's active and strategic management of her own career that she explores the position of female subjects in the polity as more than objects of exchange, specifically within the context of a civil war. The figures of Cornelia and Cleopatra have received contradictory readings from recent scholars. Joyce Green MacDonald maintains that Philips affirms the chaste and devoted wife Cornelia over the promiscuous and ambitious foreign queen.[20] And Karen Raber argues that the loss of her husband transforms Cornelia 'from the position of silent, invisible, domestic partner into the role of political actor'.[21] Yet in Act I, scene iii, Cleopatra is represented as much more politically astute and effective than her brother Ptolemy, joint-ruler of Egypt. She uses first Pompey, then Caesar to shore up her own sovereignty: '*Pompey* or *Caesar* will secure me now; / I now am sure my Scepter to obtain'.[22] Such a triangulation mirrors Philips's deployment of Orrery and Cotterell to further her political position. At the conclusion of the play, not only is Cleopatra praised along with Pompey, Caesar, and Cornelia, but she is praised as a *ruler* along with Caesar. Yet Philips slightly modifies her translation to convey a more ambivalent representation of Cleopatra than does Corneille's original. For example, while Corneille's Cleopatra declares that glory 'anime', animates or inspires, Philips translates the verb as 'enflame' (II.i, p. 14). The French is associated with elevation of spirit, while Philips's English strongly associates Cleopatra's idea of glory with sexual passion. By contrast to MacDonald, Sophie Tomlinson sees Cleopatra as a positive example of female rule, and maintains that Philips's translation consistently sharpens Cleopatra's agency and charisma through words such as 'will', 'wit', and 'art'[23] – although one might also argue that these words could be double-edged.

Since contemporary and near contemporary representations of Cleopatra were generally unequivocally positive, the shadings in Philips's representation of Cleopatra are all the more striking and perhaps recall Mary Sidney's more equivocal representation of a desirous Cleopatra in her *Antonius*. Although Lucan associates Cleopatra with Helen and Dido and demonizes her as a power-hungry woman ruler tainted with 'eastern' luxury and sexuality, Corneille in the *Examen*, which he wrote in 1660 for the collected edition of his works, states that in light of historical evidence, he disagreed with the reputation of Cleopatra as a lascivious woman abandoned to her pleasures (316). Thomas May in both his continuation of Lucan and *The Tragedie of Cleopatra*, first published in 1631 and reissued in the 1650s, represents Cleopatra as a sympathetic and majestic figure. In the continuation, while Caesar is 'enflamed' with 'fresh furie' for Cleopatra, the 'mistress of the State' was 'fil'd / With higher thoughts; desire of Soveraigntie / Aspiring hopes of State and Majestie' which 'controll'd / All other passions'.[24] In the *Tragedie*, Cleopatra is heroic, capable, and eloquent, especially in the final act preceding her suicide, with no trace of the comic peevishness assigned to her by Shakespeare. Finally, Madeleine de Scudéry's 1642 *Femmes Illustres* includes an oration by Cleopatra, in which she asserts her constancy, affirms liberty, and shuns bondage as represented in the threat of Caesar's triumph.

Philips's representation of Cleopatra that significantly departs from these positive contemporary versions may derive from Philips's anxiety-producing resemblance to Cleopatra, a resemblance from which Philips seeks to distance herself. For although Philips may seek to identify herself with the 'chaste' Cornelia, Cornelia's rejection of Caesar's clemency represents the opposite of the pragmatic political strategy that not only Cleopatra, but Philips too pursued, and this rejection constitutes a political dead end. Cornelia repeatedly emphasizes her hatred and desire for revenge.[25] By contrast, Philips resembles Cleopatra in that she, like Cleopatra, parlayed her connection to powerful men for her own political ends, carrying on an extensive correspondence with a man not her husband (instructing him to 'write in Italian' concerning their plans to bring her to London which she did not want her husband to understand [II: 99–100]), and disseminating poems written in praise of her and her writings by Orrery as well as the Earl of Roscommon. Moreover, Cleopatra, whose fame dwarfed that of Cornelia, resembles Philips who, despite her self-representation as modest and retiring, in fact sought and achieved celebrity as the 'matchless Orinda'.[26]

Nevertheless, Philips's sense of taint about the fame she gained through her writing is revealed in the extensive defense of herself to Cotterell that she did not condone the publication of her works: "'tis only I whom am that unfortunate person that cannot so much as think in private, that must have my imaginations rifled and exposed to play the Mountebanks, and dance upon the Ropes to entertain all the ruble [rabble?]; to undergo all the raillery of the Wits, and all the severity of the Wise, and to be the sport of some that can, and some that cannot read a Verse' (II: 129). She indicates that some suspect her of 'the wretched Artifice of a secret consent' and protests that 'whoever would have brought me those Copies corrected and amended, and a thousand points to have brought my permission for their being printed, should not have obtained it'. She concludes, 'I am so far from expecting applause for any thing I scribble, that I can hardly expect pardon; and sometimes I think that employment so far above my reach, and unfit for my Sex, that I am going to resolve against it for ever' while at the same time she asserts that she was 'betrayed' into allowing copies to be made, and that 'some infernal Spirits' have gained possession of the originals and have supplied by conjecture what they could not make out from 'the careless blotted writing' (II: 130).

Despite her protestations of inadequacy and expressions of self-censure, Philips also repeatedly claims the superiority of her own translation to that of the 'Confederates' and the superiority of her poem dedicated to Anne Hyde to Waller's. These statements concerning her rivalry with the metropolitan writers, especially in light of her self-identification with the 'dark' margins of Wales, calls attention to the relationship in *Pompey* between imperial Rome and its Egyptian colony and the actions of Cornelia and Cleopatra as they derive from their positions as a Roman widow and an Egyptian queen. The mediating actions of Cleopatra are motivated by her defensive position as a colonial subject that closely resembles that of Philips; the intransigence of Cornelia is motivated by her position as a widow of a Roman leader, one who has completely subsumed her identity under that of her husband.[27] Hence the difference between the two women and their opposing actions can be explained by Cornelia's identification with the metropole and Cleopatra's with the colony. In this respect, the implications of Cleopatra's actions are clarified when juxtaposed to those of her brother Ptolemy: Ptolemy cravenly, but unsuccessfully, seeks to ingratiate himself with Caesar by offering Pompey's head to the Roman victor. Ptolemy's violent action that capitalizes on the Roman civil war becomes an emblem for the dismemberment of the body politic. Cleopatra, by contrast, though Ptolemy's loss of Caesar's favor leads to her ascendancy as Egypt's sovereign in her brother's stead, nevertheless declines to take advantage of his strategic error. In this instance, Cleopatra refrains from instigating a civil conflict *within* Egypt by contrast to Ptolemy who was eager to take part in the Roman civil war solely to further his own political position. Cleopatra also diverges from Cornelia who is determined to carry on the civil conflict against Caesar even after her husband Pompey's death.

In 'On the Welch Language', Philips celebrates the 'British Language' (i.e., Welsh), whose decline she compares to that of Troy, Athens, and Rome, though it 'has still some great Remains to boast'.[28] By calling Welsh 'British', which around the time of the Civil War began to take its present meaning of pertaining to Great Britain, Philips calls attention to the linguistic appropriation and suppression of 'British' by the English colonizers, as well as counter-intuitively associating the decline of Welsh with the fall of metropolitan – rather than colonial – cultures. In doing so, she underscores the importance of language as a synecdoche for the political nation and national culture.[29] She further signals her sympathy with the colonized by identifying 'British'/Welsh as the language of Merlin and King Arthur, figures from Wales's mythic past that have been incorporated into and appropriated by British culture, but also as the language of the British/Welsh rebels Boadicca (Bonduca) and Caratacus who resisted their Roman colonizers.[30]

When in the *Agricola* Tacitus describes Bonduca's rebellion against the Romans, 'assault[ing] the colony itself, which they saw as the citadel of their servitude', he explains: 'for Britons make no distinction of sex in their appointment of commanders'.[31] She successfully invaded London and other cities. In the *Annals* Tacitus records that she exhorted her troops, seeking vengeance for violence against her, the rape of her daughters, and the Roman domination of Britons reduced to servility.[32] Significantly, Bonduca's speech juxtaposes and suggests the intersection of male violence against women and the imperial subjection of the colony. The *Annals* also relates the capture by the Romans of Caratacus, who spoke so eloquently to the Senate – 'If you want to rule the world, does it follow that everyone else welcomes enslavement?' – that he gained their admiration and was pardoned (367).

Philips goes on to pointedly state that Arthur 'Could have compell'd Mankind to speak it [Welsh] too', by contrast to the English who compelled the Welsh to use English as their official language after Henry VIII's Act of Union. In keeping with this criticism of English colonialism, she declines to mention Welsh rebels against England, such as Owen Glendower, whose representation by Shakespeare in *1 Henry IV* closely associates him (unfavorably) with the Welsh language. The persistence of Welsh, which can be gleaned from the 1567 translation of the Book of Common Prayer and the New Testament and the 1588 publication of the Welsh Bible, and even from the 1662 Act of Uniformity, which provides 'That the Book [of Common Prayer] hereunto annexed be truly and exactly translated into the British or Welsh Tongue', is in keeping with Philips's praise of the language as exemplifying Welsh culture and nationhood.

By 1757, when Philips's poem was reprinted in *Poems by Eminent Ladies*, the English had decisively incorporated the Celtic nations as well as their languages and cultures, for example in dispatching the Scottish Highlanders, who were only permitted to wear kilts as part of the British army, to the French–Indian War that began in 1756. At the conclusion of the Seven Years War (1754–63), Britain would emerge as the preeminent colonial power. Katherine Philips's sympathy with the language and culture of the colony to which she was transplanted bears comparison to that of Elizabeth Cary, who moved to Ireland with her husband, a colonial administrator, learned Gaelic, and established a school for Irish children. Yet just as both Bonduca and Caratacus's speeches do not survive in Welsh, but are reported by Tacitus in Latin, the language of the colonizers, so Philips writes her poem praising the Welsh language in English.

By translating *Pompey* for the Dublin stage, and then taking the London stage by storm, Philips acted from the periphery of Wales and Ireland as a mediator and purveyor of French culture, which was highly prized due to the tastes of Charles II and members of his court, to England. Significantly, Corneille associates his own work with 'une muse de province' in dedicating *Horace* to Richelieu – indicating another point of identification that Philips may have had with Corneille (247). She knew that when she undertook the translation, another by Edmund Waller and other eminent men of letters attached to the court of Charles II was already underway. Yet she completed hers before 'the other translation' (II: 62, 66, 69, 70) – as she repeatedly calls it – and her version in fact prevailed. Her letters to Cotterell repeatedly express an intense rivalry with the competing English translation, produced by the 'greatest wits' who have 'clubb'd' (II: 55) together to produce it, or with 'the other Translation done by so many eminent Hands' (II: 62), by the 'united forces of all their Party' (II: 66). In also calling it the 'Confederate Translation' (II: 94), Philips casts herself as the 'one' against the 'many'; there may also be pejorative connotations – the *OED* gives as one of the definitions of 'confederate', 'in bad sense: One leagued with another for an unlawful or evil purpose; an accomplice' – combined with the association with the 'Irish confederates', Catholics who treated with the royalists out of expediency but were ultimately decimated by Cromwell's troops.[33] While Philips is undoubtedly proud of her singular authorship, it should be noted that she had a great deal of support from her own 'old-boy's network', in Maureen Mulvihill's terms:[34] the Earl of Roscommon wrote the Prologue and Sir Edward Dering the Epilogue. Moreover, Philips frequently consulted her 'Poliarchus', Charles Cotterell, concerning her translation.

Waller shared the divided political loyalties of Orrery in that he wrote 'A Panegyric to my Lord Protector' in 1655 and later indicated his shift in loyalties by composing 'Three Poems upon the Death of the Late Usurper Oliver Cromwell' and 'To the King upon his Majestys Happy Return' at the time of the Restoration. Philips is explicitly rivalrous with Waller – praised by contemporaries for his technical skill and for being 'sweet', 'soft', and 'smooth', and whose monument celebrated him as 'prince of poets'[35] – as the author of a competing poem to the Queen upon her recovery from an illness. She claims that her version was preferred, as was her version of the translation of *Pompey*. Philips recounts an incident in which Waller mocked Margaret Cavendish's 'Hunting of the Stag', though she does not explicitly connect this anecdote to her own rivalry with Waller (II: 119–20).[36] In another example of a woman writer challenging Waller, Lucy Hutchinson wrote a parodic reply to 'A Panegyric to my Lord Protector'.[37] Expressing a keen desire to have her translation appear first, Philips also wonders how the 'other Translation' will fare – 'what Opinion the Town and Court have of it' (II: 70) – and assiduously seeks to obtain a copy of the rival translation: 'I have laid out several ways to get a Copy, but cannot yet procure one, except only of the first Act that was done by Mr. WALLER' (II: 70). When she has succeeded in doing so, she delivers an unvarnished critique of it for being inaccurate: she says the other translators are taking 'great Liberty ... in adding, omitting and altering the Original as they please themselves ... a Liberty not pardonable in Translators' (II: 103), though she herself modified the translation to suit her own ends, as I have shown. She further faults the verses for being 'either flat or rough ... their Rhymes are frequently very bad, but what chiefly disgusts me is, that the Sence most commonly languishes through three or four Lines, and then ends in the middle of the fifth: ... the Lines must be spiritless and dull' (II: 103). After having delivered this scathing attack, she seeks to moderate it: 'You know me as far from Envy, as those Gentlemen are above it ... for after all I really think the worse of their Lines equal to the best in my Translation' (II: 103–4). Yet she goes on to criticize 'Mr. Waller's own Act' I, which 'choques' [shocks] her for the 'many additions & omissions of ye authors sence', leading her to conclude, 'there are as many faults as ever I saw in a good Poem' (II: 112). Philips thereby 'writes back' from the colonial margins to the metropole, and the greater theatrical success of her version vindicates her desire to assert her superiority to the authors, closely associated with the London court, who enjoy privileged positions in terms of both gender and rank.[38]

MacDonald has suggested that Philips elides cultural and political conflict, and Raber has argued that Philips 'celebrate[s] the possibility of inclusive cooperation amongst formerly factionalized segments of society'.[39] While Philips's less than complimentary statements in her letters concerning Waller and his 'confederates' and her praise of the Dublin playhouse over D'Avenant's in London and Roscommon over Fanshawe (II: 54–55) extend the cultural rivalry between Ireland and England, in *Pompey* Philips does seek to mediate political opposition. Caesar praises Pompey at the end of the play: 'Prepare to morrow for a glorious day. / ... / *Pompey* to appease, and *Cleopatra* Crown, / To her a Throne, to him let's Altars Build, / And to them both Immortal Honours yield' (V.v, p. 60). Philips elaborates on this reconciliation in her own conclusion, which follows Corneille's Act V, when she has two Egyptian Priests celebrate Pompey, who 'must be Deified' while the Chorus exhorts Caesar to 'keep the World h' has won; / And sing Cornelia's praise' (pp. 60–61). The ambiguities of topical reference also work to mediate political division. For example, Philips had praised Charles as Pompey in an earlier poem, though in this play Caesar functions as the figure for the triumphant monarch who has emerged the victor from civil war.

The entr'actes, clearly marked as Philips's addition to Corneille's play, emphasize rather than resolve these ambiguities. The Song from Act I suggests that monarchs are in need of diversion from 'Employment' and 'Care', by which the 'Mind ... is rufl'ed and Curl'd' (11), thereby announcing the work itself as intended for royal entertainment. Yet the Song following Act II depicts Caesar ambiguously as causing 'Rivers of Blood' during the civil war, and the reference to Pompey's head inevitably calls to mind Charles's execution. The chorus says of 'our Princes

Fate': 'He must be wicked to be great / Or to be just, undone', suggesting a contradiction between the successful deployment of power and justice (23–24). By contrast, in Act III, Caesar is referred to as 'Dictator' (36) and the contradiction that is accepted in the previous act is here lamented: 'What is the charm of being Great? / Which oft is gain'd and lost with Sin'. Yet the entr'acte in Act IV celebrates 'Glorious *Caesar*' as does the final chorus: 'Temples to *Pompey* raise; / Set *Cleopatra* on the Throne; / Let *Caesar* keep the world h' has won; / And sing *Cornelia's* praise' (61). The play concludes with a 'Grand Masque ... Danc'd before *Cesar* and *Cleopatra*' (61) who thus occupied the same positions as Charles II and Catherine of Braganza when the play was performed;[40] given these explicit assertions of an identification between Caesar and Charles, the negative representations of Caesar and monarchical power raise questions concerning Philips's judgment of and perspective on the monarch and monarchism, despite her accepted royalism.

Philips's *Horace* also takes as its subject a civil war, this time between Rome and Alba, a civil war in which the female characters, Sabina and Camilla, are torn between their loyalties to husbands and brothers. From the beginning of the play, Sabina's statement concerning Alba having been absorbed into Rome remarkably echoes Philips's perspective on the relationship between Wales and England. She praises '*Alba* where I began to see the light, / *Alba* my native place, and first delight' and contrasts it with Rome, the 'growing Empire' that 'By War alone must make her sinews strong'; she goes on to claim that Rome should spare Alba from its imperial conquest because '*Alba's* thy Parent': 'But spare the Town where *Romulus* had birth; / Forget not her from whom thy City draws / Her Name, and all her strength, but Walls and Laws'.[41] The characterization of Alba's defeat as enslavement underscores its colonial relationship to imperial Rome, which strikingly resembles the relationship between Wales and England that Philips set forth in 'On the Welch Language'.

The female subject's divided loyalty in the context of a civil war continues to be resonant for Philips in translating this play. Sabina articulates woman's role as mediator between the hostile parties – 'I the sole link am of your sacred knot, / Which will unty, as soon as I am not' (II.vi, p. 89) – a role Philips also assumed in seeking clemency after the Restoration for her parliamentarian husband. Revisiting the issue of divided loyalty as articulated in Philips's 'To Antenor', Sabina later expresses her 'divided cares' and 'different duties' in her roles as sister and wife. In the course of the monologue, she explicitly contradicts herself on whether she should weigh 'the Cause' or 'the Combatants', and whether she should take the side of the 'triumphant' or the 'vanquisht' (III.i, pp. 92–93). While scholarly attention has focused on Camilla, who is killed by her brother Horace as an 'enemy of Rome' for mourning her beloved, Curtius, whom Horace has killed to avenge their brothers (IV.v, p. 110), it is Sabina who articulates the vexed position of women in civil war. At the end of Act IV, after the point where Philips broke off her translation, and the point at which Denham picks it up to complete it, Horace compels his wife Sabina to subordinate herself to him: 'Let both our minds be one, and since to thine / I cannot condescend, grow up to mine'. Sabina rejects her husband's command, echoing Camilla's vehement expression of hatred for the city that demands such allegiance: 'Yet Roman Vertue I renounce, since I / To purchase that must sell humanity. / Can the deplored Sister of the dead, / Like a great Conqueror's Wife advance her head' (IV.vii, p. 114). Unlike Camilla, however, Sabina is left alive by Horace to declare, 'If neither grace nor punishment I have, / When dead I shall find quiet in my grave' (IV.vii, p. 114). The play dramatizes in Camilla and Sabina the impossible position of female subjects in civil war, as well as their critique of the dominant ideology of *romanitas*, identified with the king (Tullus) who appears at the end of the play to preside over the entombment of Camilla and her beloved as man and wife.

In *Horace* as well as in *Pompey*, Philips refuses to embrace one side of the civil war and demonize the opposing position. The critique of Rome by Sabina and Camilla in *Horace* reinforces the critique of Caesar in the entr'actes that she added to *Pompey*. While Cornelia and Cleopatra proved to be problematic in different ways for Philips as models for a female subject's negotiation of civil war, Sabina and Camilla articulate a more explicit critique of the imperial basis of civil war, especially the responsibility of kings such as Caesar and Tullus, who require and naturalize sacrifices from and of women in the name of the state.

In moving from *Pompey* to *Horace*, Philips's political position becomes more explicit; read together, and along with 'On the Welch Language', they articulate Philips's political thinking on women, civil war, and empire. It is reported that the Duke or Duchess of Monmouth – Anne Scott, also a Scottish peeress as Duchess of Buccleuch – took part in the 1668 court performance of *Horace* (reports vary concerning which spoke the prologue). Such an involvement by one of the Monmouths indicates that Philips's subject matter continued to hold significance for seventeenth-century English culture, for the move to legitimize Monmouth against the claims of the Duke of York, later James II, was already gaining ground by 1664. This political movement of course led to the Popish Plot, Exclusion Crisis, and Rye House Plot, culminating in the Monmouth Rebellion of 1685 (it was reported that Philips's verses were found in Monmouth's manuscript notebook that was seized from him after his defeat at Sedgmoor). After her husband's execution for treason, the Duchess was compelled to protect her Scottish title and inheritance from the English Crown.[42] The fate of the duchess exemplifies the consequences for women of civil war, especially as imperial power perpetuates its unequal relationship with its colonial subjects.

Notes

1. See Harriette Andreadis, *Sappho in Early Modern England: Female Same-Sex Literary Erotics, 1550–1714* (Chicago: University of Chicago Press, 2001), chapter 3; Valerie Traub, *The Renaissance of Lesbianism in Early Modern England* (Cambridge: Cambridge University Press, 2002), chapter 7. The majority of Warren Cherniak's *ODNB* entry on Philips is devoted to 'Love and Friendship'.
2. Maureen E. Mulvihill, 'A Feminist Link in the Old Boys' Network: The Cosseting of Katherine Philips', in *Curtain Calls: British and American Women and Theater, 1660–1820*, ed. Mary Anne Schofield and Cecilia Macheski (Athens, OH: Ohio University Press, 1991), 72.
3. Hero Chalmers, *Royalist Women Writers, 1650–1689* (Oxford: Clarendon Press, 2004); Catharine Gray, *Women Writers and Public Debate in 17th Century Britain* (New York: Palgrave Macmillan, 2007).
4. Chalmers, *Royalist Women Writers*, 92–97; Gray, *Women Writers and Public Debate*, 131–42.
5. Tejaswini Niranjana, *Siting Translation: History, Post-Structuralism, and the Colonial Context* (Berkeley: University of California Press, 1992), 41. Niranjana, however, is speaking in this context of the 'colonial practice of translation' whereby European translation of Indian texts produced a colonial discourse that contains the colonial subject (31); yet the 'post-colonial translator' can also call attention to the 'instability of the "original", which can be meticulously uncovered through the practice of translation' (186). See also *Post-Colonial Translation: Theory and Practice*, ed. Susan Bassnett and Harish Trivedi (London and New York: Routledge, 1999).
6. Patrick Thomas, ed., *The Collected Works of Katherine Philips* (Stump Cross: Stump Cross Books, 1990), II: 84, 117, 88, 85, 99–100, 102, 111, 124, 133. Further references to Philips's letters in the text are from this edition.
7. The earliest manuscript version is found in National Library of Wales MS 776, which was compiled after Philips's death. Thomas, ed., *Collected Works of Katherine Philips*, I: 45, 305. Thomas does not give a date for the composition of the poem (I: 67). On Philips as a 'Welsh writer in an archipelagic frame', see Sarah Prescott, 'Archipelagic Orinda? Katherine Philips and the Writing of Welsh Women's Literary History', *Literature Compass* 6 (2009): 1–10.
8. See Peter Burke's recent restatement of this view: 'Women were relatively prominent in this field, probably because translation was considered more compatible than original writing with female modesty.' 'Cultures

of Translation in Early Modern Europe', in *Cultural Translation in Early Modern Europe*, ed. Peter Burke and R. Po-Chia Hsia (Cambridge: Cambridge University Press, 2007), 12.

9. Suzanne Trill and Danielle Clarke have argued against the association of translation with femininity, both focusing on the example of Mary Sidney: see Suzanne Trill, 'Sixteenth-century Women's Writing: Mary Sidney's Psalmes and the "Femininity" of Translation', in *Writing and the English Renaissance*, ed. William Zunder and Suzanne Trill (Harlow: Longman, 1996), 140–58; Danielle Clarke, 'The Politics of Translation and Gender in the Countess of Pembroke's *Antonie*', *Translation and Literature* 6.2 (1997): 149–66. On the political significance of Anne Dowriche's translation, see Elaine Beilin, '"Some Freely Spake Their Minde": Resistance in Anne Dowriche's *French Historie*', in *Women, Writing, and the Reproduction of Culture*, ed. Mary E. Burke, Jane Donawerth, Linda L. Dove, and Karen Nelson (Syracuse: Syracuse University Press, 2000), 119–40; and Mihoko Suzuki, 'Warning Elizabeth with Catherine de' Medici's Example: Anne Dowriche's *French Historie* and the Politics of Counsel', in *The Rule of Women in Early Modern Europe*, ed. Anne J. Cruz and Mihoko Suzuki (Urbana: University of Illinois Press, 2009), 174–93.

10. Amy Scott-Douglass, 'Enlarging Margaret: Cavendish, Shakespeare, and French Women Warriors and Writers', in *Cavendish and Shakespeare: Interconnections*, ed. Katherine Romack and James Fitzmaurice (Aldershot: Ashgate: 2006), 149–74.

11. Catherine Cole Mambretti, 'Orinda on the Restoration Stage', *Comparative Literature* 37 (1985): 233–51, 239.

12. Andrew Shifflet, '"How many virtues must I hate": Katherine Philips and the Politics of Clemency', *Studies in Philology* 94.1 (Winter 1997): 103–35.

13. Included in *Poems by the Incomparable, Mrs. K. P.* (1664).

14. Jacqueline Pearson, *The Prostituted Muse: Images of Women and Women Dramatists, 1642–1737* (New York: St. Martin's Press, 1988), 122; Leah Marcus, *Puzzling Shakespeare: Local Reading and its Discontents* (Berkeley: University of California Press, 1990).

15. Chalmers, *Royalist Women Writers*, 87–89.

16. Pierre Corneille, *Oeuvres Complètes*, ed. André Stegmann (Paris: Seuil, 1963), 314. All further quotations from Corneille will be from this edition.

17. While I am largely in agreement with Chalmers (*Royalist Women Writers*), who argues that Philips advocates 'political reconciliation' (91) and that the play emphasizes the 'mediation of opposites' (93), as did the literary works of her patron Orrery, my reading stresses the strategic and structural aspect of mediation as *process*; its temporary and ongoing nature is indicated in the well-known events of Cleopatra's political actions that follow the conclusion of *Pompey*.

18. Carol Barash, *English Women's Poetry 1649–1714: Politics, Community and Linguistic Authority* (Oxford: Oxford University Press, 1996), 65.

19. Gayle Rubin, 'The Traffic in Women: Notes on the "Political Economy" of Sex', in *Toward an Anthropology of Women*, ed. Rayna Reiter (New York: Monthly Review Press, 1975), 157–210; Eve Kosofsky Sedgwick, *Between Men: English Literature and Male Homosocial Desire* (New York: Columbia University Press, 1985).

20. Joyce Green MacDonald, *Women and Race in Early Modern Texts* (Cambridge: Cambridge University Press, 2002), 129.
21. Karen Raber, *Dramatic Difference: Gender, Class, and Genre in the Early Modern Closet Drama* (Newark: University of Delaware Press, 2001), 250.
22. [Katherine Philips], *Pompey. A Tragedy* (London: John Crooke, 1663), I.iii, p. 10. Subsequent quotations from this edition are cited parenthetically in the text.
23. Sophie Tomlinson, *Women on Stage in Stuart Drama* (Cambridge: Cambridge University Press, 2005), 195.
24. Thomas May, *A Continuation of the Subiect of Lucans Historicall Poem, till the death of Iulius Caesar* (London, 1567 [1657]), 23, 25.
25. Raber, however, suggests that Cornelia's dream of her dead husband in the entr'acte following Act III 'functions as a *domestic* justification of her *political* stance with regard to Caesar' (*Dramatic Difference*, 252, emphasis in original). While Tomlinson notes the zeal of Cornelia's hatred', she nevertheless concludes: 'For all its ambivalence, 'Romanness' provides a point of affiliation and self-definition for Cornelia (*Women on Stage*, 197–98).
26. Mulvihill characterizes Philips's achievement of fame as the result of 'a remarkable literary campaign conceived and promoted by Philips herself' and her associates, and her career as one that was 'distinguished by its astute management, networking, and heretofore unacknowledged artistic individualism' ('A Feminist Link', 73).
27. Timothy J. Reiss, however, reads Corneille's Cornélie as representing 'a reasoned middle path between Rome and its destruction, between Caesar and her debt to and love for Pompey'. 'Corneille and Cornelia: Reason, Violence and the Cultural Status of the Feminine. Or, How a Dominant Discourse Recuperated and Subverted the Advance of Women', *Renaissance Drama* n.s. 18 (1987), 22.
28. Quotations from 'On the Welch Language' are from *Poems by the Most Deservedly Admired Mrs Katherine Philips The Matchless Orinda* (1667); reprinted in *Women's Political Writings*, ed. Hilda L. Smith, Mihoko Suzuki, and Susan Wiseman (London: Pickering & Chatto, 2007), III: 271–72. Prescott states: 'critics have skirted around this poem in rather an embarrassed fashion' ('Archipelagic Orinda?', 7). For discussions of this poem, cited by Prescott, see John Kerrigan, *Archipelagic English: Literature, History, and Politics, 1603–1707* (Oxford: Oxford University Press, 2008), 214, and Kate Chedgzoy, *Women's Writing in the British Atlantic World: Memory, Place and History, 1550–1700* (Cambridge: Cambridge University Press, 2007), 112.
29. See Linda Colley, *Britons: Forging the Nation, 1701–1837* (New Haven: Yale University Press, 1992), 13: 'What distinguished the Welsh was their language, a language that three out of four of them still spoke out of choice as late as the 1880s ... amongst themselves, most Welshmen and women below gentry level spoke only their own language. And for much of the time ... they seem to have regarded the English as a different people.'
30. Fletcher's *Bonduca*, first produced in 1619 and published in the Beaumont and Fletcher folio in 1647, features both Bonduca and Caratach (Caratacus), although Tacitus does not give any account of their interaction. Despite its title, the hero of Fletcher's play is Caratach, who rebukes Bonduca for 'meddl[ing] in men's affairs' (III.v). The Roman general Suetonius calls

Bonduca 'Desperate and strange' (IV.iv) while he concludes the play with his exhortation: 'through the camp, in every tongue, / The virtues of Caratach be sung!' (V.i).

31. Tacitus, *Agricola and Germania*, trans. H. Mattingly, rev. S. A. Handford (Harmondsworth: Penguin, 1970), 66.

32. Tacitus, *The Annals of Imperial Rome*, trans. Michael Grant (rev. edn, Harmondsworth: Penguin, 1974), 330. Further references are cited parenthetically in the text. See Michael Roberts, 'The Revolt of Boudicca (Tacitus *Annals* 14.29–39) and the Assertion of *Libertas* in Neronian Rome', *American Journal of Philology* 109 (1988): 118–32.

33. On 'Philips and Puritanism', see Chalmers, *Royalist Women Writers*, 120–28.

34. Mulvihill, 'A Feminist Link', 73, 87, 89–91. See also the more recent discussion by Jane Milling, '"In the Female Coasts of Fame": Women's Dramatic Writing on the Public Stage, 1669–71', *Women's Writing* 7.2 (2000): 270–77.

35. Warren Cherniak, *Oxford Dictionary of National Biography*, s.v.

36. Though not commenting on Philips's reference to Cavendish, Chalmers discusses the two writers together in terms of their shared emphasis on 'feminine withdrawal [that] reflect[s] the Interregnum royalist need to represent the space of retirement or interiority as the actual centre of power' (*Royalist Women Writers*, 105).

37. See David Norbrook, 'Lucy Hutchinson versus Edmund Waller: An Unpublished Reply to Waller's *Panygyrick to my Lord Protector*', *Seventeenth Century* 11.1 (1996): 61–86.

38. Dorothea Frances Canfield (*Corneille and Racine in England: A Study of the English Translations of the Two Corneilles and Racine, with Especial Reference to their Presentation on the English Stage* [New York: Columbia University Press, 1904]) praises Philips as 'the best of Restoration translators, and perhaps the best who ever translated French tragedy' (42), and judges her version to be 'incomparably better' than the translation by Waller et al. which she considers to be 'much less intelligible' (62).

39. Raber, *Dramatic Difference*, 249.

40. Barash, *English Women's Poetry*, 80.

41. Katherine Philips, *Poems by the most deservedly admired Mrs. Katherine Philips the Matchless Orinda. To which is added Monsieur Corneille's Pompey and Horace* (London: J. M. for H. Herringman, 1667), I.i, p. 70. All subsequent quotations from *Horace* are taken from this edition.

42. Tim Harris, *Oxford Dictionary of National Biography*, 'James Scott'; Eirwen E. C. Nicholson, *Oxford Dictionary of National Biography*, 'Anne Scott'; Mulvihill, 'A Feminist Link', 99. Milling ('"In the Female Coasts of Fame"', 276) states that the Monmouths and the other performers, Captain O'Bryan and Henry Savile 'had a hand in the downfall of Clarendon and were at this point probably identified with the anti-Yorkist camp', though she goes on to connect the performance of *Horace* not with domestic politics but with the recently concluded second Dutch war and 'the complex negotiations to limit French expansionist policies'.

16
English Women's Writing and Islamic Empires, 1610–1690

Bernadette Andrea

While much of the current scholarship on England and Islamic culture, politics, and religion deals with writing by men, especially travel narratives and drama, women's role in this transcultural encounter continues to be underemphasized.[1] In response, this chapter will examine English women writers from the early seventeenth century (Mary Wroth), the mid-century (the royalist Margaret Cavendish and the radical sectarians Katherine Evans and Sarah Chevers), and the end of the century (Delarivier Manley). This survey establishes that English women, marginalized by gender, identified with the Islamic 'other' in a way not possible for their male counterparts. At the same time, as participants in the English imperial project, they increasingly came to register their allegiances toward patriarchal orientalism. This tension informs the debates at the turn of the eighteenth century about the rights of 'freeborn Englishwomen', resulting in the emergence of feminist orientalism. However, counter-orientalist challenges also emerged, starting with Manley and, following her lead, Mary Wortley Montagu.

Lady Mary Wroth and the romance of empires

Although tentative trade missions were launched into Muslim regions prior to Elizabeth I's reign (1558–1603), sustained Anglo-Ottoman relations effectively started in the 1580s. The Queen issued a series of letters to the Ottoman sultan and other highly ranked members of his court as part of these negotiations, the most significant of which for a gendered analysis are her letters to the Ottoman Queen Mother, Safiye. These letters become the basis, not only of the beginnings of English men's trade in the region, but of English women's engagement with the Islamic world in the early modern period.[2]

Elizabeth's successor – James I (r. 1603–25) – was far less amenable to Anglo-Ottoman relations and women's humanist endeavors.[3] Yet, it was during his reign that the first original (as opposed to translated) prose romance and sonnet sequence by an English woman – Lady Mary Wroth (*c*.1587–*c*.1651) – appeared in print. Wroth retains the Elizabethan era's fascination with the Ottoman Empire, adding the early seventeenth-century interest in the Persian Safavids bordering the Ottomans. She also expands the 'imaginative geography' of her romance into Asia (including Natolia and Tartaria) and other eastern regions (such as Babylon).[4] In the published first part of her romance, *The Countess of Montgomery's Urania* (1621), Wroth puts these Islamic empires 'under erasure' to promote a purely imaginary Holy Roman Empire spanning Eurasia.[5] In the manuscript continuation of this romance, she incorporates the historical figure of the 'first' Persian in England – Lady Teresa Sampsonia Sherley – into her imperialist fantasy of female agency. This assertion of agency in the context of Jacobean backlash highlights the tentativeness of Elizabeth's macro- and micro-political negotiations. At the same time, it reveals continuities in early modern English women's identifications with their counterparts from the Islamic world as a means to challenge patriarchy in their own realm.

In both parts of her prose romance, Wroth encompasses East and West under an anachronistic Holy Roman Empire, a 'phantom' projection of 'universal imperialist hope' for emerging Western empires in the period.[6] However, the Holy Roman Empire presented as the field of action in *Urania* was ruled by the Ottomans from the middle of the fifteenth century, when Constantinople fell to Mehmed II, known as 'el-Fatih' or the Conqueror (r. 1444–46; 1451–81), until the end of the seventeenth century, when the Treaty of Karlowitz (1699) initiated the Ottoman retreat from the regions Wroth describes. Underlying the imaginative geography of *Urania*, then, is the reality of Ottoman imperialism in Eastern *and* Western Europe and the Western European response as expressed through the wish-fulfillment of romance. To cite a pivotal instance, the Mediterranean island of Cyprus is selected as the site where the Morean (Greek) princess Pamphilia is paired with the prince of Naples, Amphilanthus, who is destined to become the Holy Roman Emperor. This union is celebrated by the mass conversion of the islanders to Christianity, an anomaly in the otherwise classical first part of the romance. But Cyprus, captured in 1571, remained an Ottoman stronghold well into the seventeenth century, with its colonial administration predominantly Muslim and the masses primarily Greek Orthodox Christians, who initially preferred the Ottomans to their former Latin Catholic rulers. The multiple erasures of this scene thereby implicate Pamphilia through her role as a proper Renaissance woman in Amphilanthus's imperialist drive to incorporate the 'barbarous' island of Cyprus into his revived Holy Roman Empire.[7]

In the second part of the romance, Wroth continues her negotiation of conflicting early modern discourses of empire by introducing a series of dispossessed Persians and Central Asians to complicate the first part's erasure of the Ottomans. The ostensible female heir to the Persian throne, who as an Eastern Christian seeks alliances with the West, epitomizes this transition. The ambivalent religious and racial identities Wroth ascribes to this character, whose father is Tartar and mother is Persian, correspond to that of the aforementioned Lady Sherley, a Christian(ized) Circassian subject of Shah Abbas I wedded to the English adventurer, Robert Sherley.[8] The narratives of Persia, Tartaria, and Pamphilia, locales stretching from the far northeast corner to the far southwest corner of Central Asia, become further entangled through their representatives in the romance: the Persian Sophy (shah) and the Persian princess; Rodomandro, the king of Tartaria who appears later in the romance; and Pamphilia, who has since become the ruler of her eponymous realm on the westernmost edge of Asia.[9] The realm of Pamphilia, in Anatolia, layers classical (Greco-Roman), Christian (Pauline), and, in Wroth's era, Islamic (Ottoman) histories. Rodomandro, who is eventually betrothed to Pamphilia, adds another layer as an Eastern Christian. What we see in the second part of the romance, therefore, is an arguably proto-orientalist desire for a 'multicultural' Christian empire that incorporates East and West even as it effaces the reality of contemporaneous Islamic empires.

Simultaneously, Wroth's romance articulates emerging orientalist, and even racist, dichotomies at a time when England was imagining imperial possibilities, as in Richard Hakluyt's foundational compilation *The Principal Navigations, Voyages, Traffiques and Discoveries of the English Nation* (1598–1600), rather than establishing them.[10] As such, it projects increasingly sharp ontological divisions onto an imaginary geography that sought to assimilate differences into an imperialist paradigm. Rodomandro, characterized as black, yet having 'hands soe white', signals this shift in racialized terms.[11] As Kim Hall observes, 'Rodomandro's white hands suggest the possibility of his alliance with Pamphilia even as his "sunn-burnt" body marks the couple as mismatched in some way.'[12] Furthermore, while he is incorporated as a Christian into the central coupling linking East (Rodomandro) and West (Pamphilia), an undercurrent of uncertainty about his ability to assimilate troubles Pamphilia, who marries him with reluctance. Thomas Fuller's description of Lady

Sherley, who receives the double-edged compliment of having 'more of *Ebony*, then *Ivory*, in her Complexion, yet amiable enough, and very valiant, a quality considerable in that Sex, in those Countries', echoes Wroth's description of Rodomandro as black and white and of the Persian princess as excessively white.[13] Reading both parts of Wroth's romance across this uneven transition in early seventeenth-century English discourses of empire – as supplicants eastward, but as colonists westward – highlights the centrality of English women's engagement with Islamdom to early modern constructions of race. In this case, the Muslim other, whether Tartar, Persian, or Turk, remains 'white', although ambivalently so. Montagu's praise a century later of 'fair' Ottoman ladies, often of mixed European and Asian descent, and her derogatory description of 'not quite black' North African women as 'baboons' becomes explicable as the culmination of this tendency.[14]

English trade, captives, wives, and strumpets

As we have seen, Lady Sherley, a Central Asian (Circassian) woman who traveled with her husband (the 'Persian' ambassador of English provenance) across Europe on several occasions, offers a rare example of agency through the extensive discourse that developed around her. However, the transit of English women to Persia and Persian women to England as part of her entourage has been wholly neglected in analyses of this encounter. The trip from London to Persia on an East India Company ship, for instance, included 'Sir *Robert Sherley*, the Ambassadour. *Teresha*, his Ladie, a *Circasian*. Sir *Thomas Powell*. *Tomasin* his Ladie. *Leylye*, a *Persian* Woman', along with other English and Persian men.[15] Related records show that Powell lived with his Persian wife in Herefordshire.[16] Moreover, 'three or four English women' accompanied the Sherleys on their return trip to Persia; the absence of further accounts concerning them might indicate that they did not return to England.[17] As Imtiaz Habib establishes in his groundbreaking analysis of *Black Lives in the English Archives, 1500–1677*, women and men of African descent married into the lower ranks of English society during the early seventeenth century.[18] Although less visible, perhaps because Persians were generally designated 'white', women from the Islamic empires were similarly assimilated. That English transactions with Persia subsided after the anomalous Sherley episode, not resuming until the nineteenth century, perhaps also explains the hitherto unnoticed assimilation of Persian women into English society and English women into Persian society during the first two decades of the seventeenth century.[19]

Over the next two decades, English women entered the Ottoman Empire and the Islamic regions of the Mediterranean primarily as merchants' and ambassadors' wives, in addition to counting among the captives of the Barbary slave trade. Jane, wife to Peter Wych, the ninth ambassador to Constantinople (Istanbul), who assumed his post in April 1628 and left in 1639, numbers among the first English women to reside in the Ottoman Empire.[20] While contemporaneous accounts provide few details of her residence, John Bulwer's *Anthropometamorphosis* (1653) refers to her experiences two decades earlier. In keeping with the theme of this compendium, subtitled *Man Transform'd: or, The Artificial Changeling*, Bulwer adduces her as a cross-cultural spectacle of the absurdity of English women's practice of wearing disabling stays to reduce their waists and enlarge their hips. This episode conveys her response, albeit indirectly, to 'the *Sultanesse*', who 'asked her whether all English women were so made and shaped about those parts'. In Bulwer's words, 'my Lady *Wych* answered, that they were made as other women were', verifying her explanation by revealing 'her naturall and reall shape'.[21] This trace of the voice of an English woman resident in Istanbul, along with the unveiling of her lower parts, provides an early example of the reverse gaze Montagu later elaborates as a critique of English patriarchy prompted by the perspective of Ottoman women.[22]

Another account of Montagu's precursor, Lady Wych, comes from William Seaman, who sojourned in the Ottoman Empire during the 1630s. Seaman was 'the first Englishman to write a Turkish grammar, though he wrote it in Latin: *Grammatica Linguae Turcicae* (Oxford, 1670)'.[23] He earlier translated from original sources *The reign of Sultan Orchan, second King of the Turks* (1652), dedicating it to Lady Wych (later Merick), not simply 'because (during my youth) I began the study of the Turkish Language, while I was a servant of your Family at *Constantinople*', but because he considers her a worthy interlocutor. As he continues, 'when I consider your *Ladiships* excellent parts, and accomplishments, height'ned by your experience in the general knowledge of things, acquired during your residence in the chief City of that great Empire: I am rather imbold'ned to tender it [this translation] to you, as one well qualified to judge of so unwonted a subject'.[24] We can only speculate about the extent of her acculturation, including acquiring proficiency in the Turkish language. However, Seaman's address suggests she may have been as avid a student of the language as the more famous Montagu, who sought to acquire Turkish despite her much briefer residence of only two years, by contrast to Lady Wych's sojourn of a decade.[25]

Another example from these decades is the 'Lady' of Sir Sackville Crowe, the tenth English ambassador to Constantinople.[26] His tenure, from 1633 to 1647, overlapped with the beginning of the wars between the English King and Parliament leading to the abolition of the monarchy. A staunch royalist, Crowe's nomination by the King was notoriously undermined by the parliamentary faction in control of the Levant Company. Crowe's machinations in retaliation, which involved pitting Turkish authorities against English merchants, resulted in his seizure at the ambassador's residence and transport to the Tower of London, where he was imprisoned until monarchy was restored in 1660. Sources indicate 'Crowe's wife was treated with equal severity, and compelled to embark for England at two days' notice.'[27] Other records suggest the presence of English women in the centers of the Levant Company (Constantinople, Smyrna, Aleppo) led to accusations of disruption and dissolution. Although they were generally labeled 'whores' and 'strumpets', whether married or not, their presence in the official records may indicate a certain subaltern agency for those women who were denied access to the sanctioned avenues of politics and trade that made the careers of English men in the East.[28] Hence, while we do not have details of Lady Crowe's expulsion, which could be simply for her association with the fallen ambassador, her own actions may have played a part in her speedy removal. Along with the British women captured as part of the Barbary slave trade, whom Nabil Matar has discussed in *Britain and Barbary, 1589–1689*, the agency of these less encumbered women must be more fully incorporated into future accounts of early modern English women and the Islamic world.[29]

Quaker women in England's first Mediterranean colony

Tangier under the English (*c*.1662–84) – as its most celebrated chronicler, Samuel Pepys, Chief Secretary to the Admiralty, records – contained 'nothing but vice in the whole place of all sorts, for swearing, cursing, drinking and whoring'.[30] Presented to Charles II shortly after the Restoration as part of Catherine of Braganza's dowry (along with Bombay), this Mediterranean port became a unique arena for English women's agency in the region. Because 'the expressed desire of the King [was] that Tangier should be not only a naval station and a centre for commerce, but also the starting-point of an extensive English colony in Africa', English men were given permission for their wives and children to accompany them.[31] Yet, making English women partners in this colonial project opened avenues for their agency in unexpected ways.

Whereas Pepys generally considered such women to be whores, the fuller record of the short-lived Tangier colony shows them participating in a public sphere that was fiercely political. Venues such as the 'House of Pleasure ... where the Ladies, the Officers, and the better sort of people, do refresh and divert themselves with Wine, Fruits, and a very pretty Bowling-Base', the plays they attended, and the dinner parties they hosted, enabled some women on the island to exercise their influence within this fractious colony.[32]

Ironically, the outward itinerary of the most celebrated English women chroniclers of the region during the mid-century brought them to Tangier as the colony was barely established. These women could not be more different from Pepys, who supervised the colony's closure, and the dissolute crowd that fascinated him. Rather, Katherine Evans and Sarah Chevers were aggressively proper Quaker women who had just been released from the Maltese Inquisition.[33] Having survived their three-year imprisonment in Malta, where they were held after ignoring the repeated warnings of the English consul not to proselytize on this militantly Catholic island, the two women immediately resumed their mission upon landing at Tangier. They not only condemned the dissolute English, who mostly belonged to the Church of England, but they sought to travel to the besieged frontier of the colony to convert the Moors. We can assess the general English reaction through Evans and Chevers's record of their outgoing voyage: 'But our own Countrey-men were much worse than most of them [the Catholic Maltese, including 'the *Inquisitor's* own brother'], so that they bid us go back to *Malta* again; and said the *English would use us worse than the Maltezes.*'[34] Mary Fisher, whose parallel mission brought her into the camp of the Ottoman sultan, experienced similar treatment from the English at Smyrna.[35]

Typically, even though upon reaching Tangier the captain beseeched them not to 'go a-shoar till he had spoke with the Governour's Excellency', Evans and Chevers immediately proceeded 'a-shoar as we were moved of the Lord', where they preached against 'the Abominations of the wicked in that place; none worse than Englishmen for swearing, lying, pride, drunkenness, whoredoms, and such like' (257). Having cleared their conscience in front of the English governor, 'in a few dayes after it was laid upon us of the Lord, to go forth to meet the *Moors* their Enemies, which laid siege against them, and they were such a bloody savage people, that it seemed a very hard thing to us' (259). At this time, the Moroccans under the waning Saadi dynasty were resisting English incursions; the succeeding Alaouite dynasty under Moulay Ismail ibn Sharif, whose efforts Pepys documents, would regain

Tangier. The women's momentum was halted by the governor's warnings, at which time they 'were made willing to bear and to wait upon the Lord to perswade his heart to let us go' (260). Once the Moroccans (Moors) concluded a peace treaty with the English colonists and withdrew their forces, the women's mission became moot. They nevertheless end with the assurance: 'but we do believe if we had gone forth among them before they come to treat with them, the Lord our God who liveth for ever, would have preserved us, and we should have been returned, to the conviction of many, and to the astonishment of all the whole Garison, for his own glory' (261). Considering their mission complete, they left Tangier on the next ship and returned to England as active and respected members of the Quaker community.

Like other radical sectarians from the English Civil War period, Evans and Chevers were not asserting an autonomous individual agency, but believed themselves to be speaking and acting as vehicles for the divine word. This apparently negative agency may not be amenable to 'a theory of female authorship' derived from the succeeding canon of British women novelists – and it certainly maddened the English consul on Malta as he sought to secure the women's release – but it needs to be acknowledged as a formative aspect of the English engagement with Islam in all its aspects.[36] These Quaker women, rather than the literata Mary Wortley Montagu more than sixty years later, should be seen as the 'starting point' for studies of early modern English women writing about their travels to the Islamic world.[37]

English women staging Islam

Symptomatically for the second half of the seventeenth century, both the suppression of the public stage by the Puritans in 1642 and its restoration along with the King in 1660 were represented through shifting signifiers of Islamic society, culture, and history distorted by English ignorance and prejudice. As Matthew Birchwood demonstrates in *Staging Islam in England: Drama and Culture, 1640–1685*, Oliver Cromwell, leader of the forces conventionally labeled 'puritan', was frequently represented as an English 'Turk' for his sedition and sectarianism.[38] The English kings on either side of the Interregnum (1649–60) were also represented through orientalist tropes, usually combining sensualism and absolutism as an anachronistic blend of Persian Sassanids (classical pre-Islamic) and Safavids (contemporary Islamic). The first production to breach 'the Puritan ban on theatrical performances' – William Davenant's *The Siege of Rhodes* (1656) – likewise featured a Muslim

character as its protagonist.[39] Based on the successful siege of the eastern
Mediterranean island by the Ottoman Sultan Süleyman the Magnificent
in 1522, which resulted in the Knights of Rhodes being displaced to the
western Mediterranean island of Malta, it is considered paradigmatic
for Restoration drama. John Dryden's *The Conquest of Granada* (1670),
which epitomized 'the new genre of the heroic play', follows Davenant's
lead.[40] As Birchwood concludes, 'Islam was an ever-present touchstone
for a whole range of writers struggling to find meaning in the chaos' of
this century of revolution, even though 'it was far from being a fixed
or stable point of reference'.[41] However, women dramatists remain con-
spicuously absent from the range of writers adduced in this and similar
treatments of English stagings of Islam, despite the exemplars from this
period.

For instance, the first and second parts of *Loves Adventures*, the lead
plays in Margaret Cavendish's 1662 volume, feature a cross-dressed
heroine, Affectionata, whose adventures in foreign battlefields are paralleled by the vicissitudes of women battling predatory men at home. The
first mention of 'the Turkes' comes from 'two Merchants', who elaborate: 'I hear the Lord *Singularity* [the general] hath given the Turkes a
great defeat, he is both a wise, prudent, and valiant man' (11; 31).[42] This
representation of Western victories over the Turks is quickly reversed as
these men plunge into the dissolution that observers from Biddulph to
Pepys documented for English men abroad: 'Nay faith Captain, we do
not only lose our health, but wast[e] our wealth, for what booties we get
from the Turks, the Courtezans gets from us' (49; 74). In a further plot
twist, one of the commanders describes how Affectionata, disguised as
the 'adopted Son' of the general, 'made such a massacre of the Turks,
as they lay as thick upon the ground, as if they had been mushrooms'
(50; 76). A second commander furthers this fantasy of female invin-
cibility, without realizing he is praising a woman, when he remarks,
''Tis strange, and doth amaze me with wonder, to think how such a
Willow-twig could bore so many mortal holes in such strong timber'd
bodies as the Turks' (50; 76). It is this victory over the Turks that results
in Affectionata's promotion to 'Lieutenant-General of the whole Armie,
and one of the Council of War' (51; 77), enabling her to counter, albeit
selectively, the patriarchal abuses about which the other female characters complain. It also allows her to set the terms for her marriage in
the final scene, a requisite of the comic genre, to none other than the
general. Beyond the critique of patriarchal abuses Cavendish develops
and the feminist response she proposes, we should consider this scene
against the realities of Ottoman dominance in the period. Cavendish's

feminism may be seen as proto-orientalist in the same way as Wroth's fantasy of a universal Christendom spanning contemporary Islamic empires in that it complicates dichotomies of self and other along gender lines in the context of shifting responses to Turks, Persians, and Mughals. Yet, it also anticipates the full-fledged orientalism of the 'first feminists' who articulated a discourse of English women's natural rights against the foil of Muslim women's inherent oppression, a fallacy they borrowed from male travel writers' fantasies about the seraglio or harem.[43]

Other instances in Cavendish's *oeuvre* include the discussion of polygamy in *The First Part of the Play call Wits Cabal* (1662), with Monsieur Sensuality linked to 'the *Turks* government' as 'the only government for such men as would have many Wives, Concubines, and Slaves' (250); the debate over whether women have 'rational souls' in *The Unnatural Tragedy* (1662), which is framed with the opening reference to Turkey (327); and the opening reference to 'the great Mogul' in *The Publick Wooing* (1662), where the theme of polygamy is reprised with reference to '*Solomon* and the great *Turk*' (283). *A Comedy of the Apocriphal Ladies* (1662) subjects this theme to an ironic critique by voicing it through the 'Duke of Inconstancy', who having been widowed determines to 'be like the Great Turk, [to] have many Wives' (639). His interlocutor, concerned more with securing English patriarchal succession than with defending Islam, counters that 'the great Turk hath but one chief Wife, the rest are but as Concubines' (639). In other words, he is just like an upper-class English man, monogamous with numerous mistresses.[44] The same irony informs *The Bridals*, from Cavendish's 1668 collection, where Monsieur Adviser jests with Monsieur Take-Pleasure, 'Why, I think you are a good fellow, and love a Mistress well; but I do not think you are the Grand Signor' (17; 180). The bantering, which reveals both men to be fools, focuses on the seraglio and men's varying degrees of access to it, all of which are shown to be based on fantasy.

Cavendish's challenge to men's constructions of the seraglio or harem continues in her utopian romance, *The Description of a New World, called the Blazing World* (1666, reissued in 1668).[45] Here, the representation of this space is markedly feminocentric and even homoerotic. It houses the empress of this utopia and her scribe, none other than 'the Duchess of Newcastle' (181), who are united in the body of her husband, the Duke of Newcastle, as 'platonic lovers, although they were both female' (183). The exchange between the empress and the duchess about 'the Grand Signior', or Ottoman sultan, shows the latter correcting the misconception that he was an absolutist sovereign even as the duchess

praises the English king over the sultan (191). This conversation precedes the meeting between 'those two female souls' in the body of the
duke (190), so that he 'had three souls in one body; and had there been
some such souls more, the duke would have been like the Grand Signior
in his seraglio, only it would have been a platonic seraglio' (194). This
description raises the problem of female competition in polygamous
households, only to dismiss it because 'no adultery could be committed amongst Platonic lovers' (194–95). This seraglio becomes a space
for female conversation, with the duke providing entertainment in the
form of 'scenes, songs, music, witty discourses, pleasant recreations, and
all kinds of harmless sports' (195). Cavendish again shows herself oscil-
lating between, on the one hand, challenging orientalist stereotypes, as
when she critiques the fallacy of the absolutist sultan and represents the
harem as a feminocentric space and, on the other, endorsing them, as
when she praises the English king as more just than the Ottoman sultan
and raises the specter of female competition and jealousy among harem
women. This gendered response on the cusp of the shift in English
views of the Ottoman Empire is therefore crucial to understanding the
encounter with Islam in the period.[46]

Along with the more familiar epithet 'Astrea', Aphra Behn by the
end of the seventeenth century had been designated 'Loves great
Sultana'.[47] However, she more closely follows Davenant, Dryden, and other
Restoration male playwrights in her single play focusing on Islamicate
themes: *Abdelazer; Or, the Moor's Revenge* (1676). Its plot reprises that of
Lust's Dominion or the Lascivious Queen (1567), attributed to Christopher
Marlowe: the African general is vengeful and wicked; the Spanish queen
is lascivious and murderous. As Bridget Orr summarizes, 'there is little
greatness in Behn's representation of the ongoing conflict between the
Moors and the Spaniards'.[48] Her more popular prose narrative *Oroonoko;
or, The Royal Slave* (1688), which follows an African prince captured
into New World slavery, does not identify its characters as Muslim.
However, it does operate on an orientalist register with its description of
the harem in the court of '*Coramantien*, a Country of *Blacks* so called'.[49]
Despite the scarcity of characters or themes related to Islam in Behn's
oeuvre, her career set the stage, literally and figuratively, for the epochal
season of 1695/96, which debuted a group of playwrights dubbed 'the
female wits', two of whose plays had explicitly Islamicate themes. The
first, Delarivier Manley's *The Royal Mischief*, drew on *The Travels of Sir
John Chardin into Persia and the East Indies* (1686); the second, Mary Pix's
Ibrahim, the Thirteenth Emperor of the Turks, drew on Paul Rycaut's *The
History of the Turkish Empire* (1687).[50] Other plays by 'the female wits'

deal with cross-cultural encounters touching on Turkey and Spain, which bore the traces of its Islamic past, including Catharine Trotter's *Agnes de Castro*; Pix's *The Spanish Wives*; and Manley's *The Lost Lover; or, The Jealous Husband*. Western fantasies about the Ottoman sultan's seraglio, frequently used to satirize the Restoration court, thus informed the theatrical debut of 'the female wits' not only by providing themes, but also by shaping their reception as women transgressing patriarchal norms. Corresponding to the debates among the 'first feminists', these playwrights vacillate between the orientalist position emerging at the turn of the eighteenth century and the counter-orientalist challenge epitomized by Montagu's *Turkish Embassy Letters* two decades later.[51]

Feminist orientalism and its discontents

Manley, with the other 'female wits', marks the terminus of early modern English women's initial engagement with Islam. At the same time, her involvement in the burgeoning debate about women's rights in relation to England's accelerating imperialist ambitions, framed against the 'decline' of the Ottoman Empire, opens a new phase that culminated in the hegemony of feminist orientalism over the course of the eighteenth century. Early in this century, Manley and Pix continued their engagement with Islamicate themes, with Manley's *Almyna: Or, the Arabian Vow* (performed in 1706; published in 1707) arguably the earliest literary response to the first full English translation of the Arabic classic, *Alf Layla wa Layla* (*The 1001 Nights*, also known as the *Arabian Nights' Entertainments*).[52] Pix's *The Conquest of Spain*, while more characteristic of nascent liberal feminism's orientalism, engages the history of Islamic Spain by rewriting William Rowley's *A Tragedy Called All's Lost by Lust* (1633) with more attention to the gendered nuances of race and empire.[53] Susanna Centlivre, who hinges her plays on the 'Liberties of an English wife' as opposed to Eastern, and especially Islamic, gender oppression, confirms the trend toward articulating feminist demands through orientalist discourses.[54] Whereas Manley's plays did not sustain enough interest to generate a steady income, leading to her shift to prose writing, Centlivre was one of the most successful playwrights of the era, with two of her plays among the 'four non-Shakespearian comedies written before 1750 ... still being regularly performed' by the end of the nineteenth century.[55] Clearly, her feminist orientalist message was more amenable to theater audiences than Manley's challenges. Although Montagu in her *Turkish Embassy Letters*, composed from 1716 to 1718 but not published in their final form until 1763, seconded

Manley's challenges to feminist orientalism, the bulk of eighteenth-century English women's plays and novels with Islamicate themes represent the reverse trend. Hannah Cowley's play *A Day in Turkey* (1792) might countenance a conservative brand of feminist agency in the harem;[56] however, it is finally Mary Wollstonecraft's *A Vindication of the Rights of Woman* (1792), epitomizing 'the fullest explicit feminist orientalist perspective', that determined the course of mainstream anglocentric feminism in subsequent centuries.[57]

Notes

1. Bernadette Andrea, 'Travels Through "Islam" in Early Modern English Studies', *Clio: A Journal of Literature, History and the Philosophy of History* 35 (2006): 225–43.
2. Bernadette Andrea, *Women and Islam in Early Modern English Literature* (Cambridge: Cambridge University Press, 2007), 12–29.
3. Daniel Vitkus, *Turning Turk: English Theater and the Multicultural Mediterranean, 1570–1630* (New York: Palgrave Macmillan, 2003), 32; Barbara Kiefer Lewalski, *Writing Women in Jacobean England* (Cambridge, MA: Harvard University Press, 1993), 2–3.
4. Edward W. Said, *Orientalism* (New York: Vintage, 1979), 54–55; Andrea, *Women and Islam*, 131 n. 3. See also 'Index of Places', in Mary Wroth, *The Second Part of the Countess of Montgomery's Urania*, ed. Josephine A. Roberts, completed by Suzanne Gossett and Janel M. Mueller (Tempe: Renaissance English Text Society, 1999), 574–75.
5. Andrea, *Women and Islam*, 30–42.
6. Frances A. Yates, *Astraea: The Imperial Theme in the Sixteenth Century* (London: Routledge, 1975), 1.
7. Mary Wroth, *The First Part of The Countess of Montgomery's Urania*, ed. Josephine Roberts (Binghamton: Center for Medieval and Early Renaissance Studies, 1995), 47.
8. Andrea, *Women and Islam*, 42–52.
9. Bernadette Andrea, 'Persia, Tartaria, and Pamphilia: Ideas of Asia in Mary Wroth's *The Countess of Montgomery's Urania, Part II*', in *The English Renaissance, Orientalism, and the Idea of Asia*, ed. Walter S. H. Lim and Debra Johanyak (New York: Palgrave Macmillan, 2010), 23–50.
10. Andrea, *Women and Islam*, 133 n. 10.
11. Wroth, *Second Part*, 42.
12. Kim F. Hall, *Things of Darkness: Economies of Race and Gender in Early Modern England* (Ithaca: Cornell University Press, 1995), 210.
13. Thomas Fuller, *The History of the Worthies of England* (London, 1662), 107. This is in the section on 'Sussex', which is separately paginated. Wroth, *Second Part*, 168.
14. Mary Wortley Montagu, *Turkish Embassy Letters*, ed. Malcolm Jack (Athens, GA: University of Georgia Press, 1993), 89, 118, 149, 151.
15. Walter Payton, '*A Iournall of all principall matters passed in the twelfth Voyage to the East India ... Anno 1612*', in *Purchas His Pilgrimes*, by Samuel Purchas (London, 1625), 488.

16. Boies Penrose, *The Sherleian Odyssey* (London: Simpkin Marshall, 1938), 189.

17. William Foster, '1612–16, Nicolas Withington', in *Early Travels in India, 1583–1619* (London: Oxford University Press, 1921), 188–233, citing 212.

18. Imtiaz Habib, *Black Lives in the English Archives, 1500–1677: Imprints of the Invisible* (Aldershot: Ashgate, 2008), 95–96.

19. Mohammad Nezam-Mafi covers both periods in 'Persian Recreations: Theatricality in Anglo-Persian Diplomatic History, 1599–1828', PhD dissertation, Boston University (1999).

20. Gerald M. MacLean, *The Rise of Oriental Travel: English Visitors to the Ottoman Empire, 1580–1720* (New York: Palgrave Macmillan, 2004), examines the earlier and 'strange case of Anne, Lady Glover', wife of Thomas Glover, who was ambassador from 1606 to 1611 (221–25). She was 'the first English ambassadorial wife to live in the capital' (223). He indicates that 'Lady Glover was herself accompanied by at least two maids' (222), one of whom may have been impregnated by the ambassador. Although MacLean states he found 'very little evidence' for Lady Glover's life (222), he offers a fascinating study of her death and its aftermath. MacLean briefly discusses Lady Wych (225).

21. John Bulwer, *Anthropometamorphosis: Man Transform'd: or, The Artificial Changeling* (London, 1653), 547.

22. For the most famous episode, see Montagu, *Turkish Embassy Letters*, 57–60.

23. Geoffrey Lewis, 'Turks and Britons over Four Hundred Years', in *Four Centuries of Turco-British Relations: Studies in Diplomatic, Economic and Cultural Affairs*, ed. William Hale and Ali Ihsan Bagis (Walkington: The Eothen Press, 1984), 123–38, citing 128. Lewis incorrectly locates the dedication to Lady Wych (later Merick) in Seaman's *Grammatica* (128–29), which is actually dedicated to Robert Boyle. Seaman dedicates his earlier book on Turkish matters to Lady Merick, which I discuss in this section.

24. William Seaman, 'The Epistle Dedicatory', *The reign of Sultan Orchan, second King of the Turks, Translated out of Hojah Effendi, an eminent Turkish historian* (London, 1651), n.p.

25. Andrea, 'Travels Through "Islam"', 241–42. See also Hülya Adak, 'Aligning the "Original" with the "Target": Translating Ottoman Poetry', in 'Intersubjectivity: Halide Edib (1882–1964) or the "Ottoman/Turkish Woman" as the Subject of Knowledge', PhD dissertation, University of Chicago (2001), 33–49.

26. Her transportation to Istanbul is mentioned in *Subtilty and Cruelty: Or a True Relation of the Horrible and unparalleld abuses and intolerable Oppressions, exercised by Sir Sackvile Crow, His Majesties Ambassador at Constantinople, and his Agents* (London, 1646), sig. A3.

27. Alfred C. Wood, *A History of the Levant Company* [1935] (London: Frank Cass, 1964), 92 n. 2.

28. Gerald MacLean, *Looking East: English Writing and the Ottoman Empire Before 1800* (New York: Palgrave Macmillan, 2007), 84. MacLean also discusses English men's liaisons with 'local women' (254 n. 26) and English women in Tangier later in the century (91–94).

29. Nabil Matar, *Britain and Barbary, 1589–1689* (Gainesville: University Press of Florida, 2005), 76–110. See also Daniel Goffman, *Britons in the Ottoman Empire, 1642–1660* (Seattle: University of Washington Press, 1998), who

mentions 'that in the 1650s Ambassador Bendysh's wife and five children lived with him in Istanbul (and his wife died there), we know nothing more' (226 n. 25). It is this 'inoculating critique' that I am questioning, on which see Dympna Callaghan, 'Re-Reading Elizabeth Cary's *The Tragedie of Mariam, Faire Queene of Jewry*', in *Women, 'Race', and Writing in the Early Modern Period*, ed. Margo Hendricks and Patricia Parker (London: Routledge, 1994), 163; cf. 9. Callaghan's epigraph – 'we should note ... that the practice of including an inoculating critique of its own blind spots, so as to allow business to proceed as usual, has become a common tactic in contemporary political criticism' – comes from Tania Modelski, *Feminism Without Women: Culture and Criticism in a 'Postfeminist' Age* (New York: Routledge, 1991), 6.

30. Samuel Pepys, *The Tangier Papers of Samuel Pepys*, ed. Edwin Chappell (London: Navy Records Society, 1935), 89. MacLean, *Rise of Oriental Travel*, describes Tangier as England's 'first African colony' (181).

31. E. M. G. Routh, 'The English at Tangier', *The English Historical Review* 26.103 (1911): 469–81, citing 469.

32. George Philips, *The Present State of Tangier* (London, 1676), 31. See Routh, 'The English at Tangier', 474–77.

33. Andrea, *Women and Islam*, 61–77.

34. Katherine Evans and Sarah Chevers [Cheevers], *A True Account of the Great Tryals and Cruel Sufferings undergone by those two faithful Servants of God* (London, 1663), 255. This is the expanded second edition; the first edition was published in 1662. Further references are cited parenthetically in the text.

35. Andrea, *Women and Islam*, 54–61.

36. Margaret J. M. Ezell, *Writing Women's Literary History* (Baltimore: Johns Hopkins University Press, 1993), 21.

37. Andrea, *Women and Islam*, 118–21; 132 n. 9.

38. Matthew Birchwood, *Staging Islam in England: Drama and Culture, 1640–1685* (Cambridge: D. S. Brewer, 2007), 4, 56–64.

39. Derek Hughes, 'Heroic Drama and Tragicomedy', in *A Companion to Restoration Drama*, ed. Susan J. Owen (Oxford: Blackwell, 2001), 195–210.

40. Susan J. Owen, Preface to *Companion to Restoration Drama*, xiv; Birchwood, *Staging Islam*, 103, 129.

41. Birchwood, *Staging Islam*, 182; Christopher Hill, *The Century of Revolution, 1603–1714* (New York: Norton, 1980).

42. Page numbers refer, first, to the seventeenth-century editions – Margaret Cavendish, *Playes* (London, 1662) and *Plays, Never before Printed* (London, 1668) – and, if included, to *The Convent of Pleasure and Other Plays*, ed. Anne Shaver (Baltimore: Johns Hopkins University Press, 1999).

43. Andrea, *Women and Islam*, 80–85.

44. For this theme in Manley's prose works, see Andrea, *Women and Islam*, 105–17.

45. All references will be to Margaret Cavendish, *The Blazing World and Other Writings*, ed. Kate Lilley (London: Penguin, 1994). For the Ottoman references in this utopia, see Rosemary Kegl, '"The world I have made": Margaret Cavendish, Feminism, and the *Blazing-World*', in *Feminist Readings of Early Modern Culture*, ed. Valerie Traub, M. Lindsay Kaplan, and Dympna Callaghan (Cambridge: Cambridge University Press, 1996), 119–41, esp. 132–34.

46. For this shift, see Aslı Çırakman, *From the 'Terror of the World' to the 'Sick Man of Europe': European Images of Ottoman Empire and Society from the Sixteenth Century to the Nineteenth* (New York: Peter Lang, 2002).

47. Janet Todd, *The Secret Life of Aphra Behn* (New Brunswick: Rutgers University Press, 1996), 320.

48. Bridget Orr, *Empire on the English Stage, 1600–1714* (Cambridge: Cambridge University Press, 2001), 171.

49. Aphra Behn, *Oroonoko*, ed. Catherine Gallagher (Boston: Bedford/St. Martin's Press, 2000), 41.

50. Andrea, *Women and Islam*, 85–99.

51. Ibid., 78–79.

52. Ibid., 99–104.

53. Pilar Cuder-Dominguez, 'The Islamization of Spain in William Rowley and Mary Pix: The Politics of Nation and Gender', *Comparative Drama* 36 (2002): 321–36. See also Bernadette Andrea, *Delarivier Manley and Mary Pix: English Women Staging Islam, 1696–1707* (Centre for Reformation and Renaissance Studies/University of Toronto, forthcoming).

54. Susanna Centlivre, *The Artifice* (London, 1723), 103. For Centlivre's articulation of liberalism and feminism, see Annette Kreis-Schinck, *Women, Writing, and Theater in the Early Modern Period* (Madison: Fairleigh Dickinson University Press, 2001), 71–82, 179–86.

55. Jacqueline Pearson, *The Prostituted Muse: Images of Women and Women Dramatists, 1642–1737* (New York: St. Martin's Press, 1988), 202.

56. Humberto Garcia, 'Hannah Cowley, the Female Wits, and the *Unfeminine* Politics of the Turkish Harem', in 'Islam in the English Radical Protestant Imagination, 1660–1830', PhD dissertation, University of Illinois at Urbana-Champaign (2007), 221–63.

57. Joyce Zonana, 'The Sultan and the Slave: Feminist Orientalism and the Structure of *Jane Eyre*', *Signs: Journal of Women in Culture and Society* 18 (1993): 592–617, citing 599. See also Bernadette Andrea, 'Islam, Women, and Western Responses: The Contemporary Relevance of Early Modern Investigations', *Women's Studies: An Interdisciplinary Journal* 38.3 (2009): 273–92.

Select Bibliography

Primary texts

Behn, Aphra. [Fontenelle, M. de (Bernard Le Bovier)]. *A Discovery of New Worlds From the French Made English by Mrs. A. Behn.* London, 1688.
——. *Complete Works.* Ed. Janet Todd. 7 volumes. London: Pickering; Columbus: Ohio State University Press, 1992–96.
——. *Love-Letters Between a Nobleman and his Sister.* Ed. Janet Todd. London: Penguin, 1996.
——. *Oroonoko and Other Writings.* Ed. Paul Salzman. Oxford: Oxford University Press, 1998.
Boothby, Frances. *Marcelia, or the Treacherous Friend* (1670). Brown Women Writers Project.
Bradstreet, Anne. *The Tenth Muse. Complete Works.* Ed. Joseph R. McElrath, Jr. and Allan P. Robb. Boston: Twayne, 1981.
Carleton, Mary. *Mary Carleton.* Ed. Mihoko Suzuki. Aldershot: Ashgate, 2006.
Cary, Elizabeth. *The History of The Life, Reign, and Death of Edward II. Works by and attributed to Elizabeth Cary.* Ed. Margaret W. Ferguson. Aldershot: Scolar, 1996.
——. *The History of the Life, Reign, and Death of Edward II.* Purkiss, *Renaissance Women.* 79–237.
——. *Lady Falkland: Life and Letters.* Ed. Heather Wolfe. Cambridge: Renaissance Texts from Manuscript, 2001.
——. 'The Rainge and deathe off Edwarde the Seconde. The highe and Fall of his too greate Favorites Gaveston and Spencer. February 2°. 1627. By E.F.' Ms 361. Fitzwilliam Museum, Cambridge.
——. *The Tragedie of Mariam, The Faire Queene of Jewry.* Cerasano and Wynne-Davies, *Renaissance Drama by Women.* 43–75.
——. *The Tragedy of Mariam: The Fair Queen of Jewry with The Lady Falkland Her Life: By One of her Daughters.* Ed. Barry Weller and Margaret W. Ferguson. Berkeley: University of California Press, 1994.
——. *The Tragedie of Mariam.* Ed. Stephanie Hodgson-Wright. Peterborough, ON: Broadview, 2000.
Cary, Mary. *The Little Horns Doom & Downfall.* London, 1651. Selections in Smith, Suzuki, Wiseman, *Women's Political Writings.* II: 181–200.
——. *A New and More Exact Mappe.* London, 1651.
——. *The Resurrection of the Witness.* London, 1648.
——. *A Word in Season to the Kingdom of England.* London, 1647. Smith, Suzuki, Wiseman, *Women's Political Writings.* II: 169–80.
Cavendish, Jane and Elizabeth Brackley. *The Concealed Fancies.* Cerasano and Wynne-Davies, *Renaissance Drama by Women.* 127–56.
——. *A Pastoral.* 'Poems, Songs, a Pastorall and a Play', Bodleian Library Rawlinson MS Poet 16.
——. *A Pastoral.* Greer, *Kissing the Rod.* 106–15.

Cavendish, Margaret. *Bell in Campo and the Sociable Companions.* Ed. Alexandra G. Bennett. Peterborough, ON: Broadview, 2002.

——. *The Blazing World and Other Writings.* Ed. Kate Lilley. London: Penguin, 1992.

——. *The Convent of Pleasure and Other Plays.* Ed. Anne Shaver. Baltimore, MD: Johns Hopkins University Press, 1999.

——. *Grounds of Natural Philosophy.* London, 1668.

——. *The Life of the (1st) Duke of Newcastle and Other Writings by Margaret Duchess.* London: J. M. Dent, 1916. Selections in Smith, Suzuki, Wiseman, *Women's Political Writings.* I: 249–334.

——. *Nature's Pictures.* London, 1656.

——. *Observations upon Experimental Philosophy.* Ed. Eileen O'Neill. Cambridge: Cambridge University Press, 2001.

——. *Orations of Divers Sorts.* London, 1662. Selections in *Political Writings.* Ed. Susan James. New York: Cambridge University Press, 2003. Smith, Suzuki, Wiseman, *Women's Political Writings.* I: 335–84.

——. *Paper Bodies: A Margaret Cavendish Reader.* Ed. Sylvia Bowerbank and Sara Mendelson. Peterborough, ON: Broadview, 2000.

——. *Philosophical Fancies.* London, 1653.

——. *The Philosophical and Physical Opinions.* London, 1655.

——. *Philosophical Letters.* London, 1664.

——. *Playes Written by the Thrice Noble, Illustrious and Excellent Princess, the Lady Marchioness of Newcastle.* London, 1662.

——. *Plays, Never before Printed.* London, 1668.

——. *Poems and Fancies.* London, 1653.

——. *The Sociable Companions or, the Female Wits.* Ed. Amanda Holton. Oxford: Seventeenth Century Press, 1996.

——. *Sociable Letters.* Ed. James Fitzmaurice. Peterborough, ON: Broadview, 2004.

——. *A True Relation of my Birth, Breeding, and Life.* In *The Life of the (1st) Duke of Newcastle.*

——. *The Worlds Olio.* London, 1655. Selections in Smith, Suzuki, Wiseman, *Women's Political Writings.* I: 214–48.

Cellier, Elizabeth. *Elizabeth Cellier.* Ed. Mihoko Suzuki. Aldershot: Ashgate, 2006.

——. *A Scheme for the Foundation of a Royal Hospital … for its Maintenance of a Corporation of Skillful Midwives.* Smith, Suzuki, Wiseman, *Women's Political Writings.* III: 150–57.

——. *To Dr ---. an answer to his queries concerning the Colledg of Midwives.* London, 1688.

Chidley, Katherine. *Katherine Chidley.* Ed. Katharine Gillespie. Aldershot: Ashgate, 2009.

Clifford, Anne. *The Diaries of Lady Anne Clifford.* Ed. D. J. H. Clifford. Stroud: Sutton, 1990.

——. *The Diary of Anne Clifford, 1616–1619: A Critical Edition.* Ed. Katherine O. Acheson. New York: Garland, 1995.

——. 'The Great Book'. Selections in Smith, Suzuki, Wiseman, *Women's Political Writings.* I: 5–107.

——. *The Memoir of 1603 and the Diary of 1616–1619.* Ed. Katherine O. Acheson. Peterborough, ON: Broadview, 2006.

Conway, Anne. *The Conway Letters: The Correspondence of Anne, Viscountess Conway, Henry More, and their Friends, 1642–1682.* Ed. Marjorie Hope Nicolson. Rev. Sarah Hutton. Oxford: Clarendon Press, 1992.

——. *The Principles of the Most Ancient and Modern Philosophy.* Ed. Allison P. Coudert and Taylor Corse. Cambridge: Cambridge University Press, 1996.

Davies, Eleanor. *The Prophetic Writings of Lady Eleanor Davies.* Ed. Esther S. Cope. New York: Oxford University Press, 1995.

Ephelia. *Ephelia.* Ed. Maureen Mulvihill. Aldershot: Ashgate, 2003.

——. *Female Pens on Several Occasions.* London,1679.

Evans, Katherine and Sarah Chevers. *A True Account of the Great Tryals and Cruel Sufferings undergone by those two faithful Servants of God.* London, 1663.

Fanshawe, Ann. *Memoirs.* Ed. John Loftis. Oxford: Clarendon Press, 1979.

Fell Fox, Margaret. *A Declaration and Information from Us the People of God.* Smith, Suzuki, Wiseman, *Women's Political Writings.* III: 3–9.

——. *Women's Speaking Justified.* London, 1666.

Fielding, Susan. 'Letters'. Quoted Cecilia Countess of Denbigh. *Royalist Father and Roundhead Son.* London: Methuen, 1915. Smith, Suzuki, Wiseman, *Women's Political Writings.* II: 319–20.

Finch, Anne. *Miscellany Poems with Two Plays by Ardelia.* Folger Shakespeare Library, MS N. b.3.

——. *The Poems of Anne, Countess of Winchelsea.* Chicago: University of Chicago Press, 1903.

Halkett, Anne. *Lady Anne Halkett: Selected Self-Writings.* Ed. Suzanne Trill. Aldershot: Ashgate, 2007.

——. *Memoirs.* Ed. John Loftis. Oxford: Clarendon Press, 1979.

Harley, Brilliana. *Letters of Brilliana Harley.* Ed. Thomas Taylor Lewis. London: Camden Society, 1854.

——. 'Letters'. Smith, Suzuki, Wiseman, *Women's Political Writings.* I: 118–202.

Hutchinson, Lucy. *Lucy Hutchinson's Translation of Lucretius: De rerum natura.* Ed. Hugh De Quehen. Ann Arbor: University of Michigan Press, 1996.

——. *Memoirs of the Life of Colonel Hutchinson with a Fragment of Autobiography.* Ed. N. H. Keeble. London: J. M. Dent; Rutland, VT: Everyman, 1995.

——. *Order and Disorder.* Ed. David Norbrook. Oxford: Blackwell, 2001.

James, Elinor. *Elinor James.* Ed. Paula McDowell. Aldershot: Ashgate, 2005.

Jocelin, Elizabeth, *Mother's Legacy to her Unborn Child.* London, 1624. Facsimile in Travitsky, *Mother's Advice Books.*

Jones, Sarah. *The Relation of a Gentlewoman Long Under Persecution by the Bishops.* London, 1642.

——. *This is Lights Appearance in the Truth.* London, 1650.

——. *To Sions Lovers, Being a Golden Egge, to avoide Infection.* London, 1644.

Kent, Elizabeth Grey, Countess of. *A Choice Manual of Rare and Select Secrets in Physick and Chyrurgery.* London, 1653.

Lanyer, Aemilia, *The Poems of Aemilia Lanyer: Salve Deus Rex Judaeorum.* Ed. Susanne Woods. New York: Oxford University Press, 1993.

Leigh, Dorothy. *The Mother's Blessing.* London. Facsimile in Travitsky, *Mother's Advice Books.*

Munda, Constantia. *The Worming of a mad Dogge.* London, 1617. Facsimile in O'Malley, *Defenses of Women.*

Osborne, Dorothy. *Dorothy Osborne: Letters to Sir William Temple, 1652–54*. Ed. Kenneth Parker. Aldershot: Ashgate, 2002.

Palmer, Julia. *The 'Centuries' of Julia Palmer*. Ed. Victoria Burke and Elizabeth Clarke. Nottingham: Nottingham Trent University, 2001.

Philiatros [Talbot, Alethea]. *Natura Exenterata*. London, 1655.

Philips, Katherine. *The Collected Works of Katherine Philips*. 3 vols. Ed. Patrick Thomas. Stump Cross: Stump Cross Books, 1990–93.

Polwhele, Elizabeth. *The Faythfull Virgins*. Bodleian Library MS. Rawl. Poet. 195.

———. *The Frolick's: or The Lawyer Cheated*. Ed. Judith Milhous and Robert Hume. Ithaca: Cornell University Press, 1977.

———. *The Frolick's: or, the Lawyer Cheated an New Comedey, the first Coppy written by Mrs. E.P.* Cornell University Library Rare Manuscript Collection, Kroch Library 4600Bd. MS/43 MRC.

Poole, Elizabeth. *An Alarum of War, given to the Army, and to their High Court of Justice (so called)*. London, 1649. Smith, Suzuki, Wiseman, *Women's Political Writings*. II: 53–65.

———. *An(other) Alarum of War*. London, 1649.

———. *A Vision Wherein is Manifested the Disease and Cure of the Kingdome*. London, 1648. Smith, Suzuki, Wiseman, *Women's Political Writings*. II:47–52.

Primrose, Diana. *A Chaine of Pearle, Or a Memoriall of the peerles Graces, and Heroick Vertues of Queene Elizabeth of Glorious Memory*. London, 1630.

Pulter, Hester. 'Poems Breathed forth By the Nobel Hadassas'. Selections in Millman and Wright, *Early Modern Women's Manuscript Poetry*. 110–27.

Richardson, Elizabeth. *A Ladies Legacie to her Daughters*. London: Thomas Harper, 1645.

Sharp, Jane. *The Midwives Book Or the Whole Art of Midwifry Discovered*. Ed. Elaine Hobby. New York: Oxford University Press, 1999.

Southwell, Anne. *The Southwell-Sibthorpe Commonplace Book: Folger Ms. V.B. 198*. Ed. Jean Klene. Medieval and Renaissance Texts and Studies, 1997.

Sowernam, Ester. *Ester hath hang'd Haman*. London, 1617. Facsimile in O'Malley, *Defenses of Women*.

Speght, Rachel. *The Polemics and Poems of Rachel Speght*. Ed. Barbara Kiefer Lewalski. New York: Oxford University Press, 1996.

Stuart, Arbella. *The Letters of Lady Arbella Stuart*. Ed. Sara Jayne Steen. New York: Oxford University Press, 1994.

Trapnel, Anna. *Anna Trapnel's Report and Plea*. London, 1654.

———. *The Cry of a Stone*. Ed. Hilary Hinds. Medieval Texts and Studies, 2000.

———. *A Legacy for Saints*. London, 1654.

———. *Strange and wonderful newes from White-Hall*. London, 1654. Smith, Suzuki, Wiseman, *Women's Political Writings*. II: 281–85.

Venn, Anne. *A Wise Virgin's Lamp Burning*. London, 1658.

Weamys, Anna. *A Continuation of Philip Sidney's Arcadia*. Ed. Patrick Cullen. New York: Oxford University Press, 1994.

Wharton, Anne. *Love's Martyr, or Witt above Crowns*. BL Add MS 28, 693.

———. *The Surviving Works of Ann Wharton*. Ed. G. Greet and S. Hastings. Stump Cross: Stump Cross Books, 1997.

Whitrowe, Joan. *The Humble Address of the Widow Whitrowe to King William*. Smith, Suzuki, Wiseman, *Women's Political Writings*. III: 203–11.

Wroth, Mary. *The First Part of The Countess of Montgomery's Urania*. Ed. Josephine A. Roberts. Binghamton, NY: Center for Medieval and Early Renaissance Studies, 1995.

———. *The Second Part of the Countess of Montgomery's Urania*. Ed. Josephine A. Roberts, completed by Suzanne Gossett and Janel Mueller. Tempe, AZ: Renaissance English Text Society, 1999.

———. *Loves Victory*. Cerasano and Wynne Davies, *Renaissance Drama by Women*. 90–126.

———. *The Poems of Lady Mary Wroth*. Ed. Josephine A. Roberts. Baton Rouge: Louisiana State University Press, 1983.

Anthologies

Andrea, Bernadette, ed. *English Women Staging Islam, 1696–1707: The Plays of Delarivier Manley and Mary Pix*. Center for Reformation and Renaissance Studies/University of Toronto Press, 2011 (forthcoming).

Aughterson, Kate, ed. *Renaissance Woman: A Sourcebook. Constructions of Femininity in England*. London: Routledge, 1995.

Baines, Barbara J., ed. *Three Pamphlets on the Jacobean Antifeminist Controversy*. Delmar, NY: Scholars' Facsimiles & Reprints, 1978.

Cerasano, S. P. and Marion Wynne-Davies, eds. *Renaissance Drama by Women: Texts and Documents*. London: Routledge, 1996.

Clarke, Danielle, ed. *Renaissance Women Poets: Isabella Whitney, Mary Sidney, and Aemilia Lanyer*. Harmondsworth: Penguin, 2000.

Cody, Lisa Forman, ed. *Writings on Medicine*. Aldershot: Ashgate, 2002.

Fitzmaurice, James, Josephine A. Roberts, Carol L. Barash, Eugene R. Cunnar, and Nancy A. Gutierrez, eds. *Major Women Writers of Seventeenth-Century England*. Ann Arbor: University of Michigan Press, 1997.

Garman, Mary, Judith Applegate, Margaret Benefiel, and Dortha Meredith, eds. *Hidden in Plain Sight: Quaker Women's Writings, 1650–1700*. Wallingford, Penn: Pendle Hill, 1996.

Graham, Elspeth, Hilary Hinds, Elaine Hobby, and Helen Wilcox, eds. *Her Own Life: Autobiographical Writings by Seventeenth-century Englishwomen*. London: Routledge, 1989.

Greer, Germaine, Susan Hastings, Jeslyn Medoff, and Melinda Sansone, eds. *Kissing the Rod: An Anthology of Seventeenth-Century Women's Verse*. New York: Farrar, Straus & Giroux, 1988.

Henderson, Katherine Usher and Barbara F. McManus, eds. *Half Humankind: Contexts and Texts of the Controversy about Women in England, 1540–1640*. Urbana: University of Illinois Press, 1985.

Hodgson-Wright, Stephanie, ed. *Women's Writing of the Early Modern Period, 1588–1688: An Anthology*. New York: Columbia University Press, 2002.

Hudson, Roger, ed. *Grand Quarrel: Women's Memoirs of the English Civil War*. Phoenix Mill: Sutton, 2000.

Mahl, Mary and Helen Koon, eds. *The Female Spectator: English Women Writers before 1800*. Bloomington: Indiana University Press, 1977.

Millman, Jill Seal and Gillian Wright, eds. *Early Modern Women's Manuscript Poetry*. Contributing eds. Victoria E. Burke, Elizabeth Clarke, Marie-Louise Coolahan, and Jonathan Gibson. Manchester: Manchester University Press, 2005.

O'Malley, Susan Gushee, ed. *Defenses of Women: Jane Anger, Rachel Speght, Esther Sowernam and Constantia Munda.* Aldershot: Ashgate, 1996.

Ostovich, Helen and Elizabeth Sauer, eds. *Reading Early Modern Women: An Anthology of Texts in Manuscript and Print, 1550–1700.* New York: Routledge, 2004.

Purkiss, Diane, ed. *Renaissance Women: The Plays of Elizabeth Cary, The Poems of Aemilia Lanyer.* London: Pickering, 1994.

Salzman, Paul, ed. *Early Modern Women's Writing: An Anthology, 1560–1700.* Oxford: Oxford University Press, 2000.

Shepherd, Simon, ed. *The Women's Sharp Revenge: Five Women's Pamphlets from the Renaissance.* London: Fourth Estate, 1985.

Smith, Hilda L., Mihoko Suzuki, and Susan Wiseman, eds. *Women's Political Writings, 1610–1715.* 4 vols. London: Pickering & Chatto, 2007.

Stevenson, Jane and Peter Davidson, eds. *Early Modern Women Poets: An Anthology.* New York: Oxford University Press, 2001.

Travitsky, Betty, ed. *Mother's Advice Books.* Aldershot: Ashgate, 2001.

——, ed. *The Paradise of Women: Writings by Englishwomen of the Renaissance.* New York: Columbia University Press, 1989.

Wynne-Davies, Marion. *Women Poets of the Renaissance.* London and New York: Routledge, 1999.

Secondary texts

Achinstein, Sharon. 'Women on Top in the Pamphlet Literature of the English Revolution'. *Women's Studies* 24 (1994): 130–61.

Alexander, Gavin. 'Constant Works: A Framework for Reading Mary Wroth'. *Sidney Newsletter and Journal* 14 (1996–97): 5–32.

Andrea, Bernadette. 'Islam, Women, and Western Responses: The Contemporary Relevance of Early Modern Investigations'. *Women's Studies* 38.3 (2009): 273–92.

——. 'Persia, Tartaria, and Pamphilia: Ideas of Asia in Mary Wroth's *Urania*, Part II'. *The English Renaissance, Orientalism, and the Idea of Asia.* Ed. Walter S. H. Lim and Debra Johanyak. New York: Palgrave Macmillan, 2010. 23–50.

——. *Women and Islam in Early Modern English Literature.* Cambridge: Cambridge University Press, 2007.

Andreadis, Harriette. *Sappho in Early Modern England: Same-Sex Literary Erotics, 1550–1714.* Chicago: University of Chicago Press, 2001.

Archer, Jayne. 'A "Perfect Circle": Alchemy in the Poetry of Hester Pulter'. *Literature Compass* 2.1 (2005): 1–14. <DOI: 10.1111/j.1741-4113.2005.00160.x>

Ballard, George. *Memoirs of Several ladies of Great Britain Who have been Celebrated for their Writings or Skill in the Learned Languages, Arts and Sciences.* Ed. Ruth Perry. Detroit: Wayne State University Press, 1985.

Ballaster, Rosalind. *Seductive Forms: Women's Amatory Fiction from 1684 to 1740.* Oxford: Clarendon Press, 1992.

Barash, Carol. *English Women's Poetry, 1649–1714: Politics, Community and Linguistic Authority.* Oxford: Oxford University Press, 1996.

Barroll, Leeds. 'Looking for Patrons'. Grossman, *Aemilia Lanyer.* 29–48.

Baston, Jane. 'History, Prophecy, and Interpretation: Mary Cary and Fifth Monarchism'. *Prose Studies* 21.3 (December 1988): 1–18.

Battigelli, Anna. *Margaret Cavendish and the Exiles of the Mind*. Lexington: University Press of Kentucky, 1998.

Beilin, Elaine. *Redeeming Eve: Women Writers of the English Renaissance*. Princeton: Princeton University Press, 1992.

Bell, Maureen. 'Elizabeth Calvert and the Confederates'. *Publishing History* 32 (1992): 5–49.

——. 'Hannah Allen and the Development of a Puritan Publishing Business, 1646–51'. *Publishing History* 26 (1989): 5–66.

——. '"Her usual practices": The Later Career of Elizabeth Calvert'. *Publishing History* 35 (1994): 5–64.

——. 'Mary Westwood, Quaker Publisher'. *Publishing History* 23 (1988): 5–66.

——. 'Women in the English Book Trade, 1557–1700'. *Leipziger Jahrbuch zur Buchgeschichte* 6 (1996): 13–45.

——. 'Women and the Opposition Press after the Restoration'. *Writing and Radicalism*. Ed. John Lucas. London: Longman, 1996. 39–60.

Bennett, Alexandra. '"Now let my language speake": The Authorship, Rewriting and Audience(s) of Jane Cavendish and Elizabeth Brackley'. *Early Modern Literary Studies* 11 (2005): 3.1–13.

Brant, Clare and Diane Purkiss, eds. *Women, Texts and Histories: 1575–1760*. London: Routledge, 1992.

Brayman Hackel, Heidi. *Reading Material in Early Modern England: Print, Gender, and Literacy*. Cambridge: Cambridge University Press, 2005.

Britland, Karen. *Drama at the Courts of Queen Henrietta Maria*. Cambridge: Cambridge University Press, 2006.

Broad, Jacqueline. *Liberty and the Right of Resistance: Women's Political Writings of the English Civil War Era*. Amsterdam: Springer Netherlands, 2007.

Brod, Manfred. 'Politics and Prophecy in Seventeenth-Century England: The Case of Elizabeth Poole'. *Albion* 31.3 (1999): 395–412.

Burke, Mary E., Jane Donawerth, Linda L. Dove, and Karen Nelson, eds. *Women, Writing, and the Reproduction of Culture in Tudor and Stuart Britain*. Syracuse: Syracuse University Press, 2000.

Burke, Victoria E. and Jonathan Gibson, eds. *Early Modern Women's Manuscript Writing: Selected Papers from the Trinity/Trent Colloquium*. Aldershot: Ashgate, 2004.

Callaghan, Dympna. 'Re-Reading Elizabeth Cary's *The Tragedie of Mariam, Faire Queene of Jewry*'. *Women, 'Race', and Writing in the Early Modern Period*. Ed. Margo Hendricks and Patricia Parker. London: Routledge, 1994. 163–77.

Camden, Carroll. *The Elizabethan Woman: A Panorama of English Womanhood, 1540–1640*. Houston: Elsevier Press, 1952.

Campbell, Julie and Anne Larsen, eds. *Early Modern Women and Transnational Communities of Letters*. Aldershot: Ashgate, 2009.

Carrell, Jennifer. 'A Pack of Lies in a Looking Glass: Lady Mary Wroth's *Urania* and the Magic Mirror of Romance'. *SEL* 34 (1994): 79–107.

Cerasano, S. P. and Marion Wynne-Davies, eds. *Readings in Renaissance Women's Drama: Criticism, History, and Performance*. London and New York: Routledge, 1998.

Chalmers, Hero. *Royalist Women Writers, 1650–1689*. Oxford: Clarendon Press, 2004.

Chan, Mary and Nancy E. Wright. 'Marriage, Identity, and the Pursuit of Property in Seventeenth-Century England: The Cases of Anne Clifford and

Elizabeth Wiseman'. Wright, Ferguson, Buck, *Women, Property, and the Letters of the Law*. 162–82.

Chedgzoy, Kate. 'Female Prophecy in the Seventeenth Century: The Instance of Anna Trapnel'. *Writing in the English Renaissance*. Ed. William Zunder and Suzanne Trill. London: Longman, 1996. 238–54.

——. *Women's Writing in the British Atlantic World: Memory, Place and History, 1550–1700*. Cambridge: Cambridge University Press, 2007.

Clarke, Danielle. *The Politics of Early Modern Women's Writing*. Harlow: Longman, 2001.

Clarke, Elizabeth, director. 'Constructing Elizabeth Isham 1608–1654'. University of Warwick. http://www2.warwick.ac.uk/fac/arts/ren/projects/isham/

Clucas, Stephen. 'The Duchess and the Viscountess: Negotiations between Mechanism and Vitalism in the Natural Philosophies of Margaret Cavendish and Anne Conway'. *In-between: Essays and Studies in Literary Criticism* 9.1–2 (2000): 125–36.

——, ed. *Princely Brave Woman: Essays on Margaret Cavendish, Duchess of Newcastle*. Aldershot: Ashgate, 2003.

Coolahan, Marie-Louise. '"We live by chance, and slip into Events": Occasionality and the Manuscript Verse of Katherine Philips'. *Eighteenth-Century Ireland* 18 (2003): 9–23.

Cope, Esther S. *Handmaid of the Holy Spirit: Dame Eleanor Davies, Never Soe Mad a Ladie*. Ann Arbor: University of Michigan Press, 1993.

Corporaal, Marguerite. 'Wicked Words and Vicious Voices: The Reconstruction of Tragic Subjectivity by Renaissance and Early Restoration Women Dramatists'. PhD Thesis. University of Groningen, 2003.

Cotton, Nancy. *Women Playwrights in England*. Lewisburg: Bucknell University Press, 1980.

Crawford, Patricia. 'Women's Published Writings, 1600–1700'. Prior, *Women in English Society*. 211–74.

——. *Women and Religion in England, 1500–1720*. London: Routledge, 1993.

Cuder-Dominguez, Pilar. 'The Islamization of Spain in William Rowley and Mary Pix: The Politics of Nation and Gender'. *Comparative Drama* 36 (2002): 321–36.

Dailey, Barbara Ritter. 'The Visitation of Sarah Wight: Holy Carnival and the Revolution of the Saints in Civil War London'. *Church History* 55.4 (December 1986): 438–55.

Davies, Stevie. *Unbridled Spirits: Women of the English Revolution, 1640–1660*. London: Women's Press, 1998.

Davis, Lloyd. 'Women's Wills in Early Modern England'. Wright, Ferguson, Buck, *Women, Property, and the Letters of the Law*. 219–36.

Davis, Natalie Zemon. 'Gender and Genre: Women as Historical Writers, 1400–1820'. *Beyond Their Sex: Learned Women of the European Past*. Ed. Patricia H. Labalme. New York: New York University Press, 1980. 153–82.

Daybell, James, ed. *Early Modern Women's Letter Writing, 1450–1700*. New York: Palgrave Macmillan, 2001.

——, ed. *Women and Politics in Early Modern England, 1450–1700*. Aldershot: Ashgate, 2004.

Diamond, Elin. 'Gestus and Signature in Aphra Behn's *The Rover*'. Todd, *Aphra Behn*. 49–56.

Dolan, Frances. *Whores of Babylon: Catholicism, Gender and Seventeenth-Century Print Culture*. Ithaca: Cornell University Press, 1999.

Donovan, Josephine. *Women and the Rise of the Novel, 1405–1726*. New York: St. Martin's Press, 1999.

Dowd, Michelle M. and Julie A. Eckerle, eds. *Genre and Women's Life Writing in Early Modern England*. Aldershot: Ashgate, 2007.

Dubrow, Heather. '"And Thus Leave Off": Reevaluating Mary Wroth's Folger Manuscript V.a.104'. *Tulsa Studies in Women's Literature* 22 (2003): 273–91.

Duffy, Maureen. *The Passionate Shepherdess: Aphra Behn, 1640–1689*. London: Jonathan Cape, 1977.

Eales, Jacqueline. 'Patriarchy, Puritanism and Politics: The Letters of Lady Brilliana Harley (1598–1643)'. Daybell, *Women and Politics*. 143–58.

Eardley, Alice. 'Recreating the Canon: Women Writers and Anthologies of Early Modern Verse'. *Still Kissing the Rod?* Ed. Elizabeth Clarke and Lynn Robson. Special issue of *Women's Writing* 14 (2007): 270–89.

Erickson, Amy Louise. *Women & Property in Early Modern England*. London: Routledge, 1993.

Ezell, Margaret J. M. 'Ann Halkett's Morning Devotions: Posthumous Publication and the Culture of Writing in Late Seventeenth-Century Britain'. *Print, Manuscript, and Performance: The Changing Relations of the Media in Early Modern England*. Ed. Arthur F. Marotti and Michael D. Bristol. Columbus: Ohio State University Press, 2000. 215–31.

——. 'Domestic Papers: Manuscript Culture and Early Modern Women's Life Writing'. *Genre and Women's Life Writing in Early Modern England*. Ed. Julie A. Eckerle and Michelle M. Dowd. Aldershot: Ashgate, 2007. 33–48.

——. 'The Laughing Tortoise: Speculations on Manuscript Sources and Women's Book History'. *English Literary Renaissance* 38.2 (2008): 331–55.

——. 'Never Boring, or Imagine My Surprise: Interregnum Women and the Culture of Reading'. *Imagining Selves: Essays in Honor of Patricia Meyer Spacks*. Ed. Rivka Swenson and Elise Lauterbach. Newark: University of Delaware Press, 2009. 155–69.

——. *The Patriarch's Wife: Literary Evidence and the History of the Family*. Chapel Hill: University of North Carolina Press, 1987.

——. *Social Authorship and the Advent of Print*. Baltimore: Johns Hopkins University Press, 1999.

——. '"To be your daughter in your pen": The Social Function of Literature in the Writings of Elizabeth Brackley and Lady Jane Cavendish'. *Huntington Library Quarterly* (1988): 281–96.

——. 'Women and Writing'. Pacheco, *Companion*. 77–94.

——. *Writing Women's Literary History*. Baltimore: Johns Hopkins University Press, 1993.

Fara, Patricia. *Pandora's Breeches: Women, Science, and Power in the Enlightenment*. London: Pimlico, 2004.

Ferguson, Margaret W. *Dido's Daughters: Literacy, Gender, and Empire in Early Modern England and France*. Chicago: University of Chicago Press, 2003.

—— and Mihoko Suzuki. 'Literacy, Literature, and Social Status'. *Palgrave Advances in Early Modern Women's Writing*. Ed. Suzanne Trill. New York: Palgrave Macmillan, 2011 (forthcoming).

Feroli, Teresa. *Political Speaking Justified: Women Prophets and the English Revolution.* Delaware: University of Delaware Press, 2006.

Findlay, Alison, Stephanie Hodgson-Wright with Gweno Williams. '"The Play is Ready to be Acted": Women and Dramatic Production 1550–1670'. *Women's Writing* 6.1 (1999): 129–48.

——. *Women and Dramatic Production, 1550–1700.* Harlow: Longman, 2000.

——. *Women Dramatists, 1550–1670: Plays in Performance.* Lancaster: Women and Dramatic Production with Lancaster University Television, 1999.

Foster, Donald. 'Resurrecting the Author: Elizabeth Tanfield Cary'. *Privileging Gender in Early Modern England.* Ed. Jean R. Brink. Special issue of *Sixteenth Century Essays & Studies* 23 (1993): 141–73.

Frye, Susan and Karen Robertson, eds. *Maids and Mistresses, Cousins and Queens: Women's Alliances in Early Modern England.* New York: Oxford University Press, 1998.

Gallagher, Catherine. 'Embracing the Absolute: The Politics of the Female Subject in Seventeenth Century England'. *Genders* 1 (March 1988): 24–39.

Gentles, Ian. 'Chidley, Katherine (fl. 1616–1653), religious controversialist and Leveller'. *Oxford Dictionary of National Biography.* Oxford: Oxford University Press, 2004–07.

——. 'London Levellers in the English Revolution: The Chidleys and Their Circle'. *Journal of Ecclesiastical History* 29.3 (1978): 281–309.

George, Margaret. *Women in the First Capitalist Society: Experiences in Seventeenth-Century England.* Urbana: University of Illinois Press, 1988.

Gill, Catie. *Women in the Seventeenth-Century Quaker Community: A Literary Study of Political Identities, 1650–1700.* Aldershot: Ashgate, 2005.

Gillespie, Katharine. *Domesticity and Dissent in the Seventeenth Century: English Women's Writing and the Public Sphere.* Cambridge: Cambridge University Press, 2004.

——. 'A Hammer in Her Hand: The Separation of Church from State and the Early Feminist Writings of Katherine Chidley'. *Tulsa Studies in Women's Literature* 17.2 (1998): 213–33.

Goldberg, Jonathan. *Desiring Women Writing.* Stanford: Stanford University Press, 1997.

Goreau Angeline. *Reconstructing Aphra: A Social Biography of Aphra Behn.* New York: Dial Press, 1980.

G[osse], E[dmund]. 'Behn, Afra, Aphra, Aphara, or Ayfara 1640–1689'. *DNB* CD Rom. Oxford University Press, 1995.

Grant, Douglas. *Margaret the First.* Toronto: University of Toronto Press, 1957.

Gray, Catharine. *Women Writers and Public Debate in 17th-Century Britain.* New York: Palgrave Macmillan, 2007.

Grossman, Marshall, ed. *Aemilia Lanyer: Gender, Genre, and the Canon.* Lexington: University Press of Kentucky, 1998.

Grundy, Isobel and Susan Wiseman, eds. *Women, Writing, History, 1640–1740.* London: B. T. Batsford; Athens, GA: University of Georgia Press, 1992.

Guibbory, Achsah. 'The Gospel According to Aemilia: Women and the Sacred'. Grossman, *Aemilia Lanyer.* 191–211.

Hackett, Helen. *Women and Romance Fiction in the English Renaissance.* Cambridge: Cambridge University Press, 2000.

Hageman, Elizabeth H. 'Treacherous Accidents and the Abominable Printing of Katherine Philips's 1664 Poems'. *New Ways of Looking at Old Texts*. Ed. W. Speed Hill. Tempe, AZ: Renaissance English Text Society, 2004. 85–95.

Hall, Kim F. *Things of Darkness: Economies of Race and Gender in Early Modern England*. Ithaca: Cornell University Press, 1995.

Hallett, Nicky. 'Anne Clifford as Orlando: Virginia Woolf's Feminist Historiology and Women's Biography'. *Women's History Review* 4 (1995): 505–24.

Hammons, Pamela S. *Gender, Sexuality, and Material Objects in English Renaissance Verse*. Aldershot: Ashgate, 2010.

——. *Poetic Resistance: English Women Writers and the Early Modern Lyric*. Aldershot: Ashgate, 2002.

——. 'Polluted Palaces: Gender, Sexuality and Property in Lucy Hutchinson's "Elegies"'. *Women's Writing* 13 (2006): 392–415.

Hannay, Margaret P. *Mary Sidney, Lady Wroth*. Aldershot: Ashgate, 2010.

Harris, Frances. 'The Letterbooks of Mary Evelyn'. *English Manuscript Studies 1100–1700* 7 (1998): 202–15.

Hendricks, Margo. 'Alliance and Exile: Aphra Behn's Racial Identity'. Frye and Robertson, *Maids and Mistresses*. 259–73.

—— and Patricia Parker, eds. *Women, 'Race', and Writing in the Early Modern Period*. London: Routledge, 1994.

Higgins, Patricia, 'The Reactions of Women, with Special Reference to Women Petitioners'. *Politics, Religion and the English Civil War*. Ed. Brian Manning. London: Edward Arnold, 1973. 177–222.

Hinds, Hilary. *God's Englishwomen: Seventeenth-Century Radical Sectarian Writing and Feminist Criticism*. Manchester: Manchester University Press, 1996.

Hobby, Elaine. '"Come to Live a Preaching Life": Female Community in Seventeenth-Century Radical Sects'. *Female Communities 1600–1800*. Ed. Rebecca D'Monté and Nicole Pohl. London: Macmillan, 2000. 76–92.

——. *Virtue of Necessity: English Women's Writing, 1649–1688*. Ann Arbor: University of Michigan Press, 1988.

Holstun, James. *Ehud's Dagger: Class Struggle in the English Revolution*. London: Verso, 2000.

——, ed. *Pamphlet Wars: Prose in the English Revolution*. London: Frank Cass, 1992.

Howe, Elizabeth. *The First English Actresses: Women and Drama, 1660–1700*. Cambridge: Cambridge University Press, 1992.

Hughes, Anne. 'Gender and Politics in Leveller Literature'. *Political Culture and Cultural Politics in Early Modern England*. Ed. Susan D. Amussen and Mark A. Kishlansky. Manchester: Manchester University Press, 1995. 162–88.

——. *Women, Men and Politics in the English Civil War*. University of Keele, Centre for Local History, 1999.

Hughes, Derek. 'Race, Gender, and Scholarly Practice: Aphra Behn's *Oroonoko*'. *Essays in Criticism* 52.1 (January 2002): 1–22.

Hunter, Lynette and Sarah Hutton, eds. *Women, Science and Medicine, 1500–1700*. Phoenix Mill: Sutton, 1997.

Hutton, Sarah. *Anne Conway: A Woman Philosopher*. Cambridge: Cambridge University Press, 2004.

Jankowski, Theodora A. *Pure Resistance: Queer Virginity in Early Modern English Drama*. Philadelphia: University of Pennsylvania Press, 2000.

——. *Women in Power in the Early Modern Drama*. Urbana: University of Illinois Press, 1992.

Jones, Jane. 'New Light on the Background and Early Life of Aphra Behn'. *Aphra Behn Studies*. Ed. Janet Todd. Cambridge: Cambridge University Press, 1996. 310–20.

Jordan, Constance. *Renaissance Feminism: Literary Texts and Political Models*. Ithaca: Cornell University Press, 1990.

Jowitt, Claire. 'Imperial Dreams? Margaret Cavendish and the Cult of Elizabeth'. *Women's Writing* 40.3 (1997): 383–99.

Justice, George L. and Nathan Tinker, eds. *Women's Writing and the Circulation of Ideas: Manuscript Publication in England, 1550–1800*. Cambridge: Cambridge University Press, 2002.

Kahn, Victoria. *Wayward Contracts: The Crisis of Political Obligation in England, 1640–1674*. Princeton: Princeton University Press, 2004.

Kegl, Rosemary. '"The world I have made": Margaret Cavendish, Feminism, and the *Blazing-World*'. *Feminist Readings of Early Modern Culture*. Ed. Valerie Traub, M. Lindsay Kaplan, and Dympna Callaghan. Cambridge: Cambridge University Press, 1996. 119–41.

Kinney, Clare R. *Ashgate Critical Essays on Women Writers in English, 1550–1700*. Vol. 4. *Mary Wroth*. Aldershot: Ashgate, 2009.

——. '"Beleeve this butt a fiction": Female Authorship, Narrative Undoing and the Limits of Romance in *The Second Part of the Countess of Montgomery's Urania*'. *Spenser Studies* 17 (2003): 239–50.

Klene, Jean. '"Monument of an Endless affection": Folger MS V.b.198 and Lady Anne Southwell'. *English Manuscript Studies, 1100–1700* 9 (2000): 165–86.

Knoppers, Laura. *The Cambridge Companion to Early Modern Women's Writing*. Cambridge: Cambridge University Press, 2009.

——. 'Opening the Queen's Closet: Henrietta Maria, Elizabeth Cromwell, and the Politics of Cookery'. *Renaissance Quarterly* 60 (2007): 464–99.

Kreis-Schinck, Annette. *Women, Writing, and Theater in the Early Modern Period*. Madison, WI: Fairleigh Dickinson University Press, 2001.

Krontiris, Tina. *Oppositional Voices: Women as Writers and Translators of Literature in the English Renaissance*. London: Routledge, 1992.

——. 'Style and Gender in Elizabeth Cary's *Edward II*'. *The Renaissance Englishwoman in Print: Counterbalancing the Canon*. Ed. Anne M. Haselkorn and Betty S. Travitsky. Amherst: University of Massachusetts Press, 1990. 137–53.

Kunin, Aaron. 'From the Desk of Anne Clifford'. *ELH* 71 (2004): 587–608.

Kunze, Bonnelyn Young. *Margaret Fell and the Rise of Quakerism*. Stanford: Stanford University Press, 1994.

Lamb, Mary Ellen. *Gender and Authorship in the Sidney Circle*. Madison: University of Wisconsin Press, 1990.

——. 'Merging the Secular and the Spiritual in Lady Anne Halkett's Memoirs'. Dowd and Eckerle, *Genre and Women's Life Writing*. 81–96.

Laroche, Rebecca. *Medical Authority and Englishwomen's Herbal Texts, 1550–1650*. Aldershot: Ashgate, 2009.

Laurence, Anne. 'A Priesthood of She-believers: Women and Congregations in Mid-seventeenth-century England'. *Studies in Church History* 27 (1990): 345–63.

——. *Women in England, 1500–1760: A Social History*. New York: St. Martin's Press, 1994.

Lewalski, Barbara Keifer. *Writing Women in Jacobean England*. Cambridge, MA: Harvard University Press, 1993.

Loewenstein, David. 'Scriptural Exegesis, Female Prophecy, and Radical Politics in Mary Cary'. *SEL* 46.1 (Winter 2006): 133–53.

Longfellow, Erica. 'Lady Anne Southwell's Indictment of Adam'. Burke and Gibson, *Early Modern Women's Manuscript Writing*. 111–33.

———. *Women and Religious Writing in Early Modern England*. Cambridge: Cambridge University Press, 2004.

Looser, Devoney. *British Women Writers and the Writing of History, 1620–1820*. Baltimore: Johns Hopkins University Press, 2000.

Ludlow, Dorothy. '"Arise and Be Doing": English Preaching-Women, 1640–1660'. Ph.D. Dissertation. Indiana University, 1978.

———. 'Shaking Patriarchy's Foundations: Sectarian Women in England, 1641–1700'. *Triumph Over Silence: Women in Protestant History*. Ed. Richard L. Greaves. Westport: Greenwood Press, 1985. 93–123.

MacDonald, Joyce Green. *Women and Race in Early Modern Texts*. Cambridge: Cambridge University Press, 2002.

Mack, Phyllis. *Visionary Women: Ecstatic Prophecy in Seventeenth-Century England*. Berkeley: University of California Press, 1992.

Malcolmson, Cristina. '"The Explication of Whiteness and Blackness": Skin Color and the Physics of Color in the Works of Robert Boyle and Margaret Cavendish'. *Fault Lines and Controversies in the Study of Seventeenth-Century Literature*. Ed. Claude J. Summers and Ted-Larry Pebworth. Columbia: University of Missouri Press, 2002. 187–203.

——— and Mihoko Suzuki, eds. *Debating Gender in Early Modern England, 1500–1700*. New York: Palgrave Macmillan, 2002.

Mambretti, Catherine Cole. 'Orinda on the Restoration Stage'. *Comparative Literature* 37 (1985): 233–51.

Markley, Robert. 'Behn and the Unstable Conditions of Social Comedy'. *The Cambridge Companion to Aphra Behn*. Ed. Derek Hughes and Janet Todd. Cambridge: Cambridge University Press, 2005. 98–117.

Matchinske, Megan. 'Holy Hatred: Formations of the Gendered Subject in English Apocalyptic Writing, 1625–1651'. *ELH* 60 (1993): 349–77.

———. *Women Writing History in Early Modern England*. Cambridge: Cambridge University Press, 2009.

———. *Writing, Gender and State in Early Modern England: Identity Formation and the Female Subject*. Cambridge: Cambridge University Press, 1998.

McEntee, Ann Marie. 'The [Un]Civill-Sisterhood of Oranges and Lemons: Female Petitioners and Demonstrators, 1642–53'. Holstun, *Pamphlet Wars*. 92–111.

Mendelson, Sara, ed. *Ashgate Critical Essays on Women Writers in English, 1550–1700*. Vol. 7. *Margaret Cavendish*. Aldershot: Ashgate, 2009.

———. *The Mental World of Stuart Women: Three Studies*. Amherst: University of Massachusetts Press, 1987.

———. 'Stuart Women's Diaries and Occasional Memoirs'. Prior, *Women in English Society*. 136–57.

——— and Patricia Crawford. *Women in Early Modern England*. Oxford: Clarendon Press, 1998.

Merchant, Carloline. *The Death of Nature: Women, Ecology, and the Scientific Revolution*. San Francisco: Harper & Row, 1980.

Merrens, Rebecca. 'A Nature of "Infinite Sense and Reason": Margaret Cavendish's Natural Philosophy and the "Noise" of a Feminized Nature'. *Women's Studies* 25 (1996): 421–38.

Miller, Naomi J. 'Hens should be served first: Prioritizing Maternal Production in the Early Modern Pamphlet Debate'. Malcolmson and Suzuki, *Debating Gender*. 161–84.

Miller, Shannon. *Engendering the Fall: John Milton and Seventeenth-Century Women Writers*. Philadelphia: University of Pennsylvania Press, 2008.

Milling, Jane. '"In the Female Coasts of Fame": Women's Dramatic Writing on the Public Stage, 1669–71'. *Women's Writing* 7.2 (2000): 270–77.

Mulvihill, Maureen E. 'A Feminist Link in the Old Boys' Network: The Cosseting of Katherine Philips'. *Curtain Calls: British and American Women and Theater, 1660–1820*. Ed. Mary Anne Schofield and Cecilia Macheski. Athens: Ohio University Press, 1991. 71–104.

Myers, Anne M. 'Construction Sites: The Architecture of Anne Clifford's Diaries'. *ELH* 73 (2006): 581–600.

Nevitt, Marcus. *Women and Pamphlet Culture in Revolutionary England, 1640–1660*. Aldershot: Ashgate, 2006.

Norbrook, David. 'Hutchinson, Lucy (1620–1681)'. *Oxford Dictionary of National Biography*. Oxford University Press, September 2004; online edn, January 2008.

———. 'Lucy Hutchinson versus Edmund Waller: An Unpublished Reply to Waller's *Panygyrick to my Lord Protector*'. *Seventeenth Century* 11.1 (1996): 61–86.

———. 'Margaret Cavendish and Lucy Hutchinson: Identity, Ideology and Politics'. *In-between: Essays and Studies in Literary Criticism* 9.1–2 (2000): 179–203.

———. 'Women, the Republic of Letters, and the Public Sphere in the Mid-Seventeenth Century'. *Criticism* 46.2 (2004): 223–40.

O'Day, Rosemary. 'Tudor and Stuart Women: Their Lives through their Letters'. Daybell, *Women and Politics*. 127–42.

Owen, Susan J. '"Suspect my loyalty when I lose my virtue": Sexual Politics and Party in Aphra Behn's Plays of the Exclusion Crisis'. Todd, *Aphra Behn*. 57–72.

Pacheco, Anita, ed. *A Companion to Early Modern Women's Writing*. Oxford: Blackwell, 2002.

Patton, Brian. 'Revolution, Regicide, and Divorce: Elizabeth Poole's Advice to the Army'. *Place and Displacement in the Renaissance*. Ed. Alvin Vos. Binghamton: Medieval & Renaissance Texts & Studies, 1995. 133–45.

Pearson, Jacqueline. *The Prostituted Muse: Images of Women and Women Dramatists, 1642–1737*. New York: St. Martin's Press, 1988.

Perry, Curtis. '"Royal Fever" and "The Giddy Commons": Cary's *History of the Life, Reign, and Death of Edward II* and the Buckingham Phenomenon'. Wolfe, *Literary Career*. 71–88.

Phillippy, Patricia. *Painting Women: Cosmetics, Canvases, and Early Modern Culture*. Baltimore: Johns Hopkins University Press, 2005.

Phillips, Patricia. *The Scientific Lady: A Social History of Women's Scientific Interests, 1520–1918*. New York, St. Martin's Press, 1990.

Plowden, Alison. *Women All on Fire: The Women of the English Civil War*. Stroud: Sutton, 2004.

Prescott, Sarah. 'Archipelagic Orinda? Katherine Philips and the Writing of Welsh Women's Literary History'. *Literature Compass* 6 (2009): 1–10.

—— and David Shuttleton. *Women and Poetry, 1660–1750*. New York: Palgrave Macmillan, 2003.

Prior, Mary, ed. *Women in English Society, 1500–1800*. New York: Methuen, 1985.

Purkiss, Diane. 'Material Girls: The Seventeenth-Century Gender Debate'. Brant and Purkiss, *Women, Texts and Histories*. 69–101.

Quilligan, Maureen. 'The Constant Subject: Instability and Female Authority in Wroth's *Urania* Poems'. *Soliciting Interpretation: Literary Theory and Seventeenth-Century English Poetry*. Ed. Elizabeth D. Harvey and Katharine Eisaman Maus. Chicago: University of Chicago Press, 1990. 307–35.

——. *Incest and Agency in Elizabeth's England*. Philadelphia: University of Pennsylvania Press, 2005.

Raber, Karen, ed. *Ashgate Critical Essays on Women Writers in English, 1550–1700*. Vol. 6. *Elizabeth Cary*. Aldershot: Ashgate, 2009.

——. *Dramatic Difference: Gender, Class, and Genre in the Early Modern Closet Drama*. Newark: University of Delaware Press, 2001.

——. 'Warrior Women in the Plays of Cavendish and Killigrew'. *SEL* 40.3 (Summer 2000): 413–33.

Reeves, Margaret. 'History, Fiction, and Political Identity: Heroic Rebellion in Aphra Behn's *Love-Letters Between a Nobleman and His Sister* and *Oroonoko*'. *1650–1850: Ideas, Æsthetics, and Inquiries in the Early Modern Era* 8 (2003): 269–94.

Rich, Adrienne. 'Foreword'. *The Works of Anne Bradstreet*. Ed. Jeannine Hensley. Cambridge, MA: Harvard University Press, 1967. ix–xxii.

Richetti, John J. '*Love Letters Between a Nobleman and His Sister*: Aphra Behn and Amatory Fiction'. *Augustan Subjects: Essays in Honour of Martin C. Battestin*. Ed. Albert J. Rivero. Newark: University of Delaware Press, 1997. 13–28.

Rogers, John. *The Matter of Revolution: Science, Poetry, and Politics in the Age of Milton*. Ithaca: Cornell University Press, 1996.

Romack, Katherine and James Fitzmaurice, eds. *Cavendish and Shakespeare: Interconnections*. Aldershot: Ashgate: 2006.

Rose, Mary Beth. *Gender and Heroism in Early Modern Literature*. Chicago: University of Chicago Press, 2002.

Ross, Deborah. *The Excellence of Falsehood: Romance, Realism, and Women's Contribution to the Novel*. Lexington: University Press of Kentucky, 1991.

Ross, Sarah. 'Tears, Bezoars and Blazing Comets: Gender and Politics in Hester Pulter's Civil War Lyrics'. *Literature Compass* 2.1 (2005): 1–14. <DOI: 10.1111/j.1741-4113.2005.00161.x>

Rubik, Margaret. *Early Women Dramatists, 1550–1800*. London: St. Martin's Press, 1998.

Salzman, Paul. 'Early Modern (Aristocratic) Women and Textual Property'. Wright, Ferguson, Buck, *Women, Property*. 162–82.

——. *Reading Early Modern Women's Writing*. Oxford: Oxford University Press, 2006.

Sarasohn, Lisa. 'A Science Turned Upside Down: Feminism and the Natural Philosophy of Margaret Cavendish'. *Huntington Library Quarterly* 47.4 (Autumn 1984): 289–307.

Schiebinger, Londa. *The Mind Has No Sex? Women in the Origins of Modern Science*. Cambridge, MA: Harvard University Press, 1989.

——. *Nature's Body: Gender in the Making of Modern Science*. Boston: Beacon Press, 1993.

Schleiner, Louise. 'Lady Falkland's Reentry into Writing: Anglo-Catholic Consensual Discourse and her *Edward II* as Historical Fiction'. *The Witness of Times: Manifestations of Ideology in Seventeenth-Century England*. Ed. Katherine Z. Keller and Gerald J. Schiffhorst. Pittsburgh: Duquesne University Press, 1993. 201–17.

Schnell, Lisa. 'Breaking "the rule of *Cortezia*": Aemilia Lanyer's Dedications to *Salve Deus Rex Judaeorum*'. *Journal of Medieval and Renaissance Studies* 27.1 (1997): 77–101.

——. '"So Great a Diffrence is There in Degree": Aemilia Lanyer and the Aims of Feminist Criticism'. *Modern Language Quarterly* 57.1 (1996): 23–35.

Schwoerer, Lois G. *Lady Rachel Russell, 'One of the Best of Women'*. Baltimore: Johns Hopkins University Press, 1988.

——. 'Women and the Glorious Revolution'. *Albion* 18.2 (Summer 1986): 195–218.

Scott-Douglass, Amy. 'Enlarging Margaret: Cavendish, Shakespeare, and French Women Warriors and Writers'. Fitzmaurice and Romack, *Cavendish and Shakespeare*. 149–74.

Seelig, Sharon Cadman. *Autobiography and Gender in Early Modern Literature: Reading Women's Lives, 1600–1680*. Cambridge: Cambridge University Press, 2006.

Shell, Alison. 'Popish Plots: *The Feign'd Curtizans* in Context'. Todd, *Aphra Behn*. 30–49.

Shifflet, Andrew. '"How many virtues must I hate": Katherine Philips and the Politics of Clemency'. *Studies in Philology* 94.1 (Winter 1997): 103–35.

Smith, Barbara and Ursula Appelt, eds. *Write or be Written: Early Modern Women Poets and Cultural Constraints*. Aldershot: Ashgate, 2001.

Smith, Hilda L. *All Men and Both Sexes: Gender, Politics, and the False Universal in England, 1640–1832*. University Park: Pennsylvania State University Press, 2002.

——. *Reason's Disciples: Seventeenth-Century English Feminists*. Urbana: University of Illinois Press, 1976.

——. 'Women Intellectuals and Intellectual History: Their Paradigmatic Separation'. *Women's History Review* 16.3 (July 2007): 353–68.

—— ed. *Women Writers and the Early Modern British Political Tradition*. Cambridge: Cambridge University Press, 1998.

—— and Susan Cardinale, eds. *Women and the Literature of the Seventeenth Century: An Annotated Bibliography based on Wing's Short-title Catalogue*. New York: Greenwood, 1990.

Smith, Nigel. 'The Rod and the Canon'. *Women's Writing* 14.2 (2007): 232–45.

Sondergard, Sidney L. *Sharpening Her Pen: Strategies of Rhetorical Violence by Early Modern English Women Writers*. Selinsgrove, PA: Susquehanna University Press, 2002.

Spencer, Jane. *Aphra Behn's Afterlife*. Oxford: Oxford University Press, 2000.

——. *The Rise of the Woman Novelist: From Aphra Behn to Jane Austen*. Oxford: Basil Blackwell, 1986.

Staves, Susan. *A Literary History of Women's Writing in Britain, 1660–1789*. Cambridge: Cambridge University Press, 2006.

Stephens, Isaac. 'The Courtship and Singlehood of Elizabeth Isham, 1630–1634'. *Historical Journal* 51 (2008): 1–25.

Stevenson, Jane. 'Still Kissing the Rod? Whither Next?' *Women's Writing* 14.2 (2007): 290–305.

——. *Women Latin Poets: Language, Gender, and Authority from Antiquity to the Eighteenth Century*. Oxford: Oxford University Press, 2005.

Stone, Lawrence. *The Family, Sex, and Marriage in England, 1500–1800*. New York: Harper & Row, 1977.

Straznicky, Marta. *Privacy, Playreading, and Women's Closet Drama, 1550–1700*. Cambridge: Cambridge University Press, 2004.

Suzuki, Mihoko. 'Anne Clifford and the Gendering of History'. *Clio: A Journal of Literature, History, and the Philosophy of History* 30 (2001): 195–229.

—— ed. *Ashgate Critical Essays on Women Writers in English, 1550–1700*. Vol. 5. *Anne Clifford and Lucy Hutchinson*. Aldershot: Ashgate, 2009.

——. 'Elizabeth, Gender, and the Political Imaginary of Seventeenth-Century England'. Malcolmson and Suzuki, *Debating Gender*. 231–53.

——. 'The Essay Form as Critique: Reading Cavendish's *The World's Olio* through Montaigne and Bacon (and Adorno)'. *Prose Studies: History, Theory, Criticism* 22.3 (December 1999): 1–16.

——. '"Fortune is a Stepmother": Gender and Political Discourse in Elizabeth Cary's *History of Edward II*'. Wolfe, *Literary Career*. 89–105.

——. 'Margaret Cavendish and the Female Satirist'. *SEL* 37.3 (1997): 483–500.

——. *Subordinate Subjects: Gender, the Political Nation, and Literary Form in England, 1588–1688*. Aldershot: Ashgate, 2003.

——. 'What's Political in Seventeenth-Century Women's Political Writing?' *Literature Compass* 6 (2009): 1–15.

Thomas, Keith, 'Women and the Civil War Sects'. *Past and Present* 13 (1958): 42–62.

Tinkham, Audrey. '"Owning" in Lanyer's *Salve Deus Rex Judaeorum* ("Hail God King of the Jews")'. *Studies in Philology* 106.1 (2009): 52–75.

Todd, Barbara. 'The Remarrying Widow: A Stereotype Reconsidered'. Prior, *Women in English Society*. 54–92.

Todd, Janet, ed. *Aphra Behn*. New York: St. Martin's Press, 1999.

——. *The Secret Life of Aphra Behn*. New Brunswick, NJ: Rutgers University Press, 1996.

——. *The Sign of Angellica: Women, Writing and Fiction, 1660–1800*. New York: Columbia University Press, 1989.

Tomlinson, Sophie. *Women on Stage in Stuart Drama*. Cambridge: Cambridge University Press, 2005.

Traub, Valerie. *The Renaissance of Lesbianism in Early Modern England*. Cambridge: Cambridge University Press, 2002.

Trill, Suzanne, Kate Chedgzoy, and Melanie Osborne, eds. *Lay by your needles Ladies, Take the Pen: Writing Women in England, 1500–1700*. London: Arnold, 1997.

Trubowitz, Rachel. 'Female Preachers and Male Wives'. Holstun, *Pamphlet Wars*. 112–33.

Walker, Kim. *Women Writers of the English Renaissance*. New York: Twayne, 1996.

Wall, Wendy. *The Imprint of Gender: Authorship and Publication in the English Renaissance*. Ithaca: Cornell University Press, 1993.

Watts, Ruth. *Women in Science: A Social and Cultural History*. London: Routledge, 2007.

Whitaker, Katie. *Mad Madge: The Extraordinary Life of Margaret Cavendish, Duchess of Newcastle*. New York: Basic Books, 2003.

Wiesner-Hanks, Merry E. 'A Renaissance Woman (Still) Adrift in the World'. *Early Modern Women: An Interdisciplinary Journal* 1 (2006): 137–57.

Wilcox, Helen and Sheila Otway. 'Women's Histories'. *Cambridge Companion to Writing of the English Revolution*. Ed. N. H. Keeble. Cambridge: Cambridge University Press, 2001. 148–61.

Williams, Ethyn Morgan, 'Women Preachers in the Civil War'. *Journal of Modern History* 1.4 (1929): 561–79.

Williamson, George C. *Lady Anne Clifford*. Kendal: Titus Wilson, 1922.

Wiseman, Susan. *Conspiracy and Virtue: Women, Writing and Politics in Seventeenth-Century England*. Oxford: Oxford University Press, 2007.

——. 'Gender and Status in Dramatic Discourse: Margaret Cavendish, Duchess of Newcastle'. Grundy and Wiseman, *Women Writing History*. 159–77.

——. 'Unsilent Instruments and the Devil's Cushions: Authority in Seventeenth-century Women's Prophetic Discourse'. *New Feminist Discourses*. Ed. Isobel Armstrong. London: Routledge, 1992. 176–96.

Wolfe, Heather, ed. *The Literary Career and Legacy of Elizabeth Cary, 1613–1680*. New York: Palgrave Macmillan, 2007.

Woodbridge, Linda. *Women and the English Renaissance: Literature and the Nature of Womankind, 1540–1620*. Urbana: University of Illinois Press, 1984.

Woods, Susanne. *Lanyer: A Renaissance Poet*. New York: Oxford University Press, 1999.

—— and Margaret P. Hannay, eds. *Teaching Tudor and Stuart Women Writers*. New York: Modern Language Association, 2000.

——, Margaret P. Hannay, Elaine Beilin, and Anne Shaver. 'Renaissance Englishwomen and the Literary Career'. *European Literary Careers*. Ed. Patrick Cheney and Frederick de Armas. Toronto: University of Toronto Press, 2002. 302–23.

Woolf, Virginia. *A Room of One's Own*. New York: Harcourt Brace, 1927.

Wright, Joanne H. 'Not Just Dutiful Wives and Besotted Ladies: Epistemic Agency in the War Writing of Brilliana Harley and Margaret Cavendish'. *Early Modern Women: An Interdisciplinary Journal* 4 (2009): 1–26.

——. 'Reading the Private in Margaret Cavendish: Conversations in Political Thought'. *British Political Thought in History, Literature and Theory*. Ed. David Armitage. Cambridge: Cambridge University Press, 2006. 212–34.

Wright, Nancy E., Margaret W. Ferguson, and A. R. Buck, eds. *Women, Property, and the Letters of the Law in Early Modern England*. Toronto: University of Toronto Press, 2004.

Wynne-Davies, Marion. *Women Writers and Familial Discourse in the English Renaissance: Relative Values*. New York: Palgrave Macmillan, 2007.

Index

Numbers in **bold** refer to figures

history writing, 2, 17, 21, 87, 105,
108, 196, 197, 298
fiction and, 15, 204–11, 214–15
narrative historiography, 7, 17, 206,
210
Hobbes, Thomas, 16, 87, 244, 245,
246, 247, 262
Hobby, Elaine, 9, 18, 44
Hodgson-Wright, Stephanie, 193, 194
Holbourne, Anne, 147
Holy Roman Empire, 288
homoeroticism, 7, 12, 270, 296
homosexuality, 12
see also eroticism; lesbianism;
sexuality
honor, 258, 259
Hooke, Robert, 246
Micrographia, 246
Hooton, Elizabeth, 5
Howard, Anne, 107
Howard, Sir Charles, 107
Howard, Thomas, Baron of Escrick, 107
Howe, Elizabeth, 190
Howell, James, 115, 125
Familiar Letters, 125
Hudson, Roger, 256
Hughes, Derek, 221
Hunter, Lynette, 238, 240, 248
Hutchinson, Colonel John, 5, 101
Hutchinson, Lucy, 5, 8, 9, 19–20, 34,
38–9, 41, 103, 171, 176, 177, 246,
279
history and, 17
letter writing, 126
Narrative of the Fall, 64, 71–4, 75, 76
print publication, 100, 101, 102
as translator, 38, 243–5, 248, 279
works: 'Meditations upon the
Creation and the Fall', 71–2; 'The
Night', 101; *Order and Disorder*, 5,
38, 71–2, 74, 101; translation of
De Rerum Natura (Lucretius), 5,
38, 101, 243–5
Hutton, Sarah, 238
Hyde, Anne, Duchess of York, 274, 276

iconoclasm, 82
identity
literary, 33–44, 156, 157, 190

obscured, 156–8
women's, 2, 11, 67, 69, 196
imitatio, 160
'Independency' (church government),
83, 90
International Margaret Cavendish
Society, 7, 19
Interregnum, 1, 3, 4–5, 6, 12, 13, 20,
294
see also Commonwealth; Cromwell,
Oliver
Ireland, 270, 272, 278, 280
Ireton, Bridget, 4
Isham, Elizabeth, 105, 106, 107, 112
n.38
manuscript writing, 105–7
'My Booke of Rememberance',
105
Isham, Judith, 106, 107
Islamic Empires, 287–99
English trade, 290–2
feminist orientalism, 298–9
Mary Wroth and , 287–90
Quaker women and, 292–4
staging, 294–8

Jacobean period, 3, 13, 20–1, 288
Jacobitism, 6, 190
Jacobite poetry, 270
James, Elinor, 6, 13
James I, 2, 11, 35, 48, 69, 81, 121,
211, 288
James II, 6, 108, 192, 210, 212, 213,
240, 282
James, Isaac, 139
James, Susan, 16
Jankowski, Theodora, 12, 21, 38,
192
Jessy, Henry, 84
*The Exceeding Riches of Grace
Advanced by the Spirit of Grace, In
an Empty Nothing Creature*, 84
Jewish Lurianic Kabbaleh, 247
Jinner, Sarah, 12–13
An Alamanack or Prognostication,
12–13
Jocelin, Elizabeth, 3, 43
*Mother's Legacie for her Unborne
Childe*, 3, 43

CPSIA information can be obtained at www.ICGtesting.com
Printed in the USA
LVOW072117290212

271086LV00004B/1/P